Lecture Notes in Artificial Intellig

Edited by R. Goebel, J. Siekmann, and W. Wah

Subseries of Lecture Notes in Computer Science

Huib Aldewereld   Virginia Dignum
Gauthier Picard (Eds.)

Engineering Societies in the Agents World X

10th International Workshop, ESAW 2009
Utrecht, The Netherlands, November 18-20, 2009
Proceedings

 Springer

Series Editors

Randy Goebel, University of Alberta, Edmonton, Canada
Jörg Siekmann, University of Saarland, Saarbrücken, Germany
Wolfgang Wahlster, DFKI and University of Saarland, Saarbrücken, Germany

Volume Editors

Huib Aldewereld
Virginia Dignum
Universiteit Utrecht
Institute for Computing and Information Sciences
Padualaan 14, P.O.Box 80.089
3508 TB Utrecht, The Netherlands
E-mail: {huib,virginia}@cs.uu.nl

Gauthier Picard
École Nationale Supérieure des Mines de Saint-Étienne
Industrial Engineering and Computer Sciences
158, cours Fauriel
42023 SAINT-ÉTIENNE cedex 2, France
E-mail: gauthier.picard@emse.fr

Library of Congress Control Number: 2009937937

CR Subject Classification (1998): I.2.11, I.2, D.2, K.4, D.1.3, H.3.4

LNCS Sublibrary: SL 7 – Artificial Intelligence

ISSN   0302-9743
ISBN-10   3-642-10202-6 Springer Berlin Heidelberg New York
ISBN-13   978-3-642-10202-8 Springer Berlin Heidelberg New York

springer.com

© Springer-Verlag Berlin Heidelberg 2009
Printed in Germany

Typesetting: Camera-ready by author, data conversion by Scientific Publishing Services, Chennai, India
Printed on acid-free paper   SPIN: 12788255   06/3180   5 4 3 2 1 0

Preface

The 10th international workshop "Engineering Societies in the Agents' World" (ESAW 2009), was held in Utrecht, The Netherlands, during November 18–20, 2009. In the tradition of its predecessors, ESAW 2009 was committed to the idea of multi-agent systems (MAS) as highly interconnected *societies of agents*, paying particular attention to the social aspects, methodologies and software infrastructures that tackle the emergent complexities of MAS.

The idea for the ESAW workshop series was born 10 years ago, in 1999, among the members of the working group on "Communication, Coordination and Collaboration" of AgentLink, the 1st European Network of Excellence on Agent-Based Computing, out of a critical discussion about the general mindset of the agents community. Central to this discussion is the need for proper consideration of systematic aspects of MAS, acknowledging the importance of a multi-disciplinary approach, that takes into account the social, environmental and technological perspectives. These issues that are as actual today as they were in 1999, which is confirmed by the steady interest in the ESAW workshop series that previous editions took place in:

- Berlin, Germany, 2000 (LNAI 1972)
- Prague, Czech Republic, 2001 (LNAI 2203)
- Madrid, Spain, 2002 (LNAI 2577)
- London, UK, 2003 (LNAI 3071)
- Toulouse, France, 2004 (LNAI 3451)
- Kusadasi, Turkey, 2005 (LNAI 3963)
- Dublin, Ireland, 2006 (LNAI 4457)
- Athens, Greece, 2007 (LNAI 4995)
- Saint-Etienne, France, 2008 (LNAI 5485)

This 10th workshop was devoted to the discussion of technologies, methodologies and models for the engineering of complex applications based on MAS, and brought together researchers and contributions from both within and outside the agents' field – from software engineering, distributed systems, social sciences, and others – so as to promote cross-fertilization among different research areas. By focussing on the social aspects of MAS, ESAW 2009 concentrated on the space of agent interaction, rather than on intra-agent issues, and on the technology and methodology issues rather than on the pure theoretical aspects.

Taking the notion of agent a step further, to include humans and robots, ESAW 2009 focused on heterogeneous societies where humans, artificial agents and robots can interact in a transparent and seamless fashion. In this sense, ESAW 2009 was pleased to host the HART Workshop on "Supporting Joint Activity in Human-Agent-Robot Teamwork" as a satellite event, on November 21, 2009.

The following themes were addressed during the three-day meeting:

- *Social Aspects of Agent Societies*: this session drew parallels between human and artificial societies.
- *Self-Organization*: this session discussed issues of adaptation, emergence and self-organization.
- *Organization and Autonomy*: organizations as first-class entities are one of the main topics in societies of agents. Papers in this session discussed normative frameworks, individual autonomy, and virtual communities.
- *Software Engineering and Architectures*: the presentations in this session concerned methodologies, architectures and design approaches to agent societies.

This focus on social aspects of agent societies was also visible in the two invited talks. Rosaria Conte, head of LABSS (Laboratory of Agent-Based Social Simulation) at the ISTC (Institute for Cognitive Science and Technology) in Rome, talked about "The Immergence of Norms in Agent Worlds". In this talk, a normative agent architecture was presented and shown to account for a complex bidirectional dynamics of norms as social phenomena that emerge because of and to the extent that they immerge in the agents mind. Jacques Ferber, Professor of Computer Science at the University of Montpellier II, introduced the idea of "Thinking Integral: How to Build Complex Systems That Live with People and Exhibit Collective Intelligence." In this talk, Jacques presented a model to describe both virtual and human organizations, and how this conceptual tool can be used to design complex architectures where collective intelligence may arise from the collaboration of many individuals, either humans or agents.

We received 31 submissions for the workshop, of which 13 were accepted as full papers and 5 as short contributions, after careful review by at least three independent reviewers. During the workshop, short papers were presented as posters.

This edition also included an demonstration session, during which 6 agent-based technologies and works were shown. This proceedings include extended abstracts of all demonstrations. Domain areas presented in the demonstration session ranged from P2P applications, virtual environments, MAS tools, simulation testbeds, and results from ongoing projects.

The organization of ESAW 2009 would have not been possible without the financial help of:

- Almende, Rotterdam
- D-CIS Lab, Delft
- BNVKI: Benelux Association for Artificial Intelligence
- FIPA: IEEE Standards Organization for Agents and Multi-Agent Systems
- SIKS: Dutch Research School for Information and Knowledge Systems
- NWO: Netherlands Organization for Scientific Research
- Utrecht University, Department of Information and Computing Sciences

We would like to thank the Steering Committee for their guidance, the Programme Committee and the additional reviewers for the insightful reviews, and the Local Organizing Committee for arranging an enjoyable event. We would also like to thank all the researchers who submitted a paper to the workshop.

September 2009

Huib Aldewereld
Virginia Dignum
Gauthier Picard

Conference Organization

Programme Chairs

Huib Aldewereld
Virginia Dignum
Gauthier Picard

Steering Committee

Marie-Pierre Gleizes	IRIT Université Paul Sabatier, France
Andrea Omicini	DEIS Universita di Bologna, Italy
Paolo Petta	Austrian Research Institute for AI, Austria
Jeremy Pitt	Imperial College London, UK
Robert Tolksdorf	Free University of Berlin, Germany
Franco Zambonelli	Universita di Modena e Reggio Emilia, Italy

Programme Committee

Alexander Artikis	NCSR "Demokritos", Greece
Federico Bergenti	Universita di Parma, Italy
Carole Bernon	IRIT Université Paul Sabatier, France
Holger Billhardt	Universidad Rey Juan Carlos, Spain
Guido Boella	Universita degli Studi di Torino, Italy
Olivier Boissier	École des Mines de Saint-Étienne, France
Tibor Bosse	VU University Amsterdam, The Netherlands
Jeff Bradshaw	IHMC, USA
Cristiano Castelfranchi	ISTC-CNR, Italy
Luca Cernuzzi	Universidad Catolica "Nuestra Senora de la Asuncion", Paraguay
Rem Collier	University College Dublin, Ireland
Mehdi Dastani	Universiteit Utrecht, The Netherlands
Paul Davidsson	Blekinge Institute of Technology, Sweden
Yves Demazeau	IMAG, France
Jurriaan van Diggelen	TNO, The Netherlands
Frank Dignum	Universiteit Utrecht, The Netherlands
Oguz Dikenelli	Ege University, Turkey
Nicoletta Fornara	Università della Svizzera Italiana, Switzerland
Paul Feltovich	IHMC, USA
Paolo Giorgini	University of Trento, Italy
Davide Grossi	University of Amsterdam, The Netherlands
Antony Karageorgos	Technological Educational Institute of Larissa, Greece

Matthias Klusch	DFKI GmbH, Germany
Eric Matson	Purdue University, USA
Frédéric Migeon	IRIT Université Paul Sabatier, France
Simon Miles	King's College London, UK
Tim Miller	University of Melbourne, Australia
Eugénio Oliveira	University of Oporto, Portugal
Sascha Ossowski	Universidad Rey Juan Carlos, Spain
Julian Padget	University of Bath, UK
Juan Pavon Mestras	Universidad Complutense de Madrid, Spain
Loris Penserini	Universiteit Utrecht, The Netherlands
Alessandro Ricci	Universita di Bologna, Italy
Birna van Riemsdijk	Delft University of Technology, The Netherlands
Juan Antonio Rodriguez-Aguilar	IIIA, Spain
Jaime Simão Sichman	University of São Paolo, Brazil
Leon van der Torre	University of Luxembourg, Luxembourg
John Tranier	Universiteit Utrecht, The Netherlands
Wamberto Vasconcelos	University of Aberdeeen, UK
Laurent Vercouter	École Nationale Supérieure des Mines de Saint-Étienne, France
Mirko Viroli	Universita di Bologna, Italy
Danny Weyns	Katholieke Universiteit Leuven, Belgium
Pinar Yolum	Bogazici University, Turkey

Local Organization

Hado van Hasselt	Universiteit Utrecht, The Netherlands
Loris Penserini	Universiteit Utrecht, The Netherlands
Michal Sindlar	Universiteit Utrecht, The Netherlands
John Tranier	Universiteit Utrecht, The Netherlands
Tom van der Weide	Universiteit Utrecht, The Netherlands
Joost Westra	Universiteit Utrecht, The Netherlands

Table of Contents

Part 1: Invited Talks

The Immergence of Norms in Agent Worlds 1
   Rosaria Conte, Giulia Andrighetto, and Marco Campennì

Thinking Integral: How to Build Complex Systems That Live with
People and Exhibit Collective Intelligence 15
   Jacques Ferber

Part 2: Self-organisation

A Space-Based Generic Pattern for Self-Initiative Load
Balancing Agents 17
   Eva Kühn and Vesna Sesum-Cavic

A Goal-Oriented Approach for Modelling Self-organising MAS 33
   Mirko Morandini, Frédéric Migeon, Marie-Pierre Gleizes,
   Christine Maurel, Loris Penserini, and Anna Perini

Engineering Agent Organisations in a Business Environment 49
   Dimitris Traskas and Julian Padget

Peer-to-Peer Overlay Network Based on Swarm Intelligence 65
   Vesna Sesum-Cavic and Eva Kühn

Part 3: Software-Engineering and Architectures

Agent Architectures for Compliance 68
   Brigitte Burgemeestre, Joris Hulstijn, and Yao-Hua Tan

Incorporating BDI Agents into Human-Agent Decision Making
Research 84
   Bart Kamphorst, Arlette van Wissen, and Virginia Dignum

Programming Organization-Aware Agents: A Research Agenda 98
   M. Birna van Riemsdijk, Koen Hindriks, and Catholijn Jonker

Energy Trade-Offs in Resource-Constrained Multi-Agent Systems 113
   Hugo Carr, Jeremy Pitt, Anthony Kleerekoper, and David Blancke

Part 4: Social Aspects of Agent Societies

Engineering Social Reality with Inheritance Relations................. 116
   Huib Aldewereld, Sergio Alvarez-Napagao, Frank Dignum, and
   Javier Vázquez-Salceda

Determining the Trustworthiness of New Electronic Contracts 132
  Paul Groth, Simon Miles, Sanjay Modgil, Nir Oren,
  Michael Luck, and Yolanda Gil

Trust Based Evaluation of Wikipedia's Contributors 148
  Yann Krupa, Laurent Vercouter, Jomi Fred Hübner, and
  Andreas Herzig

Evolutionary Role Model for Multi-Agent Systems 162
  Erdem Eser Ekinci and Oğuz Dikenelli

Part 5: Organisation and Autonomy

Replication Based on Role Concept for Multi-Agent Systems 165
  Sebnem Bora and Oguz Dikenelli

Knowledge Management in Role Based Agents 181
  Hüseyin Kır, Erdem Eser Ekinci, and Oguz Dikenelli

Balancing Organizational Regulation and Agent Autonomy: An
MDE-Based Approach 197
  Loris Penserini, Virginia Dignum, Athanasios Staikopoulos,
  Huib Aldewereld, and Frank Dignum

Cooperative Sign Language Tutoring: A Multiagent Approach 213
  İlker Yıldırım, Oya Aran, Pınar Yolum, and Lale Akarun

Assistance Layer in a P2P Scenario 229
  Jordi Campos, Maite López-Sánchez, and Marc Esteva

Navigational Web-Interfaces from Formal Tropos Specification 233
  Komminist Weldemariam

Part 6: Demonstrations

ALIVE: A Framework for Flexible and Adaptive Service
Coordination 236
  J.S.C. Lam, W.W. Vasconcelos, F. Guerin, D. Corsar, A. Chorley,
  T.J. Norman, J. Vázquez-Salceda, S. Panagiotidi, R. Confalonieri,
  I. Gomez, S. Hidalgo, S.A. Napagao, J.C. Nieves, M. Palau Roig,
  L. Ceccaroni, H. Aldewereld, V. Dignum, F. Dignum, L. Penserini,
  J. Padget, M. De Vos, D. Andreou, O. Cliffe, A. Staikopoulos,
  R. Popescu, S. Clarke, P. Sergeant, C. Reed, T. Quillinan, and
  K. Nieuwenhuis

An Organisational Adaptation Simulator for P2P Networks 240
  Jordi Campos, Marc Esteva, Maite López-Sánchez, and
  Javier Morales

PreSage-MS: Metric Spaces in PreSage 243
    Hugo Carr, Alexander Artikis, and Jeremy Pitt

Normative Multi-Agent Organizations: A Programming Language and
Its Interpreter 247
    Mehdi Dastani

Hybrid Teams in Virtual Environments: Samurai Joins the
Training Team... 250
    Jurriaan van Diggelen, Tijmen Muller, and Karel van den Bosch

Joint Activity Testbed: Blocks World for Teams (BW4T) 254
    *Matthew Johnson, Catholijn Jonker, Birna van Riemsdijk,
    Paul J. Feltovich, and Jeffrey M. Bradshaw*

Author Index 257

The Immergence of Norms in Agent Worlds

Rosaria Conte, Giulia Andrighetto, and Marco Campennì

LABSS - Istituto di Scienze e Tecnologie della Cognizione - CNR,
via S. Martino della Battaglia
44, 00185 Rome, Italy
{rosaria.conte,giulia.andrighetto,marco.campenni}@istc.cnr.it
http://labss.istc.cnr.it

Abstract. In this paper, after a short review of the dichotomous view of norms usually seen as either regular behaviors or obligations issued by authorities, norms are proposed to be defined as recognized, represented and reasoned upon prescriptive commands. A normative agent architecture – EMIL-A – is presented and shown to account for a complex bidirectional dynamics of norms as social phenomena that emerge because and to the extent that they immerge in the agents' minds. Simulations run using EMIL-A will be discussed to illustrate the advantages of the present treatment of norms, over either side of the dichotomy.

1 Introduction

How build up social order in agent worlds? Are we satisfied with current approaches to the emergence of norms? Unfortunately not, as a number of questions are still open. In particular, it is possible to envisage a dichotomy in the scientific treatment of norms. On one hand, social scientists view norms as *regular behaviours*, possibly enforced by social expectations and sanctions. On the other hand, philosophers of law and logicians conceptualise norms as *obligations issued* by definite authorities. Hence the first set of questions, *how keep normative behaviour distinct from normal conduct on one hand and acquiescence under menace on the other*?

As a flexible, adaptive form of social order is crucial in agent worlds, a second set of questions needs to be addressed, i.e. *how do norms emerge, change and get adapted to new circumstances*? In the approach presented here, norms will be conceptualised as social and cognitive phenomena undergoing a complex dynamics, in which the social process of emergence and the mental process of immergence are intertwined in a circular fashion. The interplay between the mental and the social dynamics allows norms to emerge and change. Observable conformity is only the tip of the normative iceberg. The crucial dynamics lies in the minds of the agents, beneath the line of observation. Norms cannot emerge in society unless they previously immerge in the mind, i.e. get converted into mental representations. Agents abiding with norms, or violating them, act on a set of specific, norm-related, mental representations.

The mental dynamics of norms brings about a third set of questions: *how should we characterize the agents from among which norms can emerge*? Current BDI models of normative agents tackle the questions as to how people represent, reason upon, abide with or violate norms, but they do not address an earlier problem, i.e. how can norms emerge among BDI type of agents.

H. Aldewereld, V. Dignum, and G. Picard (Eds.): ESAW 2009, LNAI 5881, pp. 1–14, 2009.

In this paper, we intend to present an integrated and highly dynamic view of norms showing why and how it enables to answer the three sets of questions listed above, by means of agent based simulation.

2   The Normative Gap

Theories of norms are grounded on two, unrelated notions, *regularities* and *obligations*. Regularities, or behavioural norms, are spontaneously emerging social phenomena. Obligations, or institutional norms, are deliberately issued prescriptions. Behavioural norms are often found in the moral variant, as good or prosocial conduct, or in the statistical variant, as frequent, normal behaviours. Institutional norms are obligation-based, and collapse on legal norms, issued by specified institutional authorities.

Behavioural regularities and institutional obligations are complementary phenomena. None or poor attempt of integration has been made so far. However, the gap is neither desirable nor inevitable. In the rest of the paper an integrated approach will be proposed, based on mental representations: social norms, just like legal norms, are recognized, represented and reasoned upon as prescriptive commands. Only a theory that explores the impact of norms on the minds of agents can explain the link between different typologies of norms.

The work presented is based on artificial societies. Agent-based Simulation is an ideal tool for exploring the two-way dynamics of norm emergence because it is relatively free of epistemological assumptions. Thus processes of immergence and emergence can be explored in a way that is very difficult in any other way. In this way the relationship between cognition and social dynamics can start to be teased apart in a truly dynamic manner.

3   A 2-Way Dynamics of Norms

In a view of norms as two-sided, external (social) and internal (mental) objects ([1][2][3][4]), norms come into existence only when they emerge, not only *through* the minds of the agents involved, but also *into* their minds. In other words, they work as norms only when the agents recognize them, reason and take decisions upon them as norms. The emergence of norms implies their immergence into the agents' minds. Only when the normative, i.e. prescriptive, character of a command or other action is recognized by the agent, a norm gives rise to a normative behaviour of that agent. Thus, for a norm-based behavior to take place, a normative belief has to be generated into the minds of the norm addressees, and the corresponding normative goal has to be formed and pursued. Our claim is that a norm emerges as a norm only when it immerges into the minds of the agents involved; in other words, when agents recognize it as such.

In previous works ([5][6][7][8][9]), we described the process of norm emergence as a gradual and complex dynamics by which the macro-social effect, in our case a specific norm, emerges in the society *while* immerging in the minds of the agents producing it, generating a number of intermediate loops. Thus, before any global effect emerges, specific local events affect the generating systems, their beliefs and goals, in such a way that agents influence one another into converging on one global macroscopic effect. Emergence of social norms is due to the agents' behaviors, but the agents' behaviors are due the the mental mechanisms controlling and (re)producing them (immergence). Of course, our view of norms calls for a cognitive architecture of normative agents, which is not new to the field of agents and multiagent systems (think of the BOID architecture, for example). In the next section, an analysis of our normative architecture, EMIL-A, is presented.

4 Normative Agents

In order to model and operationalize the process of norm immergence, autonomous intelligent agents need to be endowed with internal mechanisms and mental representations allowing norms to affect their behaviours. Such representations are commonly realized by architectures inspired to the modular architecture of Artificial Intelligence approaches. Nowadays, there is no unequivocal concept for the design of normative agents. The development of normative architectures is a burgeoning research field. However, architectures of normative agents are predominantly inspired in some way by BDI (Belief-Desire-Intention) architectures, introduced by the pivotal work of Rao and Georgeff ([10]), which can be regarded as the point of departure for further developments. The BDI framework is intended to model human intelligent action and decision-making. A particular striking example of this approach is a straightforward extension of the BDI architecture to normative reasoning, denoted as BOID (Belief-Obligations-Intentions-Desires) agent architecture (see [11]), which includes obligations among its mental components.

The normative architecture we present in this section, EMIL-A, is inspired to BOID as it entails the representation of normative beliefs and goals based on obligations. However, unlike BOID, EMIL-A includes a module for norm-recognition, allowing the agent to process incoming inputs and possibly converting them into norms.

4.1 EMIL-A Architecture

Our normative architecture EMIL-A (see [6], for a detailed description) is meant to show that norms not only regulate behaviour but also act on different aspects of the mind. EMIL-A consists of mechanisms and mental representations allowing agents i) to form normative beliefs and goals, and decide whether to realize them or not and ii) to be more or less reactive to external inputs by means of short cuts. EMIL-A is accessed through the norm recognition module: before an input is recognized as normative, the norm cannot immerge in the minds of agents and, as a consequence, cannot affect their behaviours and emerge in society. We consider existent normative architectures not sufficiently flexible and adaptable to be really plausible; we believe that the future of normative architectures is closely related to the development of hybrid architectures.

4.1.1 Normative Mental Representations
In This Section, We Shall Endeavour to Clarify Some Components of the Mental Processing of Norms.

Normative belief[1]. First of all, a norm becomes a belief, namely the belief that a given behaviour in a given context for a given set of agents is forbidden, obligatory, permitted, etc. More precisely, the belief should be that "there is a norm prohibiting, prescribing, permitting that..." ([12][13][2][3]). Indeed, norms are aimed at and issued for generating the corresponding beliefs. In other words, norms must be acknowledged as such in order to properly work. Of course, a normative belief does not imply that a given norm has in fact been deliberately issued by some sovereign. Social norms are often set up by virtue of unwanted effects. However, once emerged, a given social norm is believed to be based upon some normative authority, if only an anonymous and impersonal one ("You are wanted, expected (not) to do this..."; "It is generally expected that..."; "This is how things are done...", etc.).

Normative Goal. However, a believer is not yet a decider: beliefs are necessary but insufficient conditions for norms to be complied with. What is it that leads agents to accept a norm, which by definition prescribes a costly behaviour?

In the BDI approach intentions and actions originate only from desires. On the contrary, a great deal of our actions are not elicited by our desires but by external pressures and requests. Duties and norms are one of the external sources of our goals. How is this possible? How can norms generate goals?

From a cognitive point of view, goals are internal representations triggering-and-guiding action at once: they represent the state of the world that agents want to reach by means of action and that they monitor while executing the action ([14]). Under the effect of social inputs, goals can be generated anew via cognitive factors, as goals *relativized* to other mental states (e.g., social beliefs). A goal is relativized when it is held because and to the extent that a given world-state or event is hold to be true or is expected ([15]). When goals are positive or pro-social, the process of generation is called *goal-adoption* (see [1]). By this means, an autonomous agent (adopter) will have another agent's (adoptee) goal as hers, on condition that she, the adopter, comes to believe that the adoptee's achievement of his goal will increase the chances that the adopter will in turn achieve one of her previous goals. I will probably lend my car to my room mate tonight, if I want to invite my fiancé for dinner.

There seems to be a correspondence between the process from a belief about an ordinary request to the decision of accepting such a request, i.e. the aforementioned process of *social goal adoption*, and the process leading from a normative belief to a normative goal (*norm adoption*): a normative goal of a given agent x about action a is a goal that x happens to have as long as she has a normative belief about a. More specifically, x has a normative goal only if she believes to be subject to a norm.

Norm Recognizer. The norm recognition module is the main entrance, so to speak, to the EMIL-A architecture. Before an input is recognized as normative, the norm cannot immerge in the minds of agents and, as a consequence, cannot emerge in society. Agents need to be able to discriminate between norms and other social phenomena, such as coercion, ordinary requests, conventions, etc. Our claim is that

---

[1] In EMIL-A, normative beliefs, together with normative goals, are organized and arranged in the normative board according to their respective salience. By *salience* we refer to the norm's degree of activation, which is a function of the number of times a given norm enters the agent's decision-making.

other normative architectures did not render justice to the recognition procedure (see [9][8]). Simplifying, a given norm is recognized if current input

- matches with a norm already stored in our (normative) memory;
- leads to a new norm being inferred or induced by the agent on the grounds of given indicators.

In the first case, the agent is facilitated by schemata, scripts, or other pragmatic structures ([16][17][18][19]; see [20] for an overview) the norm is embedded in (see [11], for a description). Once these are activated for any reason, the corresponding normative beliefs, expectations and behavioural rules are prompted.

The second option is followed when such scripts, and consequently the corresponding pattern matching operations, are not possible. The agent has no corresponding norm. This is why the norm recognition module is needed. Indeed, the norm-recognizer that we are going to describe tries to answer the question as to how agents tell new norms, not yet stored in their memory (see also [21]). Telling norms implies agents' ability to take an observed or communicated social input as normative, and consequently to form a new normative belief.

EMIL-A module for norm recognition consists of a normative frame by which the received inputs are elaborated and interpreted, and a long term memory - called normative board - where normative beliefs and normative goals once formed are stored and ordered by salience.

The Normative Board. When EMIL-A has to deal with an external input, such as a NO SMOKING sign, the norm recognition module will explore the N-Board. Suppose a corresponding normative belief is found (DO NOT SMOKE WHEN PROHIBITED), a normative belief is fired that will follow the path described previously.

The normative board is an archive in the long term memory where active norms are stored, arranged according to the *salience* gained. Difference in salience has the effect that a subset of norm-related representations interferes more frequently and strongly with the general cognitive processes of the agent. To decide which action to execute, the agent will search through the normative board: if more than one item is found out, the most salient norm will be chosen.

If a norm is never adopted by the agent, its salience begins to decrease, and sooner or later the normative belief will decay. On the contrary, a norm that is frequently processed by the decision-maker, will increase in salience. Salience may increase to the point that the norm becomes internalized, i.e. converted into an ordinary goal, or even in an automated conditioned action, a routine. In such a case, the norm will exit the normative board.

4.2 Value Added of EMIL-A

So far, the study of norm emergence has been identified with the study of behavioural regularities. However, not all the regularities are mandatory, and not all the norms are observed. Hence, the logical and pragmatic priority is how agents find out what are the *normative* regularities. Only afterwards, it makes sense to model the reasons why they conform to them. The value added of EMIL-A is to account for this specific aspect of norm-based regulation, how agents find out the norms they decide whether or not to conform to.

Norm recognition is an important requirement of norm-emergence. In previous works (see also [5][7]), emergence has been defined as a gradual and complex dynamics by which the macro-social effect, in our case a specific norm, is brought about in society *while* immerging in the minds of the agents, generating it through a number of intermediate loops.

Unlike moral dispositions, norm-recognition is poorly sensible to subjective variability, and rather robust. It allows us to (a) account for the universal appearance of norms in human and primate societies; (b) render justice to the intuition that humans violate norms, but have little problems in finding them out; (c) account for the evolutionary psychological evidence (see [22][23]) that agents easily apply counterfactual reasoning to social rules, but find it difficult to do so with logical ones; finally, (d) explain why, as pointed out by developmental psychological data, norm acquisition follows a stable ontogenetic pattern starting quite early in childhood ([24][25][26][27][28][29][30]).

In short, the intuition behind our normative architecture is twofold: on one hand, the emergence of norms is based upon a universal capacity to tell norms; on the other, this capacity is supported by a norm frame, an internal "model of a norm", which agents use as a processing instrument in norm recognition.

The emphasis laid on the innate and universal features of EMIL-A should not be mistaken, leading to think that no space is left to subjective variability. If norm recognition is a must, equally accomplished by a vast majority of agents, moral attitudes - i.e. the results of normative and moral experience accumulated during lifetime that affect different normative procedures - are not. They are definitely subjective.

Furthermore, the reinforcement effects that occur on different EMIL-A procedures vary among agents. Personal experience, for example, impacts on norm salience. Analogously, the normative frame, being in constant interaction with the social environment and the other procedures, is liable to their influence. In these terms, a normative architecture is allowed to elegantly ignore the culture/nurture controversy.

5 Simulating Norm Emergence

Some simulation studies about the emergence of social norms have been carried out, for example Epstein and colleagues' study of the emergence of social norms ([31]), and Sen and Airiau's study of the emergence of a precedence rule in the traffic ([32]). In these studies, social norms are essentially seen as conventions, that is, behavioural conformities that do not imply explicit agreements among agents, and do emerge from their individual interests. Within this perspective, the function of norms is found in allowing participants in coordination games to choose one among equivalent alternative equilibriums. Agents repeatedly interact with other agents in social scenarios. Such interactions can be formulated as stage games with multiple equilibriums ([33]), which make coordination uncertain. Norms gradually emerge from interactional practice, essentially through mechanisms of imitation and social learning, establishing who should do what. So far, simulation-based studies have been applied to investigate which norm is chosen from a set of alternative equilibriums. In this framework agents are not provided with normative minds, but with strategic reasoning. No attention is paid to norm immergence, and therefore to the role of mental mechanisms in norm-emergence.

A rather different sort of question arises about the emergence of social norms when no alternative equilibriums are available for selection. This is a matter still not widely investigated and references are scanty if any ([34]). We propose that a possible answer to the puzzling questions posed above ought to be searched for by examining the interplay of communicated and observed behaviours, and the way these are interpreted and represented into the minds of the observers. If any new behaviour α is interpreted as obeying a norm, a new normative belief is generated into the agent's mind and a process of normative influence will be activated ([35]). We suggest that normative recognition represents a crucial requirement of norm emergence and innovation, as processes resulting from both agents' interpretations of one another's behaviours, and transmission of such interpretations to one another.

5.1 The Norm Recognition Module at Work

Our Norm Recognizer (see [9][8] for a detailed description) consists of a long term memory, the normative board, and in a working memory, presented as a three layers architecture. The normative board contains normative beliefs, ordered by salience. The difference in salience between normative beliefs and normative goals has the effect that some of these normative mental objects will be more active than others and they will interfere more frequently and with more strength with the general cognitive processes of the agent[2]. The working memory is a three layer architecture, where *social inputs* are elaborated. These inputs are represented on an ordered vector, consisting of four elements: the source (x); the type of input through which the message is presented (T)[3]; the addressee (y); the action transmitted (a). Agents observe or communicate social inputs. Once received the input from another agent, the agent will compute, thanks to its norm recognition module, the information in order to generate/update her normative beliefs.

  Here follows a brief description of how this normative module works. Every time a message containing a deontic (D), for example, "You must answer when asked", or a normative valuation (V), for example " It is impolite to not answer when asked", is received, it will directly access at the second layer of the architecture, giving rise to a candidate normative belief "One must answer when asked", which will be temporally stored at the third layer. This will sharpen agents' attention: further messages with the same content, especially when observed as open behaviors, or transmitted by assertions

---

[2] At the moment, the normative beliefs' salience can only increase, depending on how many instances of the same normative belief are stored in the Normative Board. This feature has the negative effect that some norms become highly salient, exerting an excessive interference with the decisional process of the agent. We are now improving the model, adding the possibility that, if the normative belief is inactive for a certain amount of time, its salience will decrease.

[3] It can consist either in a *behaviour* (B), i.e. an action or reaction of an agent with regard to another agent or to the environment, or in a *communicated* message, transmitted through the following holders: assertions (A), i.e. generic sentences pointing to or describing states of the world; requests (R), i.e. requests of action made by another agent; deontics (D), partitioning situations between good/acceptable and bad/unacceptable; normative valuations (V), i.e. assertions about what it is right or wrong, correct or incorrect, appropriate or inappropriate (i.e. *it is correct to respect the queue*).

(A), for example "When asked, Paul answers", or requests (R), for example "Could you answer when asked?", will be processed and stored at the first level of the architecture. Beyond a certain normative threshold (which represents the frequency of corresponding normative behaviors observed, e.g. n% of the population), the candidate normative belief will be transformed in a new (real) normative belief, that will be stored in the normative board. The normative threshold can be reached in several ways: one way consists in observing a given number of agents performing the same action (alpha) prescribed by the candidate normative belief, e.g. agents answering when asked. If the agent receives no other occurences of the input action (alpha), after a fixed time t, the candidate normative belief will leave the working memory.

Aiming to decide which action to produce, the agent will search through the normative board: if more than one item is found out, the most salient norm will be chosen.

6 The Simulation Model

The simulation model we designed is aimed to find out the sufficient (even if not necessary) conditions for existing norms to change. In particular, we want to show if a simple cultural or material constraint can facilitate norm innovation. We wonder if under such a condition, agents provided with a module for telling what a norm is can generate new (social) norms by forming new normative beliefs, irrespective of the most frequent actions. To see this, we imagined a simple case in which subpopulations are isolated in different contexts for a fixed period of time. The metaphor here is any physical catastrophe or political upheaval that divides one population into two separate communities. The recent European history has shown several examples of this phenomenon.

In our simulation model, the environment consists of four scenarios, in which the agents can produce three different kinds of actions. We define two context-specific actions for every scenario, and one action common to all scenarios. Therefore, we have nine actions. Suppose that the first context is a postal office, the second an information desk, the third our private apartment, and so on. In the first context the action *stand in the queue* is a context-specific action, whereas in the second a specific action could be *occupy a correct place in front of the desk*. A common action for all of the contexts could be, *answer when asked*. Each of our agents is provided with a personal agenda (i.e. a sequence of contexts randomly chosen), an individual and constant time of permanence in each scenario (when the time of permanence is expired, the agent moves to the next context) and a window of observation (i.e. a capacity for observing and interacting with a fixed number of agents) of the actions produced by other agents. Norm Recognizers are also provided with the three-layer architecture described above, necessary to analyze the received information, and a normative board in which the normative beliefs, once arisen, are stored. The agents can move across scenarios: once expired the time of permanence in one scenario, each agent moves to the subsequent scenario following her agenda. Such irregular flow (each agent has a different time of permanence and a different agenda) generates a complex behavior of the system, tick-after-tick producing a fuzzy definition of the scenarios, and tick-for-tick a fuzzy behavioral dynamics.

We have modeled two different kinds of environmental conditions. In the first set of simulations, agents can move through contexts (following their personal agenda and in accordance with the personal time of permanence). In the second set of simulations, from a fixed time t, agents are obliged to remain in the context they have reached, till the end of the simulation: in this case agents can explore the contexts exchanging messages with one another and observing others' behaviors. When they reach the last context at time *t*, they can interact with same-context agents till the end of the simulation. We hope this second setting allows us to show that the mere statistical frequency is sufficient (but not necessary) to the agents' convergence on the common action.

At each tick, the Norm Recognizers (NRs), paired randomly, interact exchanging messages. These inputs are represented on an ordered vector, as said above. NRs produce different behaviors: if the normative board of an agent is empty (i.e. it contains no norms), the agent produces an action randomly chosen from the set of possible actions (for the context in question); in this case, also the modal by means of which the action is presented is chosen randomly. Vice versa, if the normative board contains some norms, the agent chooses the action corresponding to the most salient among these norms. In this case the action produced is presented with one of these modals: deontic (D), normative valuation (V) or behavior (B). This corresponds to the intuition that if an agent has a normative belief, there is a high propensity (in this chapter, this has been fixed to 90% of cases) for her to transmit it to other agents under strong modals (D or V) or open behavior (B). We run several simulations for different values of the threshold, testing the behaviors of the agents in the two different experimental conditions.

6.1 Results and Discussion

We briefly summarize the simulation scheme. The process begins by producing actions (and types of inputs) at random. The process is synchronic. The process is more and more complex runtime: agent i provides inputs to the agent who precedes her ($k=1$), issuing one action and one modal. Action choice is conditioned by the state of her normative board. When all of the agents have executed one simulation update, the whole process restarts at the next step.

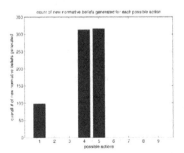 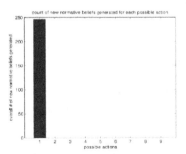

Fig. 1. (a-b). Overall number of new normative beliefs generated for each type of possible action - with (left) and without (right) external barrier

First of all we present the results obtained when imposing the external barrier. Then, we present the results obtained when no barrier was imposed; finally we compare the former with the latter results.

Figure 2(a) and Figure 2(b) show the trend of new normative beliefs generation runtime for a certain value of the norm threshold (threshold = 99), which is a good implementation of our theory: each line represents the generation of new normative beliefs corresponding to an action (i.e. each line corresponds to the sum of different normative beliefs present in all of the agents). To be noted, a normative belief is not necessarily universally shared in the population. However, norms are behaviors that spread thanks to the spreading of the corresponding normative belief. Therefore, they imply shared normative beliefs.

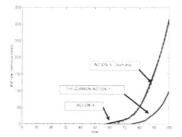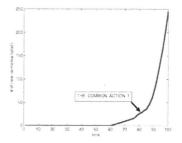

Fig. 2. (a-b). New normative beliefs generated runtime - with (left) and without (right) external barrier

Figures 3(a) and 3(b) are very similar (even if in the no-barrier variant - Figure 3(b), we find less regularity in the end of the dash line which represent the number of performed actions for the common action). In these plots, we cannot appreciate significant differences pointing to the normative beliefs acting on the effective behaviors: we cannot distinguish the clear effect corresponding to the agents' convergence on a specific norm (namely, we do not see that the dash line is significantly increasing).

Indeed, if we run longer simulations, we can appreciate the consequences of the results of our investigation: in Figures 4(a) and 4(b) we can observe two different (but related) effects: (i) more or less at the same time both in the barrier and no barrier condition, a convergence on the common action (dash line) is forming, much more significant in second case than in the first one; (ii) however, in the barrier condition, other lines of convergence are also emerging (increasing). If we observe Figure 5(a) and Figure 5(b) we can appreciate that in the first case (the case with barriers) we find a very very low convergence rate; but, in the second case (the case without barriers) we find a high convergence rate.

This corresponds to what is shown in in Figure 2(a) and Figure 2(b) on one hand, and Figure 1(a) and Figure 1(b) on the other: with external barrier, we can see that the higher overall number of new normative beliefs generated does not correspond to the common action (action 1) and the trend of new normative beliefs generated runtime shows the same results.

With no external barrier, instead, only normative beliefs concerning the common action (action 1) are generated.

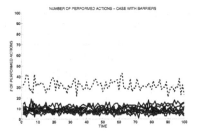

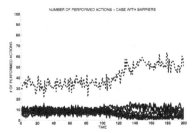

Fig. 3. (a-b). Actions performed by NRs - with (left) and without (right) external barrier. On axis X, the number of simulation ticks (100)is indicated and on axis Y the number of performed actions for each different type of action. The dash line corresponds to the action common to all scenarios.

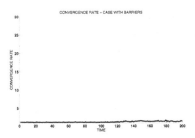

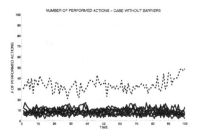

Fig. 4. (a-b). Actions performed by NRs - with (left) and without (right) external barrier. On axis X, the number of simulation ticks (200) is indicated and on axis Y the number of performed actions for each different type of action. The dash line corresponds to the action common to all scenarios.

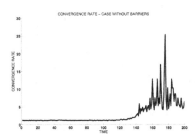

Fig. 5. (a-b). On axis X, the flow of time is shown; on axis Y the value of convergence rate in both cases with (left) and without (right) external barrier

We have shown how our model allows new norms, which do not corresponding to the common action to emerge. Some rival norms now compete in the same social settings. Obviously, they will continue to compete, unless some further external event or change in the population (e.g. the barrier removal) will cause agents to start migrating again. It would be interesting to observe how long the rival norms will survive after barrier removal, whether and when one will out-compete the others, and if so, which one. It should be said that, as we observe a latency time for a normative belief to give rise to a new normative behaviour, we also expect some time to elapse before a given behaviour disappears while and because the corresponding belief, decreasingly fed by observation and communication, starts to extinguish as well. We might call such a temporal discrepancy *inertia* of the norm. Both latency and inertia are determined by the twofold nature of the norm, mental and behavioural, which reinforce each other, thus preserving agents' autonomy: external barriers do modify agents' behaviours, but only through their minds.

More than emergence, our simulation shows a norm innovation process; in fact, Figure 3(a) shows that, starting around tick=60, two normative beliefs appear in the normative boards and the overall number of these two new normative beliefs generated is three times higher than the overall number of normative beliefs concerning the common action 1. We might say that, if stuck to their current location by external barriers, norm recognizers resist the effect of majority and do not converge on one equilibrium only. Rather, they will form as many normative beliefs as there were competing beliefs on the verge of overcoming the normative threshold before the agents had been stuck to their locations.

No such effect is expected among agents whose behavior depends only from the observation of others. In sum, is statistical frequency sufficient for a norm to emerge? Beside action 1, common to the four contexts, other norms seem to emerge in our simulation. Normative agents can recognize a norm; infer the existence of a norm by its occurrences in open behavior under certain conditions (see the critical role of previous deontics); and finally spread a normative belief to other agents. Future studies are meant to investigate on the effect of barrier removal and the inertia of normative beliefs.

7 Concluding Remarks

Does the theory presented answer the questions raised in the introduction? In principle, it allows the first set of questions to be answered, as we present a normative agent architecture, and show by means of simulation its value added with regard to concurrent, simpler, but less efficient agent models. But what about the former two sets of questions, concerning the link between different types of norms and their dynamics in society? We believe the view we have proposed accounts for both these questions in a rather innovative way.

As to integration, the paper presents a view of norms that discerns normal from normative behaviour at the same time filling the gap between legal and social norms. The solution we have proposed consists of agents' capacity to recognize a subset of the communicative or behavioural inputs they transmit to one another as normative, and autonomously decide to convert them into normative outputs.

As to norm dynamics, not only the spread of behavioural regularities and good social conduct are accounted for – what is allowed also by simpler models – but also what Ullmann-Margalit called prescribed behaviour ([36]), accounting for the mandatory character attributable to any norm, including conventions, as Margaret Gilbert acutely pointed out.

Did we answer the questions posed in a conclusive manner? Did we answer all of the interesting questions that one might pose with regard to norms? Of course, not. In particular, we have not taken into sufficient account the processes leading to incorporate norms into action schemata ([37]), or those leading to an automated normative will being formed (which Josh Epstein calls thoughtless compliance), or factors and processes leading to several different forms of norm internalization, from internalized norms to automated normative actions. In future works, we intend to integrate these ideas into our agent architecture in order to explore the effect of norm internalization on norm compliance and other relevant indicators of social order.

Acknowledgments. This work was supported by the EMIL project (IST-033841), funded by the Future and Emerging Technologies program of the European Commission, in the frame-work of the initiative Simulating Emergent Properties in Complex Systems.

References

1. Conte, R., Castelfranchi, C.: Cognitive and social action. University College of London Press, London (1995)
2. Conte, R., Castelfranchi, C.: From conventions to prescriptions. Towards a unified theory of norms. AI&Law 7, 323–340 (1999)
3. Conte, R., Castelfranchi, C.: The Mental Path of Norms. Ratio Juris 19(4), 501–517 (2006)
4. Conte, R., Castelfranchi, C.: The mental path of norms. Ratio Juris 19(4), 501–517 (2006)
5. Castelfranchi, C.: Simulating with cognitive agents: The importance of cognitive emergence. In: Sichman, J.S., Conte, R., Gilbert, N. (eds.) MABS 1998. LNCS (LNAI), vol. 1534, pp. 26–44. Springer, Heidelberg (1998)
6. Andrighetto, G., Campennì, M., Conte, R., Paolucci, M.: On the Immergence of Norms: a Normative Agent Architecture. In: Proceedings of AAAI Symposium, Social and Organizational Aspects of Intelligence, Washington, DC, November 8-11 (2007)
7. Conte, R., Andrighetto, G., Campenni', M., Paolucci, M.: Emergent and immergent effects in complex social systems. In: Proceedings of AAAI Symposium, Social and Organizational Aspects of Intelligence, Washington, DC (2007)
8. Campennì, M., Andrighetto, G., Cecconi, F., Conte, R.: Normal = Normative? The role of intelligent agents in norm innovation. Mind & Society (2009), doi:10.1007/S11299-009-0063-4
9. Andrighetto, G., Campennì, M., Cecconi, F., Conte, R.: The Complex Loop of Norm Emergence: a Simulation Model. In: Takadama, K., Revilla, C.C., Deffuant, G. (eds.) The Second World Congress on Social Simulation, Aspects of Intelligence, Washington, DC. LNCS (LNAI). Springer, Heidelberg (2008) (forthcoming)
10. Rao, A.S., Georgeff, M.P.: Social plans: Preliminary report. In: Werner, E., Demazeau, Y. (eds.) Decentralized AI 3 - Proceedings of the Third European Workshop on Modelling Autonomous Agents and Multi-Agent Worlds (MAAMAW 1991), pp. 57–76. Elsevier Science Publishers B.V., Amsterdam (1992)
11. Broersen, J., Dastani, M., Hulstijn, J., Huang, Z., van der Torre, L.: The BOID architecture. Conflicts between beliefs, obligations, intentions and desires. In: Proceedings of the fifth international conference on Autonomous Agents, Montreal, Quebec, Canada, pp. 9–16 (2001)
12. von Wright, G.H.: Norm and Action. A Logical Inquiry. Routledge and Kegan Paul, London (1963)
13. Kelsen, H.: General Theory of Norms. Hardcover (1979)

14. Conte, R. (ed.): Rational, goal governed agents. Encyclopedia of Complexity and Systems Science. Springer, Heidelberg (2009)
15. Castelfranchi, C.: Prescribed mental attitudes in goal-adoption and norm adoption. Artif. Intell. and Law 7(1), 37–50 (1999)
16. Wason, P., Johnson-Laird, P.: Psychology of Reasoning: Structure and Content. Harvard University Press, Cambridge (1972)
17. Schank, R.C., Abelson, R.P.: Scripts, plans, goals, and understanding: An inquiry into human knowledge structures. Lawrence Erlbaum Associates, Hillsdale (1977)
18. Fiske, S.T., Taylor, S.E.: Social cognition, 2nd edn. McGraw Hill, New York (1991)
19. Barsalou, L.W.: Perceptual symbol systems. Behavioral and Brain Sciences 22, 577–660 (1999)
20. Markus, H., Zajonc, R.B.: The cognitive perspective in social psychology. In: Lindzey, G., Aronson, E. (eds.) Handbook of social psychology, 3rd edn., pp. 137–229. Random House, New York (1985)
21. Sripada, C., Stich, S.: A Framework for the Psychology of Norms. In: Carruthers, P., Laurence, S., Stich, S. (eds.) The Innate Mind: Culture and Cognition, pp. 280–301. Oxford University Press, Oxford (2006)
22. Cosmides, L., Tooby, J.: Cognitive adaptations for social exchange. In: Barkow, J., Cosmides, L., Tooby, J. (eds.) The adapted mind. Oxford University Press, New York (1992)
23. Cosmides, L., Tooby, J.: Can evolutionary psychology assist logicians? A reply to Mallon. In: Sinnott-Armstrong, W. (ed.) Moral psychology, pp. 131–136. MIT Press, Cambridge (2008)
24. Bandura, A.: Social cognitive theory of self-regulation. Organizational Behavior and Human Decision Processes 50, 248–287 (1991)
25. Nucci, L.P.: Education in the Moral Domain. Cambridge University Press, Cambridge (2001)
26. Cummins, D.D.: Evidence for deontic reasoning in 3- and 4-year olds. Memory and Cognition 24(6), 823–829 (1996)
27. Piaget, J.: The moral judgment of the child. The Free Press, New York (1965)
28. Kohlberg, L.: Justice and reversibility. In: Kohlberg, L. (ed.) Essays on Moral Development, vol. 1. Harper and Row (1981)
29. Kohlberg, L., Turiel, E.: Moral development and moral education. In: Lesser, G. (ed.) Psychology and educational practice. Scott Foresman (1971)
30. Shweder, R., Mahapatra, M., Miller, J.: Culture and moral development. In: Kagan, J., Lamb, S. (eds.) The Emergence of Morality in Young Children. The University of Chicago Press (1987)
31. Epstein, J.: Generative Social Science. Studies in Agent-Based Computational Modeling. Princeton University Press, Princeton (2006)
32. Sen, S., Airiau, S.: Emergence of norms through social learning. In: Proceedings of the Twentieth International Joint Conference on AAAI (2007)
33. Myerson, R.B.: Game Theory: Analysis of Conflict. Harvard University Press (1991)
34. Posner, R., Rasmusen, E.: Creating and enforcing norms, with special reference to sanctions. Int. Rev. Law Econ., 369–382 (1999)
35. Conte, R., Dignum, F.: From Social Monitoring to Normative Influence. JASSS 4(2) (2001)
36. Ullmann-Margalit, E.: The Emergence of Norms. Clarendon Press, Oxford (1977)
37. Bicchieri, C.: The Grammar of Society: The Nature and Dynamics of Social Norms. Cambridge University Press, New York (2006)

Thinking Integral: How to Build Complex Systems That Live with People and Exhibit Collective Intelligence

Jacques Ferber

LIRMM – University of Montpellier II, 161 rue Ada,
34592 Cedex 5, Montpellier, France
ferber@lirmm.fr

Multi-agent systems have been proposed for the development of complex software systems as a way to handle complexity (Jennings 2001). It has also been advocated that basic agent oriented systems do not have the power to cope with large software and that it is crucial to use organizations centered multi-agent systems (OCMAS) (Ferber et al. 2004 ; Dignum 2009).

The AGR family (Ferber & Gutknecht, 1998; Ferber et al. 2004) has been one of the first to give a simple and detailed account of what an OCMAS should be, and has been the conceptual basis for the MadKit platform (MadKit 2004). The Moise+ has also shown its importance in the field by providing a general framework for groups, roles, goal-driven agents and norms (Hübner, Sichman & Boissier, 2002). Other OCMAS models may be seen in (Coutinho et al. 2009). It has also been shown that it is possible to give a precise and formal semantics of organizations in an operational form (Dastani et al. 2009).

Recently we have proposed a new conceptual framework and a generic model for multi-agent systems called MASQ (Ferber et al. 2009, Stratulat et al. 2009), which constitutes an abstraction of the various aspects of a MAS, generalizing the AGR approach and incorporating the institutional work of Searle (Searle 1995). This model is based on a 4-quadrant conceptual framework, where the analysis and design of a system is performed along two axes: an interior/exterior dimension and an individual/collective dimension. We will give a conceptual definition of this approach and we will show that it is possible of applying it to practical problems in the computer science fields. We will give some ideas about its use as a methodological tool and also how this model could be used to represent human organizations, through the various diagrams and notations that are proposed.

Collective intelligence, which is how intelligence emerges from the interaction of several entities, has been recently proposed as a conceptual tool to analyze and design new decentralized forms of human collaboration through the use of electronic technologies. In this "coordinate and cultivate" form of management (Malone 2004), it is necessary to have new conceptual models to take into account interactions of many kind. In this talk, we will show how MASQ may be used to describe both virtual and human organizations, and how it is possible with this conceptual tool to design complex architectures where collective intelligence may arise from the collaboration of many individuals, either humans or agents.

H. Aldewereld, V. Dignum, and G. Picard (Eds.): ESAW 2009, LNAI 5881, pp. 15–16, 2009.

References

Coutinho, L., Sichman, J., Boissier, O.: Modelling Dimensions for Agent Organization. In: Dignum, V. (ed.) Multi-agent Systems: Semantics and Dynamics of Organizational Models. IGI

Dastani, M., Tinnemeier, N.A.M., Meyer, J.-J.C.: A Programming Language for Normative Multi-Agent Systems in Virginia Dignum. In: Multi-agent Systems: Semantics and Dynamics of Organizational Models. IGI (2009)

Dignum, V.: The Role of Organization in Agent Systems. In: Dignum, V. (ed.) Multi-agent Systems: Semantics and Dynamics of Organizational Models. IGI (2009)

Ferber, J., Gutknecht, O.: A Meta-Model for the Analysis and Design of Organizations in Multi-Agent Systems. In: Proceedings of the 3rd International Conference on Multi Agent Systems (ICMAS 1998), pp. 128–135. IEEE Computer Society, Los Alamitos (1998)

Ferber, J., Gutknecht, O., Michel, F.: From Agents to Organizations: An Organizational View of Multi-Agent Systems. In: Giorgini, P., Müller, J.P., Odell, J.J. (eds.) AOSE 2003. LNCS, vol. 2935, pp. 214–230. Springer, Heidelberg (2004)

Ferber, J., Stratulat, T., Tranier, J.: Towards an Integral Approach of Organizations: the MASQ approach. In: Multi-Agent Systems in Virginia Dignum (ed.), Multi-agent Systems: Semantics and Dynamics of Organizational Models. IGI (2009)

FIPA, The Foundation of Intelligent Physical Agents (2005), http://www.fipa.org

Jennings, N.R.: An agent-based approach for building complex software systems. Commun. ACM 44(4), 35–41 (2001)

Hübner, J., Sichman, J., Boissier, O.: A model for the structural, functional, and deontic specification of organizations in multiagent systems. In: Bittencourt, G., Ramalho, G.L. (eds.) SBIA 2002. LNCS (LNAI), vol. 2507, pp. 118–128. Springer, Heidelberg (2002)

MadKit. A Multi-Agent Development Kit (2004), http://www.madkit.net

Malone, T.W.: The Future of Work: How the New Order of Business Will Shape Your Organization, Your Management Style, and Your Life. Harvard Business School Press (2004)

Searle, J.R.: The Construction of Social Reality. Free Press (1995)

Stratulat, T., Ferber, J., Tranier, J.: MASQ (2009) - Towards an Integral Approach of Agent-Based Interaction. In: AAMAS 2009 (2009)

A Space-Based Generic Pattern for Self-Initiative Load Balancing Agents

Eva Kühn and Vesna Sesum-Cavic

Vienna University of Technology, Institute for Computer Languages,
Space Based Computing Group, Argentinierstr. 4, 1040, Wien, Austria
{eva,vesna}@complang.tuwien.ac.at

Abstract. Load-Balancing is a significant problem in heterogeneous distributed systems. There exist many load balancing algorithms, however, most approaches are very problem specific oriented and a comparison is therefore complex. This paper proposes a generic architectural pattern for a load balancing framework that allows for the plugging of different load balancing algorithms, reaching from unintelligent to intelligent ones, to ease the selection of the best algorithm for a certain problem scenario. As in complex network environments there is no "one-fits-all solution", also the integration of several different algorithms shall be supported. The presented pattern assumes autonomous agents and decentralized control. It can be composed towards arbitrary network topologies, foresees exchangeable policies for load-balancing, and uses a black-board based communication mechanism to achieve high software architecture agility. The pattern has been implemented and first instantiations of it with three algorithms have been benchmarked.

Keywords: Load balancing, self-organization, autonomous agents, coordination patterns, intelligent algorithms, complex distributed systems.

1 Introduction

The rapid growth of computer systems and their complexity imposes the necessity to reconsider dynamic load balancing (LB) in order to improve the performance of the overall distributed system and to achieve the highest level of productivity. LB can be described as finding the best possible workload (re)distribution and addresses ways to transfer excessive load from busy (over-loaded) nodes to idle (under-loaded) nodes. LB can take place at *local node level* allocating load to several core processors of one computer, as well as at *network level* distributing the load among different nodes. At the local level, the determining factor for load distribution is the balanced utilization of all core processors. At the network level, one must take into consideration the time needed for transferring data from a busy node to an idle node and estimate the priority of transferring, especially when the transfer itself requires more time to complete than the load assignment.

H. Aldewereld, V. Dignum, and G. Picard (Eds.): ESAW 2009, LNAI 5881, pp. 17–32, 2009.

The problem becomes even more complex in heterogeneous systems. Networks are growing constantly and therefore the intensive need of including self-* properties (self-organization, self-management, self-repairing, self-configuring, self-grouping, self-learning, self-adaptation, etc.) arise to deal with increasing complexity. We can find a wide range of LB approaches (see section 2), however, our objections address the lack of: Provisioning a general framework, autonomy and self-* properties, and arbitrary configurations. *Provisioning of a General Framework:* Existing LB approaches are very problem specifically oriented (see section 2). As there is no "one-fits-all solution, in order to find a best solution for a problem, a generalized framework is needed that allows for testing and tuning different LB algorithms for a specific problem and environment. The framework shall support easy and dynamic exchange of algorithms as well as combinations of different algorithms. The architecture shall be agile, so that neither new requirements on LB algorithms, nor other assumptions on the network infrastructure, nor the dynamic joining and leaving of agents do become "architecture breakers". Note that a framework itself doesn't solve the LB problem but serves as a necessary basement for LB algorithms. It abstracts the general requirements in a flexible software architecture. *Autonomy and Self-* Properties:* Increased complexity of software systems, diversity of requirements, and dynamically changing configurations, force to find new solutions based on self-organization, autonomic computing and autonomous (mobile) agents. Intelligent algorithms require autonomous agents which are advantageous in situations that are characterized by high dynamics, not-foreseeable events, and heterogeneity. *Arbitrary Configurations:* LB can be required to manage the load among local core processors on one node, as well as in a network (intranet, internet, cloud). A general LB framework must be able to cope with all these demands at the same time and offer means to abstract hardware and network heterogeneities.

In this paper, we present an extensible coordination pattern called SILBA (Self-Initiative Load Balancing Agents) with pluggable LB algorithms and autonomic (multi) agents. The main contribution of this paper is the design of a reusable and agile architectural pattern and its independence on the problem at hand. Section 2 gives a classification of existing LB algorithms. Section 2 describes the SILBA pattern and how it can be extended towards arbitrary network configurations. Section 3 presents the implementation of a LB framework based on the SILBA pattern, using a space-based middleware. In section 5, we choose some well-known algorithms (both unintelligent and intelligent) as examples, map them to SILBA, and show some benchmarks. In section 6 we summarize the results and further research work.

2   Classification of LB Algorithms

There are many different approaches that cope with the LB problem. As a first classification, we shortly listen the most important ones and classify them according to the underlying LB algorithm:

The *first* group consists of different conventional approaches without using any kind of intelligence, e.g.: Sender Initiated Negotiation and Receiver Initiated

Negotiation [27], Gradient Model [30], Random Algorithm [14], and Diffusion Algorithm [9]. In Sender algorithm, LB is initiated by an overloaded node. This algorithm has a good performance for low to moderate load level while in Receiver algorithm, LB is initiated by an under-loaded node and this algorithm has a good performance for moderate to heavy load level. Also the combination of these two algorithms (Symmetric) is possible. Gradient Model is based on dynamically initiated LB requests by the under-loaded node. The result of these requests is a system wide gradient surface. Overloaded nodes respond to requests by migrating unevaluated tasks down the gradient surface towards under-loaded nodes. In Random Algorithm each node checks the local workload during a fixed time period. When a node becomes over-loaded after a certain time period, it sends the newly arrived task to a randomly chosen node without taking in consideration whether the target node is overloaded or not. Only the local information is used to make the decision. The principle of diffusion algorithms is keeping the process iterate until the load difference between any two processors is smaller than a specified value. The *second* group includes theoretical improvements of LB algorithms using different mathematical tools and estimations [5] without focus on implementation and benchmarks. The *third* group contains approaches that use intelligent algorithms like evolutionary approaches [7], and ant colony optimization approaches ([20], [41]). Evolutionary approaches use the adjustment of some parameters specific for evolutionary algorithms to achieve the goal of LB. Ant colony optimization approach is used in [20] for a graph theoretic problem formulated from the task of computing load balanced clusters in ad hoc networks. These approaches mainly try to improve only one of the components of the whole LB infrastructure, namely the LB algorithm. In this paper we will propose a framework that allows for the integration of different kinds of algorithms. However, a particular focus is on autonomous agents based control. There exist interesting approaches for solving the LB problem by using agent-based models. According to multi-agent systems, LB can be either static or mobile [18]. In static LB, tasks cannot be migrated elsewhere once they have been launched on a specific server. In mobile LB, a task may migrate to another server, utilizing the agent's mobility. In [26], it is shown that mobile LB outperforms the static case with a 3-40 % improvement over the static placement scheme.

	framework abstraction	no framework
agents based	[22](*), [42], [39], [35]	[16], [38](*), [24], [19]
without agents	[3], [2]	[17], [45], [25], [34], [31]
		[46], [43], [44](*), [33]

The above table gives another type of classification according to the criterion whether an approach uses agents or not ([11] identifies essentials of different multi-agent architectural styles (MAS) and shows how MAS can be characterized and evaluated), as well as whether an approach introduces a general framework (taking in the consideration both structured P2P and unstructured P2P networks as well as grid). Those papers that use a very specific LB algorithm are marked with "(*)". For example [34] puts the focus on DHT-based P2P systems only. First, let us discuss the articles that offer both, *agents and framework*: [22] uses a very problem-specific LB algorithm and concentrates on parallel database systems. In [42], a dynamic model of agent-based LB on grids is presented with the goal of exploring the effects of agents' strategies on the quality of LB. The results describe the dynamic behavior of LB on grids as well as modeling and predicting LB behavior. But the model used for abstraction is not very generic. It is more an agent based LB than we can say that it is a framework in our sense. [39] is not generic and in particular designed for parallel database systems. [35] uses agents and states that the approach is a generic one to implement any kind of dynamic LB algorithm in a heterogeneous cluster using software agents. However, it strictly uses only sender-initiated algorithms and no generalization is shown that allows plugging in also other algorithms.

Second, one relevant representative of each other category is presented: *Agents, no framework:* [19] presents an extension of the AMBLE model, an awareness model which manages LB by means of a multi-agent based architecture, with the aim to establish a cooperative LB model for collaborative grid environments. This model, named C-AMBLE (Cooperative Awareness Model for Balancing the Load in grid Environments) applies some theoretical principles of multi-agents systems, awareness models, and third party models, to promote an efficient autonomic cooperative task delivery in grid environments. *No agents, framework:* In [2], the design of a flexible LB framework is described and runtime software system for supporting the development of adaptive applications on distributed-memory parallel computers, i.e., the Implicit Load Balancing component of the PREMA runtime system is presented. An indication of the flexibility of the PREMA system has been given by implementing several LB policies. The four policies shown here scratch the surface of the scheduling methods possible. *No agents, no framework:* In [33], LB at the middleware level allows more flexibility than existing solutions based at lower system levels. However, it requires an execution infrastructure and mechanisms to be integrated seamlessly. DLBS (Dynamic Load Balancing Service) brings new solutions regarding large scale LB for middleware-based applications. DLBS offers a multi-criteria and easily customizable LB service. It consists of a scalable monitoring infrastructure, a connection manager (integrated into the middleware) and customizable LB strategies.

3   SILBA Pattern

The SILBA pattern is domain independent and can be used on different levels: local, with static and dynamic routing, and combining several routing strategies. It is composed of several sub-patterns that are described in this section. Its basic principle is autonomous agents that operate in a peer-to-peer network with a dynamically changing amount of work and decide on their own when to pick up or push back work. Let us first define the necessary notions, components, and assumptions used for the definition of the pattern:

A **peer node** (or node for short) is a computing device that itself might consist of several core processors.

A **request** consists of a task to be performed given in a standard format like XML or WSDL, a request identifier, a client identifier, a role describing the capacities and skills a worker must have in order to be able to process the task, a priority given in absolute terms, an informal or semantic description of the task, a timeout date, and a URL indicating a location where the answer shall be put.

An **autonomous agent** (or agent for short) is a software program that is self-responsible to be up and running. An agent implements a certain reactive and continuous behaviour [12]. Agents can move from node to node, and they can dynamically join and leave. So-called *worker agents* perform requests, decide autonomously when they act and which request they take (first or at all). Different roles determine which requests they may execute. At a certain point in time, a worker agent is associated with a node. If it fails, an automatic fail-over shall take place. Other agents occurring in SILBA are *allocation agents* and *routing agents* (see section 3.2 and 3.3).

A **client** issues requests at any reachable node in the network with an indicator, how it wants to be informed about the results and where the results shall be placed. The load that is produced by the clients can vary and peak times must be handled through the addition of resources (e.g. agents and computing nodes). Clients may either synchronously wait for the answer, or continue their job, picking up the answer later (asynchronicity). Thus, a client might go off-line and get the answer later, if they are re-connected.

In this paper, we define a **network** to connect nodes logically thus forming an overlay. Networks can be clustered into "super networks". However, as we underneath have to assume physical network links, a network can be disrupted and become partitioned into sub-networks.

A **design pattern** [21] describes a recurring and reusable solution in software design. We are mainly interested in inter-enterprise patterns for LB.

By **framework** we understand the implementation of a complex pattern – typically composed of several sub-patterns – that represents a general, re-usable architectural solution to a certain problem scenario, in our case LB. A framework can be measured by its architecture agility.

Blackboard based communication offers a high degree of decoupling (time, reference, space) and supports agents' autonomy. Clients and agents need not know each other and can act autonomously. We therefore will follow a space-based architectural style for the design of the single SILBA patterns where the entire communication is carried out via shared spaces. The composition of space-based patterns will be done by using standardized entry formats and interaction patterns in shared spaces.

In the following we describe several patterns that finally can be composed to a LB framework.

3.1   Local Node Pattern

The local node pattern is responsible to model load generation at one node and the execution of requests by local worker agents. Workers actively compete for work. If a worker agent fails the work shall be taken over by another one. The

Fig. 1. (a) Local node pattern. (b) Node classification according to transfer policy.

basic components of the local node pattern (see fig. 1 (a)) are: clients, worker agents, load space, and answer space.

A **load space** is a place where new requests are put by clients, and where the information about all worker agents' registrations and the current load status of the node are maintained. A load originates from client(s).The requests shall be accessible in either the order they arrived, or by means of other criteria like e.g. their priority, the required worker role, or their timeout date. The load space can be queried about its current load status which can be either of under-loaded (UL), ok-loaded (OK), or over-loaded (OL) (see fig. 1 (b)). The determination about the load status is done according to a certain policy (see section 3.2) called transfer policy that shall be commutable.

An **answer space** is a place where the answers that were computed by the worker agents are put and where they can be picked up by the clients. The computation result is sent directly (not routed) to the answer space.

3.2   Allocation Pattern

The arbiter pattern is responsible to decide about LB and to redirect load between the load spaces of different local nodes. The basic components of the arbiter pattern (see fig. 2 (a)) are: load space, allocation agents, policies, and allocation space.

There are three kinds of **allocation agents**: *Arbiter agents*, *IN agents*, and *OUT agents*. Arbiter agents query the load of the load space and decide about re-distribution of work. They publish this information to the routing space in form of routing requests. Both IN and OUT agents read routing information

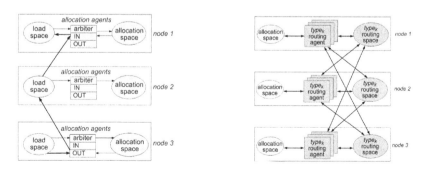

Fig. 2. (a) Allocation pattern. (b) Routing pattern.

from the allocation space and pull respectively push work from/to another node in a network to which the current node has a connection.

Transfer policy determines whether and in which form a resource should participate in load distribution and in that sense, the classification of resources is done [37]. A simple transfer policy would be to define two parameter values T_1 and T_2 (see fig. 1 (b)) which can either be assumed to be static or can be changed dynamically.

Location policy determines a suitable partner of a particular resource for LB [37]. The IN and OUT allocation agents assume that the information about the (best) partner to/from which to distribute load can be queried from the allocation space.

The **allocation space** holds information about partner nodes as computed by the location policy. This information is queried by the allocation agents and can be either statically configured or dynamically computed by so-called routing agents (see section 3.3). For the latter case, the allocation space can also be used to store information about decisions and subsequent resulting routing demands of the arbiter agent, i.e. whether load shall be get rid off or new load shall be fetched from other nodes. This might cause routing agents to become active.

3.3 Routing Pattern

The routing pattern is responsible to execute the location policy according to a special LB algorithm. The basic components of the arbiter pattern (see fig. 2 (b)) are: allocation space, routing agents, and routing space.

Routing agents perform a special routing strategy to implement a certain LB algorithm. They are either always active and continuously do their jobs, or triggered upon requests of the arbiter allocation agent. In both cases they perform the location policy by communicating with other routing agents of the same type, which thus form a dynamically structured overlay network [1].

The collaboration between routing agents of different nodes is carried out via the corresponding **routing spaces** of this type. Each kind of routing agents has its own routing space. Here, specific information as required by the applied algorithm is stored and retrieved, e.g. pheromones if we use ants, or duration of waggle dance if we use bees [36]. Eventually, the information about a best or suitable partner node is stored in an allocation space where the corresponding IN or OUT allocation agents can grab this information and distribute the load between the local node and its partner node.

3.4 Pattern Composition

The above described patterns can be composed towards more complex patterns by "hooking" them via shared spaces. They must agree on the format of entries stored in these spaces, and on the interaction patterns on these. E.g. to combine the local node pattern with the allocation pattern both must share the same load space. The arbiter agent must be able to query the load information and the IN and OUT allocation agents must understand the request entries written

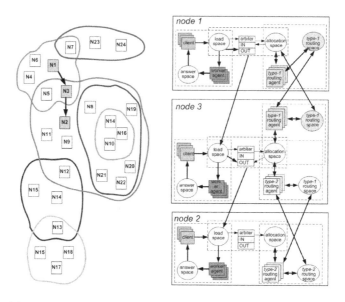

Fig. 3. (a) Network topology configuration example. (b) Pattern composition.

by the clients. This kind of composition offers more flexibility than the composition possibilities in message exchange patterns as supported by enterprise service bus middleware, where basically assemblies of patterns are build. With SILBA patterns, bi-directional control flows are possible and arbitrary logical network configurations can be easily constructed (dynamically). Fig. 3 (a) depicts 7 networks that have different relationships to each other. Nodes can belong to one or more networks, e.g., nodes N1 and N2 are part of one network each, whereas N3 belongs to two networks. Fig. 3 (b) shows the composition of the mentioned nodes N1, N2, and N3 in more detail.

4   Implementation with a Space-Based Middleware

We use a space-based architecture (extensible virtual shared memory[1] [10]) that generalizes Linda tuple based communication [15] as well as several concepts that have been proposed in the literature to make the space extensible (e.g. reactions [32], programmable behavior ([6], [13]), introduction of priority and probability tags [4]) in one single concept called *shared containers* [28].

4.1   Shared Containers and Scheduler

A shared container is a not-nested sub-space that maintains *entries*. An entry is formally defined as a multiset of labeled values called properties [10].

---

[1] The Java based open source implementation is available at www.xvsm.org

A property can be used to represent either a payload or meta-data relevant for coordination. This way the entry offers a clear separation between user data (cf. message body) and coordination data (cf. message head). Meta-model operations are: create-container, destroy-container; access operations are like in the Linda model [15] (where they are termed rd, out, and in): read, write, take, and destroy; transactional operations are: transaction-start, transaction-commit, and transaction-rollback. Operations may take a timeout parameter, specifying the time after which the operation is de-scheduled from the core with an exception, if it was not fulfilled until then. Timeout of transaction-start is an important feature that issues the entire transaction to abort if the timeout has expired. Each container has one or more *coordinators* that define the exact semantics of each operation. A coordinator is a user defineable coordination mechanism that specifies how the data in the container are accessed. Typical examples include fifo order, key selection, access via label names using the built-in relational query operators [10], template matching (cf. Linda), RDF queries, or XML querying facilities [40].

A shared data space is a collection of containers. A container is addressed via its URL in the internet. A lookup mechanism resolves a published container name to its URL. A container can refer to other (sub)containers forming a more complex coordination data structure. The asynchronous and blackboard based space-based communication model allows programmers to explicitly control interactions among processes via shared data. It is advantageous to serve for the collaboration of autonomic (multi) agents as it avoids a coupling through direct interactions between the agents ([6], [32]). All interactions of an agent are carried out via its environment [23] in a symmetric and autonomous way.

As a further extension to the classical Linda model, a scheduling mechanism exists that can start agents at a certain, dynamically configurable time schedule. The migration of an agent can therefore easily be mapped into requesting a new agent that has access to the same shared containers at another site, and then terminating the original one.

Each SILBA space is realized by an addressable container. For the implementation we assume that every container can be reached in the Internet. All containers provide the navigational, built-in XVSM query language [10] (relational operators, sorting, and counting).

4.2   Local Node Implementation

Load space is a container with an implicit coordinator termed *load coordinator*, and the answer space uses a key coordinator for the requestID. The load coordinator keeps track of every request that is inserted, when it is removed, and of all worker registrations. It implements a policy that decides about UL, OK, or OL of this node depending on the current number of workers and requests. Of course, more sophisticated transfer policies can be applied, that also take into consideration statistics information as well as operating system load, and hardware specifications. As the coordinator is pluggable, this policy can be changed at any time, even dynamically.

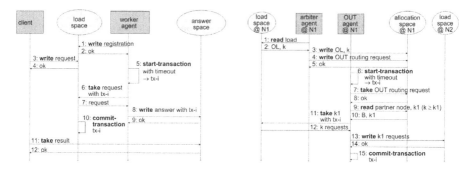

Fig. 4. (a) Local node agent interaction. (b) Allocation agent interaction.

Fig. 4 (a) shows a scenario of agent collaboration at local node level. First, each worker agent must register at the load space. It will e.g. write the following entry to the load space[2]: "[**workerId**:myID, **workerRole**:translator]". Then clients can issue requests by writing tuple like "[**job**:compile, **params**:myProg, **description**:"compile a java program", **timeout**:100, **answerURL**:myURL, **reqID**:123, **clientID**:456,**workerRole**:JavaCompiler]" into the load space.

The worker agents compete for tasks but only one will be able to execute the take operation using a new local transaction tx-i, execute the task, write the result as answer entry of the form "[**result**:resultData, **statusCode**:ok, **reqID**:123, **clientID**:456]" into the answer space using tx-i, and finally commit tx-i. If a worker that fails after having called take request and before committing the transaction tx-i, the timeout given at transaction start will fire and cause the rollback of tx-i. Failover is achieved in that another worker can take the request. Finally, the client takes the result from the answer container, correlating it with its request via the request ID, using the key coordinator for that.

4.3 Allocation Implementation

Fig. 4 (b) shows an interaction scenario of an OUT allocation agent. The arbiter agent continuously reads the load information from the load space, using the load coordinator of the container. It writes this information into the routing space. If the result is OL, it also generates an OUT routing request. The OUT agent watches for outgoing routing requests, in a newly created transaction takes a next routing request, tries to read a partner information from the allocation space, and if found, takes k1 (k1 ≤ k) requests from its load space and transfers them to the found partner site, and finally commits its local transaction. If no outgoing routing request is found, or if not (yet) partner information exists, it will abort the transaction and try later. For the case that the worker crashes, a transaction timeout is used at transaction start.

---

[2] Property labels that have been standardized for the LB scenario and must be know by agents for the interoperability of the patterns are written in boldface.

4.4   Routing Implementation

Fig. 5 shows a basic routing scheme started by node A in that an OUT routing request is found in the allocation space. The routing agent at site A – performing a certain strategy - reads this request, then it reads the routing information from its dedicated routing space (it will find here one or more neighbors depending on which algorithm it implements, e.g. ants [37], or bees ([8], [29], [36])), and routes the request to the neighbor(s). The routing agent at site B behaves in the same way and this goes so on until a routing agent at a site X finds out that its local node is OK or UL and can accept a certain amount k1 (k1 ≤ k) of requests. It will write this information directly back in a P2P manner to the originally requesting site A. This way, the location policy that resolves requests for partner nodes is implemented.

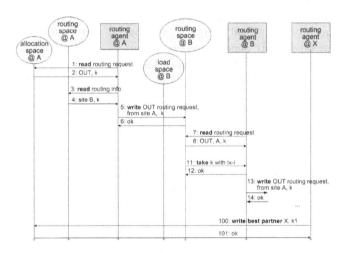

Fig. 5. Routing agent interaction

5   Examples and Benchmarks

5.1   Mapping Some Algorithms to SILBA

To demonstrate the agility of the SILBA pattern based framework, we show that algorithms can be easily exchanged, and mapped some well-known LB algorithms to SILBA:

1) *Random/Round Robin Algorithm.* Some neighbors of the current node are statically stored in the routing space at initialization phase. These neighbors are retrieved from the container, one of them is chosen randomly and the task is scheduled. Similarly, Round Robin can be mapped.

2) *Sender/Receiver/Symmetric Algorithm.* For the Sender algorithm, the OL node (Sender) initiates the routing. This can be achieved by configuring just an OUT allocation agent, but no IN allocation agent. Analogously, for Receiver

algorithm, where the UL starts to look for available tasks, an IN agent must be scheduled at the corresponding local nodes XVSM runtime. The Symmetric algorithm can be mapped by combining Sender and Receiver configurations.

3) *Adapted Genetic Algorithm (GA)*. We adapted the algorithm suggested in [47], i.e. we have no central coordinator. The routing agents of nodes implement the algorithm that means we have several GAs, performed on different nodes concurrently running. The description of the sliding window technique is remodulated – we can say that the size of window(s) is the same for all GAs and fixed to the number of nodes, where every node has the current (waiting) task as its candidate in that window. Every GA will obtain some combination according to the fitness function – they can be compared and the best one can be chosen as the final combination (at time t). The issue who will be appointed to do the actions of "comparing" and "choosing" is also done by the routing agents. They take care of that, communicate and exchange this information. Therefore, GA fires continously, i.e., every OL node and UL node can trigger GA and the procedure is repeated until all requests are done. In our case, the sliding window should not be directly dependable on a client who can put tasks somewhere in the network. A node has its load space for waiting (and new-coming) tasks which will be filled with requests from its node plus from all nodes of reachable networks each time when GA is triggered.

5.2   Benchmarks

As a proof of concept that the SILBA implementation produces reasonable results, in a first step these three different algorithms (Round Robin, Sender Negotiation, and Adapted GA) for location policies have also been implemented and benchmarked. The transfer policy (implemented by the load coordinator) was realized by relatively determined values T_1 and T_2.

The benchmarks were performed on a cluster of 4 machines. Each machine had the following characteristics: 2*Quad AMD 2,0GHz with 16 GB RAM. We simulated the network of 16 (virtual) nodes. At the beginning of each test runs, the starting state was "cold start" and all nodes were UL. The maximum number of tasks (that represented the load in the system) was 400. The obtained results can be seen in figs. 6 and 7. The benchmark time is the makespan.

Fig. 7 shows the distribution of tasks time per node, i.e. how much each node was active during the execution of a particular algorithm and how much load it had. Note: many tasks have been done in parallel, so that's why the complete benchmark(s) time(s) is (are) less than some times in fig. 7. This figure provide an additional information and analisys about the "behavior" of different algorithms, but the real comparison of algorithms is shown in fig. 6.

As a result, Round Robin algorithm activates all nodes in the network, whereas using Sender algorithm all work was done by activating only a few nodes and the rest of the network was idle. During the execution of the location policy by using the Round Robin algorithm, all nodes (except node 14) were in the state OK, and node 14 changed its state from OK to OL and vice versa. During the execution of location policy by using Sender algorithm, the majority of nodes

Algorithm	# Nodes	in ms
Round Robin	16	19893160
Sender	16	18721100
Adapted Genetic Alg.	16	9397000

Fig. 6. Benchmarking three different LB Algorithms on 16 Nodes

Node1	Node2	Node3	Node4	Node5	Node6	Node7	Node8	Node9	Node10	Node11	Node12	Node13	Node14	Node15	Node16
385100	248340	268530	573520	614370	375390	528520	296840	461530	343530	495260	385170	253960	29576790	368160	445830
7567000	9125000	4231000	9962000	12843000	2045000	8947000	3241000	9780000	12125000	11286000	9800000	9015000	450724000	8043000	9662000
55876000	4704000	4698000	4255000	8145000	4053000	2968000	3716000	4067000	4164000	4301000	4272000	4882000	4578000	3748000	3109000

Fig. 7. Row 1: Round Robin. Row 2: Sender. Row 3: Adapted GA.

were not activated, node 8 participated and stayed in OK state all the time, where nodes 1 and 14 changed their state from OK to OL and vice versa.

6   Conclusion

We presented a generic and composable load balancing (LB) pattern for worker agents having access to either one local node, or many nodes in the intranet and in the internet. The intention was to develop a self-organized LB architecture, extensible towards different LB strategies and adaptable to any kind of domain-specific problems. This objective could be solved by basing the pattern rather on a space-based architecture style than on classical message exchange patterns. The space-based collaboration allows for a high decoupling of the agents and enables their autonomic behavior. Transfer and location policies can be plugged in by means of coordinators and routing agents. Worker agents are active and autonomously deciding whether and which task to take, and whether to execute it or not; routing agents exhibit an autonomic behavior, if the transfer and location policies are based on intelligent algorithms that support self-organization. This general pattern can therefore easily be populated with a wide range of LB algorithms. New resources can be dynamically added or removed to the resource-pool at any time and the failure of one worker agent or node does not jeopardize the functioning of the whole system.

We have carried out first benchmarks that proved that an approach using active agents can be adapted to any underlying algorithm. This justifies the design of SILBA as a pattern that supports autonomic agents. The pattern supports nested networks at any level through composition. Even a mixed usage of strategies is possible. Moreover, further tuning parameters can easily be added, as the data entries and structures in the coordination space are also extensible. We considered only the time in our benchmarks, and intend to treat other important aspects of load balancing (cost of communication, communication delay etc.) in future investigations, to work on different types of metrics, to implement intelligent algorithms (e.g., swarm intelligence as proposed in [36]), and to benchmark and compare different instantiations of SILBA with each other as well as with other existing algorithms for load balancing.

Acknowledgements. We would like to thank Fabian Fischer for implementing the SILBA pattern and performing the benchmarks, and Richard Mordinyi for his helpful comments on this text.

References

1. Androutsellis-Theotokis, S., Spinellis, D.: A survey of peer-to-peer content distribution technologies. ACM Comput. Surv. 36(4), 335–371 (2004)
2. Barker, K., Chernikov, A., Chrisochoides, N., Pingali, K.: A load balancing framework for adaptive and asynchronous applications. IEEE Transactions on Parallel and Distributed Systems 15(2), 183–192 (2004)
3. Barker, K.J., Chrisochoides, N.P.: An evaluation of a framework for the dynamic load balancing of highly adaptive and irregular parallel applications. In: SC 2003: Proceedings of the 2003 ACM/IEEE conference on Supercomputing, p. 45 (2003)
4. Bravetti, M., Gorrieri, R., Lucchi, R., Zavattaro, G.: Quantitative information in the tuple space coordination model. Theor. Comput. Sci. 346(1), 28–57 (2005)
5. Bronevich, A.G., Meyer, W.: Load balancing algorithms based on gradient methods and their analysis through algebraic graph theory. J. Parallel Distrib. Comput. 68(2), 209–220 (2008)
6. Cabri, G., Leonardi, L., Zambonelli, F.: Mars: A programmable coordination architecture for mobile agents. IEEE Internet Computing 4(4), 26–35 (2000)
7. Chen, J.-C., Liao, G.-X., Hsie, S., Liao, C.-H.: A study of the contribution made by evolutionary learning on dynamic load-balancing problems in distributed computing systems. Expert Syst. Appl. 34(1), 357–365 (2008)
8. Chong, C.S., Sivakumar, A.I., Low, M.Y.H., Gay, K.L.: A bee colony optimization algorithm to job shop scheduling. In: WSC 2006: Proc. of the 38th conference on Winter simulation, pp. 1954–1961 (2006)
9. Cortés, A., Ripoll, A., Cedó, F., Senar, M.A., Luque, E.: An asynchronous and iterative load balancing algorithm for discrete load model. J. Parallel Distrib. Comput. 62(12), 1729–1746 (2002)
10. Craß, S., Kühn, E., Salzer, G.: Algebraic foundation of a data model for an extensible space-based collaboration protocol. In: 13th International Database Engineering & Applications Symposium, IDEAS (to appear, 2009)
11. Davidsson, P., Johansson, S., Svahnberg, M.: Characterization and evaluation of multi-agent system architectural styles. In: Garcia, A., Choren, R., Lucena, C., Giorgini, P., Holvoet, T., Romanovsky, A. (eds.) SELMAS 2005. LNCS, vol. 3914, pp. 179–188. Springer, Heidelberg (2006)
12. Dobson, S., Denazis, S., Fernández, A., Gaïti, D., Gelenbe, E., Massacci, F., Nixon, P., Saffre, F., Schmidt, N., Zambonelli, F.: A survey of autonomic communications. ACM Trans. Auton. Adapt. Syst. 1(2), 223–259 (2006)
13. Ducasse, S., Hofmann, T., Nierstrasz, O.: Openspaces: An object-oriented framework for reconfigurable coordination spaces. In: Porto, A., Roman, G.-C. (eds.) COORDINATION 2000. LNCS, vol. 1906, pp. 1–18. Springer, Heidelberg (2000)
14. Eager, D.L., Lazowska, E.D., Zahorjan, J.: Adaptive load sharing in homogeneous distributed systems. IEEE Trans. Softw. Eng. 12(5), 662–675 (1986)

15. Gelernter, D., Carriero, N.: Coordination languages and their significance. Commun. ACM 35(2), 97–107 (1992)
16. Georgousopoulos, C., Rana, O.F.: Combining state and model-based approaches for mobile agent load balancing. In: SAC 2003: Proceedings of the 2003 ACM symposium on Applied computing, pp. 878–885 (2003)
17. Godfrey, B., Lakshminarayanan, K., Surana, S., Karp, R., Stoica, I.: Load balancing in dynamic structured P2P systems. In: Proc. IEEE INFOCOM (2004)
18. Gomoluch, J., Schroeder, M.: Information agents on the move: A survey with load balancing with mobile agents. Software Focus 2(2) (2001)
19. Herrero, P., Bosque, J.L., Pérez, M.S.: An agents-based cooperative awareness model to cover load balancing delivery in grid environments. In: OTM Workshops (1), pp. 64–74 (2007)
20. Ho, C.K., Ewe, H.T.: Ant colony optimization approaches for the dynamic load-balanced clustering problem in ad hoc networks. In: Swarm Intelligence Symposium, Hawaii, pp. 76–83. IEEE, Los Alamitos (2007)
21. Hohpe, G., Woolf, B.: Enterprise Integration Patterns: Designing, Building, and Deploying Messaging Solutions. Addison-Wesley, Reading (2003)
22. Hu, T.-L., Chen, G., Chen, K., Dong, J.-X.: An adaptive load balancing framework for parallel database systems based on collaborative agents, vol. 1, pp. 464–468. IEEE, Los Alamitos (2005)
23. Janssens, N., Steegmans, E., Holvoet, T., Verbaeten, P.: An agent design method promoting separation between computation and coordination. In: SAC 2004: Proceedings of the 2004 ACM symposium on Applied computing, pp. 456–461 (2004)
24. Johansson, S., Davidsson, P., Kristell, M.: Four multi-agent architectures for intelligent network load management. In: Karmouch, A., Magedanz, T., Delgado, J. (eds.) MATA 2002. LNCS, vol. 2521, pp. 239–248. Springer, Heidelberg (2002)
25. Karger, D.R., Ruhl, M.: Simple efficient load balancing algorithms for peer-to-peer systems. In: SPAA 2004: Proceedings of the sixteenth annual ACM symposium on Parallelism in algorithms and architectures, pp. 36–43 (2004)
26. Keren, A., Barak, A.: Adaptive placement of parallel java agents in a scalable computing cluster, vol. 10, pp. 971–976 (1998)
27. Krueger, P., Shivaratri, N.G.: Adaptive location policies for global scheduling. IEEE Trans. Softw. Eng. 20(6), 432–444 (1994)
28. Kühn, E., Mordinyi, R., Keszthelyi, L., Schreiber, C.: Introducing the concept of customizable structured spaces for agent coordination in the production automation domain. In: The 8th Int.Conference on Autonomous Agents and Multiagent Systems, AAMAS 2009 (2008)
29. Lemmens, N., de Jong, S., Tuyls, K., Nowé, A.: Bee behaviour in multi-agent systems, pp. 145–156 (2008)
30. Lin, F.C.H., Keller, R.M.: The gradient model load balancing method. IEEE Trans. Softw. Eng. 13(1), 32–38 (1987)
31. Murata, Y., Takizawa, H., Inaba, T., Kobayashi, H.: A distributed and cooperative load balancing mechanism for large-scale p2p systems. In: SAINT-W 2006: Proceedings of the International Symposium on Applications on Internet Workshops, pp. 126–129. IEEE, Los Alamitos (2006)
32. Pietro Picco, G., Murphy, A.L., Roman, G.-C.: Lime: Linda meets mobility. In: ICSE 1999: Proceedings of the 21st international conference on Software engineering, pp. 368–377. IEEE, Los Alamitos (1999)
33. Putrycz, E.: Design and implementation of a portable and adaptable load balancing framework. In: CASCON 2003: Proceedings of the 2003 conference of the Centre for Advanced Studies on Collaborative research, pp. 238–252. IBM Press (2003)

34. Rahman, M.A.: Load balancing in dht based p2p networks. In: 5th Int. Conference on Electrical and Computer Engineering, ICECE 2008, pp. 164–171 (2008)
35. Rajagopalan, A., Hariri, S.: An agent based dynamic load balancing system, pp. 164–171 (2000)
36. Sesum-Cavic, V., Kühn, E.: Instantiation of a generic model for load balancing with intelligent algorithms. In: Hummel, K.A., Sterbenz, J.P.G. (eds.) IWSOS 2008. LNCS, vol. 5343, pp. 311–317. Springer, Heidelberg (2008)
37. Stützle, T., Hoos, H.: Max-min ant system. Future Generation Comput. Syst. 16(9), 889–914 (2000)
38. Thant, H., San, K., Tun, K., Naing, T., Thein, N.: Mobile agents based load balancing method for parallel applications. In: 6th Asia-Pacific Symposium on Information and Telecommunication Technologies, APSITT 2005 (2005)
39. Tian, J., Liu, Y., Yang, X.-H., Du, R.: Design and analysis of a novel load-balancing model based on mobile agent. In: Yeung, D.S., Liu, Z.-Q., Wang, X.-Z., Yan, H. (eds.) ICMLC 2005. LNCS (LNAI), vol. 3930, pp. 70–80. Springer, Heidelberg (2006)
40. Tolksdorf, R., Menezes, R.: Using swarm intelligence in linda systems. In: Omicini, A., Petta, P., Pitt, J. (eds.) ESAW 2003. LNCS (LNAI), vol. 3071, pp. 49–65. Springer, Heidelberg (2004)
41. Une, H., Qian, F.: Network load balancing algorithm using ants computing. In: IAT 2003: Proceedings of the IEEE/WIC International Conference on Intelligent Agent Technology, p. 428 (2003)
42. Wang, Y., Liu, J.: Macroscopic model of agent-based load balancing on grids. In: AAMAS 2003: Proceedings of the second international joint conference on Autonomous agents and multiagent systems, pp. 804–811. ACM, New York (2003)
43. Xu, M., Guan, J.: Routing based load balancing for unstructured p2p networks. Future Generation Communication and Networking 2, 332–337 (2007)
44. Xu, Z., Bhuyan, L.: Effective load balancing in p2p systems. In: CCGRID 2006: Proceedings of the Sixth IEEE International Symposium on Cluster Computing and the Grid, pp. 81–88. IEEE, Los Alamitos (2006)
45. Zhu, Y., Hu, Y.: Efficient, proximity-aware load balancing for dht-based p2p systems. IEEE Trans. on Parallel and Distributed Systems 16(4), 349–361 (2005)
46. Zoels, S., Despotovic, Z., Kellerer, W.: Load balancing in a hierarchical dht-based p2p system, pp. 353–361. IEEE, Los Alamitos (2007)
47. Zomaya, A.Y., Teh, Y.-H.: Observations on using genetic algorithms for dynamic load-balancing. IEEE Transactions on Parallel and Distributed Systems 12(9), 899–911 (2001)

A Goal-Oriented Approach for Modelling Self-organising MAS

Mirko Morandini[1], Frédéric Migeon[3], Marie-Pierre Gleizes[3], Christine Maurel[3],
Loris Penserini[2], and Anna Perini[1]

[1] FBK IRST, Via Sommarive 18, I-38100 Trento, Italy
[2] University of Utrecht, Padualaan 14, Utrecht, The Netherlands
[3] IRIT, 118 Route de Narbonne, 31062 Toulouse, France
{morandini,perini}@fbk.eu, loris@cs.uu.nl,
{migeon,gleizes,maurel}@irit.fr

Abstract. Autonomous software agents provide a promising solution to the needs of decentralised networked systems, able to adapt their behaviour in a complex and dynamically changing environment.

Current agent-oriented software engineering methodologies tend to focus on different levels to realise such a self-adapting behaviour, namely the agent individual level and the global system level. The first requires to design a goal-directed agent behaviour, the second to design agents able to optimize their coordination with other peer agents in the organization, giving rise to system-level adaptation.

In this paper we propose to extend a goal-oriented engineering methodology to deal with the modelling of organisations that are able to self-organise in order to reach their goals in a changing environment. To deliver on this aim, we combine *Tropos4AS*, an extension of *TROPOS* for adaptive systems, with concepts, guidelines and modelling steps from the *ADELFE* methodology, which provides a bottom-up approach for engineering collaborative multi-agent societies with an emergent behaviour.

The resulting MAS has self-adaptation properties, having agents that are able to change their behaviour according to changes in the environment, and having organisations that adapt themselves to changing needs. The approach is illustrated by modelling a collaborative multi-agent system for conference management.

1 Introduction

Nowadays, networked systems require decentralized and flexible configurations, which are able to support mediated services (e.g. flight booking systems) as well as peer-to-peer business/social relationships (e.g. eBay, social networking). Such software systems need to exhibit an increasing level of self-adaptivity, at the system or component level, in order to operate efficiently in a dynamically changing environment. Engineering such decentralized, self-adapting networked systems poses challenging issues for the software engineering methodologies research.

Autonomous software agents have been largely studied for their property to exhibit self-adaptive behaviours at different levels. At the level of the individual agent, the agent has ability to perceive the surrounding environment, to interpret collected information

H. Aldewereld, V. Dignum, and G. Picard (Eds.): ESAW 2009, LNAI 5881, pp. 33–48, 2009.

and to reason on it. This enables it to decide which behaviour to adopt in a context-aware manner. At the level of global (multi-agent) system, agent cooperation mechanisms can give raise dynamically to an emergent behaviour of the system.

Agent-Oriented Software Engineering methodologies propose methods and techniques to build this type of systems, but typically they tend to focus on a specific level of self-adaptivity. So, for instance the *TROPOS* methodology [3], and its extension for self-adaptivity *Tropos4AS* [13], focus on building software agents that behave in a goal-directed way and are able to dynamically switch from a behaviour to another one to avoid failure in achieving their own goals or to better meet quality requirements. On the other side, *ADELFE* [2] is an agent-oriented methodology tailored to engineer self-adaptive multi-agent societies by cooperative agents based on the AMAS theory [1]. *ADELFE* enables with a bottom-up approach to define the nominal and cooperative behaviour of the agents which leads to self-organisation and system's self-adaptation.

We study here how to engineer agent systems which can adapt autonomously to a changing environment. This system should exhibit a self-adaptive behaviour of single agents as well as a self-organising behaviour of the agent society.

In this paper, we investigate benefits from extending the *Tropos4AS* agent modelling framework with *ADELFE* modelling activities, along two main lines: *1)* extending the *Tropos4AS* modelling language meta-model by including concepts from the *ADELFE* meta-model; and *2)* revisiting the *Tropos4AS* design process by including *ADELFE* activities. For illustration, the process is applied to a conference management system example, giving a first evidence for its benefits.

The paper is organised as follows: in Section 2, the two methodologies *TROPOS* with the *Tropos4AS* extension, and *ADELFE* are briefly recalled and compared. Section 3 describes the *Tropos4AS* extension at the level of the meta-model and at the level of the design process. Section 4 illustrates the application of the resulting design approach to the conference management system example and discusses main findings from this experience. Related work is presented in Section 5, conclusions and future work in Section 6.

2   Methodological Background

2.1   Tropos and Tropos4AS: Goal-Oriented Modelling

The agent-oriented software engineering methodology *TROPOS* [3] adopts ideas from the MAS paradigm and from *i**, an organizational modelling framework for requirements analysis, founded on the 'mentalistic' notions of actor, goal, softgoal, task, resource, and social dependency between actors. The *TROPOS* modelling language is used along the whole development process: in Early Requirements Analysis (ER) the human organisational settings in which the system will be used are analysed; in Late Requirements Analysis (LR) the system-to-be is introduced and its requirements are modelled in terms of dependencies between stakeholders and the system itself; in Architectural Design (AD) the system actor is decomposed into components (*sub-system actors*), each having responsibility for the achievement of a part of the system's goals; in Detailed Design (DD) the system components and their interactions are further specified. *The*

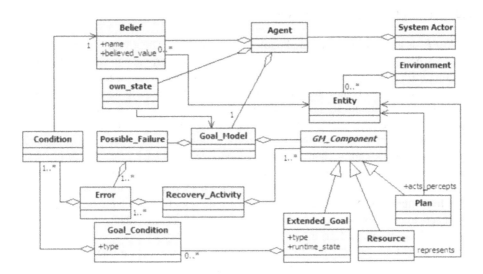

Fig. 1. The Tropos4AS metamodel, showing the composition of an agent (simplified view of the goal model)

modelling process follows a top-down approach, refining the global goals, which were delegated from the stakeholders to the system-to-be.

For the aim of this work, we give more details on the LR and AD phases. At the end of the LR phase, the system's requirements are modelled by delegation of goals and tasks from the stakeholders and users in the organisation, to the system, itself modelled as an actor. The delegated goals are then organised in the system's goal model, decomposed into more concrete goals and possibly operationalised by plans. Subsequently, as key step in AD, the system actor is decomposed into sub-actors, which will become the software agents at the implementation (in Fig. 1). This decomposition is usually done by distributing system functionalities to single subactors and gathering similar functionalities. Different architectural patterns can be applied to it, e.g. [4]. As next step, the single sub-agents' goal models are detailed, by goal analysis, decomposition and delegation.

Tropos4AS [13] extends *TROPOS* goal models to enable the description of systems that shall be able to adapt to environmental changes. *Tropos4AS* introduces modelling of an actor's perceived environment and of possible failures that can be identified and prevented by recovery activities. Moreover, goals can be annotated to define the runtime goal achievement behaviour, with various goal types and conditions related to the environment, for goal creation, achievement and failure. The resulting design model is mapped into implementation language constructs to derive a code skeleton.

Fig. 1 shows details from the *Tropos4AS* metamodel, illustrating the composition of a single *Tropos4AS* agent, an actor identified as sub-system actor at *TROPOS* detailed design.

2.2   ADELFE: Cooperative Agents

ADELFE[1] is an agent-oriented methodology for designing Adaptive Multi-Agent System (AMAS) [1]. MAS developed according to *ADELFE* provide an emergent global function [10]. It is qualified as emergent because it is not coded inside the agent. To obtain this emergent behaviour, the AMAS theory [5] propones to design agents with the ability to autonomously and locally modify their interactions in order to react to changes in their environment. This system is self-organising and is able to adapt to its environment. According to the AMAS principles, interactions between agents depend on their local view and on their ability to "cooperate" with each other. Every internal part of the system (agent) pursues an individual objective and interacts with agents it knows by respecting cooperative techniques which lead to avoid or to remove Non Cooperative Situations (NCS) like conflict, concurrence etc. Facing a NCS, a cooperative agent acts to come back to a cooperative state and permanently adapts itself to unpredictable situations while learning on others.

The *ADELFE* methodology covers the phases of usual software design from the requirements to the implementation, with the addition of specific activities to support the design of adaptive multi-agent systems.

The modelling process follows a bottom-up approach, defining the cooperation rules and activities of the single agents, leading to an emergent behaviour of the system.

In the analysis phase, *ADELFE* gives guidelines to decide if the application is adapted to an implementation following the AMAS principles. Furthermore, it provides guidance to identify cooperative agents among all the entities defined during the final requirements. Concerning the design phase, three activities are added. The first concerns the relationships between agents. The second is about the agent design. In this activity, the cooperation failures are defined. Third, a fast prototyping activity helps to build and verify the agent behaviour. Moreover, the implementation phase uses Model-Driven Engineering principles to produce code skeletons for the MAY[2] middleware.

The design phase is based on a AMAS metamodel characterising as precisely as possible the concepts involved in the AMAS principles and mandatory for *ADELFE* such as Perceptions, Actions, Aptitudes, Cooperations Rules, Non Cooperative Situations, Representations, Skills, etc. Figure 2 shows that a cooperative agent is defined with a *PerceptionModule*, a *DecisionModule* and an *ActionModule*. Decision is implemented with *Rules* tha trigger an *action* or a *skill*. These rules describe either standard behavior (with *StandardRules*) or cooperation (with *CooperativeRule*) according to *NonCooperativeSituation* type.

2.3   Comparing the Two Methodologies

Up to now, in this section we described two AOSE methodologies founding on very different principles and having a different scope. While *ADELFE* is tailored to decentralised, adaptive complex systems and follows a bottom-up approach to eventually

---

[1] ADELFE is a French acronym for "Atelier de Dveloppement de Logiciels Fonctionnalit Emergente", see http://www.irit.fr/ADELFE

[2] http://www.irit.fr/MAY

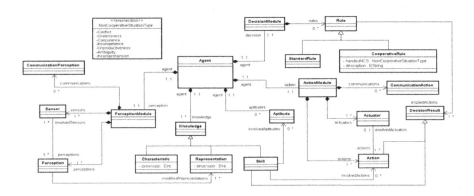

Fig. 2. Portion of the ADELFE metamodel concerning the cooperative agent

reach the global goal of the system in an emergent way through agent cooperation, *TRO-POS* claims to be a general methodology, where the system goals elicited by analysing the organisational settings, through steps of refinement and decomposition lead to program components implementable in software agents.

Albeit in both methodologies, agents are a metaphor for an autonomous entity with own goals and abilities, trying to achieve their local goals, the process of obtaining the single agent's goals presents conceptual differences: *ADELFE* agents are identified and their behaviour specified, analysing the domain entities, their role in the system and the relationships between them. They create a complex organisation by having at run-time a high number of instances for each agent type. The global goal of the system, which the stakeholders want to obtain from the software system, is modelled in use cases, but this global goal is not coded by the single agents and can only be observed, emerging from the collective behaviour.

The *TROPOS* development process starts with requirements elicitation and analysis, to capture the objectives of the stakeholders. The MAS architecture is then obtained by analysing the organisational settings with the goals and tasks delegated to the system, decomposing them and delegating their satisfaction to single roles or agents, following general engineering rules to achieve low coupling and high correlation between the tasks to be achieved by a single agent.

Next, the structure and abilities of the single agents have to be defined. In *ADELFE*, a central role is given to agent interaction and coordination, specifying behaviour rules and associated activities both for the agent's nominal behaviour (i.e. the ordinary behaviour exhibited by the agent in a working situation without problems and failures) and its cooperative behaviour (Especially focusing on how to react to collaboration problems). Moreover, the agent's belief (representation) of the outside world, and its sensors and actuators are defined.

TROPOS agents are characterised both by the goals delegated from the stakeholders, and the dependencies to other agents; the nominal behaviour is defined by its goal model, which includes plans to perform and resources to provide, to achieve goals.

By the *Tropos4AS* extensions, the goal runtime behaviour can be further specified, defining goal types and conditions on to the environment perceived by the agent. Exceptional behaviour can be defined by modelling possible failures, causing errors, and recovery activities.

Finally, In the design phase, in both *TROPOS* and *ADELFE*, further details on the implementation can be given by UML2.0 diagrams.

3   Modelling of Self-organising MAS

Tropos4AS follows a top-down approach from the system to the single agents and their behaviour, and achieves traceability by decomposition and delegation of goals through the design phases.

TROPOS requirements modelling is prominent for it's ability to capture the organisational settings where the system to develop will be integrated and the dependencies and responsibilities of the agents in the system and the actors playing different roles in the organisation.

However, *TROPOS*, as well as *Tropos4AS*, lack of support for agent organisations, i.e. for modelling the dynamics of collaboration between software agent instances in a multi-agent organisation where each modelled agent has various instances, which can also be dynamically added and removed.

The *ADELFE* methodology was created specifically for the development of such agent organisations. However, it adopts a bottom-up approach, to achieve the system's goal in an emergent way; the relationship between global goal and single agent's behaviour is not modelled and the global goal can only be observed from action and interaction of the parts.

Integrating ideas and modelling steps from *ADELFE* we enrich *Tropos4AS* for the modelling of agent organisations.

A bottom-up addition of *ADELFE* cooperation rules (which fit well into the actual concept of failure modelling) will give to the run-time agent instances the knowledge for selection of and cooperation with their peers, and thus achieve an emergent self-organising behaviour to adapt to a changing environment.

3.1   Metamodel Extension

Here, we investigate how to extend the *Tropos4AS* meta-model with concepts taken from the *ADELFE* meta-model, and revise the *Tropos4AS* design process including steps that belong to the *ADELFE* approach.

To improve modelling the interplay of an agent with the entities and actors inside and outside the software system under development, we explicitly add the concept of agent's knowledge about itself and about its environment.

ADELFE provides modelling of the agent's knowledge by characteristics (facts the agent is sure about), representations of the environment as perceived through sensors, and the agent's skills (Fig. 2). We integrate characteristics and representations (corresponding to the agent's belief) in the extended model. Information captured by *Skills*, *Aptitudes*, the agents *Actions* and its nominal behaviour, encoded in *Rules*, is mainly covered by the *TROPOS* goal model, a main component of the *Tropos4AS* metamodel (Fig. 1).

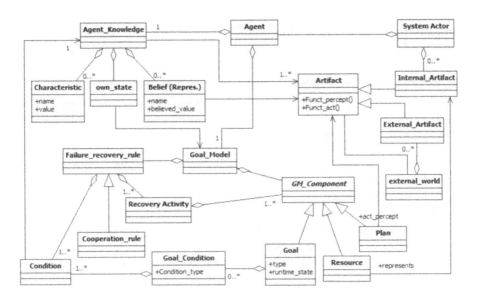

Fig. 3. Metamodel for adaptive, cooperative agents, which extends the TROPOS4AS meta-model with ADELFE concepts (simplified view of the goal model)

Understanding the interplay between the agent and its environment is of major importance to understand and model a system's self-adaptivity. To model the agent's environment we integrate ideas from the *Agents and Artifacts* approach [15]. Artifacts represent the non-intentional entities (*ADELFE* passive entities), in- and outside the boundary of the system to develop. They provide an interface to the external world, to the users and also to other agents, through *social artifacts* such as a whiteboard or a communication channel.

The extended metamodel is shown in Fig. 3 and defines an agent in the system (represented as a *TROPOS* system actor) with its components: goal model, knowledge (the "belief base"), the system and the external environment.

Regarding the aim of this paper, the most important step from *ADELFE*, integrated in the methodology, will be the elicitation of non-cooperative situations and modelling of the discovered so-called cooperation rules. We enhance *Tropos4AS* failure modelling by allowing to specify failure recovery with rules (class Failure_recovery_rule in Fig. 3). Cooperation rules are considered s specialization of failure recovery rules, with a well defined scope. Such failure recovery rules are composed by conditions to the agent's knowledge (on itself and its environment) and by recovery activities composed by represent a goal model fragment — a single *TROPOS Plan* (which corresponds to an *ADELFE Action*) or a more complex goal model.

3.2 Modelling Steps

We adapt the *TROPOS* modelling process to modelling of the newly introduced concepts. The proposed modelling steps are placed after the *TROPOS* Early (LR) and Late

Requirements (LR) phases, described in [17]. As result of the LR phase, the requirements are modelled in terms of strategic dependencies between stakeholders, such as users and other external actors, to the software system, which is also modelled as an actor. The system actor has its own goals, plans, resources which are derived along these dependencies. This model is given as input to the following modelling steps.

Step 1. With the LR model in input (an example in Fig. 4), define the system from the *ADELFE* viewpoint (*ADELFE* activity 12): identify passive and active entities in- and outside the system to develop, and identify from the active entities the autonomous agents participating in the collective task. Output: an AMAS-ML System-Environment diagram (Fig. 5).

Step 2. In the *TROPOS* AD phase, guide the decomposition of the system actor identified in the LR diagram, into sub-actors (the agents in the system), according to the agents identified in the AMAS-ML system-environment diagram. The *TROPOS* system will include agents participating to this global task and agents achieving non-collective goals delegated by some stakeholder, or that have to supervise the collective task. The actors participating in self-organisation are highlighted (Fig. 6).

Step 3. With the *TROPOS* model resulting from *Step 2* in input, detail the high-level **nominal behaviour** of the single agents in the system by defining their goal and plan dependencies, and detailing their goal models by *TROPOS* goal analysis, until finding the plans to achieve the goals. The environment perceived by the agent is modelled considering the passive entities identified in the previous step, and the resources modelled in Tropos LR. From the dependencies and interactions between entities, the perception and action functionalities of the artifacts in the environment can be identified. Beliefs describe the agent's perception of these artifacts. This step is no more detailed here as it is not central to self-organisation.

Step 4. With the *Tropos4AS* model of Step 3 in input, which includes the dependencies between agents, focus on the collective task and define the necessary interactions, following *ADELFE* activity 13. Give special attention to failures that can arise from perturbations in the interaction between agents (which are cooperative by definition). The **exceptional behaviour** of each agent is now detailed by identifying non-cooperative situations that can arise. It is captured by conditions on the agent's knowledge together with the recovery activities to execute (an example in Table 1). These rules guide the single agent's self-organising behaviour, with activities that can be categorised in three groups: change of the own behaviour (*tuning*), change of partnership (*reorganisation*), and creation/deletion of agents (*evolution*).

Next, following the *Tropos4AS* process, the goal model built in step 3 can be detailed, adding conditions, goal types and relationships, to define a more detailed nominal behaviour, and modelling possible failures not ascribed to collaboration. Modelling can continue with *TROPOS* Detailed Design (DD), detailing plans (*capability level*) and low-level interactions by UML diagrams [17], obtaining models that can be directly used as input for the implementation phase. For example, following a mapping as in [12], goal models can be mapped to *Jadex* agent code, artifacts to Java classes and failure conditions, including cooperation rules, to goal conditions.

4   Application to an Example

The design process is shown on a conference management system (CMS) example, described in [6], a case study used several times for agent systems developed with different agent-oriented software engineering methodologies [7].

A conference management system involves several stakeholders and has to satisfy users playing various roles, such as authors, reviewers, program committee members and the publisher. In the submission phase, authors need to be supported, and subsequently, *R4P* suitable reviewers have to be found for each paper, distributing the workload evenly. For this, each paper is described by *KP* keywords providing its main expertise area. Each reviewer describes its expertise fields with *KR* keywords and should review at most *P4R* papers.

Reviews have to be collected and evaluated to decide about acceptance or rejection of each submission, and finally the authors have to be notified, and the corrected camera ready papers collected and formatted. The prepared proceedings have then to be handed out to the publisher for printing. Fig. 4 shows the corresponding *TROPOS* LR diagram.

We want to obtain a system composed by agents associated to each physical entity or role that has the need of autonomous decision and interaction, e.g. one for each paper, reviewer, etc. These agents are not "personal agents" acting selfish for the benefit of their relative stakeholder, but agents belonging to the system that are trusted and cooperative.

Interesting phases from the point of view of self-organisation between agents (which will then result in a system-mediated collaboration between physical actors or entities) are the assignment of papers to reviewers, the collection of reviews and the decision of paper acceptance. We focus on the scenarios involving the reviewers. The reviewing process can possibly also be exposed to different kinds of unwanted perturbations. For example, unavailable reviewers, an unbalanced amount of papers in a particular area with a small number of competent reviewers, or withdrawn for any reason. Despite these eventualities could, in this small example, also be handled deterministically, they give a good example to show how a robust system should self-adapting, to meet its

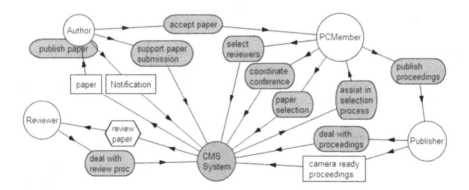

Fig. 4. *TROPOS* Late Requirements (LR) analysis: Definition of the system's objectives. Notice, that dependencies between actors entail a flow of information in the opposite direction.

objectives. We now show the modelling process, going through the steps defined in Section 3.2.

4.1   Architecture

Following Step 1, we analyse the diagram in output of the *TROPOS* LR phase (Fig. 4). We identify 7 active and 2 passive entities. The active entities participating in the system's collective task are the `paper` and `reviewer agents`, representing the single submitted papers and the reviewers (Fig. 5).

We give to the PC chair agent – an agent in *TROPOS*, and an active entity in *ADELFE* (but not one participating to the collective task) – the charge to observe the society and to decide when a stable and optimal state is reached, in which all papers are assigned to reviewers. It will also be able to advise reviewer agents to relax some constraints (e.g., allocation of more than P4R papers per reviewer).

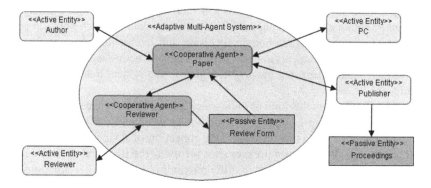

Fig. 5. Adelfe system-environment diagram showing the participating entities and the cooperative agents, inside the system boundary, related to the review assignment scenario

Guided by the agents and active entities identified in Fig. 5, following Step 2 we decompose the `CMS system` in (Fig.4) into four sub-actors: `paper agent` and `reviewer agent`, which take part in the collective task of paper-review assignment, will be associated to the single physical papers and reviewers. The `program chair` agent and the `proceedings agent` get their goals delegated from the physical actors playing the respective role in the organisation where the system is deployed and have thus also to be part of the software system (Fig. 6).

4.2   Detailed Design

In Step 3, the goals delegated from the stakeholders to the system are refined in the goal models of each sub-actor. Goals are decomposed until they can be operationalised by plans. Also, new dependencies between the different sub-actors arise (Fig. 7).

Tropos4AS provides the means for capturing the nominal goal achievement behaviour, defining when a goal will be activated, achieved, or dropped, capturing its

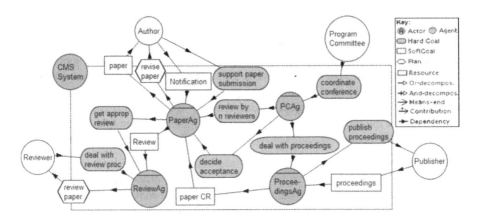

Fig. 6. TROPOS diagram of the multi-agent architecture

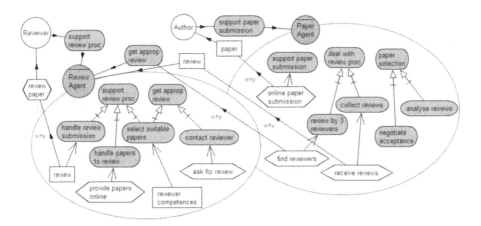

Fig. 7. Details form the goal models of the sub-actors paper and reviewer. Key in Fig. 6.

representation of the environment and linking its execution to environmental changes. For example, the goal `get approp review` is created after *R4P* reviewers were assigned to a paper; achieved when *R4P* reviews are collected; and failed if a review is missing at the deadline.

Individual goals/objectives of agents. In order to give a detailed view, we limit to the scenario of paper assignment to reviewers. Without a centralised distribution of papers to reviewers, the relative agents have to find a relevant allocation between papers and reviewers by self-organising to achieve an optimal distribution of papers and a timely collection of appropriate reviews, being robust for possible perturbations.

In Step 4, from the *TROPOS* model in output of step 3, we refer the local goals and the interactions (goal, task and resource dependencies) of the agents participating in the collective task, whose details will now be further modelled following the *ADELFE* process.

In order for any paper to meet reviewers, we design the system environment as a big room (a grid in practice) where reviewers can stand on at most one square. Paper agents can move on it to find matching reviewers. This approach was already experimented for a dynamic time-tabling elaboration with good results [18]. Furthermore, we define the notion of criticality of the `paper agent`, which is a criteria to know which one is under greatest number of constraints. It describes its difficulty to find a reviewer; it corresponds to the number of reviewers who have been met but are not relevant.

Nominal behaviour. Reviewer agents are placed on the grid and don't move. Paper agents are initially placed randomly on the grid and move in order to find reviewers and store their place under some constraints such as a reviewer cannot accept a paper if he is also author of the paper. Each paper agent remembers last N reviewer agents that it met, where it met them and what are the keywords associated to each.

Cooperative behaviour. The behaviour for the cooperation between the agent instances at run-time is defined by defining the agent's reaction to situations that are recognised to be "non-cooperative". This behaviour is expressed by collaboration rules containing activating conditions and associated recovery activities. Table 1 contains possible non-cooperative situations, and the collaboration rules, composed by a state and conditions, and the recovery activity to perform.

Take the example of the paper agent (Non-cooperative situation *PaperNCS3* in Table 1): If a paper finds a reviewer that fits to its keywords but is already associated to P4R papers, the less critical of them is asked to find a new reviewer (reviewer conflict).

Table 1. Description of main NCS for Paper-agents and Reviewer-agents. They will be modelled by cooperation rules.

Name	State	Description	Conditions	Recov. Activities
PaperNCS1	Exploration	A paper is getting closer to a reviewer already busy with another paper	Searching reviewer	Move in a different direction to find another reviewer
PaperNCS2	Exploration	Two reviewers are perceived	One of them is already busy	Move towards the reviewer that is free
PaperNCS3	Reviewer conflict	A paper found a reviewer that is already associated to *P4R* papers	Reviewer associated to *P4R* papers	Ask the less critical paper to search for another reviewer
PaperNCS4	Highly Critical	Paper agent is very critical and adequacy with reviewer is not null (but $< KP$)	High criticality and $0 < $ adequacy $< KP$	Association with reviewer is concluded
RevNCS1	No Matching	Matching keywords with an arriving paper is not obtained	Not enough matching keywords	Reviewer gives links to relevant neighbour agents
RevNCS2	Search Promotion	Reviewer agent promotes "mutual search" by asking paper agent what reviewers were already met	No matching keywords between the two	Remember paper agent's reviewers met.

So, if a paper agent is very critical and adequacy (keywords matching) is not null, the association with the reviewer must be established. At the reviewers side, when a paper agent arrives, adequacy is computed. If matching is not obtained, the reviewer gives hints for other reviewers in its neighbourhood which could have enough matching keywords.

To conclude self-organisation at a point that a suitable configuration is achieved, the (single instance) `PC chair` agent observes the papers, which expose their criticality and their state, ranging from satisfied to unsatisfied.

4.3 Discussion

The resulting design can be compared with a standard *TROPOS*, Prometheus and O-MaSE design of the CMS, as published in [7]. Despite it is divided into different agents, the *TROPOS* architecture achieved by a top-down decomposition of the system to sub-systems is centralised and not a MAS of collaborating agents, as specified also in the requirements. For the same example, also the Prometheus methodology provides a similar solution, while O-MaSE gives a MAS architecture similar to ours, with personal agents to support the stakeholders, but centralised review assignment and paper selection.

If the system to develop is adapted to an AMAS approach (as verified in the first steps of *ADELFE*), such as this example, the proposed combined approach promotes the development of decentralised, distributed MAS for problem solving, and gives the possibility to deal with self-organisation of the collaboration links between agent instances, at a class (agent or role) level, which is not clearly representable in *TROPOS*.

The application of this approach combining the two modelling paradigms and meta-models is therefore restricted to a particular subset of systems, but provides higher expressivity; modelling also gains from the detailed guidelines available in *ADELFE* to identify system entities and agents and to define inter-agent cooperation.

However, there are different drawbacks. The emergent behaviour coming from the bottom-up approach to self-organisation, performed by modelling the single reactions to non-cooperative situations, can be validated only by empirical study, which is out of scope of this paper. Thus, the link between this bottom-up approach and the objective of the system is still not straight-forward. Still, we think that by combination with the top-down *TROPOS* goal analysis and decomposition, we are able to shrink the gap between global system goals and cooperation rules.

A verification of such systems, particularly a verification of the emergent behaviour arising from cooperation rules, can only be achieved by testing. The approach proposed by Nguyen et al [14] derives *testing goals* from *TROPOS* goals and generates test scenarios by an automated, evolutionary technique.

5   Related Work

Currently, the works on methodologies focusing on self-organisation in multi-agent systems tends to increase. Tom de Wolf and Tom Holvoet have proposed a full lifecycle methodology customising the Unified Process [19]. At the requirement analysis phase, identification of macroscopic properties which must be shown by the running system is added to the classical steps. Then, the design phase is customised with two steps: one for deciding whether or not it is relevant to use a self-organising system and the other for exploiting existing practices and experiments. At the verification and testing phase, an empirical approach based on iterative development feedback is proposed. This method does not provide tools in order to choose existing approach to code self-organisation. The interesting and original part of this method is that it focuses on the system validation.

In [4] the authors present a case study of a decentralised multi-agent system for ambient intelligent scenarios, motivating the need of novel organizational structures of agents that result more flexible than traditional ones, e.g. broker and matchmaker, in order to deal with context changes. The architectural design phase has been conducted by the *TROPOS* modelling language in order to include the social surroundings needed to better characterize MAS architectural requirements. The resulting structure, *Implicit Organisation*, includes the self-organising property for the reassignment of the mediator role, i.e., the architectural requirement of disintermediation. Nevertheless, [4] does not detail the agent coordination level.

Gerhenson [11] proposes a domain-independent methodology for designing and controlling self-organizing systems. This iterative and incremental methodology includes several steps: Representation, Modelling, Simulation, Application and Evaluation, which are interrelated. The main point of this method is that the distributed control is also specified in order to always influence (by reducing friction and promoting synergy) the system and ensuring it will produce the desired behaviour. The work is more a philosophical work aiming at understanding these complex systems but also at designing them.

Another example of framework for engineering self-adaptive and self-organising systems is MetaSelf [8] which takes into account the design and the run-time levels. At the analysis phase, the requirements related to the properties of the components of the studied systems, the rules (local and global) that guide their behaviour and how the process development has to be carried out are identified. Depending on these properties, the relevant self-* architectural patterns and adaptation mechanisms are selected during the design phase. During the implementation phase, the run-time infrastructure, components, policies and metadata are developed. These frameworks rely on established general principles that fit any kind of self-* system but some guides for developers are missing.

Gardelli [9] presents an approach to engineer self-organising MAS from the early design phases. The architectural pattern adopted is based on the Agents and Artefacts metamodel. Designing a self-organising MAS consists in embedding the self-organisation mechanisms in environmental agents and properly designing their interactions with the artefacts of the environment. The design approach comprises three-steps. Modelling first provides an abstract model of the system in which user agents, artefacts and environmental agents are characterised. The second step uses stochastic simulation to study the system dynamics through statistical analysis of results, considering that proper parameters are provided for artefacts and agents. The last step consists in tuning them until the desired dynamics appears. This proposal is mainly a guide for early-designing systems based on self-organising patterns that already exist such as natural ones.

6 Conclusion and Future Work

To promote the development of a decentralized, collaborative MAS, this work proposes to enhance the goal-driven AOSE methodology *TROPOS* with concepts and modelling steps from *ADELFE* methodology. The synergy of both software engineering methodologies allows the characterisation of a decentralised MAS by the definition of intra-agent coordination properties and enhances the expressivity of the *TROPOS* modelling language. The designer is now guided along a top-down goal-oriented modelling process analysing the intentions of the system's stakeholders, which is enhanced with specific design steps devoted to the bottom-up specification of agent coordination. The resulting agents are able to rearrange their cooperations, leading the MAS to optimise the achievement of its current organisational goal, bringing forth global emergent behaviour.

Traceability of requirements through the design phases until the definition of the agents behaviour is improved, reducing the conceptual gap by maintaining the concept of goal until detailed design and –if a BDI platform is used for the implementation, e.g. by a mapping as in [16]– even until run-time. This traceability is important especially if requirements change during system development and maintenance.

Future work concerns detailing the complete modelling process, leading to a goal-oriented methodology where the requirements analysis for adaptive systems can be conducted both at agent level and at organisation level. Besides, we want to further investigate on the benefits of including *TROPOS* goal modelling steps in the *ADELFE* methodology in order to improve the traceability of requirements through the design phases.

References

1. Bernon, C., Camps, V., Gleizes, M.-P., Picard, G.: Engineering Adaptive Multi-Agent Systems: The ADELFE Methodology. In: Henderson-Sellers, B., Giorgini, P. (eds.) Agent-Oriented Methodologies, pp. 172–202. Idea Group, NY (2005)
2. Bernon, C., Gleizes, M., Peyruqueou, S., Picard, G.: ADELFE: A Methodology for Adaptive Multi-agent Systems Engineering. In: Petta, P., Tolksdorf, R., Zambonelli, F. (eds.) ESAW 2002. LNCS (LNAI), vol. 2577, pp. 156–169. Springer, Heidelberg (2003)
3. Bresciani, P., Giorgini, P., Giunchiglia, F., Mylopoulos, J., Perini, A.: Tropos: An Agent-Oriented Software Development Methodology. Autonomous Agents and Multi-Agent Systems 8(3), 203–236 (2004)
4. Bresciani, P., Penserini, L., Busetta, P., Kuflik, T.: Agent Patterns for Ambient Intelligence. In: Atzeni, P., Chu, W., Lu, H., Zhou, S., Ling, T.-W. (eds.) ER 2004. LNCS, vol. 3288, pp. 682–695. Springer, Heidelberg (2004)
5. Capera, D., George, J.-P., Gleizes, M.-P., Glize, P.: The AMAS Theory for Complex Problem Solving Based on Self-organizing Cooperative Agents. In: TAPOCS 2003 at WETICE 2003, Linz, Austria, June 9-11. IEEE CS, Los Alamitos (2003)
6. DeLoach, S.A.: Modeling organizational rules in the multi-agent systems engineering methodology. In: Canadian Conference on AI, pp. 1–15 (2002)
7. DeLoach, S.A., Padgham, L., Perini, A., Susi, A., Thangarajah, J.: Using three aose toolkits to develop a sample design. Int. J. Agent-Oriented Softw. Eng. 3(4), 416–476 (2009)

8. Frei, R., Serugendo, G.D.M., Barata, J.: Designing self-organization for evolvable assembly systems. In: Brueckner, S.A., Robertson, P., Bellur, U. (eds.) SASO, pp. 97–106. IEEE Computer Society, Los Alamitos (2008)
9. Gardelli, L., Viroli, M., Casadei, M., Omicini, A.: Designing self-organising environments with agents and artefacts: a simulation-driven approach. IJAOSE 2(2), 171–195 (2008)
10. Georgé, J.-P., Edmonds, B., Glize, P.: Making self-organising adaptive multiagent systems work. In: Bergenti, F., Gleizes, M.-P., Zombonelli, F. (eds.) Methodologies and Software Engineering for Agent Systems, pp. 319–338. Kluwer Academic Publishers, Dordrecht (2004)
11. Gershenson, C.: A general methodology for designing self-organizing systems. CoRR, abs/nlin/0505009 (2005)
12. Morandini, M., Penserini, L., Perini, A.: Automated mapping from goal models to self-adaptive systems. In: Demo session at the 23rd IEEE/ACM International Conference on Automated Software Engineering (ASE 2008), September 2008, pp. 485–486 (2008)
13. Morandini, M., Penserini, L., Perini, A.: Towards goal-oriented development of self-adaptive systems. In: SEAMS 2008: Workshop on software engineering for adaptive and self-managing systems, Leipzig, Germany, pp. 9–16. ACM, New York (2008)
14. Nguyen, C.D., Miles, S., Perini, A., Tonella, P., Harman, M., Luck, M.: Evolutionary testing of autonomous software agents. In: The Eighth International Conference on Autonomous Agents and Multiagent Systems (AAMAS 2009), pp. 521–528. IFAAMAS (2009)
15. Omicini, A., Ricci, A., Viroli, M.: *Agens Faber*: Toward a theory of artefacts for MAS. Electr. Notes Theor. Comput. Sci. 150(3), 21–36 (2006)
16. Penserini, L., Perini, A., Susi, A., Morandini, M., Mylopoulos, J.: A Design Framework for Generating BDI-agents from Goal Models. In: 6th Int. Conf. on Autonomous Agents and Multi-Agent Systems (AAMAS 2007), Honolulu, Hawaii, pp. 610–612 (2007)
17. Penserini, L., Perini, A., Susi, A., Mylopoulos, J.: High variability design for software agents: Extending tropos. ACM Transactions on Autonomous and Adaptive Systems (TAAS) 2(4) (2007)
18. Picard, G., Bernon, C., Gleizes, M.-P.: ETTO: Emergent Timetabling Organization. In: Pěchouček, M., Petta, P., Varga, L.Z. (eds.) CEEMAS 2005. LNCS (LNAI), vol. 3690, pp. 440–449. Springer, Heidelberg (2005)
19. Wolf, T.D., Holvoet, T.: Towards a methodology for engineering self-organising emergent systems. In: Czap, H., Unland, R., Branki, C., Tianfield, H. (eds.) SOAS. Frontiers in Artificial Intelligence and Applications, vol. 135, pp. 18–34. IOS Press, Amsterdam (2005)

Engineering Agent Organisations in a Business Environment

Dimitris Traskas and Julian Padget

Department of Computer Science
University of Bath, BATH BA2 7AY, UK
dtraskas@googlemail.com, jap@cs.bath.ac.uk

Abstract. Motivated by demands from the commercial world for software systems that can assist in the reorganisation of processes for the purpose of reducing business complexity, we discuss the benefits and challenges of the multi-agent approach. We concentrate on the engineering aspects of large scale multi-agent systems and begin our exploration by focusing on a real world example from the call centre industry. The critical call routing process seems appropriate and useful in presenting our ideas and provides a good starting point for the development of agent organisations capable of self-management and coordination. The main contributions of this work can be summarised as the demonstration of the value of agent organisational models that do not replicate the typical hierarchical structures observed in human organisations and that a quite basic peer-to-peer structure produces very similar performance indicators to a mature simulator that uses conventional techniques, suggesting further improvements may readily be realized.

1 Introduction

Over the last few decades the commercial world has become increasingly complex in an attempt to respond to rising consumer demands for more competitive products and services. Existing systems need to adapt and evolve rapidly in order to become more effective and flexible resulting in highly dynamic environments. Many businesses attempt to solve the complexity problem with simplification; essentially reducing the number of products and services offered or even the size of their customer base. The desired outcome of this approach is to simplify the processes and systems in place—however reduced performance and profits can also result.

In this paper we attempt to tackle the problems identified directly using multi-agent systems as the base technology and formal models of organisations as the informing theory in order to develop prototype solutions capable of operating in such dynamic environments. Our long term goal is the development of large scale agent societies interconnecting different areas of the business and capable of delivering their inherent benefits. The effective application of these systems in the business world depends heavily on three key factors: (i) the general framework that will be used to develop and deploy them, (ii) the modeling approach followed during the design process, and (iii) the organisational models used.

H. Aldewereld, V. Dignum, and G. Picard (Eds.): ESAW 2009, LNAI 5881, pp. 49–64, 2009.

We explore the multi-agent approach using a real world example from the call centre domain and client data provided by our sponsor. Concentrating on the critical call routing process we provide a brief analysis of the problem and the key business objectives. Since agents are well suited to represent self-contained, autonomous modules of software capable of making independent decisions and taking actions proactively we investigate their use in developing the dynamic organisations required. An initial architecture is modeled based on the obvious hierarchical structure of call centres and compared by means of simulation with a decentralised alternative using the key performance indicators (KPIs) common in this domain. The hierarchical model is required to establish a baseline with which we can develop comparisons when working with alternative designs.

The remainder of this paper is laid out as follows: in the next section (2) we outline the business case for a multi-agent system in the call centre domain succeeded by (3) the modeling approach followed and the organisational models developed. In section (4) we present the experiments and metrics used to validate and present the performance of the agent systems developed. Section (5) presents comparisons of the various metrics derived from running the simulations on synthetic and real-world datasets and discusses our findings. Finally section (7) summarises the main conclusions of the paper and outlines future work.

2   Call Centre Case Study

Call centres are fundamental to the operation of numerous large organisations, emergency and government agencies and all types of customer service providers[9]. They constitute a vital component of and interdependency between many economies around the world, employing millions of people. As such, improvements in their management and performance would seem likely to have a significant impact. WorkForce Management (WFM) systems and a number of techniques borrowed from queueing theory through to artificial intelligence and simulation are used to forecast future inbound call volumes, allocate shifts efficiently or experiment with alternative business models. All along, the aim is to optimise performance and maintain the desired service level while preserving a balance between costs and service.

However call centre management and critical aspects of it such as the call routing process which we focus on in this paper, are becoming increasingly complicated due to the growing complexity of businesses. Call centres are getting bigger, physical colocation is becoming impractical and there are more interacting factors that complicate decision-making. Often the effects of poor call centre management are perceived as unsatisfactory levels of service offered to customers, inefficient allocation of resources which leads to increased running costs or high staff turnover.

We believe an appropriate response to these problems is to enable the construction of distributed virtual call centres, that take on much of the responsibility for their organisation and management and are able to adapt both to changes in load (environment) and changes in requirements. Control should become expressible through KPIs and QoS relationships and not by directly modifying the rules of the processes in place. Furthemore evaluation of alternative business models should become practical and cost effective with the virtual call centre serving the purpose of an experimentation testbed capable of simulation and application. The overall characteristics of multi-agent systems motivated us to investigate their use as the base technology for implementing the software systems required. In addition the MAS paradigm seems appropriate for conceptualizing and designing highly dynamic models that can operate across multiple business and technology domains.

In the next few sections we analyse the call routing process and discuss its role in meeting business objectives. We subsequently demonstrate the agent-based modeling approach to the problem followed by the implementation of the prototype systems.

2.1 Call Routing Process

The term 'call-routing' is probably most commonly associated with telecommunications networks, where the task is to avoid hot-spot creation, maximise throughput and minimise latency. Popular approaches to this problem to include swarm routing [4] and stigmergic optimisation [5].

Call-routing in call centres is a somewhat different problem that is more akin to distributed resource discovery and allocation. Conventional implementations of call-routing in call centres are tightly controlled, centralised systems of asynchronous components, where all the decision-making is embedded in a single element—the call router—that communicates with the call-handlers (typically known as agents in the call-centre literature: here we use the term "handler" to alleviate confusion with the term (software) agent).

During the call routing process a call arrives from the telecommunications network and is ready for allocation by the 'Automatic Call Distributor' (ACD) part of the 'Computer Telephony Integration' (CTI) system. The ACD processes a set of business rules which determine which call has the highest priority. These rules use the call type or skill – as it is usually referred to in this industry – to identify the work with the highest criticality for the business in terms of performance. Another parameter used is handler availability, the resources waiting the longest without work will be at the top of the allocation list excluding those on breaks. The 'longest available handler' algorithm is common in most call centres although the simpler random allocation is not unusual either. If there is no available handler the call is inserted into a queue of calls that are ordered by waiting time and skill priority. Whenever a new resource becomes available the ACD gets notified and begins the allocation process for the list of calls currently in the queue. If customers wait too long and terminate their link with the ACD the call gets registered as abandoned and removed from the queue.

It becomes apparent that the ACD is a critical component of the call centre and any change requires expert knowledge and experience. Resource planning teams are able to manipulate the call routing scripts in order to improve performance and employ a number of techniques such as simulation and queueing theory (Erlang-C) to experiment with alternative operational models. However we have observed a number of problems through personal experience in this industry. Many call centres operate within tight time scales and budgets and are managed by poorly trained management staff. Collecting accurate data that will assist managers during the planning process is a difficult task and depends heavily on reliable data sources and reporting tools. It is common to have data misinterpretations or encounter legacy software that cannot coexist with newly installed systems. As a result it is harder to develop precise simulation models and inform the decision making process. Additionally the centralised nature of the Call Router presents a single point of failure and a bottleneck with the increased demand of requests by the business.

We aim to address the problem from the MAS perspective and adopt agents in representing the key elements of the call routing process. Our objective is to implement a prototype system that can operate for application and simulation while using the same rules for resource discovery and allocation. Essentially business logic and rules in the form of java classes are injected within the agents and the mode of operation – application or simulation – does not affect that logic. Thus we expect improved data collection and accuracy while planning teams will have available an environment to experiment with the distribution of resources and skills or allocation rules.

3   Modelling Approach

We have encountered a number of challenges in engineering the prototype agent-based solutions we are presenting here primarily due to their scale. Borrowing techniques from the object-oriented methodology we identified the key elements of the call centre to develop a conceptual model whilst satisfying our goal of a scalable, autonomous system. The key characteristics of the call centre model are summarised below:

- The *Call Centre* consisting of customer calls, handlers and routing information.
- The *Call Distributor* or Router which receives calls and routes them to the human agents.
- The *Call* which is a packet of information used by the Call Distributor and which contains customer details, type of call and time of arrival.
- The *Skill* which is the type of call that a call handler can handle, e.g technical support.
- The *Skill Group* a grouping mechanism used to define the different skills call handlers may have e.g an insurance skill group consists of motor, home and pet insurance.
- And finally the *Call Handler* a trained worker with a set of skills or skill group able to answer customer requests.

Using this model we then designed and implemented an initial prototype multi-agent system. It is clear that the fundamental parts of the call routing process are the handler and router. These two key elements can be represented by an agent and interact as they would in the real world. An agent operating in this environment communicates using a simple set of messages such as 'accept call offer', 'reject call offer' or 'send confirmation'. Within those messages we include useful information about the caller, the time or type of call and propagate it using the message transport mechanism.

Early on we identified a number of problems with the hierarchical approach mainly due to the large number of messages being sent. For all agents to perceive the current state of their environment it was necessary to propagate information to each and every one of them. This introduces two problems, the design depends heavily on the router agent which now becomes a bottleneck and a single point of failure and also the number of messages required is now increased dramatically.

A decentralised architecture however could potentially consist entirely of handlers and not require the router agent. Handlers in this design are servers and can route the calls to the appropriate agent colleague if they behave in an unselfish manner. Nonetheless with this design there are important questions to be answered:

- Where can we store and maintain the queue of calls?
- How do we ensure that the last available handler receives the highest priority call?
- What happens when a call gets abandoned? Can we inform all the handlers of that event?
- What if two handlers decide to handle a call at the same time? Which is the entity that will prioritise?

The research area of peer to peer networks [1] provided us with a number of ideas although not directly applicable to our problem. The concept of a peer is almost indistinguishable from that of an agent so any design patterns used in this area could be useful to us too. An interesting concept is that of peer rings where information propagates in a cyclical manner. Potentially call information could be propagated this way and system integrity ensured. Another area we had some inspiration from was the work on semantic overlay networks [3] and the idea of cluster formations based on certain agent properties. A handler agent that can only answer calls of a specific type seems like a reasonable property to use for that purpose. Using the skill information we tag agents and during an initial bootstrapping phase allow them to self-organise in skill-based clusters.

In the next two sections we present both architectures in detail and present their key concepts. For the purpose of this paper we largely omit implementation details as we only need to expose a high level view of the systems developed.

3.1 The Hierarchical Model

The initial and apparently obvious architecture for the call routing process is essentially a consequence of earlier human organisational structures: a telephone operator receives calls and then routes them to the longest available handler. However, the pattern it implements is intrinsically a function of the strengths and weaknesses of *human* agents. Nevertheless, an architecture that does not conform to the expectations of stakeholders may face difficulties in being accepted.

The hierarchical model mimics the current allocation process and requires three core agents: **Administrator**, **Router** and **Handler**. The Intelligent Call Distributor (ICD) as it was initially termed, is potentially capable of operating for application and simulation. The difference lies heavily on the deployment process and the capabilities of the agent platform used.

Exploring the routing process even further we identify a Router agent receiving customer calls in random intervals and using the routing information defined in the model to search for an available handler. This routing information is in the form of skills, skill groups and priorities as defined by the business. Once an appropriate handler agent is

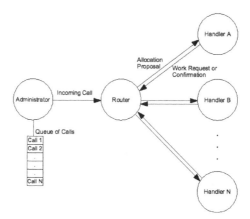

Fig. 1. Overview of the ICD architecture

found a negotiation begins with a proposal. This negotiation either leads to an allocation or the continuation of the resource discovery process. The Router queues calls that it cannot allocate to a handler and waits for the next cycle of processing. In a real world scenario a customer waiting too long will abandon the call. We account for this behaviour using a patience time model which we have developed based on the exponential distribution [10] appropriate for this kind of simulation delays. For each call that arrives we generate randomised abandonment times using the formula below:

$$\text{Time in seconds} = (-\ln(1 - r)\sigma)$$

where r is a random number between 0 and 1 and σ is the average patience time. The same model is considered suitable to generate the handling times of agent handlers. Eventually the Router will check for calls that have reached their patience time and abandon them. Our design requires the Router and Handler agents to be synchronised once an event such as a customer call arrives, achieved with the use of Finite State Machines (FSM). Below we describe in summary the key states of the Router and Handler agents.

Router Agent

1. *Receive model:* The Administrator sends skill / skill group definitions and the total number of handlers in a message.
2. *Receive call:* The Router waits for an incoming call from the Administrator.
3. *Receive work requests:* Handler agents send work requests to the Router with attached current availability, working hours and the set of skills available. The Router requires work requests from the total number of Handlers to be received in order to proceed to the call allocation phase.
4. *Allocate call:* Once all work requests are received, the Router orders the list of Handlers by availabiltiy and attempts to allocate the top call in the queue by sending a proposal message to the Handler.

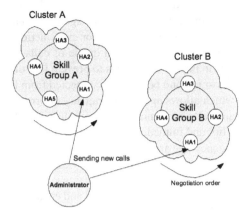

Fig. 2. An example IRN with two skill groups and clusters

5. *Receive confirmation:* If a Handler is able to handle the work proposed and available – not on a break – will send back a confirmation message otherwise a rejection. In the latter case the Router will attempt to allocate the work to a different agent following the procedures of state (4). Calls that cannot be handled are added in a waiting queue.
6. *Check abandonment:* In this final state the list of abandoned calls is checked and any call where patience time has been reached becomes abandoned.

Handler Agent

1. *Initialise:* Similar to the initial state of the Router the agent requests skill and shift information.
2. *Request work:* Handlers send work requests to the Router even if there is a possibility that they will still be busy when the next call arrives.
3. *Confirm or Reject:* If a proposal message is received, the Handler will evaluate the work offered and reply either with a confirmation or a rejection message.

3.2 A Decentralised Approach

In the absence of a Router, the Intelligent Routing Network (IRN) requires Handler agents to coordinate and find the longest available handler with the right skill to handle a call. IRN uses a semantic overlay network of skill group based clusters to allocate calls. Clusters and connections are formed during an initial bootstrapping sequence using the tagging mechanism first proposed by Holland [8]. Essentially handlers are tagged based on their skill information and grouped in clusters.

The system uses two core agents: **Administrator** and **Handler**. The key characteristics of this architecture are: (i) the formation of clusters able to handle different skills, (ii) call queues per cluster, (iii) a negotiation cycle required to process every event, (iv) a forward list used to transfer information from one agent to another, (v) state replication across all agents in a cluster. Handlers are linked in a circular list where one agent is assigned the role of the *first* agent in the cycle. This agent is required to receive a new call from the Administrator and complete a cycle for every action. When a call arrives the *first* Handler will ensure to update the local queue of calls and thus maintain the same state across all agents in the cluster. This is to prevent loss of useful routing information when an agent or host fail and become disconnected from IRN. The forward list is a simple mechanism which allows agents to wrap any information required for state updates, call allocation and call abandonment. On completion of the update process the agent will check availability and immediately send the forward list and current call to the next Handler. Once the message arrives back to the first Handler a cycle is complete and the information contained in the forward list provides the longest available agent and call to be allocated. This cyclic processing of events is required to gather all information necessary to allocate, queue or abandon a call and ensure that queues of calls are replicated across all agents in the cluster. For the purpose of page economy we present only the key states of the Handler agent below.

Handler Agent

1. *Initialise:* The agent requests initialisation data.
2. *Ping:* The agent starts sending ping messages to all agents in the network.
3. *Pong:* On receipt of a ping message the agent replies with pong and its skill group attached.
4. *Cluster formation:* Once all agents in the network have replied the agent uses skill group information to form a cluster.
5. *Process new call:* The first Handler in the negotiation cycle receives a new call and checks the skill and current availability. The local waiting queue gets updated accordingly and ordered by the longest waiting call. All this information is forwarded to the next agent in the cycle.
6. *Allocate call:* When a call completes one negotiation cycle information collected is used to determine who is the longest available Handler. A new negotiation cycle begins to clear all local queues from the call and allocate it. If there are more calls to handle and available agents a new cycle begins to allocate it, otherwise calls are tested for abandonment. A negotiation cycle is also required to abandon-clear calls from all queues.
7. *Process forwarded call:* On receipt of a forwarded call Handler availability is tested and added to the forward list. If this is the last agent in the cycle then the information collected is used to allocate the call.
8. *Abandon call:* When a customer's patience time is reached a call becomes abandoned and added in the forward list which is forwarded to the cluster.

4   Experiments

For validation purposes we conducted a number of simulation experiments with different scales and using synthetic and empirical data. We compared the performance of the two solutions with that of an industry-standard call centre simulator from CACI

Ltd[1] called Call Centre Workshop (CCW) and actual data provided by one of CACI's clients. CCW is a commercial product used by a significant number of clients from the software, retail, banking, insurance and mobile phone sectors. For our experiments we used a set of performance metrics to validate and compare the results such as Service Level (SL%), Calls Handled and Calls Abandoned, Queue Length and handler Utilisation per interval [9]. These are the standard metrics used by call centre managers and planning teams to measure business performance and assist in the decision making process. Service Level is the percentage of calls answered within a business-specific time frame. This time frame is called Telephone Service Factor (TSF) and is usually in the range of 20-30 seconds. Service Level can be used to measure intra-day, daily and weekly performance and is normally defined as:

$$SL\% = \frac{\text{Calls Answered before TSF}}{\text{Calls Answered} + \text{Calls Abandoned}} \times 100$$

Utilisation is defined as the percentage of time handlers that are busy per interval in a day and Queue Length defined as the number of calls queued per interval. Other metrics that are common in the call centre domain are Average Handle Time (AHT), Average Patience Time (APT) which is the average time customers wait on the phone before they abandon and Average Answer Time (ASA). We created synthetic datasets with an aim to test the agent prototypes and allow all different scenarios to be handled by the agents. An example synthetic model used has four skills, variable call density and shift breaks during afternoon hours in order to demonstrate the expected drop in service level and the increase of abandonment. The attributes of the model used can be seen in table 1.

Table 1. Synthetic Model (4 skills, 10 handlers, 1420 calls)

Skills	TSF (secs)	Priority	AHT (secs)	APT (secs)
LOANS	20	1	120	180
MORTGAGES	20	1	180	240
PET INSURANCE	20	1	120	360
MOTOR INSURANCE	20	1	240	120

The second phase of the experimentation process was the use of real customer data. We have data available from a number of clients but in many cases the computational cost of running such simulations is prohibitive. Typical scenarios require 5,000 handler agents and 400,000 calls in a day just to simulate one run of the call allocation process.

The call centre selected for our experiments is significantly smaller and part of one of the UK's leading mobile phone retailers. The client provided us with actual data from one of their main call centres which we use to simulate one day with 560 Handlers, 43,365 incoming calls and 13 different skills. Calls received are considered to be within service level if they have been answered within 20 seconds from the time of arrival. Skill handling times were varied through the day, while customer patience times are estimated on average to be 180 seconds.

---

[1] http://www.caci.co.uk

For the purpose of this work we set-up a very simple call routing model with no skill priorities and a direct mapping of skills to skill groups. We then loaded the data mentioned above in ICD and IRN and repeated the exact same process in CCW. The average handling and patience times were used to generate randomly the time it takes for a handler to handle a call and a customer to abandon it using the exponential distribution models discussed earlier. We executed the simulation for 5 runs and compared our results with those of CCW as well as the actual service level values. The client's resource planning team calculated the actual service level values after collecting all the data necessary stored for that day in the ACD database and using the same routing model with us. Unfortunately they were not able to provide other performance metrics such as utilisation or queuelength that would be very useful for our experimentation thus we only demonstrate a comparison of service level.

4.1   Call Centre Workshop (CCW)

CCW allows the user to develop simulation models of call centres and specify through its user interface skills and skill groups, the number of handlers working on every period, average handling and patience times and call allocation rules. Using a standard workflow language CACI has developed a library of workflows for call centre processes that are used in the simulation depending on the routing and queueing selected. When the simulation begins: (i) handler resources are created, (ii) random calls generated for each interval based on the specified call density, (iii) a routing workflow selected and (iv) a simulation loop initialised. Each new call from the list is treated as a discrete event and sent to the workflow for further processing. Through that process the call is checked for skill, skill priority and sent to the longest available handler for allocation. Any call that has not been allocated is queued until the next event comes and the clock moves forward. An important step in the workflow is the check for abandonment, essentially if the customer has reached her patience limits the call becomes abandoned. During the simulation a Data Collector retrieves low level raw data that is subsequently parsed to produce the performance metrics described in earlier sections. The routing workflows used are standard for most simulations however CCW allows modelers to customise the process based on business requirements. The ICD, IRN and CCW simulators follow exactly the same business rules and constraints required for our experiments in order to prove that the agent approach is equally effective.

5   Results and Discussion

Below we present comparisons with the metrics produced from the synthetic model experiments. The graph in figure 3 shows changes in service level throughout the day with a target service level of 80% represented by the green (horizontal) line, a common target across many businesses and sectors. We wanted to demonstrate that the systems behave as expected when incoming call volumes remain at high levels at certain periods in the day while at the same time agents start their breaks. As it was anticipated we notice a dramatic decrease of service during early morning and afternoon hours. The overall variance of the daily average of service level between the ICD and CCW was

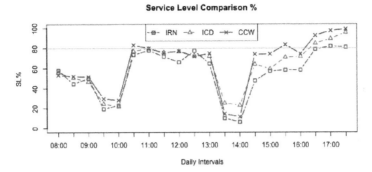

Fig. 3. Service Level plot of hierarchical and decentralised agent-based systems compared with CCW

3% and between IRN and CCW 9.6% which we believe is within the acceptable range of 3%-10% of an operational model[11].

To further validate our model and confirm that the systems behave as they should we also calculated the number of calls handled and abandoned through the day as we can see in figure 4. We notice that between 13:00 and 14:30 the number of calls handled drops significantly, that is because we have reduced the number of available agents by 60% at a very busy time in our hypothetical call centre. However the number of calls abandoned increases during that same period reflecting the inability of the business to service customers queueing for a very long time. The Resource utilisation plot demonstrates that agents are generally very busy due to high volume of inbound calls and, as expected, their availability drops between 13:00 and 14:30.

Finally the results shown in figure 5 demonstrate the performance of ICD and IRN using the real world model and, we believe, they show a satisfying variance of 7.5% between the daily average service level of the ICD and actuals and 5.8% between the IRN and actuals. The prototypes appear to have sufficient accuracy considering the complexity of the problem, the volume of data and the unknown parameters of the client's routing process. It would be very useful of course to use more metrics as service level is a high level indicator and can sometimes hide some of the detail required.

The results presented in this section confirm that the multi-agent prototypes developed are effective and inspire us to further experimentation. There are however inefficiencies that became apparent during the course of this study. The frameworks available for the development of large scale multi-agent systems are limited. We begun our development with an object-oriented design of the call centre which allowed us to identify the key agents. It would be useful during that phase to model the interactions of the agents outside the agent platform and detect problems with the logic and state of the agents that could bring the system to a deadlock or race condition. We lack the modeling tools and methods that will allow not only us but also high level users of such systems to manipulate and investigate the agents without coming into contact with the low level implementation details.

Our first hierarchical prototype was developed using the JADE [2] agent platform but due to scalability problems we continued our work with Cougaar which stands for

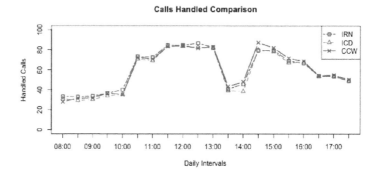

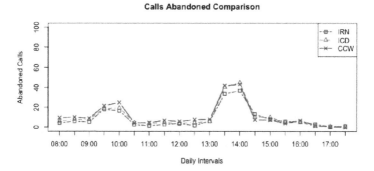

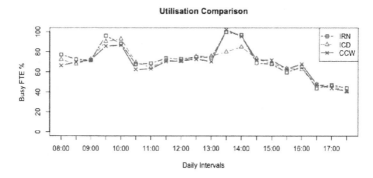

Fig. 4. Calls Handled, Abandoned and Utilisation comparison plots

'Cognitive Agent Architecture' [7]. Cougaar is the product of an eight-year DARPA-funded research project and developed to meet demanding scalability, reliability and survivability needs. Agents in Cougaar contain plug-in components — rather than behaviours — and interact with each other via a blackboard-based publish and subscribe mechanism — rather than messaging. The blackboard encourages the use of events for agent interaction and is the primary mechanism for state management and message exchange. The plug-in software components provide a domain-specific behaviour to the agent and can be added or removed at design or run-time. A simple relay mechanism

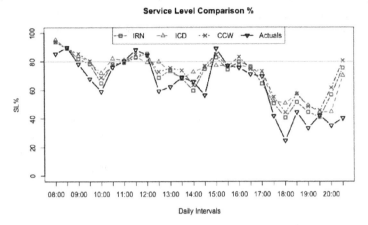

Fig. 5. Service Level plot of hierarchical, decentralised, CCW and actuals

allows the communication across agents spawned within different host machines and through the blackboard. For the purpose of our work we created different types of messages and packets of information that could be wrapped in a single message. Each agent has to subscribe to the different message types and listen for incoming messages. The platform so far has proven to be highly scalable and allowed us to deploy the real world call centre model with 560 Agent Handlers. Its threading pool model and resource handling is more rigorous than other platforms that we have examined and encourages future use. Below we provide a summary of our findings:

– We have shown that a multi-agent architecture can be used effectively to manage a business process with a real world example from the call centre industry. The agent systems can allocate inbound call volumes to resources while adhering to business rules and constraints. An inherent advantage of the proposed solutions is their dual purpose. They can operate for application and simulation offering to businesses an experimentation framework that will assist in the decision making process by evaluating alternative operational models without the imposed risk and cost of current approaches.
– We have demonstrated an approach where system architecture does not need to follow human intuition which encourages the use of a hierarchical model. Instead the solution should take advantage of the properties of agent-based organisations of self-coordination and self-management.
– The inefficiencies that become apparent with the scale of the experiments conducted indicate the need for further investigation of organisational models and frameworks. The current state of MAS technology prohibits the deployment of such systems within a commercial environment with the aim of upgrading existing infrastructure.

In general we believe that the multi-agent paradigm has many benefits to offer to the corporate world but it is imperative to look into the problems and challenges of the technology and devise new methodologies and organisational models. Although the domain of MAS advocates scalability as one of its benefits it is very difficult to find the frameworks, supporting methodologies and tools required to develop these large scale systems.

6   Related Work

Multi-Agent Systems have long been identified as a suitable framework for the development of the virtual enterprise [14]. The effective application of agents in the commercial world however has been minimal and even today with the advance of internet technologies and increase in computational power we have few examples to demonstrate. We haven't found many examples of MAS in the call centre sector and much of the research work discusses agents as a useful abstraction for modeling business processes.

The work described in [13] concentrates on the ADEPT multi-agent architecture which allows the coordination of agents across different business domains using negotiation. ADEPT operates on the basis of transforming existing business processes into a number of agencies under a hierarchy. The hierarchical structuring of agencies enables the encapsulation and abstraction of services. The example used does not need to identify the key performance indicators that are critical in the business process simulated compared to ours and does not discuss how agent societies would organise in large scale corporate environments.

In [12] the authors discuss the use of a meta-layer to assist in system adaptation without requiring any global information. A semantic overlay network is created on top of the lower level agents, however the specific tasks and roles agents can have are not necessary to establish their organisation. This is a useful approach for some problems but in the demanding business environment it is crucial to specify the exact business rules and tasks of resources such as the Call Handler. Any system deployed in a corporate scale would have to deliver good measurable performance whilst being capable of satisfying business rules and constraints and adapting to ever changing demands.

Finally in [6] we are presented with an overlay system of controller agents associated with application agents. Controllers can detect rule violations based on their observations and sanction the violators by using reputation. The main difference with the call centre example is that in our designs agents are tightly controlled and have limited freedom in their decision making process, as it is required by the business. We plan however to experiment with alternative organisational models in the future where agents have a lot more freedom to interact with each other whilst delivering good overall system performance.

7   Conclusions and Future Work

This paper advocates the multi-agent approach in the corporate environment in order to create software systems that are capable of self-organisation and management, adaptable to the ever changing requirements of businesses. More specifically we support the case for an alternative model in call centre management and investigate the call routing process, a critical operation in this domain. We develop two prototypes, a hierarchical system as a baseline model that mimics the current routing process and a decentralised one that consists of self-organising and coordinating handler agents. Using synthetic and empirical data we conduct a number of simulation experiments and show that the hierarchical prototype is capable of performing equally well with the conventional call router. The centralised manner of this design however exhibits a number of problems such as inability to scale better, a single point of failure – the Router – and incapable of adapting to changes in the process. Influenced by ideas from peer to peer computing and semantic overlay networks we progress our work and implement a decentralised routing network capable of handling call and handler prioritisation and queueing calls without the need for a central control entity. Following the same experimentation methodology we prove that this design is also equally effective when compared to our initial attempt although it presents a number of challenges.

Future work includes the investigation of alternative decentralised architectures that are flexible and efficient in tackling the problems mentioned in this study. We wish to relax the constraints and rules of our designs and experiment with agents that respond to changes in their environment using probabilistic models rather than the rule-based approach we currently employ. We also plan to conduct further research work on the methodologies and tools that will allow us to decrease development and debugging time. It is necessary to have a modeling framework that will help us produce and test new designs. Furthermore such a framework could be extended to become a high level tool for business managers who do not require to be aware of all the implementation details but wish to manipulate the logic and interactions of agents.

Acknowledgements

We wish to thank CACI Ltd for their support and for providing access to client data and the Call Centre Workshop software. We would also like to note that our findings and conclusions do not necessarily reflect those of the sponsor.

References

1. Androutsellis-Theotokis, S., Spinellis, D.: A survey of peer-to-peer content distribution technologies. In: ACM Computing Surveys (CSUR), vol. 36, pp. 335–371. ACM Press, New York (2004)
2. Bellifemine, F., Poggi, A., Rimassa, G.: Jade: a fipa2000 compliant agent development environment. In: AGENTS 2001: Proceedings of the fifth international conference on Autonomous agents, pp. 216–217. ACM, New York (2001)
3. Crespo, A., Molina, H.G.: Semantic overlay networks for p2p systems. In: Agents and Peer-to-Peer Computing, pp. 1–13. Springer, Heidelberg (2002)
4. Di Caro, G., Ducatelle, F., Gambardella, L.: Swarm intelligence for routing in mobile ad hoc networks. In: Proceedings IEEE Swarm Intelligence Symposium 2005, pp. 76–83. IEEE Computer Society, Los Alamitos (2005)
5. Dorigo, M., Caro, G.D., Gambardella, L.M.: Ant algorithms for discrete optimization. Artificial Life 5(2), 137–172 (1999)

6. Grizard, A., Vercouter, L., Stratulat, T., Muller, G.: A peer-to-peer normative system to achieve social order. In: Noriega, P., Vázquez-Salceda, J., Boella, G., Boissier, O., Dignum, V., Fornara, N., Matson, E. (eds.) COIN 2006. LNCS (LNAI), vol. 4386, pp. 274–289. Springer, Heidelberg (2007)

7. Helsinger, A., Thome, M., Wright, T.: Cougaar: a scalable, distributed multi-agent architecture. In: IEEE International Conference on Systems, Man and Cybernetics, vol. 2, pp. 1910–1917. IEEE, Los Alamitos (2004)

8. Holland, J.H.: Hidden Order: How Adaptation Builds Complexity. The Perseus Books Group (1995) ISBN-13: 9780201407938

9. Koole, G.: Call center mathematics: A scientific method for understanding and improving contact centers, http://www.math.vu.nl/~koole/ccmath/book.pdf (Verified 20080520)

10. Lilja, D.J.: Measuring computer performance: a practitioner's guide. Cambridge University Press, New York (2000)

11. Michael, C.M.M., North, J.: Managing Business Complexity — Discovering Strategic Solutions with Agent-Based Modelling and Simulation. Oxford University Press, Oxford (2007)

12. Miralles, J.C., López-Sánchez, M., Esteva, M.: Multi-agent system adaptation in a peer-to-peer scenario. In: SAC 2009: Proceedings of the 2009 ACM symposium on Applied Computing, pp. 735–739. ACM, New York (2009)

13. Norman, T., Jennings, N.R., Faratin, P., Mamdani, E.H.: Designing and implementing a multi-agent architecture for business process management. In: Jennings, N.R., Wooldridge, M.J., Müller, J.P. (eds.) ECAI-WS 1996 and ATAL 1996. LNCS, vol. 1193, pp. 261–275. Springer, Heidelberg (1997)

14. Petrie, C., Bussler, C., Survey, A.: Service agents and virtual enterprises: A survey. Survey, Internet Computing, 7 (July/August 2003)

Peer-to-Peer Overlay Network Based on Swarm Intelligence

Vesna Sesum-Cavic and Eva Kühn

Vienna University of Technology, Institute of Computer Languages
Space Based Computing Group, Argentinierstr. 4, 1040 Wien, Austria
{vesna,eva}@complang.tuwien.ac.at

Abstract. As the number of information in the Internet constantly increases and the complexity of systems rapidly grows, locating and manipulating complex data has become a difficult task. We propose a self-organizing approach that combines purely decentralized unstructured peer-to-peer (P2P) with space based computing in order to effectively locate and retrieve information from a network. The approach is inspired by swarm intelligence, is distributive and autonomous. As the scalability is a common open issue both for unstructured P2P networks and for coordination models, our approach successfully copes with that by using a biologically inspired multi-agent system. Benchmarks demonstrate powerful query capabilities with a good scalability.

Keywords: swarm intelligence, unstructured P2P, space based computing, lookup mechanisms.

1 Introduction

The highly dynamic nature of the Internet, characterized by a huge number of information often expressed as complex data, imposes the necessity for new and advanced ways for locating and retrieving of information. We propose a self-organizing architecture as a combination of unstructured P2P [1] and space based computing ([4], [9]) for searching and retrieving data concurrently. It intends to use the benefits of both paradigms. The lookup mechanism is inspired by swarm intelligence ([6], [8], [12]).

2 Architecture and Design

In our approach, a space-based architecture, called XVSM (extensible virtual shared memory)[1], based on a formal model [7], is used . It generalizes Linda tuple space communication ([4], [9]) by introducing customizable, shared data structures (*shared containers* [10]). A container stores *entries* that generalize tuples. Each container possesses so-called *coordinators* (e.g. fifo, random, template matching, key, label), and can be located and accessed via a URL. All operations on it (*read, take, write*) use this URL to refer to the container. When a container is created, it can be made publicly accessible by a name. [2] combines a structured P2P system with XVSM. In contrast, in this paper, we propose the creation of an overlay network that consists of

---

[1] Project and open source download site: www.xvsm.org

H. Aldewereld, V. Dignum, and G. Picard (Eds.): ESAW 2009, LNAI 5881, pp. 65–67, 2009.

lookup containers. A container can be published under one or more public names. The discovery of data is performed by means of swarm intelligence. For the *structure of the overlay network,* we use the scale-free network approach [3] for an initial construction. Software agents realize the *algorithms of the overlay network* acting in swarms and performing the role of artificial ants. The multi-agent system is inspired by ant colony that is distributed, self-organizing, with a high level of autonomy.

Writing of information. An ant can put the content (i) *randomly* (no need for swarm intelligence algorithms), or (ii) using *brood sorting* [5]: entries are distributed on the basis of their type (similar entries stay closer to each other). In this case, the similarity function δ is based on spatial locality. **Retrieving of information.** We implemented two different ant algorithms, an adaptation of MMAS that is combined with Local Search (2.5-Opt) and an adaptation of AntNet. We introduced the following changes: In the *ConstructSolution* procedure [8], heuristic values from the random proportional rule are interpreted as a quality of the used links, expressed in time needed to traverse a particular path from lookup container A to lookup container B by using a particular link. The possible resulting situations of ants' search for the particular data are: *no data* found, *exact data* found, and *acceptable data* found with the accuracy/error rate $< \varepsilon$, where ε is a parameter given in advance, connected to the definition of δ. The *DepositPheromone* procedure [8] is changed as follows: If an ant on its trip *) found exact data, it deposits pheromone; *) found acceptable data, it deposits less amount of pheromone, *) did not find data, then skip depositing pheromones on its trip (i.e., the values on arcs it traversed will be the same as the values on the rest of unvisited arcs in the network). String comparison (representing URLs) uses a similarity function δ, based on a spatial locality. A different amount of pheromones is deposited according to the quality of solution found. The general form δ is: $\delta = \delta$ (currentSolution, exact-Solution), that describes how good (acceptable) the found solution is, $\delta \in [0,1]$. In case of changing the type of δ, its value can be scaled into the same segment [0,1]. *DepositPheromone* procedure is changed: 1) for MMAS algorithm: $\Delta\tau = 1/MC^{best}$ where $M=1/\delta$, 2) for AntNet algorithm: $\tau := r \cdot (1-\tau) \cdot \delta$.

3   Simulation Results

We implemented two ways respectively of writing data into containers and of performing lookup and retrieval of data from containers on a cluster of 4 computers (2*Quad AMD 2,0 GHz, 16 GB RAM). A first group of benchmarks investigates the behavior of the algorithms in different combinations (Table 1) and different parameter settings [8] while trying to find the best possible combination of parameters. When comparing the two kinds of lookup, AntNet supplies the best performance in case of retrieving only one query (Fig. 1). A second group of benchmarks investigates the query capability of our system and compares it with Gnutella's lookup mechanism [1]. We can conclude that the adapted intelligent algorithms cope successfully with an increasing number of queries, compounded of several simple queries. We used the possibility of increasing the number of concurrently working ants. Our approach outperformed the Gnutella lookup by means of the obtained performance. Fig. 1 represents one test case using 80 containers.

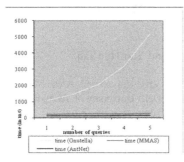

Table 1. Possible combinations

	MMAS	*AntNet*
Random	case 1	case 2
Brood sorting	case 3	case 4

Fig. 1. Different lookup mechanisms

4 Conclusion

Locating and retrieving of data in a global network implies the necessity for effective lookup mechanisms. We introduced a self-organizing approach combining decentralized unstructured P2P with space based computing, that focuses on the quality of the solutions and the time needed to obtain that solution, applies a learning principle from the nature, and outperforms Gnutella lookup. Future work will consider large size benchmarks, and other intelligent approaches, like bee intelligence [11].

References

1. Androutsellis-Theotokis, S., Spinellis, D.: A survey of peer-to-peer content distribution technologies. ACM Computer Survey 36, 335–371 (2004)
2. Bessler, S., Fischer, A., Kühn, E., Mordinyi, R., Tomic, S.: Using Tuple-Spaces to manage the Storage and Dissemination of Spatial-temporal Content. Journal of Computer and System Sciences (to appear, 2009)
3. Caldarelli, G.: Scale-Free Networks. Oxford University Press, Oxford (2007)
4. Carriero, N., Gelernter, D.: Linda in Context. CACM 32(4), 444–458 (1989)
5. Casadei, M., Menezes, R., Viroli, M., Tolksdorf, R.: A Self-organizing Approach to Tuple Distribution in Large-Scale Tuple-Space Systems. In: Hutchison, D., Katz, R.H. (eds.) IWSOS 2007. LNCS, vol. 4725, pp. 146–160. Springer, Heidelberg (2007)
6. Di Caro, G., Dorigo, M.: AntNet: Distributed Stigmergetic Control for Communications Networks. JAIR 9, 317–365 (1998)
7. Craß, S., Kühn, E., Salzer, G.: Algebraic Foundation of a Data Model for an Extensible Space-Based Collaboration Protocol. In: IDEAS, Calabria, Italy (to appear, 2009)
8. Dorigo, M., Stützle, T.: Ant Colony Optimization. MIT Press, Cambridge (2005)
9. Kühn, E.: Virtual Shared Memory for Distributed Architectures. Nova Science Publ. (2001)
10. Kühn, E., Mordinyi, R., Keszthelyi, L., Schreiber, C.: Introducing the Concept of Customizable Structured Spaces for Agent Coordination in the Production Automation Domain. In: AAMAS, Budapest, Hungary (2009)
11. Sesum-Cavic, V., Kühn, E.: Instantiation of a Generic Model for Load Balancing with Intelligent Algorithms. In: Hummel, K.A., Sterbenz, J.P.G. (eds.) IWSOS 2008. LNCS, vol. 5343, pp. 311–317. Springer, Heidelberg (2008)
12. Tolksdorf, R., Menezes, R.: Using Swarm Intelligence in Linda Systems. In: Omicini, A., Petta, P., Pitt, J. (eds.) ESAW 2003. LNCS (LNAI), vol. 3071. Springer, Heidelberg (2004)

Agent Architectures for Compliance

Brigitte Burgemeestre[1], Joris Hulstijn[1], and Yao-Hua Tan[1,2]

[1] Faculty of Economics and Business Administration, Vrije Universiteit, Amsterdam
[2] Department of Technology, Policy and Management, Delft University of Technology
{jhulstijn,cburgemeestre,ytan}@feweb.vu.nl

Abstract. A Normative Multi-Agent System consists of autonomous agents who must comply with social norms. Different kinds of norms make different assumptions about the cognitive architecture of the agents. For example, a principle-based norm assumes that agents can reflect upon the consequences of their actions; a rule-based formulation only assumes that agents can avoid violations. In this paper we present several cognitive agent architectures for self-monitoring and compliance. We show how different assumptions about the cognitive architecture lead to different information needs when assessing compliance. The approach is validated with a case study of *horizontal monitoring*, an approach to corporate tax auditing recently introduced by the Dutch Customs and Tax Authority.

1 Introduction

A Normative Multi-agent System consists of autonomous agents who must comply to social norms [3,13,6]. Normative multi-agent systems are used to design electronic institutions [31], but can also be used to understand compliance schemes in human society. Interesting new forms of auditing and norm enforcement are *horizontal monitoring* [15] and *responsive regulation* [2,4]. Such forms of auditing are based on mutual trust and understanding, and do not only monitor compliance behaviour, but also take the underlying motivation and corporate culture into account. This may lead to more robust compliance behaviour and can save all parties a lot of effort. However, it requires different kinds of evidence than a traditional command and control approach. What are the *information needs* for assessing compliance using such 'horizontal' approaches?

How a norm is adopted and followed by an agent depends on the cognitive architecture of the agent. By a cognitive architecture we mean a structured model of the various components or modules which generate the agent's behaviour. Different ways of formulating norms make different assumptions about the underlying cognitive capabilities.

For example, in the accounting profession there is a long standing debate between advocates of *rule-based* and *principle-based* ways of formulating norms. A principle-based formulation of norms assumes that agents can reflect upon the outcomes of their actions; a rule-based formulation of norms only assumes that agents can follow procedure. Therefore agents can 'hide behind the rules' and pretend not be responsible for the consequences: "... rule-based traditions of auditing became a convenient vehicle that perpetuated the unethical conduct of firms such as Enron and Arthur Andersen" [28]. The Sarbanes-Oxley act [27] was introduced in 2002 to avoid such accounting scandals. Although originally a principle-based norm, in practice it has been given a rule-based

H. Aldewereld, V. Dignum, and G. Picard (Eds.): ESAW 2009, LNAI 5881, pp. 68–83, 2009.

interpretation. Our working hypothesis is that principle-based norms only work when a subject has adequate capabilities for norm adoption and compliance. Using cognitive agent architectures we hope to make such assumptions explicit. Sanctions form another example. The use of sanctions assumes that agents 'care' about the negative consequences and are actually able to adjust their behaviour. These assumptions are not true in all cases. For instance, artificial agents typically do not 'care'; only their owners do. Also, when agents lack expertise to improve their behaviour, sanctions are counterproductive. In such cases it is better to provide advice [2].

In this paper we investigate how agent architectures can account for compliance. We discuss several cognitive agent architectures taken from the literature. We show how the architectures can implement normative behaviour, namely by filtering or adjusting the data structures which generate behaviour (policy, plans or goals). Moreover, we show how different architectures lead to different information needs to assess whether an agent is compliant. Such information needs are required for the design of 'auditing tools' to support human auditors when assessing compliance of companies. Throughout the paper we will therefore compare agent architectures to practices in the business world. Another application is in the design of electronic institutions. There too, assumptions about the underlying agent architecture will influence compliance monitoring.

Consider an electronic service broker. Compare [31] for similar such applications. There are two kinds of artificial agents: service providers and service consumers. Agents are 'scripts' written in a programming language, which is run by the broker environment. The environment provides primitive actions for paying, communicating and delivering services. The purpose of the broker is to help consumers find providers and to help them negotiate, implement and maintain a service level agreement. Owners of participating agents pay a fixed membership fee and a percentage for each successful deal. The broker tries to make sure that (owners of) agents comply with the rules of the institution, i.e. follow the protocol and honour the service level agreements. This assurance is part of the added value of a broker. The broker must therefore monitor communications and transactions as they take place in the environment. Upon complaints or other evidence of fraud, a human investigation may be started. The main sanction is to evict perpetrators. However, sanctions always come after the fact. Therefore the broker should assess the compliance attitude of the owner of a participating agent before entrance, and do a code review of the scripts. Our information needs analysis can be used as a guideline for the set-up of such an assessment.

Our findings about information needs are illustrated and validated with a real life case study of *horizontal monitoring*, a form of auditing recently introduced by the Dutch Customs and Tax Authority (DTCA) [15]. The tax office relies as much as possible on the company's internal control system. Tax auditors only have to assess reliability of the company's internal control system, instead of the tax declarations themselves. This saves the tax office a lot of effort. To participate, the company must give tax auditors access to its records and policies. The tax office in return can give the company more certainty, for instance that a tax declaration for a preceding year is settled. The new audit approach requires different kinds of evidence and a different way of communicating.

The paper is structured as follows. In Section 2 we present three cognitive agent architectures for compliance. In Section 3 we outline the information needs for establishing compliance. In Section 4 we present the case study on horizontal monitoring.

2   Cognitive Agent Architectures

Below we discuss a number of general cognitive agent architectures. We determine what it means to be compliant given the capabilities offered by each architecture.

2.1   Perception and Action

The most simple agent architecture consists of two modules: perception and action [26]. These are linked in a feedback-control loop (Figure 1). Therefore this architecture is called a *reactive agent architecture*. The agents behaviour is determined by a data structure called *policy* π: a set of situation-action pairs $s \rightarrow a$, which specify for each possible situation s, what appropriate actions a would be. The policy is non-deterministic: several actions may be possible in a situation. The perception module determines on the basis of observations what situation the agent is likely to be in. Perception may be wrong. The agent has a (limited) memory of the previous situations it has been in. These may be called its *beliefs*. The action module simply executes the action suggested by the policy. Not all actions will be successful.

If we compare this to the business world, there are similarities with the way a company is run. The daily operations are usually determined by business processes and standardised operating procedures. Like the policy data structure, processes and procedures outline for known situations what to do.

What does it mean to be compliant given this architecture? In a reactive architecture, being compliant to a norm can in principle be implemented in two ways:

1. Adapt the perception module to send a warning signal when the next move is likely to lead to a violation, and to send an alert when detecting an actual violation. This is called *self monitoring*. Adapt the action module to suspend all actions after a warning and undo the previous move after an alert. This is called *self control*.
2. Adapt the policy data-structure and *filter out* all situation-action pairs which are known to lead to a violation. Depending on the computational complexity, such readjustment can be done either immediately after a warning or an alert, or off-line.

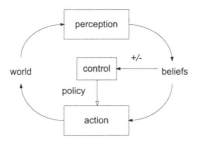

Fig. 1. Perception and Action

In an ideal world adjusting the policy is enough, but self monitoring and self control are necessary when, due to inaccurate beliefs or unsuccessful actions, the agent may find itself in or close to a violation despite the adapted policy.

The ability to monitor, evaluate and adjust future behaviour is crucial for being compliant. That means we need a *reflective agent*: an agent who has a representation of itself and can alter this representation in order to adjust its behaviour [22]. In Figure 1 this function is performed by a separate control module. Adjustments are indicated with an open arrow: $\dashrightarrow$. There are many ways to implement a reflective agent; see [29] for a survey. A very basic one would make use of *reinforcement learning*: adjusting the policy through signals from the environment [19]. After each action, the agent gets a reinforcement signal r. Violations receive a punishment ($r = -1$); other states get a reward ($r = 1$). The agent must optimise its policy π to increase the sum of reinforcement signals over a certain period. Many algorithms can solve such optimisation problems [19]. We mention a simple one as illustration (linear reward-inaction algorithm). Let p_i be the relative likelihood of taking action a_i in some given situation s according to the policy, and let α be a learning rate ($0 \leq \alpha \leq 1$). For all actions a_i, a_j which are possible in s, if action a_i succeeds ($r = 1$), then $p_i := p_i + \alpha(1 - p_i)$ and $p_j := p_j - \alpha p_j$ for $j \neq i$. When action a_i fails ($r = -1$), p_j remains unchanged for all j.

2.2 Perception, Planning and Action

The second architecture contains an additional module: planning. This module determines by what sequence of actions the agent can best achieve its goals. Therefore, this architecture is also called a *deliberative architecture*. A well known example is the BDI architecture [25]. The planning module takes two kinds of input: (1) the information produced by the perception module about the current state the agent is likely to be in, enriched with background knowledge on how to interpret situations. Again, this may be called the *beliefs* of the agent. (2) The *desires* of the agent, i.e. preferred future states of affairs, which function as potential goals. Desires may be mutually incompatible. The output of the planning module is the set of goals the agent has decided to pursue, and for which a particular plan has been adopted. These adopted goals are called *intentions*. Intentions must be mutually compatible. Following Pollack [24] and many subsequent BDI architectures, we suppose each agent is equipped with a plan library with useful *recipes*: pre-stored plans for different kinds of situations. When there are no recipes for a particular goal, a new plan must be generated from first principles.

In the business world, goals would correspond to objectives of an enterprise. Desires correspond to long term objectives, such as increasing market share or reducing time-to-market. Intentions can be compared to those objectives which have been aligned in a consistent strategy and for which processes, procedures and projects have been implemented. Plans or recipes correspond to business processes and procedures (for routine plans) or to projects (for one-off plans).

Again, such architectures are reflective: agents must be able to learn and adjust their behaviour. So when a plan fails to achieve its goals, it must be dropped or adjusted along with the plan library. This function is again performed by a separate control module. Desires or goals define the success of a plan, similar to the reinforcement signals in the previous section. The control module therefore takes goals as input.

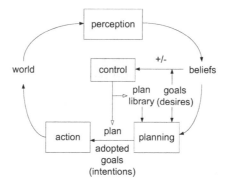

Fig. 2. Perception, planning and action

When we compare such reflective capabilities to the business world, the so called Deming Cycle comes to mind: *plan-do-check-act* [12]. Variants of this management control cycle are very influential in management approaches to quality control, risk management or information security. *Plan* and *do* correspond to our planning and action. *Check* (or study) refers to all kinds of learning and evaluation. This corresponds to our perception. *Act* refers to making decisions: altering the plan, based on the outcome of the evaluation. This is modelled here by the control module. Learning is also one of the cornerstones of capability maturity models [17]. In other words: mature organisations have the ability to learn, evaluate and adjust their behaviour.

What does it mean to be compliant in a deliberative architecture? Again, we can adjust execution by adding self monitoring and self control to the perception and action modules, or we can adjust the data-structures which generate the behaviour. The policy data structure is now replaced by goals and plans. In general, there are two ways of adjusting plans and goals to address compliance: by *filtering out* potential violations from existing plans and goals [23], or by *adopting a norm* as a new goal [6,8,13].

Filtering. We can deal with compliance in three different ways: (1) filter the plan library (no capability to violate), (2) filter the adopted plans and goals (no intention to violate), and (3) filter the potential goals (no desire to violate). Filtering the plan library (option 1) can be done off-line. It needs an algorithm to scan all recipes for potential violations. Such recipes are then *suppressed*: they receive a special status such that they will never be adopted. This is essentially the compliancy approach of Meneguzzi and Luck [23], implemented in the AgentSpeak programming language.

Option 1 assumes that possible violations can be detected out of context. But in general violations are context dependent. Consider an agent intending to "go as fast as possible given the condition of the terrain". We can't decide off-line if this plan would violate a speed limit of 30 km/h. Or consider a budget of $20. Buying fuel ($8), tires ($11) and a new mirror ($3) will add up to a violation, but it is unclear which goal constitutes 'the' violation. Therefore potential violations need to be assessed in conjunction with current beliefs and relevant other goals. This can be done under option 2. Option 3 suffers from a similar problem: potentially illegal desires cannot be detected off-line.

Norm Adoption. Instead of filtering, we can also produce compliant behaviour by adopting a norm as a source of potential goals similar to a desire. This approach is developed by [9], see also [6,13]. Adopted norms will often correspond to *maintenance goals*: goals to make sure that a desirable state of affairs subsists or that an undesirable state is avoided, by contrast to *achievement goals*, which are about reaching a new state of affairs. For example, our agent could adopt a maintenance goal to obey the speed limit. A cognitive architecture which can deal with maintenance goals contains a kind of feedback-control loop [16]. Similar to what we discussed in Section 2.1, trigger conditions will produce a warning or an alert when the goal is likely not to be maintained (self monitoring), which will lead to the blocking of current actions or repair actions being executed (self control). Moreover, any new goal about to be adopted must be filtered, to verify whether it does not conflict with current maintenance goals.

Norm adoption will often lead to conflicts. Consider an agent who is late for an appointment and must drive to as fast as possible. Which goal should get priority: keeping the appointment (achievement goal) or obeying the speed limit (maintenance goal)? Often such conflicts will have to be resolved by the designer of the system; priorities are build-into the agent. Our next architecture can deal with conflicts explicitly.

2.3 Perception, Goal Generation, Planning and Action

The third architecture adds a separate module for *goal generation*. Goal generation was introduced by Thomason [32], who observed that until then in AI, goals were simply given. Thomason realised that even before planning, it makes sense to filter goals. Goals which are incompatible with current beliefs are impossible to achieve and may lead to *wishful thinking*. Such goals should never even be generated. The idea was taken over by the BOID architecture, which distinguishes between two kinds of goals: internal motivations (desires), representing individual wants or needs, and external motivations (obligations) to model social commitments and norms [5]. All these potential goals may conflict with each other. New potential goals may also conflict with previously adopted goals (intentions). To resolve conflicts among the sets of beliefs, obligations, intentions and desires, some sort of priority order is needed. In the BOID, such a (partial) ordering is provided by the *agent type*. For instance, a so called *realistic* agent values beliefs over any kind of goals: $B > D, B > I, B > O$. This avoids wishful thinking, over-commitment or dogmatism. A *stable agent* values previously adopted goals (intentions) over new goals (desires; obligations): $I > D, I > O$. A *selfish* agent values its desires over social obligations, $D > O$, whereas an *obedient* agent will value obligations over desires: $O > D$. These orderings produce caricatures of agent behaviour. In practice, more detailed distinctions will be necessary. For instance, a stable agent might make an exception for life-saving obligations. The priority should be based on a classification of goals based on their relative value for the agent. In the business world, such a classification is often done by a risk assessment [10].

Again, the architecture is reflective: it can adjust its behaviour based on an evaluation of its relative success. What does it mean to be successful? For actions and plans, success is defined in terms of the underlying goals (desires, obligations). For selecting one goal over another, success depends on the agent type. Agent types are basic; they have no external motivation.

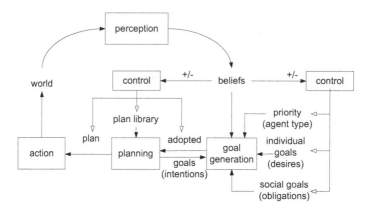

Fig. 3. Perception, goal generation, planning and action

What does it mean to be compliant in such an architecture? All previously mentioned ways of being compliant will work here too: self monitoring and self control, as well as adjusting the plans and goals or even the priority order guiding decision making. Given that resources (money, energy, time) are limited, adopting a norm as a goal means that other goals can no longer be achieved. Norms may conflict with individual desires, with reality, with previous intentions or with other norms. So norm adoption creates dilemmas; it requires a form of conflict resolution. Because agents are autonomous, we cannot ensure an agent will always adopt a norm. At least the agent should be aware of the consequences of possible violations such as sanctions or loss of reputation. When an agent nevertheless decides to violate a norm this should be a conscious decision.

How can dilemmas be resolved? A priority order determines how an agent will make choices. In the BOID, priorities are fixed by agent type. In general, the relative importance of goals is linked to *social values* [30]. In the business world, consider values like profit, safety, or quality. Such values are embedded in the corporate culture. For example, a culture which values short term profits over security – as apparent from payment and incentive schemes – will be more likely to lead to behaviour which violates a security norm, than a culture which values security over profits.

Social values may look vague, but fortunately, there has been progress in the computational representation of argumentation systems based on social values, see Atkinson et al [1]. Decision making is a form of *practical reasoning*. Crucial is what counts as a justification for an action. In a BDI architecture justification is essentially based on goals.But how are goals justified? Social values account for the fact that people may disagree upon an issue even though it would seem to be rational [30]. That means that justification becomes a matter of debate. Like in legal theory, it doesn't matter who is right; what matters is who can construct the most convincing argument and defend against counter arguments. An argument starts with a position [1]: "In the current circumstances s, we should perform action a, to achieve consequences s', which will realise some goal g, which will promote some value v." A position can be attacked by critical questions, which seek to undermine the underlying assumptions (Table 1). Critical questions provide a kind of quality test for the justification of a decision.

Table 1. Critical Questions (Atkinson et al [1])

CQ1 Are there alternative ways of realising consequences s', goal g or value v ?
CQ2 Is it possible to do action a?
CQ3 Would doing action a promote some other value ?
CQ4 Does doing action a have a side effect which demotes the value v, or some other value?
CQ5 Are the circumstances s such that doing action a will bring about goal g?
CQ6 Does goal g promote value v? Is value v a legitimate value?
CQ7 Is goal g achievable?

3   Information Needs

In this section we are concerned with the assessment of whether an agent is compliant or not. As we have seen compliance can be realised in many different ways. To demonstrate compliance to a norm, both subjects and auditors therefore need different kinds of evidence, based on the underlying cognitive architecture.

1. *perception, action.* First, evidence of the behaviour itself, i.e. original records, data and log-files testifying that violations did not occur. This is the only way to show effectiveness of monitoring. Second, evidence of the policy avoiding violations, and evidence showing that the policy is instrumental in actually producing behaviour. This can be a review of the policy specification, or data-mining techniques discovering patterns of behaviour to indicate that there is a consistency in behaviour which suggests a policy is followed. Third, evidence of changes in behaviour after sanctions or rewards were administered. Again, this would be pattern detection, showing that certain non-compliant patterns ease after the sanctions were applied.
2. *perception, planning, action.* In addition to the kinds of evidence listed above, for deliberative agents we can also look for evidence of plans and goals being compliant. Having such higher cognitive attitudes makes agents' behaviour predictable even in unforeseen situations. As evidence we need documentation on goals, plans and evidence that these goals plans are actually implemented and effective in producing behaviour.
3. *perception, planning, goal generation.* In addition to the kinds of evidence listed above, now we also look for evidence of the agents' priorities in decision making: are obligations preferred over desires? Moreover, it must be assessed whether these preferences are used for day-to-day decisions and do not comprise a paper reality. Addition evidence may concern embedded social values.

How can such evidence be collected in practice? For all architectures, evidence of behaviour is needed. This is the only way to demonstrate effectiveness of the agent's internal monitoring and control. In auditing, such evidence corresponds to statistical samples from a pool of relevant events recorded in the company's information systems or log-files. Note that taking samples requires that the company is collaborating. In an electronic institution such as the service broker discussed in the introduction, we expect that log-files and traces of interaction and (relevant aspects) of transactions are accessible for monitoring by the institution.

For the more complex architectures, evidence about the cognitive 'data structures' which generate behaviour can be used in addition to evidence of behaviour. In practice, that means evidence of policies and procedures. In auditing theory, one distinguishes three audit aspects: design, implementation and operational effectiveness [18]. The *design* of a policy or procedure should guarantee that it will prevent, detect or correct undesirable behaviour. Evidence of *implementation* of a policy or procedure checks whether it has been adopted by the board, and whether employees know about it. Finally, evidence of *operating effectiveness* of a procedure should establish whether the procedure was followed in all relevant cases for the period under investigation. Note that this differs from the usual notion of effectiveness, i.e. meeting objectives. In an electronic institution, these aspects also make sense. Auditing the design would correspond to analysing the agents' specification. Auditing implementation corresponds to verifying the way agents have been programmed. Also the security of the electronic environment matters, whether it prevents unauthorised modifications to agent scripts. Auditing operating effectiveness corresponds to analysing log-files of agents behaviour. It also depends on the continued security of the electronic environment.

To summarise, we can demonstrate compliance by:

– *evidence of compliant behaviour.* This can be established by logging and monitoring the behaviour itself. In auditing, typically representative statistical samples are taken from a set of records of events. Logging and monitoring are greatly enhanced by tools for data mining and pattern recognition.
– *evidence of norm implementation.* This can be established by reviewing the policy or the plans in a plan-base. In a company this amounts to interviews, dossier research and reviews of documentation or board meeting minutes with the purpose of verifying the existence of relevant business processes and standard operating procedures. Implementation of a procedure is typically verified by a so called line control: for one or two representative cases, follow the procedure from the "cradle to the grave" and verify whether all relevant steps have been taken. In addition, one needs to establish whether the procedure has been operationally effective for the whole period (i.e. was not temporally switched off). This can be done by selecting a representative sample of cases (e.g. incidents or events), to verify whether in all those cases the procedure has been followed.
– *evidence of norm adoption.* This is hardest to establish. It means that norms have affected decision making. Presence of adopted norms in the form of objectives can be established by a dossier review combined with interviews with management (tone at the top). For those procedures, processes and projects implemented to meet these objectives, we must then verify the appropriateness of their design: would they indeed meet the objectives generated by the norm? Critical questions, similar to the ones mentioned by Atkinson et al [1] may be used to challenge the assumptions of a decision. Also the corporate culture may be a factor to support true norm adoption.

Discussion. One may wonder why all of this is needed. After all, evidence of an agent's behaviour should be enough to determine whether the agent is compliant with the system norms. There are some reasons that evidence of norm adoption and norm implementation may be preferred. First, determining compliance through monitoring behaviour may take a lot of effort. In particular, for tax monitoring, this would involve large statistical samples from past behaviour (See Section 4). In the 'horizontal' approaches some of this effort is delegated to the subject of the norm. Second, log-files can establish that behaviour is compliant, but not why. By contrast, compliance enforced through self regulation is said to be more robust [2]. So it makes sense to collect evidence about the way in which norms have been adopted and implemented. Third, monitoring behaviour can only lead to sanctions after the fact; there is no way of providing assurance beforehand. For example, in the case of the electronic service broker, mentioned in the introduction, the broker needs to provide some kind of assurance that agents will not violate norms. This can be done by an assessment of the intentions of the owner (evidence of norm adoption), and a code review (evidence of norm implementation).

Principle-based versus rule-based. What can we say about the relative merits of principle-based or rule-based formulations of a norm? To make a comparison, we first need a concrete example of a principle and a rule. Consider the auditing principle of 'need to know': "only those people who need access to a document for their work, should be given access". When applying the principle to a specific situation, detailed models are needed of the organisational roles assigned to people, the tasks assigned to organisational roles, and the information needs associated with those tasks. In large enterprises such models are often unavailable or out of date. When they are available the models may be too restrictive, because there is a hidden trade-off between security and flexibility of the organisation. By contrast, a rule-based version of access control measures, would give a predefined checklist of those access rights which are not allowed for many common organisation roles. For instance, database administrators are not allowed to access the content of the database they manage. The problem is that a large part of such checklists is not relevant: there may not be any database administrators. Moreover, rules can be either too lenient or too strict for the situation. Still, rule-based norms are much more easy to implement and monitor.

It turns out that rule-based norms can be followed by all kinds of agents, including reactive agents. Principle-based norms, however, can only be followed by deliberative agents. When a principle is interpreted as a general (declarative) goal, which must still be adapted to the context, some form of planning is needed. When the principle involves a trade-off or dilemma, some form of ethical decision making is needed.

Sanctions. What can we say about the effectiveness of sanctions as a way of enforcing norms? For reactive agents, it is important that sanctions follow immediately after the action that caused a violation. If there is a delay, the agent will not be able to adjust the relative weights for the right action in the policy data-structure. For deliberative agents, the goals (desires) are used to evaluate the success of an action or plan. Based on this evaluation, plans may be adjusted. So to have an impact, sanctions must actually be undesired; rewards must actually be desired. Sanctions are not necessarily monetary fines. For example, for many companies, certainty about the financial situation is more important than the possibility of a fine (Section 4). Empirical research among humans has shown that external sanctions can be counterproductive [14]. In a number of day care centres, they studied the introduction of a fine for parents being late to pick up

their kids. After the fine was introduced, more parents were late. Apparently, they interpreted the fine as a kind of price, which made it morally acceptable to be late: the fine
removed their guilt. Removing the fine never restored original levels. For such reasons,
non-instrumental motivations for following a norm, such as recognition of the authority,
may lead to more robust compliance behaviour [7]. This is also one of the motivations
behind responsive regulation approaches [15,2]. Finally, sanctions assume agents have
the ability and expertise to improve their behaviour. But not all architectures have capabilities for generating a plan, say, from first principles. Similarly companies often lack
expertise concerning compliance issues. So even if they have the ability to change the
do not know in which direction to change. Also in such circumstances, sanctions may
be counterproductive. It is much more effective to provide guidance and advice on how
to improve compliance [2].

4   Case Study: Horizontal Monitoring

Horizontal monitoring is introduced as the new compliance approach for tax audits
concerning company taxation by the Dutch Customs and Tax Authority (DTCA) [15].
Companies which have shown that they have a reliable 'tax control framework', may
voluntarily enter into horizontal monitoring. This is an auditing approach based on a
relationship of mutual trust and understanding. Consider the following text from the
brochure issued by the tax office [33]:

> "Horizontal monitoring entails mutual trust between tax payer and the Tax and
> Customs Administration, indicating more clearly everyone's responsibilities
> and abilities in order to do what is right, as well as laying down and observ-
> ing reciprocal agreements. Horizontal monitoring is in line with developments
> in society, where the individual responsibilities of corporate and government
> managers and administrators are defined more clearly and upheld through su-
> pervision. Businesses must be transparent for stakeholders about the degree to
> which they achieve operational targets and the extent to which they are in con-
> trol of the processes involved. The government is an example of a stakeholder."

Data Collection. Our case study is in an initial stage. We are exploring hypotheses concerning changing information needs. The following findings concerning the tax control
framework and the horizontal monitoring philosophy are based on two interviews with
experts of horizontal monitoring within Dutch Tax and Customs Administration, as well
as on publicly available policy documents [33]. Moreover, as part of previous research
we have conducted several interviews with experts on AEO self-assessment, a compliance scheme used in customs, which is also based on Horizontal Monitoring.

The general idea of horizontal monitoring is that the tax office relies as much as possible on the company's internal controls. This is illustrated by the audit layer model of
Dutch Tax shown in Figure 4. The model is nicknamed the 'onion model' because it
represents auditing effort as consecutive layers which can be peeled off. The kernel is
formed by the business processes. Reliability of the business processes is mostly established by the internal control framework. Reliability of the internal control framework

Fig. 4. Audit layer model (Dutch Tax and Customs Administration)

is maintained by the internal audit department of the company. The internal controls are audited yearly by the external accountant as part of the financial audit. This means that the tax office now only has to assess reliability of the company's internal controls, internal auditing and external auditing, rather than having to establish reliability of the original records and business processes underlying the tax declarations. Only for specific tax issues do tax officers need to make visits and collect full evidence. To facilitate such 'meta-auditing', the company must provide access to all kinds of information about business processes and internal controls. The tax office in return can give the company more certainty, for instance that a tax declaration for a certain year is settled.

Mutual trust and understanding may sound nice, but there are real changes in the way companies are being treated. Below we list a number of illustrative changes.

1. *Demonstrating to be 'in control'.* When entering into a horizontal monitoring relationship, the tax office must establish the reliability of the company's internal control framework. This forms the basis for their 'trust' in the company's record keeping. COSO provides a well known standard for setting up an internal control framework [10]. The standard recommends: (1) a control environment where integrity and ethical values are supported from the top management throughout the organisation. (2) risk assessment is performed to identify and manage risks relevant to the organisation. (3) Control activities such as policies, procedures and processes are implemented to ensure a company carries out management directives. Examples include approvals, verifications, reconciliations, reviews of operating performance, security of assets and segregation of duties. (4) Relevant company data contained in the information system should be communicated in the organisation and to the relevant stakeholders. (5) Ongoing monitoring to assess the quality of a companys internal control systems. When a company has implemented a control framework like COSO it can demonstrate to the tax administration that it is in control of its business processes.
2. *No hunt for mistakes.* Under the tax control framework the tax office will not try and find as many mistakes as possible in a company's tax declaration; given the complexity of the legislation this is not difficult to do. Confronting a well meaning company year after year with the mistakes they have made, is counterproductive. Instead the tax office will try to help companies avoiding such mistakes in the future. This involves clear communication about what is expected of a company.

3. *Open communication.* Another issue regards the interpretation of the tax code. The Dutch corporate tax – by design – contains some space for interpretation. Companies are allowed to interpret the rules in their favour. However, grossly unreasonable interpretations are not considered acceptable. What is considered acceptable, differs from case to case. Currently, this creates uncertainty for companies. Under the new tax control framework, companies may seek advice with their tax office, to find out in advance whether their interpretation is considered acceptable. Such advance information sharing can save both parties a lot of work.

4. *Up to date tax assurance.* In corporate taxes it is customary to audit retrospectively. The tax officials are entitled to look back in the records to check for tax violations. A company can be fined by the tax administration for an error that occurred a few years ago. Resolving disputes is a long process resulting in high costs for both parties. In horizontal monitoring the company and the tax office agree to solve all historical issues when they start the relation. New issues are supposed to be solved immediately when they occur. A company no longer needs to worry about past tax issues and is assured that sanctions for historical violations will not be imposed.

These examples show that a relation based on mutual trust and understanding imposes requirements on the interaction between both parties as well as on the internal processes of the company. A company can demonstrate compliance by the implementation of an internal control system and open communication of the results. We show how different assumptions about the cognitive architecture(internal control system, ability to differentiate between compliant and violating behaviour, embedded plan-do-check-act cycle) lead to different information needs (emphasis on advice on norm interpretation instead of norm violations, new and timely data instead of historical data, information on implementation of norms, control procedures) when assessing compliance (principle based instead of rule based). We thus observe that a more mature agent architecture is needed to handle the new control approach of Dutch tax.

As part of the case study, we have looked at the internal auditing guidelines used by Dutch Tax to instruct auditors on the tax control framework [33]. It turns out that auditors are instructed to use evidence regarding decision making and implementation of decisions, in addition to the usual transaction based evidence. To demonstrate compliance, evidence about the design, implementation and operational effectiveness of cognitive data structures like procedures is needed. In practice this means that a company should provide tax auditors with detailed process descriptions, working procedures as they are implemented, and evidence that the procedures are known and applied.

5   Related Research

There is a growing body of research about compliance. We can only mention a few works that may be of interest.

In the field of multi-agent systems, the work by Meneguzzi and Luck [23] is similar to our work. They understand compliance as a filter of the plan library, implemented in AgentSpeak. The norm adoption approach has been advocated both Conte and by Dignum [8,9,13]. These architectures have influenced the BOID architecture of Section 2.3. Moreover, we believe that any architecture for norm adoption should be able to handle maintenance goals, see Hindriks and Van Riemsdijk [16].

Regarding reflective programming, there has been progress on systems for automated reconfiguration [11]. This work focuses on mechanisms for monitoring and diagnosis, in order to reconfigure its activities. They also need a declarative specification of objectives (i.e. goals) to evaluate the 'success' of an activity against.

Compliance can often be guaranteed by the design of business processes. Lu et al [21] discuss how to use business process management systems (BPMs) to automatically monitor and enforce compliance to norms and standards. Like us, this work combines formal reasoning and the agent metaphor with the actual practice of companies.

Finally, there is an interesting parallel between our information needs and the work of Lewicki and Bunker [20] who distinguish three sequential stages of trust. *Calculus-based trust* is based on the consistency of behaviour and involves a continuous evaluation by the actors of the punishment for violating trust and the rewards for preserving it. *Knowledge-based trust* occurs when one has enough knowledge about the other party's needs and preferences to understand them and to predict their likely behaviour. *Identification-based trust* is based on identification with the others' desires and intentions. There is a mutual understanding and appreciation of each others' wants, such that parties are able to act to the benefit and on behalf of the other.

One would expect a correspondence between the information needs for trust establishment and for assessing compliance. There are indeed many similarities, but a full mapping is not possible. For instance, Lewicki and Bunker put adoption of the other's intentions and desires under identification-based trust, where we would expect this to be part of the goal-based model. Social values or cultural cues, which we would expect under identification-based trust, are not mentioned by Lewicki and Bunker.

6   Conclusions

Compliance of agents has mostly been discussed at the inter-agent level; however, the intra-agent level is also important. After all, different kinds of norms make different assumptions about the cognitive architectures of the agents who must comply with the norm. In this paper we have tried to make such assumptions explicit by presenting three cognitive agent architectures from the literature and by indicating in which ways compliance can be implemented in these architectures. The architectures are: perception-action, perception-planning-action and perception-goal-generation-planning-action. All of these architectures also require reflective capabilities: to learn, evaluate and adjust behaviour based on experience.

Conceptually, compliance can be implemented either

- by a filter, restricting cognitive 'data-structures' like policies, plans and goals so that no violations will occur, or
- by norm adoption, where the norm itself is added as a goal or plan, so that the rest of the agent architecture will ensure execution.

The cognitive architecture of an agent has an impact on the evidence needed to assess whether the agent is compliant.

- For reactive architectures, we need log-files of behaviour, to demonstrate that the agent behaves consistently, manages to avoid violations and seek preferred states.

– For goal-based architectures, also evidence of the plans and goals may be used in establishing compliance. In particular, when an agent states that it has as a goal to be compliant, and when evidence about its plans and actual behaviour demonstrate that the agent is 'in control' of its own behaviour, we may trust that the agent will indeed behave in a compliant way.
– Finally, for value-based architectures that allow for ethical decision making, we may also use evidence of the social values of the agent, and how they are effective in actual decision making. However, the causal influence of stated values on actual decisions is hard to demonstrate. Therefore, such compliance is similar to the establishment of trust. Similar to identification-based trust [20], identification of the values of an agent may be based on cultural 'cues'.

Regarding the debate between rule-based versus principle-based norms, principle-based systems are much harder to implement and monitor. Principle-based systems require that subjects and auditors have a deliberative agent architecture, and often also the possibility to deal with trade-offs by ethical decision making. This could explain why principle-based norm systems may degenerate into rule-based systems.

Regarding the use of sanctions, we can say that sanctions assume agents are both willing and able to adjust their behaviour. This means that sanctions must really be undesired; also internal sanctions (guilt) may work. When agents lack expertise to improve their behaviour, giving advice may be more effective than sanctions.

The analysis has been validated in a case study of horizontal monitoring, a new auditing approach established by Dutch Tax. This auditing approach is based on mutual trust and understanding. It assumes companies have an interest in being compliant. Traditional command and control often works counterproductive. Instead of hunting mistakes in tax declarations, auditors must now give advice to companies on how to avoid misstatements. However, because it is principle-based, horizontal monitoring assumes that companies have an internal decision making structure which is at least goal-based and preferably also allows for ethical decision making. The case study shows that, in addition to evidence of behaviour, horizontal monitoring also requires evidence that compliance issues are taken into account during internal decision making.

References

1. Atkinson, K., Bench-Capon, T., McBurney, P.: Computational representation of practical argument. Synthese 152(2), 157–206 (2006)
2. Ayres, I., Braithwaite, J.: Responsive Regulation: Transcending the Deregulation Debate. Oxford University Press, Oxford (1992)
3. Boella, G., Verhagen, H., van der Torre, L.: Introduction to the special issue on normative multiagent systems. Journal of Autonomous Agents and Multi Agent Systems 17(1), 1–10 (2008)
4. Braithwaite, V.: Responsive regulation and taxation: Introduction. Law and Policy 29(1), 3–10 (2007)
5. Broersen, J., Dastani, M., Hulstijn, J., Van der Torre, L.: Goal generation in the BOID architecture. Cognitive Science Quarterly 2(3-4), 431–450 (2002)
6. Conte, R., Castelfranchi, C.: Cognitive and Social Action. UCL Press, London (1995)
7. Castelfranchi, C.: Prescribed mental attitudes in goal-adoption and norm-adoption. Artificial Intelligence and Law 7(1), 37–50 (1999)

8. Conte, R., Castelfranchi, C.: From conventions to prescriptions: towards an integrated view of norms. Artificial Intelligence and Law 7(4), 323–340 (1999)
9. Conte, R., Castelfranchi, C., Dignum, F.: Autonomous norm acceptance. In: Rao, A.S., Singh, M.P., Müller, J.P. (eds.) ATAL 1998. LNCS (LNAI), vol. 1555, pp. 99–112. Springer, Heidelberg (1999)
10. COSO. Internal control integrated framework. Technical report, Committee of Sponsoring Organizations of the Treadway Commission, COSO (1992)
11. Dalpiaz, F., Giorgini, P., Mylopoulos, J.: An architecture for requirements-driven self-reconfiguration. In: van Eck, P., et al. (eds.) CAiSE 2009. LNCS, vol. 5565, pp. 246–260. Springer, Heidelberg (2009)
12. Deming, W.E.: Out of the Crisis. MIT Center for Advanced Engineering Study (1986)
13. Dignum, F.: Autonomous agents with norms. Artificial Intelligence and Law 7, 69–79 (1999)
14. Gneezy, U., Rustichini, A.: A fine is a price. Journal of Legal Studies 29(1), 1–17 (2000)
15. Gribnau, H.: Soft law and taxation: The case of the Netherlands. Legisprudence 1(3) (2008)
16. Hindriks, K., van Riemsdijk, M.B.: Satisfying maintenance goals. In: Baldoni, M., Son, T.C., van Riemsdijk, M.B., Winikoff, M. (eds.) DALT 2007. LNCS (LNAI), vol. 4897, pp. 86–103. Springer, Heidelberg (2008)
17. Humphrey, W.S.: Characterizing the software process: A maturity framework. Technical Report CMU/SEI-87-TR-11, Carnegie Mellon University (1987)
18. IAASB. Audit sampling: Redrafted international standard on auditing (ISA 530). International Federation of Accountants, IFAC (2008)
19. Kaelbling, L.P., Littman, M.L., Moore, A.W.: Reinforcement learning: A survey. Journal of Artificial Intelligence Research 4, 237–285 (1996)
20. Lewicki, R.J., Bunker, B.B.: Developing and maintaining trust in work relationships. In: Trust in organizations, pp. 114–139. Sage Publications, Thousand Oaks (1996)
21. Lu, R., Sadiq, S., Governatori, G.: Measurement of compliance distance in business work practice. Information Systems Management 25(4), 344–355 (2009)
22. Maes, P.: Concepts and experiments in computational reflection. In: Proceedings OOPSLA, pp. 147–155 (1987)
23. Meneguzzi, F., Luck, M.: Norm-based behaviour modification in BDI agents. In: Proceedings of AAMAS 2009, pp. 177–184 (2009)
24. Pollack, M.E.: Plans as complex mental attitudes. In: Cohen, P., Morgan, J., Pollack, M. (eds.) Intentions in Communication, pp. 77–103. MIT Press, Cambridge (1990)
25. Rao, A.S., Georgeff, M.P.: Modeling rational agents within a BDI-architecture. In: Allen, J., et al. (eds.) Proceedings of KR 1991, pp. 473–484 (1991)
26. Russell, S.J., Norvig, P.: Artificial Intelligence: A Modern Approach, 2nd edn. Prentice Hall, New York (2003)
27. Sarbanes, Oxley: Sarbanes-oxley act of 2002. Public Law 107 - 204, Senate and House of Representatives of the United States of America (2002)
28. Satava, D., Caldwell, C., Richards, L.: Ethics and the auditing culture: Rethinking the foundation of accounting and auditing. Journal of Business Ethics 64, 271–284 (2006)
29. Schut, M.C.: Scientific Handbook for Simulation of Collective Intelligence, version 2. Available under Creative Commons License (2007), www.sci-sci.org
30. Searle, J.: The Construction of Social Reality. The Free Press, New York (1995)
31. Sierra, C.: Agent-mediated electronic commerce. Journal Autonomous Agents and Multi-Agent Systems 9(3), 285–301 (2004)
32. Thomason, R.: Desires and defaults: A framework for planning with inferred goals. In: Cohn, A.G., et al. (eds.) Proceedings of the International Workshop on Knowledge Representation (KR 2000), pp. 702–713. Morgan Kaufmann, San Mateo (2000)
33. Visser, E.: Tax control framework. Dutch Tax and Customs Administration (2008)

Incorporating BDI Agents into Human-Agent Decision Making Research

Bart Kamphorst, Arlette van Wissen, and Virginia Dignum

Institute of Information and Computing Sciences, Utrecht University, the Netherlands

Abstract. Artificial agents, people, institutes and societies all have the ability to make decisions. Decision making as a research area therefore involves a broad spectrum of sciences, ranging from Artificial Intelligence to economics to psychology. The Colored Trails (CT) framework is designed to aid researchers in all fields in examining decision making processes. It is developed both to study interaction between multiple actors (humans or software agents) in a dynamic environment, and to study and model the decision making of these actors. However, agents in the current implementation of CT lack the explanatory power to help understand the reasoning processes involved in decision making. The BDI paradigm that has been proposed in the agent research area to describe rational agents, enables the specification of agents that reason in abstract concepts such as beliefs, goals, plans and events. In this paper, we present CTAPL: an extension to CT that allows BDI software agents that are written in the practical agent programming language 2APL to reason about and interact with a CT environment.

1 Introduction

Decision making has since long been an area of interest to scholars from all kinds of disciplines: psychology, sociology, economics and more recently, computer science. A lot of research has been done on finding, isolating and formalizing the factors that are involved in decision making processes of both humans and computer agents [18] [11] [22]. The Colored Trails (CT) framework [10] is designed to aid researchers in this purpose. It is developed (i) to study interaction between multiple actors (humans or software agents) in a dynamic environment and (ii) to study and model both human and agent decision making. CT allows for a broad range of different games to be implemented, such as one-shot take-it-or-leave-it negotiation games [7], iterated ultimatum games [27] and, of late, dynamic games with self-interested agents [26].

Currently, CT software agents are *computational agents* implemented in the object oriented programming language Java. In this paper, we will use the term 'computational agent' to refer to software agents that determine their strategy by use of algorithms, probabilities or game theory. We will use this term to distinguish these agents from agents that use concepts from folk psychology to define strategies. CT agents are usually tailored either to display one type of behavioral strategy, such as egoism or altruism [27], or to maximize their utility for every action [16]. However, even though computational agents perform well in some scenarios, they lack

H. Aldewereld, V. Dignum, and G. Picard (Eds.): ESAW 2009, LNAI 5881, pp. 84–97, 2009.

the *explanatory power* to help understand the reasoning processes involved in decision making. Computational agents may make optimal decisions based on a clever probabilistic algorithm, but they will generally not show you how they did it.

In order to gain more insights into the actual reasoning processes that lie behind a decision of a software agent, the agents must be endowed with a richer model of reasoning. Based on Bratman's theory of rational actions in humans [2], agents can be constructed that reason in abstract concepts such as beliefs, goals, plans and events [3]. These types of agents are often referred to as Belief, Desire and Intention (BDI) agents. Ideally, agents are able to display *reactivity, proactiveness* and *social abilities* [32]. That is, they should be able to perceive and respond to the environment, take initiative in order to satisfy their goals and be capable to interact with other (possibly human) actors. For an agent to have an effective balance between proactive and reactive behavior, it should be able to reason about a changing environment and dynamically update its goals. Having social abilities requires it to respond to other agents, for example by cooperating, negotiating or sharing information. Working in a team for instance requires agents to plan, communicate and coordinate with each other. A BDI architecture lends itself well to implement these requirements in an intuitive yet formal way [9].

The BDI approach has proved valuable for the design of agents that operate in dynamic environments. It offers a higher level of abstraction by explicitly allowing beliefs to have a direct impact upon the agents behavior. This means the agents can respond flexibly to changing circumstances despite incomplete information about the state of the world and the agents in it [6]. Since BDI uses 'mental attitudes' such as beliefs and intentions, it resembles the kind of reasoning that we appear to use in our everyday lives [30]. To interact successfully, agents can benefit from modeling the mental state of their environment and their opponent [23]. Additionally, BDI models provide a clear functional decomposition with clear and retractable reasoning patterns. This can provide more helpful feedback and more explanatory power.

This paper presents middleware that lets software agents with a BDI decision structure interact with humans and other software agents in CT. The software presented in this article, CTAPL, allows BDI software agents that are written in the practical agent programming language 2APL to reason about and interact with a CT environment and the actors within the environment. CTAPL is a platform designed for the implementation of various interaction scenarios between BDI agents, computational agents, humans and heterogeneous groups. Although the framework of CTAPL has been developed, we are currently in the preliminary stages of evaluating CTAPL by building BDI agents whose performance can be compared to the performance of computational CT agents.

2   Related Work

The BDI model of agency does not prescribe a specific implementation [25]. We therefore do not claim that 2APL is the only suitable agent language for decision making research. There exist several different implementations that differ from each other in the logic they use and the technology they are based on. More often than not, the logics that are used are not formally specified in the semantics of the BDI programming language. 2APL differs from most agent languages (e.g., JACK [28] and Jadex [21]) in that it is defined with exact and formal semantics [3]. In addition to being theoretically well-motivated, 2APL provides easy implementation of external environments (see Section 4.1 for a more in-depth discussion of these environments), enabling different environments and frameworks to be connected to it.

The study of mixed-initiative interactions requires some kind of negotiation environment for the interactions to take place. Most environments are domain-specific and focus on specific tasks to be evaluated. Multi-agent decision making environments are mostly designed for agent simulation based on human performance. Examples of these environments are OMAR [5] and GENIUS [14]. The CT framework is very flexible in that it can be used to implement domains ranging from highly abstract to rich and complex scenarios. However, using BDI agents in decision making environments is certainly not limited to CT and it would be interesting to see how well BDI agents can be incorporated into other negotiation environments.

Literature shows that there are frameworks constructed for BDI agents [19] and recent work focuses on the development of a multi-agent simulation platform that supports different agent-oriented programming languages [1]. However, these frameworks are designed for very specific domains and are therefore not broadly applicable. CTAPL allows for the implementation of a range of different interaction domains in which BDI agents, computational agents and humans can interact. We are not aware of any other existing generic framework that allows computational agents and BDI agents to interact with each other and with humans in negotiation environments.

3   Colored Trails

Throughout the remainder of the paper we will illustrate various aspects of the CT framework using a decision making scenario that was presented in [27]. In this scenario the agents do not have to cope with any uncertainties about the world except the strategy of the opponent. Furthermore, it is a game that can be easily be divided into goals and subgoals. That is, players can create their own decision recipe trees that do not involve probabilities. This game is therefore very suitable to be implemented in CT as well as in the BDI constructs of 2APL. The game consists of an implementation of the ultimatum game (UG) [13], in which two players (here referred to as Alice and Bob) interact to divide their colored chips in order to take a path to the goal.

3.1   The Framework

CT [10] is a flexible research platform developed by Grosz and Kraus to investigate decision-making in group contexts. CT implements a server-client architecture. Figure 1 represents the conceptual design of CT: A is the set of software agents

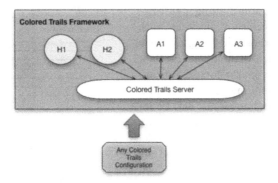

Fig. 1. The Colored Trails framework

and $\{A_1 \ldots A_i\} \in A$. H is the set of human actors and $\{H_1 \ldots H_i\} \in H$. Through an administrative shell a configuration file is loaded that specifies the properties of the game. Once the configuration file is loaded, the server starts the game.

The standard CT environment consists of a board of colored squares, one or more goals, two or more players (these can be both humans and software agents) and a set of colored chips per player. Players may move across the board by handing in colored chips that correspond to the colored squares of their taken path. They are allowed to negotiate in order to obtain useful chips. The size of the board, the colors of the squares, the number of players and the number of goals are a few examples of the many variables that can be set in the configuration file. The configuration file also specifies when and in what way players may communicate with each other and what information each player has about the current state of the world. CT thus allows for games of both *imperfect* and *incomplete information*. CT also allows for the "specification of different reward structures, enabling examination of such trade-offs as the importance of the performance of others or the group as a whole to the outcome of an individual and the cost-benefits of collaboration-supporting actions" [10]. Given the large number of variables that can be modified, a great variety of domains can be implemented in CT.

Figure 2 shows the configuration of the ultimatum game that was mentioned earlier. The board consists of 5 × 5 colored squares and two players, Alice and Bob, who each have full visibility of the board and of the other player's position, goal and chips. This means they do not have to cope with any uncertainty, other than the strategy of the opponent. On the board, the position of both players and their goal is visible. The chips (displayed in the 'Player Chips Display' at the bottom of the screen) represent the resources the players have and can divide amongst themselves. A player is either a proposer and required to propose the split of the chips, or a responder and required to respond to an offered proposal.

3.2   What's Missing?

The CT framework was specifically designed to investigate human-agent interactions: "A key determinant of CT design was the goal of providing a vehicle for comparing the decision-making strategies people deploy when they interact with other people with those they deploy when computer systems are members of their groups."[10] If a scenario focuses on analyzing decision making in interactions between humans and agents, it can be interesting and helpful if the agents reason in a similar way as humans (say they) do. These agents help us understand how they interact and what motivates their decisions, by enabling us to look more closely at their reasoning process. On top of that, agents that are based on models that take into account the same social principles that humans also base their decision on (such as fairness and helpfulness), were shown to explore new negotiation opportunities [15] and find solutions that correspond to solutions found by humans [4]. The information about the agent's reasoning process can be used to create agents that are able to support humans in decision making tasks.

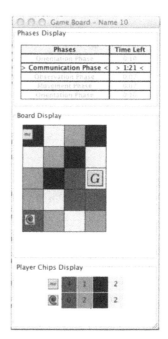

Fig. 2. The Configuration of a Colored Trails Game

BDI structures reflect the collaborative decision making process of humans more closely and at a more realistic level than the more algorithmic approaches [29]. The possibility of having BDI agents within the CT framework also allows for comparisons between how people interact with BDI agents and with computational agents. Currently, the CT framework is only suitable for computational agents written in Java. What is missing from CT is a way to have BDI agents interact in CT domains.

4   2APL

4.1   The Platform

2APL (pronounced double-a-p-l) is a practical agent programming language designed to implement agents that can explicitly reason with mental concepts such as beliefs, goals (desires) and plans (intentions) [3]. Figure 3 shows the conceptual design of 2APL. Like CT, the 2APL platform implements a server-client architecture, where A is the set of BDI agents written in the 2APL programming language and $\{A_1 \ldots A_i\} \in A$. Each agent A_n can communicate with all other agents via a *send action*. All communication between agents goes through the 2APL server.

The 2APL language has both a formal syntax and a formal semantics, which makes it possible to check programs on the satisfiability of their (formal)

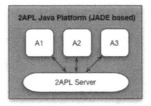

Fig. 3. The 2APL platform

specifications and constraints. Furthermore, it integrates both declarative and imperative programming styles. Goals and beliefs are stated in a declarative way, while plans and external environments are implemented in an imperative programming style. The declarative programming is well-suited for the implementation of reasoning and the updating of the mental states of the agents. The imperative part enables the implementation of plans, flow of control and allows for the interaction with existing imperative programming languages. (For a more detailed discussion of the implementation of beliefs, goals and plans in 2APL, see [3].) The 2APL platform also allows for *external environments*. These environments are modular extensions that agents can have access to through *external actions*. External environments serve as an interface to the Java programming language which allows programmers (i) to build custom environments for agents to interact in and (ii) to easily add functionality to the 2APL Platform.

Example 1 illustrates a specific reasoning pattern of the UG example in 2APL. Alice might have a different strategy of reacting to proposals received from Bob than Bob has of reacting to Alice's proposals. It might be the case that Alice is egoistic and only accepts proposals if it leaves herself better but Bob worse off, while Bob is more altruistic and also accepts proposals that favor Alice. In 2APL this can be expressed in terms of goals, subgoals and belief updates. This example shows what happens if Alice receives a proposal. The method 'makeResponse(MSGID)' is called when Alice receives a new proposal and she has an ID. If Alice has the goal to win and to respond to proposals (meaning that she is currently the responder in the game), then she will check whether accepting an offer that Bob has proposed is both beneficial for her and harmful for Bob. If this condition is met, she will accept the proposal and put this in her belief base. Otherwise, she will reject the proposal and put this in her belief base. Statements that transfer knowledge to the belief base can be identified by the first letter of the name of the method, which is always a capitol. In this case, the statement 'Responded(TYPE, MSGID, accept)' is a belief update rule (as defined in 2APL), which will update the belief base with the fact that the agent responded with 'accept' to a particular proposal. Since in the following round Alice will be a proposer, she now updates her goal base by dropping the subgoal of responding to proposals and accepting the goal of making proposals.

Example 1 (Performing   high   level   task-specific   reasoning: *makeResponse(MSGID))*

```
makeResponse (MSGID) <- received (TYPE, MSGID, open) and
    agentId (MYID) | {
if  ( G(win) and G(respond) ) then {
        if  ( B(scoreAfterExchange (MYID, SCORE) >
        scoreCurrentChips (MYID))
            and B(scoreAfterExchange (BOBID, SCORE) <
        scoreCurrentChips (BOBID) ) then {
            response (MSGID, accept);
            Responded (TYPE, MSGID, accept)
    } else {
            response (MSGID, reject);
            Responded (TYPE, MSGID, reject)
    }
        dropGoal (respond);
        adopta (propose)
    }
}
```

4.2   What's Missing?

Although the 2APL platform in principle allows external environments to have a graphical user interface (GUI) with which humans can interact with the 2APL agents, external environments are in practice mostly designed to examine the agents' behavior and reasoning processes. The environments provided by 2APL are not very well-suited to study human-agent interaction, because the scenario often focuses on helping the agent to learn or display certain behavior. However, since BDI systems have the advantage that they use similar concepts of reasoning as humans do, it would be very interesting to study their behavior in heterogeneous settings comprising of both agents and humans. This requires an empirical testbed that enables the implementation of both abstract and more real-world domains in which humans and agents can interact. CT is very suitable for this purpose.

In many scenarios, the BDI model has proven to be a useful tool and several successful applications use BDI structures [29] [20]. According to Georgeff, "the basic components of a system designed for a dynamic, uncertain world should include some representation of Beliefs, Desires, Intentions and Plans [...]" [8]. However, one of the main criticisms against BDI systems is that it cannot deal properly with learning and adaptive behavior. However, recent attempts have been made to extend BDI languages with learning components [12]. Extensions to the existing BDI framework can be easily evaluated in CT, since agents have to adapt to a dynamic environment and can learn from interactions with humans. "The CT architecture allows games to be played by groups comprising people, computer agents, or heterogenous mixes of people and computers. [...] As a result, CT may also be used to investigate learning and adaptation of computer decision-making strategies in both human and computer-agent settings" [10]. Another criticism concerns the gap between the powerful BDI logics and practical systems [17].

To conclude, the 2APL platform is currently missing a uniform way to let humans interact with the BDI agents. Combining 2APL and CT enables researchers to study BDI agents in a setting of human-agent interaction.

5 CTAPL

From the previous sections, two issues can be distilled. The first is that the CT framework in its current state lacks a clear-cut way to build agents with a rich model of reasoning needed to help better understand the reasoning processes involved in decision making. Secondly, although the 2APL platform offers a BDI agent programming language that provides agents with such a rich model of reasoning, the 2APL platform is in itself not very suitable for human-agent interaction experiments. CTAPL is designed to overcome both problems. CTAPL is middleware that allows BDI agents, written in 2APL, to participate in a CT environment in which heterogeneous actors can interact. CTAPL allows for both the interaction between BDI agents and humans and between BDI agents and computational agents. It is even possible to have a mixed group of BDI agents, computational agents and humans interact. Because of this, CTAPL is a very suitable platform to evaluate the performance of BDI agents.

5.1 Conceptual Design

Figure 4 shows the conceptual design of CTAPL. The top layer represents the 2APL platform. As with any 2APL setup, it consists of a server and one or more BDI agents $(A_1 \ldots A_i)$. The bottom layer represents the CT framework, with software agents and human actors. In CTAPL however, the CT agents are not fully functional, reasoning agents. Instead, $GA_1 \ldots GA_i$ are mere hooks for the BDI agents to communicate with the CT environment. Each agent A_n thus corresponds with hook GA_n. The 2APL platform is extended by an external environment that instantiates (i) the hooks for each 2APL agent and (ii) a Java Thread that continually listens whether agents have received any new messages from the server. In CTAPL the communication between agents flows through the CT messaging system instead of directly through the 2APL server.

5.2 Implementation

CTAPL consists of four major components: a 2APL external environment, a MessageListener class, a set of hooks in CT in the form of generic Java CT agents and higher level 2APL code that 2APL agents have to use in order to communicate with the CT framework. In the upcoming subsections the four components will be discussed individually.

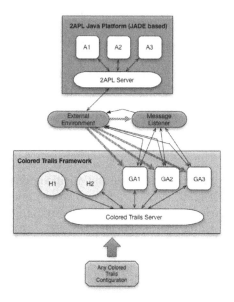

Fig. 4. The conceptual design of CTAPL

2APL Agents. The 2APL agents are designed to perform all higher level reasoning about the game. Through external actions the agents can pass information to and request information from the CT environment. CTAPL provides a 2APL API that defines BDI constructs for all external actions that are available in the CTAPL external environment (see Section 5.2). For instance, the procedural rule[1] *getPosition(ID)*, shown in Example 2, allows agents to retrieve the position of another actor on the board. This method can be called without restrictions, as demonstrated by the guard of this method, which is 'true'. First, the method calls upon the 'getPosition(ID)' method in the CT environment. The environment returns the result of this call, which is captured in the variable POS. Subsequently, it is checked whether the POS value meets the required form of two coordinates. These coordinates are then put in the belief base with the belief update rule 'Position(ID,X,Y)'.

Example 2 (Requesting information from the external environment: *getPosition(ID)*)

```
getPosition(ID) <- true | {
    @ctenv(getPosition(ID), POS);
    B(POS=[X,Y]);
    Position(ID,X,Y)
}
```

---

[1] For more on procedural rules in 2APL, see [3].

The agent programmer can include the constructs from the API by putting an *Include: filename* statement on the first line of the 2APL file that defines the reasoning patterns of the specific BDI agent. This statement creates a union between the code from the API and the agent code designed by the agent programmer. Other extensions such as general beliefs and plans specified by the programmer may also be put into separate files that can then be included by all agents.

The External Environment. The external environment consists of several classes, written in Java with the 2APL API, that have been packaged as a Java archive (jar). External environments are the default way in the 2APL platform of providing agents with an environment in which to interact. Normally, an external environment is a closed system that defines all the external actions an agent can perform within the environment. In CTAPL however, the external environment functions as a proxy between the 2APL agents and the hooks in CT. For instance, the environment ensures that the procedural rule *getPosition(ID)* from Example 2 will call the *getPosition(ID)* method of the CT hook that corresponds with the 2APL agent in question and returns the value to the 2APL agent. If Alice – programmed in 2APL – wants to know Bob's position, the 2APL code will call the CT environment to extract this information.

CT Generic Agents. The generic agent functions solely as a hook for 2APL to communicate with the CT server. The class *GenericAgentImpl* contains all the basic functionality that CT offers its regular agents. Examples of basic methods are *getChips()*, *getPosition()* and *setClientName(String name)*. Example 3 shows the getPosition(ID) method in CT, to give an impression of the functionality. First, the set of players is collected by the method 'getPlayers()', which is defined in the CT API. The method then cycles through the set of all players to find the one with the right ID. Then the position of this player is collected by 'getPosition()', which is also defined in the CT source code. The method now stores this position value and returns it to the environment, where the method was called.

Because the agent functions as a hook to the 2APL platform, GenericAgentImpl also implements higher level methods such as *getBoard()*, *getPlayers()* and *getPlayerByPerGameId(int pergameid)*. If CT is extended by new methods specifically designed for a specific experiment, the generic agent class can be subclassed to implement the additional methods.

The Message Listener. The Message Listener component is a Java Thread instantiated by the external environment that continuously polls each CT Generic Agent for new messages that the agent may have received.[2] This information is then passed through the external environment onto the 2APL agents using the

---

[2] Technically, the Message Listener is part of the external environment. However, because it is a Threaded class and serves a very specific purpose, it is considered a separate component of CTAPL.

Example 3 (The CT functionality: *getPosition(ID)*)

```
public RowCol getPosition(int id) {
    Set<PlayerStatus> players = client.getPlayers();
    RowCol position = null;
    for (PlayerStatus player : players ) {
        if (player.getPerGameId() == id) {
            // the getPosition() method is defined in
                the CT API
            position = player.getPosition();
            break;
        }
    }
    return position;
}
```

2APL built-in construct *throwEvent(APLFunction event, String ... receivers)*. This construction allows the BDI agents to passively gain knowledge about messages that have been sent to them. The 2APL agent code specifies what to do when messages are received.

6   Discussion

Currently, the authors are in the process of implementing an egoistic BDI agent in 2APL that interacts within a scenario similar to the one described in [27]. A proof of concept has already been developed that shows that the framework of CTAPL functions properly by relaying information from 2APL to CT and visa versa. Once the implementation of the egoistic BDI agent is complete, the authors will evaluate it by comparing its performance with that of the egoistic agent from [27]. We expect the BDI agent to perform *at least* as well as the original agent.

CT allows for environments in which uncertainties, probabilities and utilities play an important role. Due to the highly abstract philosophical origins of BDI, such concepts are typically not included in BDI models. One might therefore object against the use of 2APL in CT by raising the question how 2APL would handle such concepts. In defense of CTAPL two things may be said. The first is that this objection holds for almost all approaches that use BDI structures. The question posed brings forth a long-existing tension between those who favor BDI models and those who favor computational (decision and game theoretic) approaches to building software agents [31]. The burden of solving this tension does not lay with CTAPL because it is written as an extension to the already existing framework of CT. The authors of this paper do not claim that BDI agents should be preferred over computational agents in all cases. Instead, we have argued that BDI agents can be a valuable addition to decision making research with CT when the focus is on understanding the reasoning processes involved.

Second, the 2APL platform does offer a clear, modular way to capture uncertainties, probabilities and utilities. External environments may be written that provide computational methods. By allowing BDI agents access to these environments, the agents can request a certain value to be calculated. The agents can then reason with the outcome. Consider the case in which Alice does not know what chips Bob has. Alice may now access an external environment to calculate the probability of Bob having the chips Alice needs. Alice can then use this information to make her offer. So even though the probability is calculated using a computational algorithm, Alice uses her own beliefs, desires and intentions to interpret that value. In this way the 2APL agents are able to reason about uncertainties, probabilities and utilities.

7   Future Work

Currently no work has been done to deploy BDI agents in CT scenarios in which agents have to deal with (i) utilities and (ii) uncertainties about the world. As we discussed in section 6 traditional BDI systems are not well equipped to cope with uncertainties. Current BDI approaches simply do not provide tools for quantitative performance analysis under uncertainty. Future research will have to show whether these difficulties can be overcome by either using external environments to implement computational features that BDI agents can utilize, or by using hybrid approaches such as BDI-POMDP to deal with uncertainty [24].

As mentioned in section 6, the authors will use CTAPL to compare the performance of an egoistic BDI agent with that of an egoistic computational agent in a negotiation scenario similar to the one presented in [27]. Because CTAPL allows for the interaction between both types of agents, the platform is very suitable for empirically comparing BDI agents with computational agents in terms of speed, performance and explanatory power in various settings. Future work will provide more empirical insights into the advantages and disadvantages of the BDI approach. Future research with CTAPL also includes (i) building BDI agents that model human decision making processes in a setting of coalition formation with self-interested agents [26] and (ii) improving the planning mechanism of agents in a collaborative setting with uncertainty [16].

8   Conclusions

In this paper the authors have proposed a technical solution for dealing with the explanatory gap that exists when computational agents are used to investigate decision making. We have proposed that BDI based agents can assist in filling the gap because they use clear and retractable reasoning patterns. This paper has described new middleware called CTAPL that is designed to combine the strengths of a BDI-based agent approach with the Colored Trails testbed for decision making.

CTAPL makes three major contributions. First, CTAPL opens up the possibility for BDI researchers to explore existing research domains developed in CT for agent-agent interaction. Secondly, it gives BDI researchers the opportunity to have BDI agents that perform optimally in a certain environment interact with human players. Lastly, it creates the possibility for CT researchers to write agents that can qualitatively reason in terms of beliefs, goals and plans by using the 2APL agent programming language.

Acknowledgements. We thank Ya'akov (Kobi) Gal and Maarten Engelen for helpful comments and assistance with the initial setup of CTAPL. This research is funded by the Netherlands Organization for Scientic Research (NWO), through Veni-grant 639.021.509.

References

1. Bordini, R., et al.: Mas-soc: a social simulation platform based on agent-oriented programming. Journal of Artificial Societies and Social Simulation 8(3) (2005)
2. Bratman, M.: Intentions, Plans and Practical Reason. Harvard University Press (1987)
3. Dastani, M.: 2apl: a practical agent programming language. Autonomous agents and multi-agent systems 16(3), 214–248 (2008)
4. de Jong, S., Tuyls, K., Verbeeck, K.: Fairness in multi-agent systems. The Knowledge Engineering Review (2008)
5. Deutsch, S., Adams, M.: The operator-model architecture and its psychological framework. In: 6th IFAC Symposium on Man-Machine Systems. MIT, Cambridge (1993)
6. Dignum, F., Morley, D., Sonenberg, E., Cavedon, L.: Towards socially sophisticated bdi agents. In: Proceedings of the Fourth International Conference on MultiAgent Systems, Boston, MA (2000)
7. Gal, Y., Pfeffer, A.: Predicting people's bidding behavior in negotiation. In: AAMAS (2006)
8. Georgeff, M., Pell, B., Pollack, M., Tambe, M.: The belief-desire-intention model of agency. LNCS. Springer, Heidelberg (1999)
9. Grosz, B., Kraus, S.: Collaborative plans for complex group action. Artificial Intelligence 86(3), 269–357 (1996)
10. Grosz, B., Kraus, S., Talman, S., Stossel, B., Havlin, M.: The influence of social dependencies on decision-making: Initial investigations with a new game. In: AAMAS (2004)
11. Grosz, B., Pfeffer, A., Shieber, S., Allain, A.: The influence of task contexts on the decision-making of humans and computers. In: Proceedings of the Sixth International and Interdisciplinary Conference on Modeling and Using Context (2007)
12. Guerra-Hernández, A., Fallah-Seghrouchni, A.E., Soldano, H.: Learning in BDI multi-agent systems. In: Dix, J., Leite, J. (eds.) CLIMA 2004. LNCS (LNAI), vol. 3259, pp. 218–233. Springer, Heidelberg (2004)
13. Guth, W., et al.: An experimental analysis of ultimatum bargaining. Journal of Economic Behavior and Organization 3, 367–388 (1982)
14. Hindriks, K., Jonker, C., Kraus, S., Lin, R., Tykhonov, D.: Genius - negotiation environment for heterogeneous agents, Budapest, Hungary (May 2009)
15. Hogg, L., Jennings, N.: Socially intelligent reasoning for autonomous agents. IEEE Trans. on Systems, Man and Cybernatics - Part A, 381–399 (2001)

16. Kamar, E., Gal, Y., Grosz, B.: Incorporating helpful behavior into collaborative planning. In: AAMAS (2009)
17. Mora, M., Lopes, J., Viccari, R., Coelho, H.: BDI models and systems: Reducing the gap. In: Rao, A.S., Singh, M.P., Müller, J.P. (eds.) ATAL 1998. LNCS (LNAI), vol. 1555, pp. 11–27. Springer, Heidelberg (1999)
18. Newell, A., Simon, H.A.: Human Problem Solving. Prentice-Hall, Englewood Cliffs (1972)
19. Nguyen, M., Wobcke, W.: A flexible framework for sharedplans. In: Sattar, A., Kang, B.-h. (eds.) AI 2006. LNCS (LNAI), vol. 4304, pp. 393–402. Springer, Heidelberg (2006)
20. Onken, R., Walsdorf, A.: Assistant systems for vehicle guidance: Cognitive man-machine cooperation. Aerospace Science Technology 5, 511–520 (2001)
21. Pokahr, A., Braubach, L., Lamersdorf, W.: Jadex: A bdi reasoning engine. In: Multi-Agent Programming: Languages, Platforms and Applications. Kluwer, Dordrecht (2005)
22. Sanfey, A., Rilling, J., Aronson, J., Nystrom, L., Cohen, J.: The neural basis of economic decision-making in the ultimatum game. Science (300), 1755–1758 (2003)
23. Sindlar, M.P., Dastani, M., Dignum, F., Meyer, J.-J.C.: Mental state abduction of BDI-based agents. In: Baldoni, M., Son, T.C., van Riemsdijk, M.B., Winikoff, M. (eds.) DALT 2008. LNCS (LNAI), vol. 5397, pp. 161–178. Springer, Heidelberg (2009)
24. Tambe, M., et al.: Conflicts in teamwork: Hybrids to the rescue. In: AAMAS, pp. 3–11 (2005)
25. van der Hoek, W., Wooldridge, M.: Towards a logic of rational agency. Logic Journal of the IGPL 11(2), 135–159 (2003)
26. van Wissen, A., Kamphorst, B., Gal, Y., Dignum, V.: Coalition formation between self-interested heterogeneous agents (forthcoming)
27. van Wissen, A., van Diggelen, J., Dignum, V.: The effects of cooperative agent behavior on human cooperativeness. In: AAMAS (2009)
28. Winikoff, M.: Jack^{TM} intelligent agents: An industrial strength platform. In: Multi-Agent Programming: Languages, Platforms and Applications. Kluwer, Dordrecht (2005)
29. Wolfe, S., Sierhuis, M., Jarvis, P.: To bdi or not to bdi, design choices in an agent-based traffic flow management simulation. In: Proceedings of the 2008 Spring Simulation Multiconference (2008)
30. Wooldridge, M.: Intelligent agents. In: Weiss, G. (ed.) Multiagent Systems. MIT Press, Cambridge (1999)
31. Wooldridge, M.: Reasoning about Rational Agents. MIT Press, Cambridge (2000)
32. Wooldridge, M., Jennings, N.: Intelligent agents: Theory and practice. The Knowledge Engineering Review 10(2), 115–152 (1995)

Programming Organization-Aware Agents
A Research Agenda

M. Birna van Riemsdijk, Koen Hindriks, and Catholijn Jonker

Technische Universiteit Delft, The Netherlands
{m.b.vanriemsdijk,k.v.hindriks,c.m.jonker}@tudelft.nl

Abstract. Organizational notions such as roles, norms (e.g., obligations and permissions), and services are increasingly viewed as natural concepts to manage the complexity of software development. In particular in the context of multi-agent systems, agents are expected to be organization-aware, i.e., to understand and reason about the structure, work processes, and norms of the agent organization in which they operate. In this paper, we analyze which kinds of reasoning an agent should be able to do to function in an organization. We categorize these kinds of reasoning with respect to several dimensions, and distinguish three general approaches on how these might be integrated in existing agent programming languages. Through this, we provide a research agenda on what needs to be addressed when developing techniques for programming organization-aware agents.

1 Introduction

Software systems are becoming increasingly complex. One of the main challenges in the field of software engineering is to develop tools and techniques for managing this complexity [41]. A central role is played by development methodologies and programming languages, which can help managing complexity by providing appropriate *concepts and abstractions* in terms of which an application can be analyzed, designed, and implemented. Searching for the "most appropriate" (most convenient, most natural, most succinct, most efficient, most comprehensible, ...) programming concepts and abstractions is addressed in programming language design [5, Foreword].

In the field of multi-agent systems (MAS), several dedicated agent programming languages have been proposed [5] to support the implementation of MAS. The programming abstractions on which many of these languages focus, are aimed at programming how an agent can reach certain goals, how it should react to events occurring in its environment, and how it should communicate with other agents.

A line of research in the MAS field that has received increasing attention in the last years, is to assign an organization to the MAS with the aim of organizing and regulating it (see, e.g., [17,4,31,3,54]), in a similar way as done in human organizations. Using an *organizational specification* to organize a MAS should make the agents more effective in attaining their purpose, or prevent certain undesired behavior from occurring. An organizational specification may define

H. Aldewereld, V. Dignum, and G. Picard (Eds.): ESAW 2009, LNAI 5881, pp. 98–112, 2009.

the structure of the agent organization in terms of roles and the relations between roles, and specify the norms (e.g., obligations and prohibitions) that are to be followed by the agents of the MAS.

Agents that operate in such an organized MAS are expected to *take the specification of the organization, as well as their own position in the organization, into account when deciding what to do.* For example, an agent playing the role of supervisor can typically delegate tasks to its subordinates, but not the other way around. Agents playing the role of supervisor or subordinate should be aware of this and take this into account when deciding on action, if they are to operate effectively in the organization. While there is a growing body of work addressing the modeling and implementation of organizational specifications, little research has been done on how to program agents that use these specifications for deciding on action (see [57,11,18,12,31,40] for a few papers that do address various aspects of this). We call agents that are capable of such organizational reasoning and decision making *organization-aware agents*.

It is the aim of this paper to analyze which kinds of reasoning an agent should be able to do to function in an organization and how this might be programmed, thereby providing a starting point for research on how to program an agent's organizational reasoning.

2 Motivation and Background

In this section, we explain in more detail why we believe that it is important that agents are capable of organizational reasoning and decision making, and we provide more background on the subject.

One of the main application areas that we believe would benefit from organization-aware agents, is *simulation and training* of human organizations. Agent-based simulation is important for analyzing and training organizations, especially where learning is dangerous or where teaching is expensive [50,48,28,14,1,42,49]. The more realistic the behavior of the agents is, the better the training results will most likely be.

For example, since 9/11 a lot of research has been put into the improvement of crisis management. Agent technology plays an important role in creating computer simulations for analysis support and in developing training environments for this domain [44,46,26,49,28,27]. Software agents form a natural programming metaphor: there is a relatively close correspondence between real-world crisis management organizations and collections of autonomous agents that interact in a dynamic environment, usually with some individual or collective purpose.

As an example of the kind of organizational reasoning that is required in crisis management, consider the following scenario:

> *An explosion has occurred in a chemical plant and hazardous chemicals have leaked into the area. To prevent further injuries, it is essential that the emergency response team secures the area by setting up road blocks. Normally, this is the task of policemen, but firefighters are the first to arrive on the scene. Should the firefighters set up the road blocks?*

The firefighters operate in the context of a larger emergency response organization, for which operating procedures and role responsibilities are (partly) described in a disaster plan. The firefighters have to decide whether to take on a role that is normally played by other members of the organization (according to the disaster plan), or whether to give priority to their own goal of fighting the fire. This kind of organizational reasoning and decision making takes place frequently in organizations such as those for crisis management. Endowing agents with similar capabilities is thus highly relevant.

Other application areas where organizational reasoning can be useful, are human-agent teamwork and open systems. In human-agent teamwork, humans and agents work together to achieve joint goals. It is essential for the effective operation of a (human-agent) team to create a shared understanding between teammates [52,39,36]. This is facilitated by making agents understand how to function as part of an organization. Open systems allow agents to enter and leave the system as it operates [19,2,15]. Typical examples are e-institutions such as market places on the internet. An open system is organized by an organizational specification that is to be followed by the participating agents. Organizational reasoning and decision making facilitates the functioning of agents as part of an open system.

Existing research on *organizational modeling languages* supports the specification of organizations using the notion of "role" (see, e.g., [19,21,17,58,30,4] [31,54,33]). In this way, an organizational specification abstracts from the individual agents that will eventually play the roles, comparable to a disaster plan in crisis management: a disaster plan describes the desired structure and functioning of the crisis management organization without specifying which individuals will play the roles of policeman and firefighter in case of a crisis. Some organizational modeling languages come with implementation frameworks [20,31,45] that, for example, allow agents to access and modify the state of the organization and enforce organizational constraints by applying sanctions in case of their violation.

Given an organizational specification, it is up to the agents to operationalize it by playing the roles of the organization. A few abstract models exist on how aspects of an organizational specification may influence agent behavior [16,7,38,18,8], but little is understood on how to operationalize and combine them on the level of agent programming. First steps towards this have been made [57,11,18,12,31,40]. However, in order to program agents that take reasoned decisions on how to play their part in the organization, more advanced forms of organizational reasoning and decision making are needed as discussed in the rest of this paper.

3   Dimensions of Organizational Reasoning

In this section, we categorize forms of organizational reasoning along three main dimensions: the phases of organizational participation of the agent, the elements of organizational specifications that agent should understand, and the direction of organizational reasoning (top-down starting from an organizational specification, or bottom-up where the agents have to figure out amongst themselves how to organize). It is the aim of this section to provide a reasoned overview of kinds of organizational reasoning. We have included references that can be used as a starting point if a certain kind of organizational reasoning is studied, and we provide several examples of organizational reasoning for each of the categories, such as deciding whether to take on a role (weighing possibly conflicting interests as in the firefighter scenario), reasoning about how to fulfill norms imposed by the organization and deciding when to go against them (even though sanctions might be applied), reasoning about how to change the organization, etc.

3.1   Phases of Organizational Participation

Organizations are operationalized through the agents that play roles in the organization. In the case of open organizations where agents may enter and leave the organization, it seems evident to distinguish three phases of an agent participating in an organization: entering the organization, playing roles in the organization, and leaving the organization. If closed systems are considered, only the second phase is relevant. In each phase, different kinds of reasoning can be distinguished.

Entering the Organization. In this phase, the agent has to reason about whether it *wants* to enter the organization, and whether it has the *capabilities* to behave as the organization requires. That is, the agent needs to consider what it wants from the organization, and what the organization wants from it.[1] Since agents typically participate in an organization by playing a role in the organization, this kind of reasoning will focus on deciding whether to play a role.

In order to determine this, the agent has to reason about whether playing a certain role in the organization can help it to fulfill its own goals, and whether it can come to an agreement, e.g., with respect to the interaction protocols that will be used. For this, the agent has to *understand the specification of the role*, and should be able to relate it to its own *goals*. For example, if an agents wants to sell books, it might participate as a seller in an auction if it understands that playing the seller role will enable it to sell the books. The agent also has to determine whether it can play the role in the way required from the organization. For example, the auction might require the agent to have a bank account in the country where the auction is held, to enable easy transfer of the money earned by selling the books. In order to determine whether the agent can fulfill these norms belonging to a role, the agent has to understand them and relate them to its own capabilities. For example, if the agent currently does not have a bank account in the country where the auction is held, but it does know how to obtain such a bank account, it might decide to play the role and open up the account.

---

[1] See also [8], where the notion of social power is used as a basis for the agent to decide whether it wants to enter a group, i.e., whether the power it loses by entering is compensated by the power it gains or not.

In practice, it will often be the case that the agent and the role do not match exactly [11]. Playing the role might not enable the agent to fulfill its goals entirely, and the agent might not have all the capabilities in principle required to play the role. The agent can then *negotiate* about the terms under which it plays the role in the organization (see also [36], where goal negotiation is identified as one of the challenges of human-agent cooperation), and form a contract [17] with the organization. A related aspect is that *conflicts* may arise between some goals of the agent and requirements imposed by the role [11] (see also [53,47,56] for work on conflicting goals). For example, the agent may want to sell its books to only one buyer because it concerns a book series that the agent feels should not be separated. However, the auction does not offer the possibility to specify that the books should be sold to a single buyer. The agent will then have to reason about *priorities between its goals*, i.e., whether selling the books is more important than keeping the books together.

Playing Roles in the Organization. When the agent has decided to play a role in the organization, it has to decide how to do this. In other words, the abstract specification of the role with accompanying norms and responsibilities or goals has to be interpreted and translated to concrete actions taken by the agent. We distinguish three increasingly advanced levels of organizational reasoning related to playing roles: behaving according to the specification of the role, reasoning about violation of the specification, and reasoning about adapting the specification of the role (or other parts of the organization).

Before we discuss these levels of organizational reasoning, we remark that an agent may also be *designed* to fulfill certain roles in an organization (see, e.g., the Gaia methodology [60])[2]. An agent may then always behave according to the specification of the role by design, and no advanced forms of reasoning are required to make sure the agent complies with the specification. Generation of agent skeleton code [57] from the organizational specification can be used to ease agent developed in such a setting.[3] While this is useful for certain kinds of applications, it limits the flexibility of the MAS. We aim for domains in which increased flexibility obtained through organizational reasoning would provide additional benefits. For example, in the case of open systems it would be beneficial if the agents are capable of entering and functioning in various organizations without the programmer having to specify for each of these organizations exactly how the agent should do this. Also, in simulation of organizations one may want to simulate with different norms, organizational structures, and role specifications, in order to try out what yields better results. If the agents are able to understand the organizational specification, this provides for additional flexibility and a kind of separation of concerns: one could modify the organizational specification independently of the agents, and the agents would be able to adapt

---

[2] In [34], the ROADMAP methodology is proposed which extends Gaia, among other things by allowing agents to change roles at run-time.

[3] Although the skeletons make sure the agent behaves according to the specification, even in this approach reasoning may still be required to choose from several allowed options.

to this. The discussion in the sequel focuses on organizational reasoning in this sense.

The first level of organizational reasoning that we distinguish, *behaving according to the specification*, requires that the agent understands the role specification and is able to translate it into concrete actions that fulfill the goals of the role and do not violate the norms of the role. One of the main challenges here is to bridge the gap between the possibly abstract specification of the role, and concrete actions that the agent has to take (see also [59] for an approach to concretizing norms for electronic institutions). For example, the role specification of a policeman might specify that he should keep people away from hazardous situations. The agent playing the role of policeman then has to translate this into setting up road blocks in case hazardous chemicals have escaped from a plant. The closer the role specification is to the internal agent architecture (e.g., in [11,12] they are relatively close), the easier this translation will presumably be. If a role is specified in an organizational modeling language and the agent is programmed in an agent programming language that was not designed to work with the organizational modeling language, bridging this gap will be more difficult. Another challenge is to let the agent reason about its own behavior to prevent it from violating norms (see, e.g., [24,25] for work on how to prevent violation of goals, and [40] for an approach on how AgentSpeak(L) agents can adapt their behavior to norms). For example, if the norm is that policemen should always execute tasks in pairs, this should influence the agents' actions accordingly.

The second level, *reasoning about violation*, requires the agent to decide whether, even though it has decided to play the role, it will nevertheless violate some of the requirements imposed by the role (see also [10,7]). For example, the role of policeman might specify that it can only be played by agents that have the corresponding diploma. However, if road blocks need to be set up and policemen have not arrived yet, firefighters might decide to play the role of policemen and set up the road blocks, even though strictly speaking they are not allowed to do this. Deciding on whether to violate the role specification requires *weighing* the benefits of breaking the rules against possible negative consequences or sanctions resulting from this. Here, it should be noted that there is a difference between norm *enforcement*, which makes the violation of norms less desirable by introducing, e.g., sanctioning mechanisms, and norm *regimentation*, in which case it is made impossible to violate a norm (see, e.g., [35,55]). In the former case, an agent can decide to violate the norm and accept the sanction, while in the latter case this is not possible. Regimentation can be realized using organizational middleware in which the agent sends requests for actions that it would like to execute to the middleware, which decides whether the specific action is indeed executed. For example, in MOISE$^+$ [31] each agent is connected to a so-called "Orgbox" which forms the interface between agents and middleware, and in ISLANDER/AMELI [20] governors are used for mediating the participation of agents in an electronic institution.

The third level, *reasoning about adaptation*, requires the agent to reason about how possible changes to the specification of the role or organization as a whole might affect the functioning of the organization (see [30] for an approach that uses reorganization agents for performing reorganizations). In particular, the agent should be able to determine which changes will lead to improvements in the functioning of the organization. This might, for example, be determined by comparing the actual behavior of the organization against the prescribed behavior. Discrepancies can indicate that changes are necessary.

Besides reasoning about how to play a role in the organization, the agent should also reason about whether to take on additional roles in the organization or change roles. This is largely similar to the kind of reasoning needed when entering the organization. An additional aspect that needs to be addressed if the agent decides to take on multiple roles, is that it should reason about possible conflicts between the requirements imposed by these roles. For example, if an incident occurs, the mayor of the city might take on the role of coordinator of the rescue efforts. This role requires him to be at the crisis management centre. However, this conflicts with his role as mayor, as in that role he should be at the scene to comfort the injured people.

Leaving the Organization. In order to enter this phase, the agent has to reason about whether it still wants to participate in the organization. Reasons for leaving the organization (see also [29]) can be that the agent has achieved the goals it wanted to by being part of the organization. Another reason can be that it believes it will not be able to achieve its goals. These considerations are similar to an agent deciding whether to drop a goal in BDI agent languages: when the goal is achieved or believed to be unachievable. Another reason for the agent to leave the organization is that it is thrown out, for example because it has not adhered to the norms of the organization. Alternatively, an agent may not be allowed to leave the organization, e.g., if it has not payed yet in the case of an electronic market place.

3.2   Elements of Organizational Specifications

As explained in Section 1, an organizational specification defined in an organizational modeling language is used to organize and regulate a multi-agent system. For example, the MOISE$^+$ organizational modeling language [4,31] specifies an organization in terms of a structural dimension using the notions of roles and groups, a functional dimension that describes how global collective goals should be achieved, and a normative dimension expressing permissions and obligations for roles, related to the achievement of (sub)goals.

Agents capable of organizational reasoning should be able to understand and reason about an organizational specification. This requires agents to understand all *elements* of the organizational specification, such as the structural dimension, the functional dimension and the normative dimension in the case of MOISE$^+$. Different kinds of organizational reasoning are associated with each of these elements.

For example, the MOISE$^+$ structural dimension is related to the communication between agents. It specifies that agents playing a certain role should not communicate with agents playing some other role. Moreover, the structural dimension allows the specification of authority links between roles. This should presumably influence how agents handle and pose requests: if a higher ranked agent requests something from a lower ranked agent, the latter should usually obey (unless its reasoning determines that there are strong arguments against obeying).

3.3 Direction of Organizational Reasoning

The third dimension that we distinguish, is the direction of organizational reasoning: top down or bottom up. By top down reasoning we mean that the agents take an organizational specification as the basis for their behavior in the organization, for example by following the specified work processes. By bottom up reasoning we mean that the agents figure out amongst themselves how they should cooperate, without a predefined organization. Naturally, these can co-exist. In general, the more is specified in the organizational specification, the less room there will be for bottom-up reasoning, and vice versa. This dimension is related to the distinction made between agent-centered and system-centered [31], where the latter refers to the case where there is an explicit organizational specification. The direction of organizational reasoning refers to the kind of reasoning required from the agents in each of these cases.

In the discussion so far, we have focused mainly on top down reasoning. In bottom up reasoning, an important kind of reasoning is *reasoning about other agents*. This has received relatively little attention in the agent programming literature. Nevertheless, we mention several approaches in agent programming and other areas of MAS research that address aspects of reasoning about other agents. For example, for virtual characters in games, it is important that they are able to form an internal representation of the mental states of other players, e.g., for predicting what they might do [37,51]. A related area is plan or intention recognition [9,13,23]. There, agents try to recognize the plans or intentions of other agents (which might also be humans), based on observations of their actions and domain knowledge of certain standard procedures. Reasoning about humans is also an important part of mixed-initiative systems, in which the system collaborates with a user by sometimes taking initiative to support the user's activities (see, e.g., [43,22]). It will have to be investigated whether techniques developed in these areas can be used in the context of organized MAS for reasoning about other agents, and how this kind of bottom up reasoning can be combined with top down reasoning.

4 Programming Organization-Aware Agents

In Section 3, we have categorized kinds of organizational reasoning. In this section, we discuss general approaches for how agents could be programmed to perform organizational reasoning. Future research will have to make an effort in clearly identifying their respective strengths and weaknesses.

The first approach that we identify, is to *use existing agent programming languages* for specifying an agent's organizational reasoning. This is the approach taken in [31], where Jason is used to program agents that should function in a MOISE$^+$ organization. Jason is extended by necessary organizational actions, such as an action for adopting a role. Otherwise, no additions to Jason are made. The actions do not come with sophisticated reasoning, e.g., the action for adopting a role does not check whether the agent has the capabilities for playing the role. Plans are programmed, e.g., to specify when the agent should adopt a particular role.

The advantage of this approach is that an existing language is used, which means that a programmer who knows Jason could in principle program Jason agents that should function in an organization. The disadvantage is that the programmer is not explicitly supported in programming organization-aware agents. For example, he will have to program how an agent should determine whether it can play a role in an organization. This is a non-trivial task. Also, some aspects of organizational reasoning have to be repeated for each instance of it. For example, an agent should notify the organization if it has achieved some goal. This means that an action has to be included in each plan where a goal of the organization is reached.

The second approach we discuss here aims for a more generic approach based on the recognition that in open systems software agents can no longer be completely hard-coded as this would require the reprogramming of agents every time a virtual organization changes. The idea is that agents instead need to exchange information about virtual organizations to be able to adequately coordinate their activities. Such information exchange needs to be supported by explicitly representing the structure and norms of the organization in some declarative language. Current state of the art agent programming languages provide an agent with the capability to reason with its beliefs and goals. In order to become organization-aware the second approach would be to suggest adding dedicated capabilities to an agent that support organizational reasoning. The basic idea here would be to add an "organizational attitude" to agents besides their epistemic and motivational attitude. This can be achieved by adding dedicated organizational reasoning patterns as *software components* or plugins that will provide agents with the capability to reason about generic issues related to the organization they participate in. For example, plugins might be provided (i) for identifying the benefits of taking part in the organization, (ii) for negotiating about interaction protocols, (iii) for monitoring of norm compliance, and possibly other typical reasoning patterns.

Finally, the third - even more ambitious - approach would be to develop *new programming abstractions* for programming an agent's organizational reasoning and decision making. In this approach, the organizational reasoning would be done in a separate layer using the new programming abstractions, and the agent's cognitive reasoning and decision making (reasoning about achieving goals) in another. The latter is then programmed in existing agent programming languages. A semantic connection between both layers would have to be established. For

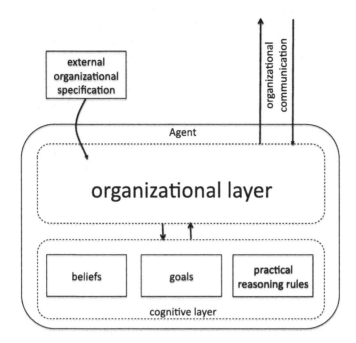

Fig. 1. Architecture for Organizational Reasoning

example, organizational reasoning and decision making involves deciding whether to take on a certain role, which typically comes with permissions and obligations to achieve goals. If the agent takes on the role, this should influence its cognitive reasoning and decision making on how to reach the accompanying goals. However, if it turns out that the agent is not able to achieve the goals after all, or decides to achieve other goals because this is more in line with its own interests, this should in turn influence its organizational reasoning and decision making. It may, e.g., have to decide to delegate some goals to other agents (see also [32,6]). An architecture for this approach is depicted in Figure 1.

Programming languages for organization-aware agents would reduce the effort needed for programming and maintaining agents. We refer to the well-known rule of thumb that programmers can code a fixed number of lines of code per hour, independently of the language in which the coding is done. Having programming constructs for organization-aware agents would allow the programmer to represent the reasoning in a concise way, reducing the amount of time needed for programming. Moreover, it would provide conceptual support, since the language would guide the programmer in its thinking about the problem. For maintenance of programs, programs written in terms of higher programming abstractions are easier to read and thus to maintain than programs written in lower-level languages. Maintenance of software is notoriously hard for those that did not write the programs themselves, and increased understandability of the code would improve maintenance.

Although we aim for applications in which an agent's ability to perform organizational reasoning is beneficial, it may not be necessary for the agent to perform all of the reasoning required to function in an organization itself. Some approaches alleviate the agent partly from having to do organizational reasoning, by letting the organizational middleware take over some aspects of this. For example, in ISLANDER/AMELI, governors can be posed questions about the institution [19], in J-MOISE+ events are sent to agents to notify them, e.g., about whether the agent has an obligation, and in [55] the agent can delegate tasks to its role, which forms the connection between the agent and the organization. Although these approaches can help explain the agent what is expected from it in a certain situation from the perspective of the organization, the agent will still have to take the decision as to what it will do. That is, either decide which of several allowed actions it takes in case of regimentation (see, e.g., [57]), or decide whether to comply with a norm if the norm is only enforced.

5   Conclusion

In this paper, we have identified kinds of organizational reasoning along three dimensions: phases of organizational participation, elements of organizational specifications, and direction of organizational reasoning. Moreover, we have identified three approaches for programming organization-aware agents: using existing agent programming languages, developing components for organizational reasoning, and developing dedicated programming abstractions for supporting organizational reasoning. Through this, we have provided a research agenda on what needs to be addressed when developing techniques for programming organization-aware agents.

Acknowledgements

We would like to thank the anonymous referees for their useful comments.

References

1. AOS group. Jack: an agent infrastructure for providing the decision-making capability for autonomous systems (whitepaper), http://www.aosgrp.com/downloads/JACK_WhitePaper_UKAUS.pdf
2. Arcos, J.L., Esteva, M., Noriega, P., Rodríguez-Aguilar, J.A., Sierra, C.: Engineering open environments with electronic institutions. Engineering applications of artificial intelligence 18(2), 191–204 (2005)
3. Baldoni, M., Boella, G., Genovese, V., Grenna, R., van der Torre, L.: How to program organizations and roles in the JADE framework. In: Bergmann, R., Lindemann, G., Kirn, S., Pěchouček, M. (eds.) MATES 2008. LNCS (LNAI), vol. 5244, pp. 25–36. Springer, Heidelberg (2008)

4. Boissier, O., Hübner, J.F., Sichman, J.S.: Organization oriented programming: From closed to open organizations. In: O'Hare, G.M.P., Ricci, A., O'Grady, M.J., Dikenelli, O. (eds.) ESAW 2006. LNCS (LNAI), vol. 4457, pp. 86–105. Springer, Heidelberg (2007)
5. Bordini, R.H., Dastani, M., Dix, J., El Fallah Seghrouchni, A.: Multi-Agent Programming: Languages, Platforms and Applications. Springer, Berlin (2005)
6. Brazier, F., Jonker, C., Treur, J.: Formalization of a cooperation model based on joint intentions. In: Mueller, J., Wooldridge, M., Jennings, N. (eds.) ATAL 1996. LNCS, vol. 1193, pp. 141–155. Springer, Heidelberg (1997)
7. Broersen, J., Dastani, M., Hulstijn, J., van der Torre, L.: Goal generation in the BOID architecture. Cognitive Science Quarterly 2(3-4), 428–447 (2002)
8. Carabelea, C., Boissier, O., Castelfranchi, C.: Using social power to enable agents to reason about being part of a group. In: Gleizes, M.-P., Omicini, A., Zambonelli, F. (eds.) ESAW 2004. LNCS (LNAI), vol. 3451, pp. 166–177. Springer, Heidelberg (2005)
9. Carberry, S.: Techniques for plan recognition. User Modeling and User-Adapted Interaction 11, 31–48 (2001)
10. Castelfranchi, C., Dignum, F., Jonker, C., Treur, J.: Deliberative normative agents: Principles and architecture. In: Jennings, N.R. (ed.) ATAL 1999. LNCS, vol. 1757, pp. 364–378. Springer, Heidelberg (2000)
11. Dastani, M., Dignum, V., Dignum, F.: Role-assignment in open agent societies. In: Proceedings of the second international joint conference on autonomous agents and multiagent systems (AAMAS 2003), Melbourne, pp. 489–496 (2003)
12. Dastani, M.M., van Riemsdijk, M.B., Hulstijn, J., Dignum, F.P.M., Meyer, J.-J.C.: Enacting and deacting roles in agent programming. In: Odell, J.J., Giorgini, P., Müller, J.P. (eds.) AOSE 2004. LNCS, vol. 3382, pp. 189–204. Springer, Heidelberg (2005)
13. Demolombe, R., Fernandez, A.M.O.: Intention recognition in the situation calculus and probability theory frameworks. In: Toni, F., Torroni, P. (eds.) CLIMA 2005. LNCS (LNAI), vol. 3900, pp. 358–372. Springer, Heidelberg (2006)
14. Dignum, F., Dignum, V., Jonker, C.: Towards agents for policy making. In: Proceedings of the 9th International Workshop on Multi-Agent-Based Simulation, MABS 2008 (2008)
15. Dignum, F., Dignum, V., Thangarajah, J., Padgham, L., Winikoff, M.: Open agent systems??? In: Luck, M., Padgham, L. (eds.) Agent-Oriented Software Engineering VIII. LNCS, vol. 4951, pp. 73–87. Springer, Heidelberg (2008)
16. Dignum, F., Kinny, D., Sonenberg, L.: From desires, obligations and norms to goals. Cognitive Science Quarterly 2(3-4), 407–430 (2002)
17. Dignum, V.: A Model for Organizational Interaction: Based on Agents, Founded in Logic. PhD thesis (2004)
18. Dignum, V., Dignum, F.: What's in it for me? Agent deliberation on taking up social roles. In: Proceedings of the second European Workshop on Multi-Agent Systems, EUMAS 2004 (2004)
19. Esteva, M., Padget, J., Sierra, C.: Formalizing a language for institutions and norms. In: Meyer, J.-J.C., Tambe, M. (eds.) ATAL 2001. LNCS (LNAI), vol. 2333, pp. 348–366. Springer, Heidelberg (2002)
20. Esteva, M., Rosell, B., Rodríguez-Aguilar, J.A., Arcos, J.L.: AMELI: An agent-based middleware for electronic institutions. In: Proceedings of the Third International Joint Conference on Autonomous Agents and Multiagent Systems (AAMAS 2004), pp. 236–243. IEEE Computer Society, Los Alamitos (2004)

21. Ferber, J., Gutknecht, O., Michel, F.: From agents to organizations: An organizational view of multi-agent systems. In: Giorgini, P., Müller, J.P., Odell, J.J. (eds.) AOSE 2003. LNCS, vol. 2935, pp. 214–230. Springer, Heidelberg (2004)
22. Ferguson, G., Allen, J.: Mixed-initiative systems for collaborative problem solving. AI Magazine 28(2) (2009)
23. Goultiaeva, A., Lespérance, Y.: Incremental plan recognition in an agent programming framework. In: Workshop on Plan, Activity, and Intent Recognition, PAIR 2007 (2007)
24. Hindriks, K.V., van Riemsdijk, M.B.: Satisfying maintenance goals. In: Baldoni, M., Son, T.C., van Riemsdijk, M.B., Winikoff, M. (eds.) DALT 2007. LNCS (LNAI), vol. 4897, pp. 86–103. Springer, Heidelberg (2008)
25. Hindriks, K., van Riemsdijk, M.B.: Using temporal logic to integrate goals and qualitative preferences into agent programming. In: Baldoni, M., Son, T.C., van Riemsdijk, M.B., Winikoff, M. (eds.) DALT 2008. LNCS (LNAI), vol. 5397, pp. 215–232. Springer, Heidelberg (2009)
26. Hoogendoorn, M., Jonker, C., Popova, V., Sharpaskykh, A., Xu, L.: Formal modelling and comparing of disaster plans. In: Proceedings of the Second International Conference on Information Systems for Crisis Response and Management (ISCRAM 2005), pp. 97–107 (2005)
27. Hoogendoorn, M., Jonker, C., van Maanen, P., Sharpanskykh, A.: Formal analysis of empirical traces in incident management. Reliability Engineering and System Safety 93, 1422–1433 (2008)
28. Hoogendoorn, M., Treur, J.: An adaptive multi-agent organization model based on dynamic role allocation. In: Proceedings of the 2006 IEEE/WIC/ACM International Conference on Intelligent Agent Technology (IAT 2006), pp. 474–481. IEEE Computer Society, Los Alamitos (2006)
29. Hormazábal, N., Cardoso, H.L., de la Rosa, J.L., Oliveira, E.: An approach for virtual organizations' dissolution. In: Proceedings of the international workshop on coordination, organization, institutions and norms in agent systems (COIN 2009@AAMAS), pp. 93–108 (2009)
30. Hübner, J.F., Sichman, J.S., Boissier, O.: Using MOISE+ for a cooperative framework of MAS reorganisation. In: Bazzan, A.L.C., Labidi, S. (eds.) SBIA 2004. LNCS (LNAI), vol. 3171, pp. 506–515. Springer, Heidelberg (2004)
31. Hübner, J.F., Sichman, J.S., Boissier, O.: Developing organised multiagent systems using the MOISE+ model: programming issues at the system and agent levels. International Journal of Agent-Oriented Software Engineering 1(3/4), 370–395 (2007)
32. Jennings, N.: Controlling cooperative problem solving in industrial multi-agent systems using joint intentions. Artificial Intelligence Journal 74(2) (1995)
33. Jonker, C., Treur, J.: From organisational structure to organisational behaviour formalisation. International Journal of Agent-Oriented Software Engineering (to appear, 2009)
34. Juan, T., Pearce, A.R., Sterling, L.: ROADMAP: extending the Gaia methodology for complex open systems. In: Proceedings of the First International Joint Conference on Autonomous Agents and Multiagent Systems (AAMAS 2002), pp. 3–10. ACM, New York (2002)
35. Kamara, L., Pitt, J., Sergot, M.: Norm-aware agents for ad hoc networks: A position paper. In: Proceedings of the AAMAS 2004 Workshop on Agents and Ubiquitous Computing (2004)
36. Klein, G., Woods, D.D., Bradshaw, J.M., Hoffman, R.R., Feltovich, P.J.: Ten challenges for making automation a "team player" in joint human-agent activity. IEEE Intelligent Systems 19(6), 91–95 (2004)

37. Laird, J.E.: It knows what you're going to do: adding anticipation to a quakebot. In: Proceedings of the fifth international conference on Autonomous Agents, pp. 385–392. ACM, New York (2001)
38. López y López, F.: Social Power and Norms: Impact on Agent Behaviour. PhD thesis (2003)
39. Mathieu, E., Heffner, T.S., Goodwin, G., Salas, E., Cannon-Bowers, J.: The influence of shared mental models on team process and performance. The Journal of Applied Psychology 85(2), 273–283 (2000)
40. Meneguzzi, F., Luck, M.: Norm-based behaviour modification in BDI agents. In: Proceedings of the eighth international joint conference on autonomous agents and multiagent systems (AAMAS 2009), Budapest, pp. 177–184 (2009)
41. Mitchell, R.J. (ed.): Managing Complexity in Software Engineering. Institution of Electrical Engineers, UK (1990)
42. Munroe, S., Miller, T., Belecheanu, R.A., Pechoucek, M., McBurney, P., Luck, M.: Crossing the agent technology chasm: Experiences and challenges in commercial applications of agents. Knowledge Engineering Review 21(4), 345–392 (2006)
43. Myers, K., Yorke-Smith, N.: Proactivity in an intentionally helpful personal assistive agent. In: Proceedings of AAAI 2007 Spring Symposium on Intentions in Intelligent Systems (2007)
44. Nair, R., Tambe, M., Marsella, S.: Team formation for reformation in multiagent domains like RoboCupRescue. In: Kaminka, G.A., Lima, P.U., Rojas, R. (eds.) RoboCup 2002. LNCS (LNAI), vol. 2752, pp. 150–161. Springer, Heidelberg (2003)
45. Okouya, D., Dignum, V.: OperettA: a prototype tool for the design, analysis and development of multi-agent organizations. In: Proceedings of the 7th international joint conference on Autonomous agents and multiagent systems (AAMAS 2008), pp. 1677–1678. International Foundation for Autonomous Agents and Multiagent Systems, Richland (2008)
46. Oomes, A.: Organization awareness in crisis management: dynamic organigrams for more effective disaster response. In: Proceedings of the First International Conference on Information Systems for Crisis Response and Management (ISCRAM 2004), pp. 63–68 (2004)
47. Pokahr, A., Braubach, L., Lamersdorf, W.: A goal deliberation strategy for BDI agent systems. In: Eymann, T., Klügl, F., Lamersdorf, W., Klusch, M., Huhns, M.N. (eds.) MATES 2005. LNCS (LNAI), vol. 3550, pp. 82–93. Springer, Heidelberg (2005)
48. Rouse, W.B., Boff, K.R.: Organizational Simulation. Wiley, Chichester (2005)
49. Schurr, N., Patil, P., Pighin, F., Tambe, M.: Using multiagent teams to improve the training of incident commanders. In: Proceedings of the fifth international joint conference on autonomous agents and multiagent systems (AAMAS 2006), Industry Track, Hakodate (2006)
50. Sierhuis, M.: Modeling and Simulating Work Practice; Brahms: A multiagent modeling and simulation language for work system analysis and design. PhD thesis (2001)
51. Sindlar, M., Dastani, M., Dignum, F., Meyer, J.-J.C.: Mental state abduction of BDI-based agents. In: Baldoni, M., Son, T.C., van Riemsdijk, M.B., Winikoff, M. (eds.) DALT 2008. LNCS (LNAI), vol. 5397, pp. 161–178. Springer, Heidelberg (2009)
52. Sycara, K., Sukthankar, G.: Literature review of teamwork models. Technical Report CMU-RI-TR-06-50, Carnegie Mellon University (2006)

53. Thangarajah, J., Padgham, L., Winikoff, M.: Detecting and avoiding interference between goals in intelligent agents. In: Proceedings of the 18th International Joint Conference on Artificial Intelligence, IJCAI 2003 (2003)
54. Tinnemeier, N.A., Dastani, M., Meyer, J.-J.C.: Orwell's nightmare for agents? Programming multi-agent organisations. In: Proceedings of the Fifth International Workshop on Programming Multiagent Systems, ProMAS 2008 (2008)
55. Tinnemeier, N.A., Dastani, M., Meyer, J.-J.C.: Roles and norms for programming agent organizations. In: Proceedings of the eighth international joint conference on autonomous agents and multiagent systems (AAMAS 2009), Budapest, pp. 121–128 (2009)
56. van Riemsdijk, M.B., Dastani, M., Meyer, J.-J.C.: Goals in conflict: Semantic foundations of goals in agent programming. Autonomous Agents and Multi-Agent Systems 18(3), 471–500 (2009)
57. Vasconcelos, W.W., Sabater, J., Sierra, C., Querol, J.: Skeleton-based agent development for electronic institutions. In: Proceedings of the First International Joint Conference on Autonomous Agents and Multiagent Systems (AAMAS 2002), pp. 696–703. ACM, New York (2002)
58. Vazquez-Salceda, J.: The Role of Norms and Electronic Institutions in Multi-Agent Systems: The HARMONIA Framework. Whitestein Series in Software Agent Technologies and Autonomic Computing. Birkhäuser, Basel (2004)
59. Vázquez-Salceda, J., Aldewereld, H., Grossi, D., Dignum, F.: From human regulations to regulated software agents' behavior. Journal of Artificial Intelligence and Law 16(1), 73–87 (2008)
60. Zambonelli, F., Jennings, N.R., Wooldridge, M.: Developing multiagent systems: The Gaia methodology. ACM Transactions on Software Engineering and Methodology (TOSEM) 12(3), 317–370 (2003)

Energy Trade-Offs in Resource-Constrained Multi-Agent Systems

Hugo Carr, Jeremy Pitt, Anthony Kleerekoper, and David Blancke

Electrical & Electronic Engineering Department,
Imperial College London, SW7 2BT, UK

1 Introduction

Sensor networks and mobile ad hoc networks are two types of open system with resource constraints, in which functionality may be compromised by a lack of resources. In this work, we investigate adaptive algorithms for power-challenged computing networks. Using simulations, we have studied how self-organization can be used to trade off energy for (acceptable) accuracy to improve longevity in a sensor network; and how perceived threat and information sensitivity can be used to trade-off energy for (acceptable) security risk in an ad hoc network.

2 Energy vs. Accuracy in Sensor Networks

In sensor networks, a trade off exists between accuracy and longevity for networks implementing in-network data aggregation functions. Given the following system:

- A set of sensor nodes $S = \{s_1, \ldots s_n, s_{sink}\}$ where s_{sink} is the sink node;
- Each sensor node, s_i, has some energy at time t, $en_i(t)$, and some, fixed, error value, er_i;
- Sensor nodes take readings such that $r_i(t) = R(t) \pm er_i$ where $R(t)$ is the correct value. The error value is applied positively or negatively at random;
- Sensor nodes form opinions such that $o_i(t) = O(\{r_1(t), r_2(t), ..., r_n(t)\})$ where $O(\dots)$ is some aggregating function of the readings received from neighbours;
- Network error is defined as $NE(t) = abs(R(t) - o_{sink}(t))$;
- Network lifetime is defined as $NL = t$ such that $\sum_{i=0}^{n} en_i(t) > 0$ and $\sum_{i=0}^{n} en_i(t+1) \leq 0$ where the summations do not include the sink node;

The requirement is to derive a method for aggregation that enables the sensors to specify an upper accuracy bound for the network error such that the network lifetime increases as the upper bound is raised, i.e. derive an algorithm for $O(\{r_1(t), r_2(t), ..., r_n(t)\})$ such that we maximise NL while ensuring that $\forall t[NE(t) \leq \epsilon]$, where ϵ is some predefined error bound.

There are three main algorithmic aspects to our proposed solution: the clustering algorithm for routing and self-organization of the aggregation tree initiated by s_{sink}, the opinion formation algorithm for in-network data aggregation (i.e. computing $o_i(t)$, for each $i \in S$), and network reformation and 'intelligent' message casting.

H. Aldewereld, V. Dignum, and G. Picard (Eds.): ESAW 2009, LNAI 5881, pp. 113–115, 2009.
© Springer-Verlag Berlin Heidelberg 2009

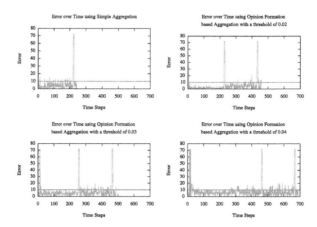

Fig. 1. Error in the aggregated reading over time under difference thresholds

The clustering algorithm is a minor variation of the protocol for forming an aggregation tree presented in [1], primarily in the assumption that transmission range is variable and the impact that data aggregation has on the cluster-head selection mechanism. We then adopt the opinion formation model of [4] for in-network data aggregation algorithm: treating the sensor nodes as agents, we can condition the interaction with social relations, such as trust and confidence thresholds, rather than simply averaging values. Finally we extend the message-passing protocols so agents (sensors) themselves determine the advisability on whether or not to transmit, and the extent whether or not it is appropriate (due to resource constraints) for the sink node to start re-dimensioning the network.

The algorithm has been simulated using the PreSage platform [2]. To test the longevity vs. accuracy trade-off, we used 500 nodes with a (max.) cluster size of 30 and ran the simulation recording the aggregated opinion at the sink node. Figure 1 compares the result of using simple aggregation against using opinion formation aggregation with different confidence thresholds. The results show that using a confidence threshold and network reformation can considerably extend the life-span of the network.

3   Energy vs. Security in Ad Hoc Networks

In ad hoc networks, a trade off exists between risk and longevity for networks implementing a number of different security policies, given that some policies require more computationally complex (and so high power) encryption algorithms. Given the following system:

- set of agents $A = \{a_1, a_2, \ldots, a_n\}$
- a set of clusters C satisfying $c_i \in C \rightarrow c_i \subseteq A$
- a pair of roles, *cluster-head* and *member*, such that there is one cluster-head per cluster and each agent is a member of at least one cluster;
- the set of social constraints (normative rules) as given by e.g. a specification in an action language (cf. [3]);

- environment variables, in particular a security level, sl, energy level el, and perceived threat level tl (derived from the information sensitivity and the detected interception rate).

The requirement is to derive a security policy that enables the agents to determine a network-level security policy from local, cluster-based interactions concerning the available energy and perceived threat.

Accordingly, we have developed an algorithm for selecting an appropriate security policy which inter-leaves data aggregation using 'gossiping' at the cluster and cluster-head level, and role-based norm-governed voting protocols for multi-agent systems [3]. We use opinion formation, based on the same model [4], to determine the need for change at the cluster level, followed by a vote (by the cluster members) for change at the cluster level; if there is a change then there is opinion formation at the cluster-head level, followed by votes within each cluster initiated by the cluster-heads. Simulation of this system is work in progress.

4 Conclusions

In both sensor networks and ad hoc networks, there is a resource-constrained environment limiting the effective computation of the constituent nodes. In both cases, we see 'brute' facts (the energy level), institutional facts determined by opinion formation (resp. data reading and perceived threat), and institutional facts determined by social rules (resp. accuracy bound and security level).

In order to trade-off the brute facts against the institutional facts to improve (resp.) accuracy and data integrity in such open systems (i.e. in the absence of global objects and common objectives), we have developed algorithms based on the interaction between and adaptation of an underlying social network with an overt organizational structure, where each informs, influences and interleaves with the other. This is the basis of what we call micro-social systems, which arise from the interleaving of social networks with norm-governed system, and may provide the basis of a common computational framework for self-organization in open resource-constrained networks.

References

1. Ding, M., Cheng, X., Xue, G.: Aggregation tree construction in sensor networks. In: IEEE Vehicular Technology Conference, vol. 4, pp. 2168–2172 (2003)
2. Neville, B., Pitt, J.: Presage: A programming environment for the simulation of agent societies. In: Hindriks, K., Pokahr, A., Sardina, S. (eds.) ProMAS 2009. LNCS (LNAI), vol. 5442, pp. 88–103. Springer, Heidelberg (2009)
3. Pitt, J., Kamara, L., Sergot, M., Artikis, A.: Formalization of a voting protocol for virtual organizations. In: Proceedings International Conference on Autonomous Agents and Multi-agent Systems (AAMAS), pp. 373–380 (2005)
4. Ramirez-Cano, D., Pitt, J.: Follow the Leader: Profiling Agents in an Opinion Formation Model of Dynamic Confidence and Individual Mind-Sets. In: Proceedings IEEE/WIC/ACM International Conference on Intelligent Agent Technology (IAT), pp. 660–667. IEEE Computer Society, Los Alamitos (2006)

Engineering Social Reality with Inheritance Relations*

Huib Aldewereld[1], Sergio Alvarez-Napagao[2],
Frank Dignum[1], and Javier Vázquez-Salceda[2]

[1] Universiteit Utrecht, The Netherlands
{huib,dignum}@cs.uu.nl
[2] Universitat Politècnica de Catalunya, Barcelona, Spain
{salvarez,jvazquez}@lsi.upc.edu

Abstract. In systems based on organisational specifications a reoccurring problem remains to be solved in the disparity between the level of abstractness of the organisational concepts and the concepts used in the implementation. Organisational specifications (deliberately) abstract from general practice, which creates a need to relate the abstract concepts used in the specification to concrete ones used in the practice. The prevailing solution for this problem is the use of *counts-as* statements. However, current implementations of counts-as view the relations expressed in this notion as static ontological classifications, which presents problems in dynamic environments where the meaning of abstract concepts can change over time. This limitation has already been solved in complex formal theoretical investigations, but the results of that study are far too complex to make a practical implementation. This paper investigates the limitations of current implementations of counts-as, and proposes a more flexible implementation based on the use of inheritance relations.

1 Introduction

A common problem in the design and implementation of complex systems (be it multiagent systems [6,16] or service-based systems [7]) is the fact that specifications of the organisation of the system generally abstract from actual practice. This creates a distinct gap between the ontology of the organisation (containing abstract concepts such as "means of transport") and the ontology of the implementation (containing concrete concepts such as "trucks"; often domain and/or implementation dependent).

A typical way to solve this is by applying refinement techniques as done in requirement engineering (see, e.g., [17]) to link the abstract model elements to concrete concepts *at design time*. However, this only solves static cases and

---

* This work has been performed in the framework of the FP7 project ALIVE IST-215890, which is funded by the European Community. The author(s) would like to acknowledge the contributions of his (their) colleagues from ALIVE Consortium (http://www.ist-alive.eu)

H. Aldewereld, V. Dignum, and G. Picard (Eds.): ESAW 2009, LNAI 5881, pp. 116–131, 2009.

cannot cope with dynamic domains where the link between the abstract and concrete concepts changes over time (due to unforeseen circumstances). Moreover, using such a method for bridging the gap does not explicitly state how the concrete and abstract concepts relate, and leaves no information for the system to reason about different implementations (or different contexts) at runtime. In critical domains such as crisis management, it is important to be able to reason about different approaches to solve a crisis and thus requires the ability to reason about different links between the abstract organisational concepts and concrete concepts used in practice.

It has been proposed already (e.g., see [1,9,10]) that an explicit representation of the links between the abstract and concrete concepts can be given by the concept of *counts-as*. The intuition of counts-as as subsumption relation (that is, as a relation pertaining to ontologies) to solve this problem was first stated in [11].

> "There are usually constraints within any institution according to which certain states of affairs of a given type count as, or *are to be classified as*, states of affairs of another type." [11]

The notion of counts-as expressed above is limited to a classificatory view of counts-as. However, the notion of counts-as is far richer than that of an ontological subsumption relation. Early studies of counts-as describe it as being used as a "constitution of social reality" [13], which, in essence, means that counts-as statements *define*, or establish, the appropriate context in which the organisation must act. In this view, a set of counts-as statements defines an institutional frame.

> "[...] 'institutions' are systems of constitutive rules. Every institutional fact is underlain by a (system of) rule(s) of the form "X counts as Y in context C"." [13]

Thus the fact that an *army truck* counts-as a *means of public transport* is not always true, but only in the context of a large scale evacuation being carried out. In fact, it can be one of the constitutive rules that defines what a *large scale evacuation* is (that is, the fact that army trucks are being used means that the evacuation must be a large-scale evacuation). This shows two additional aspects of counts-as. The aspect of something being constituted, that is, something as being the *result of constitution*, and the aspect of something *constituting* a context. All of these notions of counts-as have been formally investigated by [9] and given precise semantical senses.

When designing agent systems for complex and dynamic applications such as crisis management support (or simulation), these counts-as relations play a crucial role in the design and running of the system. While the high level specification of the organisation of the system should stay stable throughout the life cycle of the system (and thus be as abstract as possible), the actual implementation of the MAS should be flexible and adapt to changing environments and contexts. Agents should know that army trucks are not available as means of transport when a burst water pipe floods a street, but are available when the context becomes that of a large scale evacuation after a dam has been breached.

So, this type of systems should incorporate not only the classificatory part of the counts-as relation, but also should implement at least some of the constitutive elements. The constitutive part of counts-as, however, has only been researched from a theoretical (mostly formal) point of view so far; no implementations that can be used in runtime systems exist. In this paper, we explore the possibility of implementing *all* aspects of counts-as in the DROOLS rule engine.

To elucidate the need of these additional elements of counts-as we start this paper in section 2 with a brief description of the ALIVE project and a discussion of the kind of dynamic domains the ALIVE project aims to cater to. In ALIVE, the goal is to create systems that organise services in dynamic contexts to serve a specific goal or (organisational) objective. The fact that the context of the system changes at runtime means that the relations between the abstract and concrete concepts cannot be fixed on forehand, as the relations between the abstract and concrete concepts can change during the run of the system. It is also not possible to define all the different relations for all the different contexts on forehand, because not all the necessary information about all the different contexts is available. A more flexible approach is required, and counts-as provides just that. In section 3 we proceed by briefly investigating the different meanings of *counts-as* which are used as a basis for the implementation presented in section 4. Moreover, section 4 contains some considerations about how the constitutive aspects of counts-as are to be used in solving the problem of dynamic domains as encountered in the ALIVE project. We end this paper with conclusions and considerations for future extensions.

2   The ALIVE Project

The research presented in this paper is carried out within the ALIVE project. ALIVE aims to apply organisational theory to the design and implementation of software systems. The main focus of the project is to create complex systems based on the composition of (existing) services, through the addition of levels of abstraction. The advantage of added levels of abstraction to the design process of systems is two-fold: 1) it is often more intuitive to think in organisational structures and interactions while designing complex interactions for services, and the addition of the layers of abstraction allows for a gradual (fluent) transition from the system as foreseen to the actual implementation; 2) when changes happen in the environment (e.g., specific services become unavailable) the added levels of abstraction act as an explicit representation of the conceptual steps made at design, thus giving additional information on why certain interactions are as they are, which enables the system to dynamically cope with the changes. To this extend the project attempts to create a framework for software and service engineering through the combination of the latest in coordination and organisation mechanisms and model driven design. The layers of abstraction introduced by the project are the following (from bottom to top).

- The *Service Layer* augments and extends existing service models with semantic descriptions to make components aware of their social context and of the rules of engagement with other services.
- The *Coordination Layer* provides the means to specify, at a high level, the patterns of interaction between services, using a variety of powerful coordination techniques from recent research in the area.
- The *Organisation Layer* provides context for the other levels – specifying the organisational rules that govern interaction and using recent developments in organisational dynamics to allow the structural adaptation of distributed systems over time.

Adding layers of abstraction to the design process of systems, however, also creates a major problem. The different layers are not necessarily specified on the same level of abstraction which means that each are specified in terms of a different ontology. These different ontologies do not match, and in order to link the specifications of one level to the next, the ontologies have to be related somehow.

The organisational layer uses an OPERA-like formalisation for the specification of the organisational structures and interactions [6]. These structures are to be used at the Coordination Layer to be transformed into coordination plans and workflows. A possible implementation of the Coordination Layer is through the use of a multi-agent system. This solution has its advantages in that the connection between multiagent systems and organisational structures has been researched to some extent already (e.g., see [6,15]); that is to say, agents can be created on the basis of the organisational specification and designed in such a way that they comply to that specification (as proposed in, e.g., [15]). Using agents on the Coordination Layer has another advantage in the fact that agents are autonomous and can be equipped with the means to create elaborate plans to achieve pre-set goals/objectives (e.g., through the use of multiagent planning mechanisms such as TÆMS [5,12]). The link from the Coordination Layer to the Services and Service Layer can be achieved through service invocations and the design of tools for the assistance of service composition (to allow for more complex service calls and workflow enactment). The specific invocations of services or service workflows are done by the agents playing a role in the organisation.

Although this implementation via an agent system on the coordination layer (as intermediary between the organisational specification and the service practice) seems intuitive and attractive, it does not circumvent the mentioned problem of disparity between the abstract organisational concepts and the concrete (service-based) concepts. While, instead of the need to link three different levels, the problem can be reduced to linking just two levels (the agents can be programmed with either an ontology that closely matches the organisational ontology, or with an ontology close to the service one), assuming that the agents automatically and autonomously come up with the solution to bridge the gap between the abstract and concrete ontologies is unfeasible.

Bridging the gap between the abstract and concrete concepts is not the only issue, however. If that was the case, a static solution linking the two levels would suffice. However, ALIVE aims to deal with dynamic runtime elements as well, which require the links between the concepts to change *during the run of the system*. To give a concrete impression of the kind of dynamic organisations and environments that the ALIVE project aims to deal with, we briefly discuss one of the ALIVE use-cases. This use-case scenario, situated in the domain of Crisis Management, will serve as an example throughout the latter sections of the paper.

2.1   Crisis Management Scenario

One of the domains used by the ALIVE project is situated in the field of crisis management, in particular dealing with the handling of disasters in the Netherlands. In a densely populated country like the Netherlands where the threat of flooding is matter-of-fact, regional and nation-wide organisation of the management of crises was required. Crisis management in the Netherlands is organised through a nation-wide agreement on procedures called the GRIP. GRIP stands for "Gecoordineerde Regionale Incidentbestrijding Procedures", which translates to Coordinated Regional Incident handling Procedures. GRIP describes the required organisational and management needs for different levels of incidents. The five different GRIP levels are the following (in increasing severity).

GRIP-0 Routine accidents.

GRIP-1 Incidents.

GRIP-2 Large scale incidents.

GRIP-3 Disasters concerning multiple regions.

GRIP-4 Large scale disasters.

GRIP-0 handles about normal (traffic) accidents where no real coordination is required (coordination between incident handlers is done ad hoc). GRIP-1 to 4 are the real incident levels, ranging from small incidents that only have an effect in the immediate region of the incident (GRIP-1), or that have (apparent) effect regions of a nearby city (GRIP-2), nearby cities (GRIP-3), or even multiple provinces and/or the whole nation (GRIP-4). The scaling from one level to another happens in accordance with the severity of the incident (the range of the apparent affected region is wider because of changes in the incident or because the incident was more/less severe than anticipated) or because the organisational infrastructure of a higher level is deemed required to solve the incident.

Instead of using all the different GRIP levels to illustrate our approach we will focus, due to space limitations, on GRIP levels 2 and 3. The important aspect of the GRIP scenario (and which is covered by our limited scope of just viewing levels 2 and 3) is that the domain and organisation are of a dynamic nature. Therefore, the examples will show that static counts-as relations (as modelled by [1,11]) do not suffice and a more complex implementation is required.

3   The Intuitions of Counts-As

Due to the dynamic nature of the domains used by the ALIVE project, it is not sufficient to use static references between the abstract concepts in the organisational specification of the system and the concrete concepts used by the services implementing the system. Contexts change during the run of the system, and the relations between the abstract concepts and the concrete concepts need to change with them. While in a large scale incident (GRIP-2) ambulances would be used to evacuate a hospital that is being threatened to be flooded, in disaster situations (GRIP-3) the crisis management can call upon the army to assist, deploying army trucks to evacuate the hospital instead.

As mentioned in section 1, in these domains there is a need to explicitly represent the relations between the abstract and concrete concepts which can be used by agents in their reasoning. The need for an explicit representation is the first argument for using counts-as to bridge the gap instead of using refinement techniques from requirements engineering instead. But there is a second argument for using counts-as relations as well. Let us first look at the nature of counts-as before we further explain this second argument.

The different readings of counts-as can be summarised in the example seen in table 1 presented below (extracted from [9]).

Table 1. Three notions of counts-as

"In normative system Γ, happenings with severe consequences to the general safety *count as* disasters"	**Constitutive**
"It is always the case that large scale fires *count as* happenings with severe consequences to the general safety"	**Classificatory**
"In normative system Γ large scale fires *count as* disasters"	**Proper Class.**

In the example, the counts-as locution occurs three times. However, the three locutions are each of a different nature. The second premise is a (generally acknowledged) contextual classification concerning an universal context (and can thus be formalised as ontological subsumption as done in, e.g., [1,11]). The conclusion is a "new", proper contextual classification which is considered to hold with respect to the given system (this requires the extension to a context dependent counts-as as attempted in, e.g., [4,10]). But what about the first premise? The semantic ingredient of the first premise is not captured by either notions of counts-as; it is neither a contextual nor a proper contextual classification.

The first premise of table 1 is not classificatory of nature, but is what Searle referred to as the ability to "constitute social reality". The counts-as defines a context in which that counts-as relation holds. Counts-as has the ability to change the world. Not in the sense that it affects the physical reality; it makes no sense to express that "children at the age of 3 *counts-as* writers", since 3-year old children are physically unable to write. Stating that they can does not make them able to.

Instead, counts-as adds institutional/organisational semantics to real-world events and concepts (that is, the events and concepts are given meaning in the context of the institution/organisation). Doing so can, however, change the institutional/organisational capabilities of people. That is, counts-as does not change what people can or cannot do physically, but it does change what people are allowed/entitled to do institutionally. For instance, a normative system that states that "a coordinator has executive command in crisis situations" (a norm of the system) can change the organisational capabilities of a police officer in GRIP-1 because in GRIP-1 "the first police officer at the scene *counts-as* the crisis coordinator" (and again at GRIP-2 where it holds that "the mayor *counts-as* the crisis coordinator").

The rules and norms related to concepts in the social world change with the changes made by counts-as. It is this kind of change that counts-as brings to the world. It creates social facts that determine how situations should happen or how situations should be handled. Thus, the counts-as does not directly influence the world, but it influences the capabilities/rights of roles, and the way these roles interact with each other. Counts-as defines the social (normative) meaning of things; it defines the applicability of the norms on brute (real-world) concepts.

This constitutive aspect is the second argument on using counts-as rules for the specification of the links between the abstract and concrete concepts in complex and dynamic applications. In next section we will see how applying the constitutive aspect of counts-as would bring important advantages in the crisis management domain.

3.1   Constitutive Counts-As in Crisis Management

In the crisis management domain it is important that agents are able to reason about what different contexts would bring; for instance, reasoning about whether a change from GRIP-2 to GRIP-3 would allow for better solutions to solve the crisis in that the army becomes available as evacuation means. Moreover, the constitutive aspect of counts-as allows agents to change the context to affect the crisis solving. In short, constitutive counts-as allows the agents to *dynamically* change the social reality of the system, thus enabling them to scale from one GRIP-level to another when required.

This was already evident from our earlier example; while army trucks are means of transportation, they are generally not considered to be public transport, except in the case they are used in a large scale evacuation. This change in meaning of the concept public transport (in GRIP-2 it does *not* include army trucks, in GRIP-3 it *does*) has an impact on the planning possibilities of the agents in the system. The change of environment enables new (previously unavailable) means to add to their plans.

Likewise, domain restrictions change their impact on the creation of plans when the environment changes. While the abstract specification of the restrictions in the domain (both expressed in norms and in organisational specifications) remains stable over time, the dynamics of the environment (the changing of contexts) impacts the *interpretation* of those restrictions; that is, the norms and organisational specification remain fixed for all situations, but their application changes due to changes in the meaning of the abstract concepts used to express them. For example, a domain restriction could be that all agents are under the authority of the operational commander (and obliged to obey his commands). The role of operational commander can change from one GRIP to another, which also means that the organisational structure, and the rights and authorities of the agents involved changes between contexts. See [2] for a further elaboration of this kind of organisational and normative dynamics.

The constitutive elements of the counts-as comes into play in the definition of the contexts in an environment. These definitions of contexts play a major role in determining the current context. During the run of a system in a dynamic domain such as the crisis management scenario, context changes can happen. These context changes happen for two different reasons:

1. An agent in the system with the appropriate rights/power decrees that a different context is of effect.
2. The situation at hand does not conform to the constitutional definition of the current context, and a switch to another context is required.

The former kind of change has to do with notions of power and speech acts [13,11,3]. The agent with this function has the ability to create or change bridge rules in the normative system, i.e., the utterance "we can now use army trucks for evacuation" made by this agent constitutes that army trucks count as public transport and therefore affects an (indirect) change to GRIP-3.

The latter change can be observed in the environment and constitutes a kind of external trigger for changing the context. E.g., when a flooding extends the city limits it violates the proper classificatory counts-as part of the GRIP-2 definition, and the situation scales automatically to GRIP-3.

3.2   Dealing with Sub-contexts and Overlap

In order to be able to implement the above kinds of contextual reasoning in practice, we have implemented all the afore-mentioned aspects of counts-as into DROOLS rules. As we will see in section 4, this allows for ease of use and efficient reasoning by the agents in the system. However there were some issues to be tackled, mainly related with the handling of overlapping and subsuming contexts.

As described above, the constitutive counts-as rules define the social context in which the counts-as holds. This could, in practice, mean a lot of different rules defining a single social context, which could make it problematic (or rather inefficient) to use when comparing different contexts (e.g., in case when an agent wants to decide whether a scale-up from GRIP-2 to GRIP-3 is required). To deal with this inefficiency at runtime, we consider contexts to only have their unique counts-as rules (the rules that are not part of any other context). But this requires a proper handling of the occurrence of context subsumptions (i.e. context A being sub-context of context B) and context overlap (i.e. a non-void intersection between the scopes of context A and B).

Any domain contains a number of social contexts defined by constitutive counts-as rules as mentioned above. These constitutive counts-as rules define

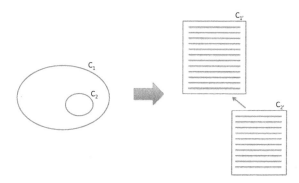

Fig. 1. Context subsumption

the classifications that *only hold for that context*. Global classifications are considered to be part of the universal context, which subsumes each defined social context (i.e., all defined contexts are a *sub-context* of the universal context). To deal with subsumed contexts and to allow for quick reasoning about what makes contexts unique, we limit the counts-as rules in a context to only those rules which are not contained in any of its *parent-contexts*. Then, by using context inheritance relations we specify that all the counts-as rules that hold in a context are those contained in its specification *and* any contained in the specification of its parents. Figure 1 shows the subsumption of context C_2 by context C_1; for instance, the social context of the GRIP procedures (C_2) being a sub-context of the social context of crisis management organisations (C_1). This basically means that the worlds in the context of GRIP are a 'refinement' of the worlds in the context of crisis management organisation; that is to say, these worlds adhere to both the classifications made by the parent context as well as to the classifications specified by the specific GRIP scenarios. Therefore, in a world in the social context of crisis management organisation, all counts-as rules of $C_{1'}$ apply, but in worlds in the social context of GRIP apply both the counts-as rules from $C_{1'}$ and $C_{2'}$. It is then easy to see that what makes the GRIP context different from the global context by looking at just the rules specified in C_2'.

Similarly, we can deal with overlapping contexts. Take, for example, the different GRIP-levels; each are a specification of the crisis management situation at a different level of severity, but they all contain elements that remain the same between them; e.g., ambulances counts-as means of evacuation in both GRIP-2 and GRIP-3. There are, however, distinctions between the separate levels as well; e.g., army trucks count-as means of evacuation only in GRIP-3, not in GRIP-2. In figure 2 it is visualised how contextual descriptions for C_1 and C_2 are split: a) a new shared, parent context (shown as $C_{1\&2}$ in the figure) that contains all counts-as rules that are shared between contexts C_1 and C_2, b) two distinct sub-contexts (shown as $C_{1'}$ and $C_{2'}$ in the figure) which contain the counts-as rules that make each original context distinct.

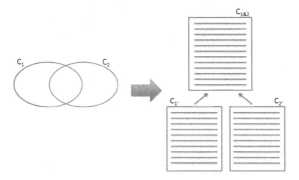

Fig. 2. Context overlap

By this split it now becomes fairly easy to determine the differences between contexts C_1 and C_2: one looks at the specific rules for each in $C_{1'}$ and $C_{2'}$, respectively. Similarly, it is easy to determine the similarities between contexts C_1 and C_2 by looking at their shared parent-context $C_{1\&2}$.

In the next section we show how this can be implemented in DROOLS.

4   Implementing Counts-As

A prototype of the counts-as has been implemented as a DROOLS rule file. DROOLS is an open-source Java-based rule engine for declarative reasoning (supporting reasoning based on the standardised Description Logic OWL-DL) [14]. Its rule engine is an implementation of the forward chaining inference Rete algorithm [8].

In DROOLS we can represent facts by adding them to the knowledge base as objects of the class *Predicate*. The following shows an example of the insertion of $Mayor(a)$ into the knowledge base to express that a (represented as object $obj3$ of the domain) is in fact a mayor.

```
Object obj3 = new Object();
ksession.insert(obj3);
ksession.insert(new Mayor(obj3));
```

The class *Predicate* is designed specifically for the prototype and is the superclass of every predicate in the system. We also defined the sub-class *Context* which means that contexts can be asserted to the knowledge base in a similar way:

```
ksession.insert(Context.GRIP2);
ksession.insert(Context.GRIP3);
```

Defining contexts as concepts in the knowledge base allows us to also refer to them explicitly and reason with them. This is an important advantage over implementations where contexts are mere labels on the counts-as relations between concepts.

In order to define the proper classificatory counts-as in a specific context, the predicate *ClassificatoryCountsAs* is introduced. This predicate allows for the expression of classificatory relations *between classes* with respect to a context.

```
ksession.insert(new ClassificatoryCountsAs
        (ChiefFire.class, OperationalCommander.class, Context.GRIP2));
ksession.insert(new ClassificatoryCountsAs
        (Mayor.class, OperationalCommander.class, Context.GRIP3));
```

The expressions above show two examples of the classificatory counts-as, where the first statement expresses that the commander of the fire brigade counts as the operational commander in GRIP-2, while the second statement expresses that in GRIP-3 the mayor counts-as operational commander, instead.

To implement the uniqueness criterium specified in subsection 3.2, which allows for more efficient runtime use of the counts-as rules, we implemented the DROOLS rule file to create internal parallel sets of contexts (based on the intuitions expressed in figures 1 and 2 in section 3.2). The first rule of figure 3 shows how this splitting is done, while the second rule of figure 3 gives an example of how one can identify in which (original) context a counts-as rule was formulated.

```
rule "creation of running contexts"
  when
    ClassificatoryCountsAs(a : c1, b : c2)
    and
    lc : TreeSet()
      from collect(ClassificatoryCountsAs(c1 == a, c2 == b))
  then
    RunningContext rc;
    rc = new RunningContext(lc);
    insertLogical(rc);
end

rule "identify running contexts"
  when
    cca : ClassificatoryCountsAs(c : context)
    and
    rc : RunningContext(countsas contains cca)
  then
    insertLogical(new RunningContextIdentifier(rc, c));
end
```

Fig. 3. Context splitting

The following shows an example of the context splitting. From three counts-as rules, of which two of them are the same for two different contexts, the result will be two contexts.

```
ksession.insert(new ClassificatoryCountsAs
        (Ambulance.class, MeansOfEvacuation.class, Context.GRIP2));
ksession.insert(new ClassificatoryCountsAs
        (Ambulance.class, MeansOfEvacuation.class, Context.GRIP3));
ksession.insert(new ClassificatoryCountsAs
        (ArmyTruck.class, MeansOfEvacuation.class, Context.GRIP3));

[...]

[GRIP2GRIP3, GRIP3]
```

The first rule of the example expresses that ambulances count as a means of evacuation in the context of GRIP-2; the second expresses that ambulances also count as a means of evacuation in the context of GRIP-3; the third rule expresses that in the context of GRIP-3 army trucks also count as a means of evacuation. After the splitting of contexts GRIP-2 and GRIP-3 containing just these three rules we end up with two contexts, namely the context which contains the rules that are present in both GRIP-2 and GRIP-3 (ambulances count as means of evacuation), and the context which gives the refinement of being in context GRIP-3, namely that army trucks also count as means of evacuation. The result being the GRIP2GRIP3 context containing the rule about ambulances being evacuation means (now unique, as there is no need to specify it twice) and the GRIP3 context containing only the rule specifying that army trucks are evacuation means. As explained in subsection 3.2, this split allows for an easy and efficient means to check the similarities and differences between the contexts GRIP-2 and GRIP-3[1].

The internal effect of a context activation is the activation of all its shared contexts (see Figure 4). With the contexts active, their counts-as rules will be instantiated as active counts-as rules in the rule engine. The counts-as rules are fired whenever there is a matching predicate. The effect of a fired counts-as rule is that for each instance of the first predicate of the rule, a new instance of the second predicate of the rule is created.

Closure is provided in the rules file by automatically detecting which context should be active based on the active counts-as rules. Figure 5 shows the rules implemented for this purpose. The first rule detects if all the proper classificatory counts-as rules for a certain shared context are instantiated, in which case that shared context will be activated automatically. The second rule checks if all the shared contexts that belong to a user defined context are active, in which case the context will be activated.

By using these rules we can identify the concept of a context (like GRIP-2) with the counts-as rules related to that context. Having this constitutive relation between a context and the counts-as rules available we can now also handle the following scenario of the crisis management.

---

[1] Note that in this example GRIP-3 ended up as a subcontext of GRIP-2 because of the limited scope of the example. In reality, there are other differences between these contexts which would show that they instead overlap.

```
rule "activate running contexts"
  when
    ContextActive(c : context)
    and
    RunningContextIdentifier(rc : runningContext, context == c)
  then
    insertLogical(new RunningContextActive(rc));
end

rule "classificatory counts-as"
  when
    rc : RunningContextActive(ca : ClassificatoryCountsAs(y1 : c1, y2 : c2))
    and
    obj : Predicate(class == y1)
  then
    insertLogical(new CountsAs(y1, y2));
end

rule "counts-as"
  when
    c : CountsAs(y1 : c1, y2 : c2)
    and
    obj : Predicate(class == y1)
  then
    Predicate instance;

    instance = (Predicate)(((Class)y2).newInstance());
    instance.setObject(obj.getObject());
    insertLogical(instance);
end
```

Fig. 4. Activation of counts-as rules

Suppose the hospital has to be evacuated due to a flooding. There are not enough ambulances available to evacuate all people in time. The commander (chief medic at the location) checks to see what can be done. He can use (special) army trucks. However, army trucks do not (in general) count-as ambulances. The commander can check (with the DROOLS implementation) that army trucks count-as ambulances in the context of GRIP-3. (They are part of constituting GRIP-3). So, the commander decides to move to the context of GRIP-3. Now he has to check what other rules constitute GRIP-3. One of them states that in GRIP-3 the mayor counts-as commander. This means that the commander has to transfer his command to the mayor.

The scenario shows that we need the context as an explicit concept and also we need the constitutive aspect of the counts-as rules that define the context in order for the commander to be able to define a switch to another context (GRIP level) and realizing the consequences of this switch. The DROOLS implementation presented above enables us to do this.

```
rule "activate running context"
  when
    rc : RunningContext(cal : countsas)
    and
    forall(ca : ClassificatoryCountsAs(a : c1, b : c2) from cal
      CountsAs(c1 == a, c2 == b)
    )
  then
    insertLogical(new RunningContextActive(rc));
end

rule "activate context by its running contexts"
  when
    c : Context()
    and
    forall(RunningContextIdentifier(rc : runningContext, context == c)
      RunningContextActive(runningContext == rc)
    )
  then
    insertLogical(new ContextActive(c));
end
```

Fig. 5. Automatic activation of contexts

5   Conclusions

Counts-as statements play a crucial role in the design of agent systems for complex and dynamic applications. They are needed to create the links between the abstract system specification and the concrete practice. These links created between the abstract and concrete ontologies are context dependent.

This paper presents an implementation of the notion of constitutive counts-as and proper classificatory counts-as as a means to solve this gap in dynamic domains. We considered all intricate theoretical aspects of counts-as in the implementation, and the implementation is made in such a way that it allows for reasoning about the differences between contexts and the effects of (possible) context changes. The implementation in DROOLS is expressive enough to create the necessary tools for the definition of contexts and the specification of context-dependent relations which are needed in complex and dynamic domains. An advantage of the DROOLS implementation is that it allows reflection on the counts-as statements, thus allowing for agents (with sufficient capabilities to do so) to reason about what changes between contexts, and even to reason about whether changing a context is a valid option to achieve their (organisational) objective(s). That means, the implementation of counts-as presented in this paper is such that it not only represents the links in different contexts, but also allows reasoning about the effects of context change.

DROOLS, in its last version, is an integrated platform supporting *rules*, *workflows*, and *events*, fully adapted to object-orientation and working under Java and .NET. Its rule engine is an implementation of the forward chaining inference Rete algorithm. The knowledge base is dynamic, supporting the addition and removal of facts and rules at runtime, and it works as a truth maintenance system with logical assertions, supporting Predicate and First-Order Logic.

DROOLS is nowadays the most powerful and efficient open-source rule engine, with a strong support from the community. One of the advantages of using DROOLS for our implementation is the possibility of contributing our results back to be included in further releases of the platform.

We are aware of only a few similar approaches towards the use of context-dependent ontological subsumption rules (i.e., [10] and [4]) that could also be used to solve the dynamic problem ontologically. While these approaches achieve similar results in the specification of ontological relations that can change depending on the current context, neither of these take any note of the definition of contexts themselves. That is, the constitutive aspect of the relation is overlooked and is not implemented. To our knowledge, this is the first attempt in implementing the constitutive aspect of counts-as.

For our current application our implementation has all properties that were needed to define contexts and be able to reason when and why to change between contexts. Although the DROOLS implementation stays quite close to the theoretical work on the counts-as some "short-cuts" had to be taken. Most notably is that contexts are defined as concepts, on the same level as "domain" concepts. Of course, the idea is that they will not be used in the same way as other concepts, because this might lead to circular definitions of contexts. As future work we will look more thoroughly at the logical properties that still can be derived using this implementation.

References

1. Aldewereld, H.: Autonomy vs. Conformity: an Institutional Perspective on Norms and Protocols. PhD thesis, Universiteit Utrecht (June 2007)
2. Aldewereld, H., Dignum, F., Penserini, L., Dignum, V.: Norm dynamics in adaptive organisations. In: Boella, G., et al. (eds.) Proc. of the 3rd Int. Workshop on Normative Multiagent Systems, NorMAS 2008 (2008)
3. Austin, J.L.: How to Do Things With Words. Harvard University Press (1962)
4. Bouquet, P., Giunchiglia, F., van Harmelen, F., Serafini, L., Stuckenschmidt, H.: Contextualizing ontologies. Journal of Web Semantics 1(4), 325–343 (2004)
5. Decker, K.S.: TÆMS: A framework for environment centered analysis & design of coordination mechanisms. In: Foundations of Distributed Artificial Intelligence, ch. 16, pp. 429–448. Wiley, Chichester (1996)
6. Dignum, V.: A Model for Organizational Interaction: based on Agents, founded in Logic. PhD thesis, Universiteit Utrecht (2004)
7. European FP-7 Project. Coordination, organisation and model driven approaches for dynamic, flexible, robust software and services engineering (ALIVE), http://www.ist-alive.eu/
8. Forgy, C.L.: Rete: A fast algorithm for the many pattern/many object pattern match problem. Artificial Intelligence 19(1), 17–37 (1982)

9. Grossi, D.: Designing Invisible Handcuffs: Formal Investigations in Institutions and Organizations for Multi-agent Systems. PhD thesis, Universiteit Utrecht (2007)
10. Grossi, D., Aldewereld, H., Vázquez-Salceda, J., Dignum, F.: Ontological aspects of the implementation of norms in agent-based electronic institutions. In: Computational and Mathematical Organization Theory, pp. 104–116. AISB (2005)
11. Jones, A., Sergot, M.: A formal characterization of institutionalised power. Journal of the IGPL 3, 427–443 (1996)
12. Lesser, V., Decker, K., Wagner, T.: Evolution of the GPGP/TÆMS domain-independent coordination framework. Autonomous Agents and Multi-Agent Systems 9(1), 87–143 (2004)
13. Searle, J.: Speech acts. An essay in the philosphy of language. Cambridge University Press, Cambridge (1969)
14. JBoss Community. JBoss drools business rules, http://www.jboss.org/drools
15. Vasconcelos, W.W., Sabater, J., Sierra, C., Querol, J.: Skeleton-based agent development for electronic institutions. In: Proc. AAMAS 2002, pp. 696–703. ACM Press, New York (2002)
16. Vázquez-Salceda, J., Dignum, V., Dignum, F.: Organising multiagent systems. JAAMAS 11(3), 307–360 (2005)
17. Wieringa, R.: Requirements Engineering: Frameworks for Understanding. John Wiley & Sons, Inc., Chichester (1996)

Determining the Trustworthiness of New Electronic Contracts

Paul Groth[1], Simon Miles[2], Sanjay Modgil[2], Nir Oren[2], Michael Luck[2], and Yolanda Gil[1]

[1] Information Sciences Institute, University of Southern California, USA
[2] Department of Computer Science, King's College London, UK

Abstract. Expressing contractual agreements electronically potentially allows agents to automatically perform functions surrounding contract use: establishment, fulfilment, renegotiation etc. For such automation to be used for real business concerns, there needs to be a high level of trust in the agent-based system. While there has been much research on simulating trust between agents, there are areas where such trust is harder to establish. In particular, contract proposals may come from parties that an agent has had no prior interaction with and, in competitive business-to-business environments, little reputation information may be available. In human practice, trust in a proposed contract is determined in part from the *content* of the proposal itself, and the similarity of the content to that of prior contracts, executed to varying degrees of success. In this paper, we argue that such analysis is also appropriate in automated systems, and to provide it we need systems to record salient details of prior contract use and algorithms for assessing proposals on their content. We use *provenance* technology to provide the former and detail algorithms for measuring contract success and similarity for the latter, applying them to an aerospace case study.

1 Introduction

Contracts are a mechanism by which multiple parties codify agreements to undertake tasks, deliver services, or provide products. Before signing a contract, it is generally true that each party expects that the others will be able to fulfil their part of the agreement. This *trust* in a party can be obtained from a variety of sources including prior dealings with the party, recommendations from associates, and the perceived ability to effectively enforce the compliance of the party. For example, when signing a mobile phone contract, the phone provider performs a credit check on the potential customer, to verify that the customer will be able to pay. Likewise, the customer may check independent internet sites to determine whether the service provided is high quality and fairly priced. Thus, the parties trust each other to perform the actions stated in the contract.

However, another trust judgment must be made in addition: one must also trust the contract *itself* [8], to believe that, for example, it correctly specifies terms of service, appropriately deals with exceptional cases, is sufficiently stringent that actions will be taken if obligations are not fulfilled. For a phone contract, the customer might look for a statement on when support will be available, whether there is an indemnification portion of the contract, or even whether the contract is presented on paper with an attractive letterhead (indicating professionalism by the provider).

H. Aldewereld, V. Dignum, and G. Picard (Eds.): ESAW 2009, LNAI 5881, pp. 132–147, 2009.

As open electronic contracting becomes prevalent, we expect issues centred around *content-based trust* (trust of artifacts based on the artifacts themselves) to arise more frequently. Clients must determine whether to place trust in a contract provided by a service even while, in many cases, such services may be unknown, or the service may introduce a new contract specific to the client.

In these cases, reputation-based mechanisms alone do not provide suitable means of measuring trust: if there are little or no grounds on which to make reputation decisions, then assessments of trust based on reputation are of limited value. Mechanism design techniques, attempting to guarantee that agents will behave in a certain way [11], are ill-suited to open systems, where new agents, which may not be analysed by the system designer and may not always act rationally, can enter the system at any time.

Contracts presented by one agent for a service may well have similarities to those proposed by other agents providing similar services, but are unlikely to be of the same form or *template*: each company (or organisation, or agent) drafts contracts in its own way. However, even without exactly matching contracts, an agent may still draw on prior experience, and judge a newly proposed contract on the basis of similarities. For example, if similar contracts to the current one turned out to be valuable or successful in the past, this may indicate future value or success. This approach requires two contract-specific mechanisms to be in place, to determine each of the following.

- The *success* of prior contracts the agent has been party to. Success is meaningful only if we have an unambiguous model of contractual behaviour, and if it is based on the events that occur during a contract's lifetime. For us to draw on salient events, we need to capture data on those events in a queryable form.
- The *similarity* of a prior contract to a newly proposed one. As above, similarity is meaningful only if we understand what a contract contains: syntactic similarity alone would not provide a meaningful measure, e.g. the obligation to do something and the obligation *not* to the same may be expressed using almost the same data are not similar contractually.

In this paper, we begin to address the problem of how a client can make a trust judgment about a contract based on the contract itself. We do so by building on several pieces of existing, though largely unconnected work on *contract modelling, content-based trust* and *provenance*. A theoretical framework for modelling contracts, and its use for representation as concrete data, is presented. As with human assessments, we enable clients to access their own prior experiences, as well as records available from others, in order to help make a trust judgement. This prior experience is expressed in the form of a *provenance graph*, which documents how contracts were constructed, where they were used, and the processes that they were related to. While the overall work is preliminary, we have provided a proof of concept implementation and evaluation. The technical contributions provided in this paper are:

- an approach to measuring the success of prior contract executions;
- an algorithm for establishing the similarity between contracts;
- a model for determining the trustworthiness of contract proposals based on the above notions of success and similarity;

– an implementation of all of the above using an existing electronic contract representation scheme and provenance model;
– a case study and evaluation of our approach in the aerospace domain.

1.1 Case Study

In this paper, we use an aerospace application as our running example and case study. We are grateful to Lost Wax for the particulars, which are part of a simulation performed by the Aerogility tool for their (aircraft engine manufacturer) customers [1].

Within the domain under consideration, aircraft operators require the manufacturers of their aircraft engines to maintain the engines during their lifetimes. Engine manufacturers in turn rely on services at particular sites to conduct any repairs. A plane with an engine requiring maintenance will be scheduled to land at a site with which the engine's manufacturer has a contract, so that repairs can take place. A service site makes use of suppliers for given parts, and engine manufacturers often wish to restrict the suppliers they use to those trusted.

As our running example, we consider proposals from new service sites to engine manufacturers to provide, and be paid for, repair of engines. The question asked by the engine manufacturer is: Should I trust this new proposal? Engine manufacturers have more or less prior experience with other sites, and may or may not have access to records about other manufacturers' experience.

2 Trust

Trusting someone or something allows the uncertainty of the world to be handled: even where aspects are unknown and may be unknowable, we do not allow this to preclude us from action. Gambetta [7] defined trust as "a particular level of the subjective probability with which an agent will perform a particular action, both before she can monitor such an action, and in a context in which it affects her own action". We apply this definition in contract-based systems as the likelihood that a contract proposal will lead to other agents (primarily other contract parties) acting in an expected and desirable way.

To understand what we should capture in a measure of trust for a contract proposal, we need to know why an agent may agree to one, including the following reasons.

– The agent believes the outcome of successful execution of the contract will be in their interests.
– The agent believes the other parties will act in accordance with the contract.
– The agent believes another contract could not easily be obtained which better represented their interests.

Castelfranchi [5] gives a more exhaustive list of reasons why an agent may attempt to meet a norm in the general case.

Content-based trust, the trust in artifacts from the artifacts themselves, is a relatively neglected area compared with mechanisms to assess trust in other agents (reviewed recently, for example, by Sabater and Sierra [19], Ruohomaa and Kutvonen [18]). Determining content-based trust was identified as an open issue by Gil and Artz in the context of the Semantic Web [8]. Content-based trust is crucially important, given that the web can be understood as a network of documents whose content people judge trustworthy or otherwise based on various factors, including context, popularity, appearance, provenance, apparent bias, etc. Content-based trust complements assessments on the trust of those providing the content made, for example, through reputation metrics.

Such evaluations also apply where actors in a process are not human but software agents, and it is therefore important to determine such assessments of trust automatically. Aside from general web documents, content-based trust is important in assessing contract proposals in an open system, where evaluations of those issuing proposals may not be sufficient for providing a basis to decide whether to accept. Gil and Artz envisaged users providing feedback on content, which would inform the trust assessments of later users. We take an equivalent approach here, where that feedback data is captured by records of success or otherwise of past contracts.

3 Electronic Contracts

To compare similarity of contracts, so we can judge how much of an influence a past contract's success should have on assessing a new proposal, there needs to be a basis for comparison. Unless contracts are expressed in a relatively uniform way, there is no way to know whether one part of the document, e.g. a clause, is comparable to another. While we cannot rely on contracts created by different agents being instantiated from the same template, we assume that all contracts can be expressed using the same conceptual structure, so can be mapped to the same data structure. We also assume that, within an application domain, contract terms can be mapped to a common ontology, allowing each part of a contract to become comparable.

For example, in our case study, we cannot assume all service sites provide contracts following the same template, as they are independent, but assume that they all rely on the same basic constructs (obligations, permissions etc.) and include some similar content, e.g. obligations to service engines when they require maintenance.

3.1 Basic Concepts

A contract is a document containing *clauses* agreed to by a set of agents, called the *contract parties*. Prior to agreement by the relevant parties, a contract document is simply a *contract proposal*. For an electronic document, agreement may be indicated in the form of digital signatures by the contract parties. Clauses specify *regulative* or *constitutive* norms influencing agent behaviour.

Constitutive norms do not form a mandatory part of a contract, but help with contract reusability and interpretation. According to Boella and van der Torre [4], the main role of a constitutive norm is to specify a *counts-as* relation between facts in the domain and terms in the contract. For example, a contract for a broadband connection may specify what counts-as fair use, in terms of observable facts such as the amount of data downloaded over the course of a month. Another important contractual notion, *role*, where an agent occupying the role takes on the regulative norms imposed on the role, may also be subsumed by the counts-as relationship. The counts-as relationship has been the subject of much analysis [12,10].

Here, we focus on regulative norms. Regulative norms are associated with a *target* agent, and specify either what the target *should* do, an *obligation*, what the target *should not* do, a *prohibition*, or what the target *may* do, a *permission*. If the target of an obligation or a prohibition does not conform to the behaviour expected by that clause, then this is a *violation* of the clause. If a clause has not been and can no longer be violated (for example, if the action required in an obligation has been performed), then we say that it has been *fulfilled*.

Some obligations or permissions may specify behaviour required or allowed when another clause is violated: *contrary-to-duty* clauses, e.g. one obligation may state "A must deliver the package to B by Thursday" while a contrary-to-duty obligation says "If A has not delivered the package to B by Thursday, it must refund B's payment."

3.2   Electronic Representation of Contracts

Many different computational representations of contracts are possible, but common formats are required for interoperability and comparison. The CONTRACT project [2] addresses this concern (among others), by encoding contracts as XML documents consisting of normative clauses that are essentially declarative specifications of agent behaviours. The model is informed by a need to meet requirements for *practical* execution of contracts and monitoring for violation of contracts by the parties involved (some features of this model are not unique to this approach, but also present in others' models [6,9]). Importantly, this execution-based motivation and XML-based representation provide us with both the stance and tools needed to develop techniques for evaluating contract similarity. We therefore adopt the CONTRACT model and representation in our work. Although we cannot provide a complete account here, we briefly outline several key qualities of the model, and leave details to other publications [16,17].

1. A contract clause is often conditional, requiring or allowing an agent to undertake an action only in specific circumstances. For example, an obligation on a service site to repair an engine only matters whenever a request for maintenance has been placed. For this reason, a practical agent should not expend resources aiming to fulfil all clauses when most do not apply at any given time.
2. These 'activating' circumstances can exist in multiple instances, sometimes simultaneously. Continuing the example, multiple requests may be placed at one time, and a single contract clause requires each request be processed.
3. No contract party can predict whether it will, in practice, be possible for them or the other parties to fulfil obligations at the time the contract is agreed. Contracts are based on expected future capabilities of agents not on certainty of achievement. For a recent example, consider passengers left stranded due to the collapse of airline and holiday companies: the obligation to return them home was agreed but the capability did not exist at the relevant time.
4. All information relating to whether a contract clause is violated or not must originate from some source. For example, in a distributed system, information about time comes from *clock* services, and there can be no guarantee in practice that the time received from any two clocks will be the same.
5. That which is obliged or permitted can always be expressed as *maintenance* of some condition (within each instantiating circumstance). Clearly the obligation to

"always drive on the left", for example, is already expressed as the maintenance of a condition. However, an obligation to achieve state S in the system before deadline condition D can be expressed as maintaining the condition: *either* achieved S *or* not yet passed D. For example, the obligation to "have repaired an engine within 7 days of the request" can be re-expressed as maintaining the state "have repaired the engine or not yet passed 7 days from the request". Generally, the obligation to perform action A before a deadline D can be re-expressed as maintaining the state of having performed A or D not yet having passed.

Taken together, these points inform the development of a model for contractual clauses using the data structure in Table 1. It should be noted that any logic may be used to specify the conditions in our contract clauses, and that it is possible to map the deontic aspect of a clause to standard conditional logics [21]. Examples of the model's use in the domain of aerospace aftermarkets are provided in Section 6.

Table 1. The model for a contractual clause used in this paper

Type	Whether this is an obligation or permission. A prohibition is modelled as an obligation not to do something, i.e. with a negative normative condition below.
Target	The contract party obliged, prohibited or permitted by the clause.
Activating Condition	The circumstances under which the clause has force, parametrised by the variables specific to each instance.
Normative Condition	The circumstances under which the obligation is not being violated or the permission is being taken advantage of, parametrised by the variables specific to each instance. Therefore, for an obligation, the target must *maintain* the normative condition so as not to be in violation of the contract.
Expiration Condition	The circumstances under which the clause no longer has force, parametrised by the variables specific to each instance.

The CONTRACT project XML-based electronic format for contracts [17] is used in our implementation. Without providing excessive detail, the key components of a contract in this format can be outlined as follows.

- References to ontologies defining the concepts used in the contract and the pre- and post-conditions of actions obliged, prohibited or permitted.
- A set of contractual roles to which contract clauses apply.
- A set of agents assigned to those roles.
- A set of clauses as modelled above.

A contract, in itself, does not express success or failure in achieving the obligations expressed within it. For that we need to know, through recorded documentation, the outcomes of agents' attempts to fulfil the contract, and the processes by which they did so. This can be called the *provenance* of the contracts' outcomes.

4 Provenance

Judgements of trust must be based on reliable data. Even when the assessed object provides the primary data, its content must be compared against something. In our case, the proposal content is compared against prior contracts, to assess the proposal based on the similarity with, and success of, those contracts. The task of acquiring this historical data is outside the scope of many approaches and so not adequately addressed. However, in a system with multiple *authorities*, where contracts need to be established to guarantee one agent's behaviour towards another, gathering such data is not trivial.

Much work [20] has been conducted on techniques for determining the *provenance* of data: the source or history of that data [14]. There are two critical issues in providing infrastructure for determining provenance. First, applications must be adapted to record documentation of what occurs in a system in such a way that it can be connected to form historical traces of data. This requires the independent agents in the system to document their activities using a suitable common data model. Second, techniques are needed to query potentially large amounts of such documentation, to elicit details relevant to the history of a given item. Additional issues, such as the reliability of documentation for provenance and its secure storage must also been considered [14].

In this paper, we exploit the documentation produced by a provenance infrastructure to find connections between prior contracts and their outcomes. This allows us to measure the success or otherwise of prior contract executions, and the compliance with, or violation of, clauses by the contract parties. The model of provenance used to evaluate our approach is based on *causal graphs*, connecting occurrences in the system as *effects* to their *causes*, whether the occurrences involved one agent or the interaction of many. Here, we are not concerned with *how* the system was adapted to record documentation, but refer readers interested in the software engineering issues elsewhere [13].

We use the Open Provenance Model (OPM) [15], developed by an international collaboration of provenance researchers. OPM documents prior occurrences in terms of *processes* that manipulate *artifacts*. A process can be seen as an individual action by an agent, while an artifact corresponds to a message sent between agents or to an object acted on while in a given state. An example is shown in Figure 1, where a part supply process receives a request for a part and generates that part, passing it to a process that takes a broken engine and produces a repaired engine. Arrows denote causal dependencies, where a process *used* an artifact or an artifact *was generated by* a process.

OPM has serialisations in formats such as XML and RDF (though they are still being refined). We use the current XML serialisation in our experiments, a sample of which is shown in Figure 2.

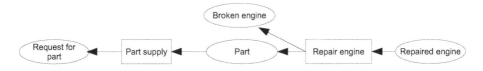

Fig. 1. Sample OPM graph fragment: artifacts are ovals, processes are boxes

5   Contract Trust Algorithm

We can view the problem of determining the trust of a previously unseen contract in different ways. As a *classification* problem, we aim to determine to which category of trust the contract belongs, e.g. we could classify a contract into 'trustworthy', 'somewhat trustworthy' or 'untrustworthy'. Or, as a *regression problem*, the goal is to compute a *trust value* for the given contract.

For either case, we can apply an approach based on the simple *k-nearest neighbour* algorithm [3]. Briefly, the algorithm can be described as follows. Given an instance, q (in our case a contract proposal) find the k instances (prior contracts) in a historical dataset that are closest to q. The instances then *vote* as to the category/value of q. In our evaluation, we use the k-nearest neighbour algorithm to perform regression that determines a numerical trust value. It is then for an agent to decide whether the trust value is adequate to accept the proposal, or to choose between multiple potential proposals. To use the k-nearest neighbour algorithm, we need to define the *features* or attributes to be used, a *distance* function, a *voting* function, and k. Below, we define each of these elements for our purposes.

5.1   Features: Measuring Success of Contracts

The historical dataset used by our algorithm is the set of prior contracts the agent has been party to. We are interested in one attribute of a contract: whether the contract was successful, defined as one in which the outcome of the process the contract governed is achieved without breaking any contractual clauses. For example, if a service site was obliged to repair an engine by a certain time according to a contract and the service does so, then the contract is successful. However, the success of a process' outcome is not a binary decision but lies in a range. For example, if the engine is fixed but the repair was delayed, the outcome of the repair process is still successful but less so than if the engine was repaired on time. Additionally, it is important to note that the outcome of a process is not merely its output; the outcome may also include effects such as repairs being late. To determine all these effects, our approach is to use documentation of a process. We write D_p^c to identify the provenance data for a process p that was the execution of a contract C.

Our algorithm relies on a success-outcome function, $s(D_p^C) = 0 \ldots 1$, that computes, given the provenance data for a process, a numeric value for the success of the process outcome. In practice, this is a series of tests performed on the provenance data to see if particular effects were present in the documentation; for example, whether penalties were paid when a clause was violated. Thus, the success-outcome function provides the value for the success attribute of each contract in the historical dataset. This is a domain-specific and often user-specific function.

The measure of success of a past contract is calculated by the agent assessing the new proposal, and so the values given to that success are otherwise arbitrary reflections of what that agent considers important. If two agents use similar calculations of success from the events recorded in the documentation, they have similar outlook on trust. Section 6.3 describes the function we use for the aerospace case study.

5.2 Distance: Measuring Similarity of Contracts

We now define a distance function to determine how close a proposal is to the prior contracts. A contract C_1's distance from another contract C_2 is a normalised similarity value. We rely on a general function, Equation 1, to produce all permutations of pairings of elements of any sets A and B:

$$map(A, B) := \left\{ P \subset A \times B \middle| \text{all elements in a pair occur only once in } P \right\}. \quad (1)$$

$map(A, B)$ is used by Equation 2 to compute the summation that maximizes the additive similarity score between two sets. Equation 2 assumes that there exists a similarity function for the elements within the provided sets. This equation is necessary because clauses and other constructs do not have a fixed comparison order.

$$max\_additive\_score(A, B) = \max\left(\left\{ \sum_{(x,y) \in P} sim(x, y) \middle| P \in map(A, B) \right\} \right) \quad (2)$$

Based on Equations 1 and 2, we define the distance function, Equation 3, as the maximum similarity score between two contracts, C_1 and C_2. The function assumes that a contract, C, is a set of clauses, hence, we can write $cl \in C$.

$$dist(C_1, C_2) = max\_additive\_score(C_1, C_2); \quad (3)$$

The similarity between two clauses, Equation 4, is defined as the similarity between the clauses conditions. We use a dot accessor notation to denote accessing each type of condition from a clause. Thus, $cl.act$ denotes accessing the activation condition from a clause. Likewise, $cl.mant$ denotes accessing the maintenance condition (the expiration condition is excluded, as it merely aids agents in knowing when clauses no longer apply, rather than affecting the semantics of what is required/permitted). Similarly, each condition contains a formula, F, that can be accessed in the same fashion. Additionally, we use the function $type()$ to allow for the retrieval of the type of a given object. In the case of the deontic statement this is whether it is an obligation or permission. In the case of other entities such as variables this is the class of that entity.

$$sim(cl_1, cl_2) \quad := \quad \frac{sim(cl_1.act, cl_2.act) + sim(cl_1.mant, cl_2.mant)}{2} \quad (4)$$

The similarity of two conditions is the similarity between the two conditions formulas as seen in Equations 5, 6, 7.

$$sim(exp_1, exp_2) := \begin{cases} 0 & \text{if } type(exp_1)! = type(exp_2) \\ sim(exp_1.F, exp_2.F) & \text{otherwise} \end{cases} \quad (5)$$

$$sim(act_1, act_2) := sim(act_1.F, act_2.F) \quad (6)$$

$$sim(mant_1, mant_2) := sim(mant_1.F, mant_2.F) \quad (7)$$

For convenience, we assume all formulas are in disjunctive normal form, i.e. each formula is a set of disjunctive clauses, DIS, and each of these is a set of conjunctive clauses, CNJ, in turn a set of atoms. The equations for determining formula similarity are given below. At each step, the combination that maximizes the similarity are chosen.

$$sim(F_1, F_2) := max\_additive\_score(F_1, F_2) \tag{8}$$

$$sim(DIS_1, DIS_2) := max\_additive\_score(DIS_1, DIS_2) \tag{9}$$

$$sim(CNJ_1, CNJ_2) := max\_additive\_score(CNJ_1, CNJ_2) \tag{10}$$

Similarity between two atoms is defined by Equation 11. Each atom consists of a relation, $a.r$, a list of variables, $a.vars$, and a list of individuals, $a.inds$. The Equations 13, 14, and 15 define similarity for each component respectively.

Note $d(x, y)$ denotes a *domain specific function* for comparison, returning a similarity score from 0 and 1. In the case study below, we used a function for time periods that states if two periods are within 5 calendar days then they are equivalent. Similarly, for two non-equal payments, if the difference is less than 2000 euros, we state a 0.75 similarity score, or 0.5 if between 2000 and 6000 difference.

$$sim(a_1, a_2) :=$$
$$\begin{cases} 0 & \text{if } |a_1.vars|! = |a_2.vars| \vee |a_1.inds|! = |a_2.inds| \\ sim'(a_1, a_2) & \text{otherwise.} \end{cases} \tag{11}$$

$$sim'(a_1, a_2) := \left(sim(a_1.r, a_2.r) \right.$$
$$+ \sum_{i=0}^{|a_1.vars|} sim(a_1.vars[i], a_2.vars[i])$$
$$\left. + \sum_{i=0}^{|a_1.inds|} sim(a_1.inds[i], a_2.inds[i]) \right) \Big/ \tag{12}$$
$$1 + |a_1.vars| + |a_1.inds|$$

$$sim(r_1, r_2) := \begin{cases} 1 & \text{if } r_1 = r_2, \\ d(r_1, r_2) & \text{if } \exists d(r_1, r_2), \\ 0 & \text{otherwise.} \end{cases} \tag{13}$$

$$sim(v_1, v_2) := \begin{cases} 1 & \text{if } type(v_1) = type(v_2), \\ 0 & \text{otherwise.} \end{cases} \tag{14}$$

$$sim(ind_1, ind_2) := \begin{cases} 1 & \text{if } ind_1 = ind_2, \\ d(ind_1, ind_2) & \text{if } \exists d(ind_1, ind_2), \\ 0 & \text{otherwise.} \end{cases} \tag{15}$$

5.3   Voting: Evaluating Trustworthiness of Proposals

Using this distance function, *k-nearest neighbour* can determine which contracts are closest to the input contract. To assign a success value to the new contract, a voting function is required. We adopt a simple normalised weighted average approach. Here, the input or proposed contract, c_p, is assigned a success value that is determined as follows: first, the sum of the success values from the k-nearest contracts is calculated, where each success value is weighted by its distance from the input contract. Then, this sum is divided by k. Because we are using this weighted approach, we can use a very high value for k because the weighting will discount any contracts that are far away from the input contract. In our tests, k is set to be equal to the entire historical dataset. Thus, Equation 16 describes the voting function, n is equal to the number of contracts in the historical dataset.

$$v(c_p) = \frac{\sum_{i=0}^{i=n} dist(c_p, c_i) s(D_p^{c_i})}{n} \tag{16}$$

k-nearest neighbour has a number of properties that make it useful for this application. In particular, it allows the agent to apply all its historical knowledge to determining the trust value of a new contract. It also removes the need for a training phase in the algorithm so that new information can be used immediately. Finally, the approach can be easily adapted to support categories of trust instead of a trust value.

6   Case Study

In our preliminary case study, we simulate the aerospace scenario through messages being sent by the various entities, indicating what they have done and what has happened. This allows compliance or violation to be determined. Now, in our particular example, we assume that an engine manufacturer is offered a contract proposal by a service site of which it has no prior experience. The manufacturer judges the contract proposal on the basis of its prior contracts with other sites. Each contract consists of the following relevant clauses.

1. An obligation on the service site to repair each engine within D days of it arriving for maintenance.
2. An obligation on the service site to pay a penalty P to the manufacturer for each repair not completed in D days (with the payment having its own deadline, not varied in this case study).
3. A set of permissions and prohibitions, one for each of a set of part suppliers, allowing or denying the service site to source parts from that supplier. We assume three relevant part suppliers exist.

The formalisation of the first of the above is characterised in Table 2, following the data structure shown in Table 1.

Table 2. Model for obligation 1 in the case study contract

Type	Obligation
Target	Service Site
Activating Condition	Engine E requires repairing at time T
Normative Condition	Engine E has been repaired or time $T + D$ has not been reached
Expiration Condition	Engine E has been repaired or time $T + D$ has been reached

6.1 Simulation

Simulations of the execution of the above contract were run, varying the following simulation factors.

- The time to repair, D, may be short or long.
- The penalty payment, P, may be high or low.
- For each part supplier, the site may be permitted or prohibited from sourcing parts from that supplier.
- The service site may be honest or dishonest.

These factors combine to influence which of four scenarios is executed in the simulation. The scenarios have the following outcomes.

1. The repairs are completed successfully using permitted part suppliers.
2. The repairs are not all completed successfully, but a penalty payment is received.
3. The repairs are not all completed successfully, and no penalty payment is received.
4. The repairs are completed but using a prohibited part supplier.

Long time to repair, high penalty payment and more permitted suppliers increase the chance of repairs being completed. Long time to repair and more permitted suppliers also increase the chance of correct part suppliers being used. Honesty increases the chances of penalties being paid when repairs are not performed.

Specifically, the following calculation is used. First, we calculate the *repair success chance* as a base probability increased if D is long, P is high, and for each permitted supplier. *Allowed supplier chance* is increased by D being long and for each permitted supplier. *Pays penalty chance* is 0.1 or 0.8 depending on whether the site is honest. Repair success chance is the probability that repair is successful. If yes, allowed supplier chance is the probability that scenario 1 occurs, else 3. If no, pays penalty chance is the probability that scenario 4 occurs, else 2.

6.2 Provenance

Each of the four scenarios above produces a different provenance graph. Each OPM graph documents the processes that occurred during the scenario, and the data produced and exchanged in that scenario, with the documentation being recorded by some or all of the agents involved. Included in that graph are the messages sent between agents, which means that the engine manufacturer can identify the critical messages sent between participants indicating success of and compliance with the contract.

- A message received by the engine manufacturer notifying of successful repair, and containing a timestamp less than the deadline, indicates that repairs were completed successfully. The absence of such a message, or a later timestamp than the deadline, indicates lack of successful repair.
- Where there was not a successful repair, a message received by the engine manufacturer notifying of payment of penalty indicates that such a payment was made. Absence of the message indicates that the payment was not made.
- A message received by the service site from a part supplier notifying of delivery of a part indicates that that supplier was used by the service site.

A snippet of the XML serialisation in the OPM for a scenario is shown in Figure 2.

```
<opmGraph xmlns="http://openprovenance.org/model/v1.01.a">
  ...
  <processes>
    <process id = "SiteServiceScenario1Process">
      <value xsi:type="xs:string" ...>ServiceSite</value>
    </process>
  ...
  <artifacts>
    <artifact id = "SiteServiceScenario1OrderPart1">
      <value xsi:type="xs:string" ...>orderPart(order1,type112)</value>
    </artifact>
  ...
  <causalDependencies>
    <used>
      <effect id    = "SiteServiceScenario1Process"/>
      <role   value = "requestReceived"/>
      <cause  id    = "EngineManufacturerScenario1Request1"/>
    </used>
    <wasGeneratedBy>
      <effect id    = "SiteServiceScenario1OrderPart1"/>
      <role   value = "requestSent"/>
      <cause  id    = "SiteServiceScenario1Process"/>
    </wasGeneratedBy>
```

Fig. 2. Snippets of documentation recorded from scenario 1 following the OPM XML schema

6.3 Success and Similarity

The success of the contract execution should depend on the outcome and reflect the importance given to different factors by the agent making the trust assessment. For the scenarios above, scenario 1 should be rated as 1.0 success; scenario 2 has 0.75 success; scenario 3 has 0.25 success; and scenario 4 has 0.0 success. Scenario 4 has the worst outcome because using a faulty part from a bad supplier is more likely to cause the plane to fail than merely not receiving maintenance. A prior contract is, then, more similar to the proposal if it has the same time to repair, same penalty payment, and same permissions and prohibitions on part suppliers.

7 Evaluation

In this section, we describe our evaluation of the efficacy of our algorithm, using the aerospace case study introduced above. In one test case, N prior contracts are generated with a random set of factors. For each contract, a scenario is selected randomly but influenced by the factors as described in Section 6.1, e.g. long time to repair increases the chance that a scenario in which repairs are completed will be chosen. The scenarios are enacted and the execution documented as provenance graphs.

A contract proposal is randomly generated just as was done for the prior contracts. The engine manufacturer uses the documentation to judge the success of each prior contract, and the similarity algorithm to judge the similarity of the content of the new proposal to each prior contract. They combine these measures, as specified in the trust algorithm above, to judge whether to trust the proposal.

We evaluate how more information on prior contracts has a beneficial effect on decisions to trust proposals. For each randomly generated proposal, we first enact it multiple times, getting an average score for its success: called the *average actual success*. We compare this with trust rating generated by our algorithm.

In our experiment, we generated 10 contract proposals. For each proposal, we computed the average actual success by enacting the proposal 100 times. We then compared this to the trust rating computed using our algorithm as we increased the number of prior contracts from 1 to 200. We measured the difference between these values after adding increments of 10 prior contracts. Figure 3 shows the average difference when combining the measures for all 10 proposals. As can be seen in the graph, the difference between these two scores steadily decreases as the number of prior contracts increases. This shows that the algorithm is effective: by calculating trustworthiness of a proposal using our algorithm, based on prior contract success and similarity, we achieve a closer and closer match to the actual success rate which would be achieved from enacting that contract. Therefore, the trust measure accurately reflects the worth to be gained by the agent by accepting the proposal.

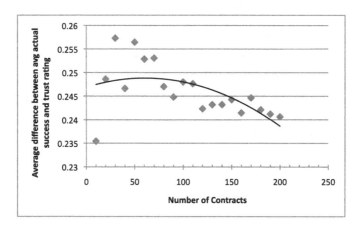

Fig. 3. The difference between trust evaluation and actual success of a proposal (Y-axis) as the number of prior contracts increases (X-axis)

8 Conclusions

Assessing a contract proposal can be difficult when there is little public information on the proposer. In this paper, we show how a content-based assessment, comparing the proposal with prior contracts based on its similarity of content to them, and the success of those prior contracts, can inform a decision on whether to trust the proposal. As shown in our results, as the number of prior contracts used in the assessment increases, the difference between the trust value and the actual outcome decreases; that is, the evaluation becomes more accurate.

Our approach relies on two pieces of technology: a contract model and its data representation on the one hand, and a model for representing the history of processes within the system (the provenance of contract enactments' outcomes) on the other. Our work effectively integrates these different aspects to provide an effective means of assessing content-based trust in contracts.

As with any approach which is improved by drawing on ever more data, optimisations need to be made to realistically scale. First, we use the k-nearest neighbour measure as an example similarity measure, but the same overall technique described here applies with other algorithms. Second, optimisations are possible even when retaining the k-nearest neighbour approach, e.g. by pre-computing the similarity of past contracts A and B, to approximate the similarity of proposal P to B based on its calculated similarity to A. In either case, this is an interesting avenue of work, for which we would not reinvent optimisations but draw on existing machine learning research.

While the work presented here considers proposals from unfamiliar agents, we may also expect to see unfamiliar contract proposals from familiar agents, i.e. those for which the agent receiving the contract has some direct or indirect reputation metrics. We cannot automatically assume that an agent providing a robust contract in one area is doing so in another area, e.g. your mobile phone provider may be excellent, but you may not wish to rely on them providing reliable medical insurance contracts. In such cases, the trustworthiness of the contract content can be complemented by the metrics regarding the agent, to ensure that we can expect the contract both to be reliably fulfilled and its effect to be as we expect and desire. A simple way to combine contract and agent trust metrics would be to perform a weighted sum. Exactly how best to weight each aspect, and how beneficial this combination would be, is a topic for future work.

Acknowledgements. The research described in this paper is partly supported by the European Commission Framework 6 funded project CONTRACT (INFSO-IST-034418). The opinions expressed herein are those of the named authors only and should not be taken as necessarily representative of the opinion of the European Commission or CONTRACT project partners. We also gratefully acknowledge support from the US Air Force Office of Scientific Research (AFOSR) with grant number FA9550-06-1-0031.

References

1. Aerogility (2009), http://www.aerogility.com/
2. IST CONTRACT project (2009), http://www.ist-contract.org

3. Aha, D.W., Kibler, D., Albert, M.K.: Instance-based learning algorithms. Machine Learning 6, 37–66 (1991)
4. Boella, G., van der Torre, L.W.N.: Regulative and constitutive norms in normative multiagent systems. In: Principles of Knowledge Representation and Reasoning: Proceedings of the Ninth International Conference (KR 2004), pp. 255–266 (2004)
5. Castelfranchi, C.: Prescribed mental attitudes in goal-adoption and norm-adoption. Artificial Intelligence and Law 7(1), 37–50 (1999)
6. Dignum, V., Meyer, J.J., Dignum, F., Weigand, H.: Formal specification of interaction in agent societies. In: Proceedings of the Second Goddard Workshop on Formal Approaches to Agent Based Systems, pp. 37–52 (2002)
7. Gambetta, D.: Can we trust trust? In: Trust: Making and Breaking Cooperative Relations, pp. 213–237. Basil Blackwell, Malden (1988)
8. Gil, Y., Artz, D.: Towards content trust of web resources. Journal of Web Semantics 5(4), 227–239 (2007)
9. Governatori, G.: Representing business contracts in ruleml. International Journal of Cooperative Information Systems 14(2-3), 181–216 (2005)
10. Grossi, D.: Designing Invisible Handcuffs. PhD thesis, Dutch Research School for Information and Knowledge Systems (2007)
11. Guerin, F., Pitt, J.: Proving properties of open agent systems. In: The First International Joint Conference on Autonomous Agents & Multiagent Systems (AAMAS 2002), pp. 557–558 (2002)
12. Jones, A.J.I., Sergot, M.: A formal characterisation of institutionalised power. Journal of the IGPL 3, 427–443 (1996)
13. Miles, S., Groth, P., Munroe, S., Moreau, L.: Prime: A methodology for developing provenance-aware applications. ACM Transactions on Software Engineering and Methodology (June 2009)
14. Moreau, L., Groth, P., Miles, S., Vazquez, J., Ibbotson, J., Jiang, S., Munroe, S., Rana, O., Schreiber, A., Tan, V., Varga, L.: The provenance of electronic data. Communications of the ACM 51(4), 52–58 (2008)
15. Moreau, L., Plale, B., Miles, S., Goble, C., Missier, P., Barga, R., Simmhan, Y., Futrelle, J., McGrath, R.E., Myers, J., Paulson, P., Bowers, S., Ludaescher, B., Kwasnikowska, N., Van den Bussche, J., Ellkvist, T., Freire, J., Groth, P.: Open Provenance Model (2009), http://openprovenance.org/
16. Oren, N., Panagiotidi, S., Vazquez-Salceda, J., Modgil, S., Luck, M., Miles, S.: Towards a formalisation of electronic contracting environments. In: Proceedings of the Workshop on Coordination, Organization, Institutions and Norms in Agent Systems at AAAI 2008, COIN 2008 (2008)
17. Panagiotidi, S., Alvarez, S., Vazquez, J., Oren, N., Ortega, S., Confalonieri, R., Jakob, M., Biba, J., Solanki, M., Willmott, S.: Contracting language syntax and semantics specification (2009), http://www.ist-contract.org
18. Ruohomaa, S., Kutvonen, L.: Trust management survey. In: Herrmann, P., Issarny, V., Shiu, S.C.K. (eds.) iTrust 2005. LNCS, vol. 3477, pp. 77–92. Springer, Heidelberg (2005)
19. Sabater, J., Sierra, C.: Review on computational trust and reputation models. Artificial Intelligence Review 24(1), 33–60 (2005)
20. Simmhan, Y., Plale, B., Gannon, D.: A survey of data provenance in e-science. SIGMOD Record 34(3), 31–36 (2005)
21. van der Torre, L., Tan, Y.: Contextual deontic logic. In: Bonzon, P., Cavalcanti, M., Nossum, R. (eds.) Formal Aspects of Context, pp. 143–160. Kluwer Academic Publishers, Dordrecht (1997)

Trust Based Evaluation of Wikipedia's Contributors

Yann Krupa[1], Laurent Vercouter[1], Jomi Fred Hübner[1,3], and Andreas Herzig[2]

[1] École Nationale Supérieure des Mines de Saint Etienne
Centre G2I, Département SMA
158, cours Fauriel, F-42023 Saint-Etienne
{krupa,vercouter,hubner}@emse.fr
[2] Institut de Recherche en Informatique de Toulouse
118 route de Narbonne, F-31062 Toulouse
herzig@irit.fr
[3] Federal University of Santa Catarina
Department of Automation and Systems Engineering
P.O. Box 476, Florianópolis, Brasil, 88040-900
jomi@das.ufsc.br

Abstract. Wikipedia is an encyclopedia on which anybody can change its content. Some users, self-proclaimed "patrollers", regularly check recent changes in order to delete or correct those which are ruining articles integrity. The huge quantity of updates leads some articles to remain polluted a certain time before being corrected. In this work, we show how a multiagent trust model can help patrollers in their task of controlling the Wikipedia. To direct the patrollers verification towards suspicious contributors, our work relies on a formalisation of Castelfranchi & Falcone's social trust theory to assist them by representing their trust model in a cognitive way.

1 Introduction

In evolutive and open systems, like participative websites as Wikipedia[1], common security measures are too complex to be applied while maintaining a good tradeoff between openness and website integrity. For example, a Role Based Access Control (RBAC) limits the system openness thus reducing participation. Moreover, role management represents a heavy administrative task. Then, it is necessary to define decentralized control mechanisms allowing scalability. A multiagent approach of this problem is therefore appropriate, in particular by means of social control via trust assessment towards other agents of the system.

The work presented here defines how a multiagent trust model, inspired by the Theory of Social Trust by Castelfranchi & Falcone [1], can be constructed to contribute to an application like Wikipedia. The content of Wikipedia is controlled by the users themselves. These users handle the modification checking,

---

[1] http://en.wikipedia.org/

H. Aldewereld, V. Dignum, and G. Picard (Eds.): ESAW 2009, LNAI 5881, pp. 148–161, 2009.

nevertheless, a few mistakes remain online for some certain time because of the sizeable activity of Wikipedia. The cognitive trust model that we propose allows to target more efficiently the contributions to check in priority by making trust assessments towards other users.

The structure of this article is the following: section 2 focuses on some of Wikipedia intrinsic mechanisms and particularly on patrollers who watch modifications. Section 3 is about trust in multiagent systems and describes the trust model used in our application. We apply this model to Wikipedia in section 4. Finally, we focus on the use of the trust model to maintain the integrity of the encyclopedia, by means of patrollers assistance, in section 5.

2   The Wikipedia Encyclopedia

The online encyclopedia Wikipedia is now famous and commonly used, it is one of the 10 most visited websites, according to the web traffic measurement website Alexa[2]. Wikipedia basic principle is that anyone can modify articles. They are constantly updated, corrected and completed. By submitting a modification, a user accepts that everything goes under free licence allowing free use and modification of the content. Those two principles make Wikipedia a free encyclopedia that is constantly moving. Wikipedia relies on collective knowledge in order to make its content evolve.

2.1   Participative But Not Anarchic

Wikipedia allows the user to correct or increase the quality of any article. The user doing such a modification is called a "contributor". Every contributor is identified either by its account, if he created one, or his IP address at the moment of the publication.

Wikipedia encourages modifications, even minimal ones, because they can bring attention to an article thus making other users contribute on this article. This has two main consequences: firstly, it allows anyone to improve or damage articles[3]. Secondly, it also allows anyone to correct other's mistakes and damages. Wikipedia relies on that collective behaviour in order to evolve.

Unlike most websites or forums, on Wikipedia all users are equal. There are some administrators that are elected by users. They have some privileges that allow them to do some maintenance tasks and block users, but they don't have "full power" over users. Thus, if an administrator is in conflict with another user on the article about darwinism for example, he cannot impose his point of view.

However, contributions must follow some explicit rules. Rules are defined by users, the same way articles are, and their application is insured by the collectivity. For example, there are rules about the conditions[4] that an article should

---

[2] http://www.alexa.com/topsites

[3] Nevertheless, some pages are protected, e.g. Barack Obama's page during the presidential campaign. Protected pages can only be modified by users that have been registered for days or months.

[4] http://en.wikipedia.org/wiki/WP:NN

meet to be on Wikipedia. The online encyclopedia is thus a website that is not anarchic, but self-governed by processes defined by the users themselves [2].

There is, for example, a process which aims to assign categories to every article. This provides a structure to the encyclopedia by placing articles inside one or multiple categories. The Tennis article is inside "racquet sport" category which is itself contained in a category named "sport".

Also, multiple roles emerge on Wikipedia, some users, like the Wikignomes who browse articles in order to add references, categories, and correct dead links, ... "Cabalists" from the Mediation Cabal try to find a compromise between users with conflicting point of view. In this article we will focus on the "Recent Changes Patroller" role, which consists in a surveillance of the recent changes on the encyclopedia to prevent damages.

2.2   The RC Patrol

The sizeable activity of users on Wikipedia play a preponderant role in its evolution. In 2009, there are about 20 modifications per minute on Wikipedia (in French)[5]. Among these modifications, there are many quality contributions, but also many damaging ones. Some people use the articles as a means of chatting by successive modifications of them. Some others just want to verify if it is really possible to modify the article by adding test messages. Finally, there are some users that just want to damage the encyclopedia, by adding insults, libelous content, or by changing the meaning of an article. Those users making voluntary damages are called "Vandals".

The RC Patrol is a group of users, with no specific power and self-proclaimed, aiming at protecting the encyclopedia from being damaged. Patrollers follow the evolution of the "recent changes" page. Their objective is to cancel as quick as possible any modification that damages article integrity. Such a cancellation is called a "revert". Reverts sometimes come with a small comment, if the patroller decides to provide one.

Taking into account the number of modifications per minute, it is impossible for the patrollers to verify in details every modification. When a vandal adds insults inside an article, there is no doubt about the goal of that modification. However, when a contributor modifies a scientific article, the verification could both take a long time and require some expertise.

Thus, the RC Patrol tries to reduce the number of modifications to check, by warning vandals and reverting their modification in order to discourage them from damaging the encyclopedia. A vandal that decides to keep on damaging the articles after having being warned will be blocked by an administrator upon the request of a patroller.

Besides vandalism, some users can add other mistakes, by lack of expertise for example. Even patrollers can make mistakes or may not agree. As a revert is also a modification, users can therefore cancel the erroneous revert.

Wikipedia is an environment in which users can act freely. This environment is open, meaning that anyone can participate. User's autonomy, system openness

---

[5] http://toolserver.org/~gribeco/stats.php

and decentralised control of Wikipedia allows to consider it as a multiagent system and to apply existing approaches for related problems in this domain, like trust towards other agents of the system.

3   The ForTrust Trust Model

In this paper, we aim at using a trust model in order to assist the RC patrollers. As Wikipedia is open and decentralized, multiagent systems are suitable for that application. In this part, we present trust in multiagent systems and the ForTrust model, a multiagent trust model based on Castelfranchi & Falcone Social Trust Theory.

3.1   Trust in Multiagent Systems

The open and decentralised context of multiagent systems is interesting in terms of flexibility, adaptability and scalability but it also brings some risks and vulnerability. Agents, potentially developed by different people and acting in an autonomous way, can freely enter or leave the system, contribute to collective activities or transmit data to other agents. Thus, they can have a selfish behaviour, meaning that they will favour their own goals without taking into account other's goals or system integrity. This kind of agent can harm the system if it doesn't know how to react against such an agent.

The problem raised by the possible presence of selfish agents leads to a trust management problem towards other agents. Grandison [3] defines trust management as "the activity of collecting, codifying, analysing and presenting evidence relating to competence, honesty, security or dependability with the purpose of making assessments and decisions regarding trust relationships for Internet applications". Such a decision must be used in addition to classical security techniques which insure authentication, confidentiality of information, . . . but that cannot garantee the behavior of transaction partners.

In multiagent systems, and generally speaking in many of the open web applications, trust management is often handled by reputation mechanisms. Some of those mechanisms work in a centralised way, for example, by using recommandations and opinions of the website users (cf. eBay[6], Amazon[7], . . .). These opinions can be presented as they are or interpreted by an aggregation function (e.g. Sporas [4]). Other mechanisms, inspired by the multiagent field, work in a decentralised manner (e.g. Repage [5]) by allowing each agent to evaluate locally its neighbour's reputation such that the agent decides whether to trust or not.

Nevertheless, reputation is a single element among others that can be used to make trust assessments. In this article, we focus more specifically on the trust *decision*.

---

[6] http://www.ebay.com/
[7] http://www.amazon.com/

3.2   Social Trust Theory

According to Castelfranchi & Falcone [1] (C & F), social trust relies on four elements: a truster i, a trustee j, an action α and i's goal φ. C & F propose a definition of trust based on four primitive concepts: capacity, intention, power and goal. They state that: "an agent i trusts an agent j for doing the action α in order to achieve φ" iff:

1. i has the *goal* φ;
2. i believes that j is *capable* of doing α;
3. i believes that j has the *power* to achieve φ by doing α;
4. i believes that j *intends* to do α.

3.3   Trust Formalisation

A formal model of trust, relative to the social trust theory by C & F has been proposed in a precedent work [6]. This model is briefly described here, details about the formalisation realised in multimodal logic (called $\mathcal{L}$) which combines dynamic logic and BDI, can be found in the article [6].

That formalisation points out the difference between *occurent* trust and *dispositional* trust. Occurent trust represents a trust decision "here and now". In this case, the truster i has goal φ and trusts j to do action α now to achieve goal φ. In this article, we will only use the occurent trust, defined this way:

$$
\begin{aligned}
Trust(i,j,\alpha,\varphi) \; &\stackrel{\text{def}}{=} \\
Goal(&i,\varphi) \; \wedge \\
Bel(&i, Act(j,\alpha)) \; \wedge \\
Bel(&i, Power(j,\alpha,\varphi))
\end{aligned}
\tag{1}
$$

That formalisation uses the four primitive concepts by C & F, the predicate $Act(j,\alpha)$ meaning that j does α. It covers both capacity and intention: $Act(j,\alpha)$ is the case when j has the capacity and the intention of doing α. Predicate *Power* means that j has the power of achieving φ by doing action α.

3.4   Trust in Inaction

Trust, as considered here, allows to represent how an agent can make a trust assessment towards another agent trusting that he will *act* in a certain manner to achieve a given goal. Nevertheless, Lorini and Demolombe [7] says we also have to consider trust in *inaction*, relating to the trust assessment made when an agent i trusts an other agent j so that j does not execute action α that can prevent i from achieving φ. Trust in inaction is defined as follows:

$$
\begin{aligned}
Trust(i,j,\sim\alpha,\varphi) \; &\stackrel{\text{def}}{=} \\
Goal(&i,\varphi) \; \wedge \\
Bel(&i, \neg Act(j,\alpha)) \; \wedge \\
Bel(&i, Power(j,\alpha,\neg\varphi))
\end{aligned}
\tag{2}
$$

Meaning that i trusts j not to do α when i has goal φ iff: i has goal φ, i believes that j has the power to prevent i from achieving φ by doing α, and i believes that j will not do α (he has no capacity or no intention).

4   Trust Decision on Wikipedia

This section defines an application of the the ForTrust model, presented in section 3, to Wikipedia. Section 4.1 identifies actors, actions and goals and the situations where a trust decision happens. The way those contributions are inferred is presented in sections 4.2 and 4.3, respectively for the case of contribution needing correction and vandalism to revert. Finally, section 4.4 presents an implementation of an assistant agent using this trust model.

4.1   Application of the ForTrust Model to Wikipedia

The ForTrust model is used on Wikipedia in order to decide whether to trust or not a contributor. Trustees (j agent in the previous section) are Wikipedia contributors. Two actions are taken into account: page *modification* and *vandalism*. Even though a vandalism is a modification, we decide to take into account these actions separately in order to simplify the formalisation. The goal that we consider here is the role of the RC patrol: maintaining pages integrity. The achievement status of this goal is estimated by the patrollers themselves who decide if a page content integrity is maintained or not.

These two actions lead to two situations where one must decide whether to trust or not a contributor. In the first case, "patroller i trusts j to modify page p while maintaining its integrity" can be formalised this way:

$$
\begin{aligned}
&Trust(i, j, modify(p), integrity(p)) \leftarrow \\
&Goal(i, integrity(p)) \wedge \\
&Bel(i, Act(j, modify(p))) \wedge \\
&Bel(i, Power(j, modify(p), integrity(p)))
\end{aligned}
\tag{3}
$$

An implication is used here instead of an equality (as used in the previous section), in order to get closer to the inference mechanisms implemented in logic programming (cf. section 4.4).

The second case, "patroller i trusts contributor j *not* to vandalize page p so that the page integrity is maintained" can be defined this way:

$$
\begin{aligned}
&Trust(i, j, \sim vandalize(p), integrity(p)) \leftarrow \\
&Goal(i, integrity(p)) \wedge \\
&Bel(i, \neg Act(j, vandalize(p))) \wedge \\
&Bel(i, Power(j, vandalize(p), \neg integrity(p)))
\end{aligned}
\tag{4}
$$

We assume that if $Trust$ cannot be inferred, it implies $\neg Trust$.

Actions and goals are now clearly identified, the next step is to develop mechanisms that allow the agent i to infer those trust assessments from past behaviours of agent j. More precisely, those mechanisms must allow i to evaluate if the predicates $Power(j, \alpha, \varphi)$ and $Act(j, \alpha)$ are true, so that i can deduce j's reliability.

4.2   Trust in Action: Modification

In this case, we will focus on the contributor's power when he publishes a modification. Intentional vandalism is not considered in this part. The trust model is used in order to evaluate if a contributor reaches the wanted goal ($integrity(p)$) when he publishes some contribution (action $modify(p)$). Contributor's capacity and intention ($Act(j, modify(p))$) are always true and the decision to trust relies on the agent belief on $Power(j, modify(p), integrity(p))$. This belief is inferred the following way:

$$
\begin{aligned}
&Bel(i, Power(j, modify(p), integrity(p)) \\
&\leftarrow category(p, c) \wedge \\
&\quad image_m(j, c) > \delta \wedge \#O^{j,c} > 0
\end{aligned}
\tag{5}
$$

where the predicate $category(p, c)$ links page p to its category c and $image_m(j, c)$ is a function that maps to each pair (agent,category) the "quality" of j contributions in that category ($image_m : AGT \times CAT \rightarrow [0, 1]$ where AGT is the set of all agents and CAT the set of all categories) and $\#O^{j,c}$ is the number of changes done by agent j in the category c. The δ threshold is used to define the minimal value of the required image in order to consider that an agent produces contributions of reasonnable quality in a given category. The image function is defined this way:

$$
image_m(j, c) = \frac{min(\bar{x}^{j,c}, \eta)}{\eta}
\tag{6}
$$

$$
\bar{x}^{j,c} = \frac{\displaystyle\sum_{\langle t_s, t_e \rangle \in O^{j,c}} t_e - t_s}{\#O^{j,c}}
$$

where $O^{j,c}$ is the set of all changes done by agent j in pages of category c. Each member of this set is a tuple $\langle t_s, t_e \rangle$ where t_s is the time of the modification, and t_e is the time when this page is modified again by another contributor. Thus, the difference between t_e and t_s represents the duration while agent j modification was not changed. Mean persistence of modifications of j in category c is given by $\bar{x}^{j,c}$. η is an upper bound for $\bar{x}$ such that if η is equal to one month, agents with $\bar{x} = 1$ month or $\bar{x} = 10$ months will get the same image. Thus, the general image of Wikipedia contributors relies on the persistence of their modifications.

In some particular cases, this metric can be noisy and therefore, a good contributor can receive negative feedback. This will happen, for example, when the contributor modifies a specific part of an article and another part of the same article is modified the following minute by another contributor. The first contributor will be regarded as a contributor with a low persistence of his modifications. But the only information source that is available is the Wikipedia website, thus it is impossible to use other metrics like the number of views per version of an article to reduce this noise. We also do not want to go into complex or unfeasable computations like the semantical analysis of the modifications.

```
1    // inference rules for Trust decision, Goal=integrity(p)
2    trust(J,modify(p),Goal)[strength(C)]  :-
3        .intend(Goal) &                        // the agent has the goal
4        act(J,modify(p))[strength(X)] &        // J has is capable and intends
5        power(J,modify(p),Goal)[strength(Y)] & // J has the power
6        C = math.min(X,Y).                     // computes trust strength
7        // trust strength is represented by annotations in hooks
8
9    trust(J,~vandalize(P),Goal)[strength(C)]  :-
10       .intend(Goal) &                        // the agent has the goal
11       act(J,~vandalize(P))[strength(X)] &
12       // J is capable and intends to not vandalize
13       power(J,vandalize(P),~Goal)[strength(Y)] & // J has the power
13       C = math.min(X,Y).
         // computes trust strength
14
15   // P integrity is a goal to maintain
16   { begin mg(integrity(P)) }
17   { end }
18
19   //rules for action (capacity and intention)
20   act(J,modify(p))[strength(1)].
21   act(J,~vandalize(P))[strength(X)]  :-
22       (1-imagev(J)) > 0.8.
23
24   // rules for power
25   power(J, modify(p), _)[strength(Y)]  :-
26       category(P,C) & imagem(J, C) > 0.5.
27       // the image function is implemented so that the 3rd term is
28       // the value for agent J in category C
29   power(J, vandalize(P), _)[strength(1)].
30
31   // computing images:
32   imagev(J,0)  :- 0 = .count(modify(_,J,_)).
33   imagev(J,X)  :- X = .count(vandalize(_,J,_,_)) / .count(modify(_,J,_)).
```

Fig. 1. Extract of *Jason* implementation

4.3   Trust in Inaction: Vandalism

This time, we need to use trust in inaction. Patrollers' goal stays the same ($integrity(p)$). Nevertheless, trust assessment does not rely on the *power* of a contributor to prevent the truster from achieving this goal by doing action *vandalize(p)* (we suppose that every contributor has that power), but on his *intention* to do it (predicate $Act(j, vandalize(p))$). Belief inference on *Act* is done as follows:

$$Bel(i, \neg Act(j, vandalize(p))) \atop \leftarrow (1 - image_v(j)) > \epsilon \wedge nc(j) > 0 \tag{7}$$

$$image_v(j) = \frac{pvt(j)}{nc(j)} \tag{8}$$

where $pvt : AGT \rightarrow \mathbb{N}$ is a function that maps each agent j to the number of modification that has been labelled as vandalism and $nc : AGT \rightarrow \mathbb{N}$ maps to the total number of modifications done by agent j. $image_v(j) = 0$ means that no change has ever been considered as vandalism. The threshold ϵ is used to define the minimal image required so that *Act* becomes true. Agents' image regarding vandalism acts does not refer to a specific category because it does not rely on a specific expertise in a category of articles.

4.4   From the Abstract Model to an Implementation

An implementation of an agent using the ForTrust model has been realized with a BDI architecture using the *Jason* language [8]. *Jason* fits well an implementation of a formal definition of trust, as defined in section 3: it is based on logic programming and BDI architecture at the same time.

Fig. 2 illustrates the main components of the agent architecture. Data structures encapsulates goals, beliefs, intentions and plan library. The *perceive* process updates the belief base from the environnement and the *act* process selects the next action to be done from the set of current intentions. Finally, the *inference* process must decide whether to trust or not an agent.

Specialisation of this agent to the Wikipedia specific context is easy while using *Jason*. Decisions to trust have to be customized and some inference rules must be added for that decisions. It is also needed to implement the perception component which analyses the "recent changes" page on Wikipedia and translates it into perceived facts.

The perception given by the architecture is then converted into first order predicates and included in the belief base whith a specific annotation indicating that they correspond to the agent perception. Older perceptions are removed consequently. Among those beliefs, the following are extracted from Wikipedia:

- $modify(p, j, t)$: agent j modified p at time t.
- $vandalize(p, j, g, t)$: change on page p by j at time t was labelled as vandalism by g.
- $category(p, c)$: page p belongs to category c.

An intitial implementation of this agent in *Jason* is presented in Fig. 1. Lines from 1 to 13 implement the trust inference mechanisms. Lines from 20 to 29 implement the inference of predicates *Act* and *Power* as defined in (7) and (5). Lines 32 to 33 implement the $image_v(j)$ function computation (8). The $image_m(j, c)$ (6) is computed in a similar manner but is not reproduced in this source code extract for simplicity reasons.

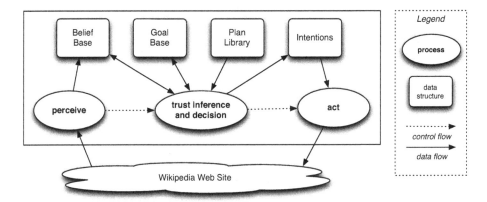

Fig. 2. General architecture for trust

5   Trust-Based Assistance to Wikipedia Patrollers

The encyclopedia quality relies directly on each user's contribution and correction to existing articles. Most important damages come from vandalism acts that consist in erasing valid content or introducing voluntarily false data inside articles or text without relation to the article topic. The case of imperfect contributions (incomplete content, wrong spelling, ...) also has an impact on the global quality. We propose to use trust in order to spot contributors that need to be frequently corrected. Trust assessment towards contributors will allow to spot untrustworthy users and target verifications towards them.

A complete automation of the decision to revert a contribution, to correct it or to block a user will be really difficult to realize. The verification task is currently handled by human patrollers because it requires a semantic interpretation of articles content, which is currently impossible to realise with a software. There are some robots which do very simple verifications, by seeking terms or characteristic regular expressions, in order to prevent the insertion of insults in articles. But they are not reliable and show a large number of false positives. Therefore, the patroller has to judge whether a contribution is a vandalism act when he thinks that the damage was intentional. This decision is subjective, and the patroller can make mistakes. For example, what if a contributor indicates a wrong date for a historical event, is it an error or voluntary damaging?

Over the 30000 daily modifications on wikipedia (French), the patrollers' task is a hard one. Fig. 3 shows the number of overall daily deletions and reverts[8]. Reverts represents only 3 to 6% of overall contributions. But it is necessary to control every contribution in order to identify the ones that are vandalism acts. Fig. 4 estimates the revert delay of a vandalism by indicating the probability that it can be reverted in a certain amount of time[8]. If approximatively 50% contributions are reverted in less than 2 minutes, a non negligible quantity (approximatively 25%) stays online longer than 1 hour and about 10% remains longer than one day. Most likely, the cause of this delay is the huge number of contributions to check.

We propose to use the ForTrust model, as described in section 4, in order to assist patrollers in their verification tasks. Our goal is to reduce their task charge by supplying them with an assistant agent which has the ability to make trust assessment in order to help the patroller targetting his verifications.

The assistant agent can therefore use its own trust model in order to classify contributions in four distinct categories:

- **VAN**: contributions that probably are vandalism;
- **COR**: contributions that may need to be corrected;
- **INT**: contributions with less chance of being reverted or corrected;
- **UKN**: the agent is not sure about these contributions.

---

[8] Data and graphics from `http://toolserver.org/~gribeco/stats-vandalism.php`, based on `http://fr.wikipedia.org/` project.

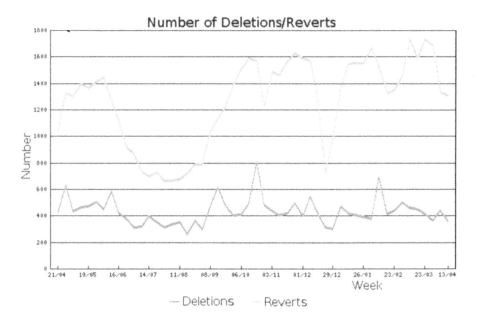

Fig. 3. Deletion and reverts on Wikipedia (retrieved on april 22nd, 2009)

Table 1. Relation between beliefs and decisions (i is the patroller, j is the contributor and p the modified page)

Decision	Assistant Agent's beliefs
VAN	$\neg\,Trust(i,j,\sim vandalize(p), integrity(p)) \;\wedge\; nc(j) > 0$
COR	$Trust(i,j,\sim vandalize(p), integrity(p)) \;\wedge$
	$\neg\,Trust(i,j,modify(p), integrity(p))$
INT	$Trust(i,j,\sim vandalize(p), integrity(p))\wedge$
	$Trust(i,j,modify(p), integrity(p))$
UKN	$nc(j) = 0$

The classification of a contribution in one or another category depends on the trust assessment that the agents makes towards the contributor. Table 1 summarizes the relationship between decision and agent beliefs.

This table illustrates the advantages of a cognitive model for an assistant agent for the patrollers. The use of C & F socio-cognitive theory allows to describe to a human user the reasons that brings the agent to a trust or distrust decision. Here, we aim to distinguish between distrust regarding an intentional vandalism and distrust regarding a low skill contribution. The assistant agent does not replace the patroller but gives advice by telling him that some contributions do not need to be checked (those in category **INT**). It could also completely mask the

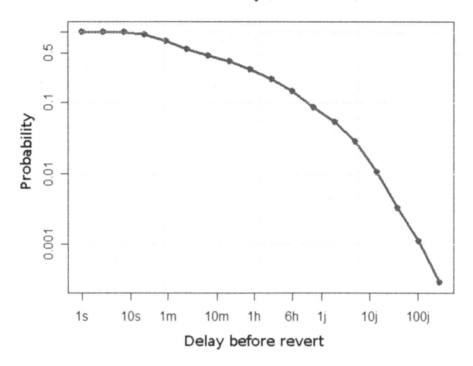

Fig. 4. Probable delay before revert

INT contributions in order to reduce significantly the amount of contributions to verify.

It is interesting to note that the trust model of an assistant agent is constantly evolving and can review its trust assessment. For example, if a contributor stops being a vandal and decides to contribute correctly, the trust model will change its trust value accordingly after a certain time. On the other hand, trusted contributors may not be verified directly by patrollers and a trusted contributor that has turned vandal may not be spotted immediately. Eventually, every contribution is checked, as the "classical" means of article surveillance still are available:

– The Watchlist is a list managed by the user that displays all changes that have been done on the articles selected by the user.
– The Projects: Some users participate in projects and regularly checks articles contained in the project to ensure their correctness.
– Article Browsing: Mistakes and vandalisms can be detected by users that are simply gathering information on Wikipedia.

Once the vandal has been spotted, the assistant agent will adjust its trust value and the contributor could be marked as untrusted.

6   Conclusion

In this article, we presented an application allowing Wikipedia patrollers to automatically filter recent changes in order to verify only those performed by untrustworthy contributors. This is obtained by providing to the patrollers an assistant agent that can make trust assessments based on the contributor's supposed capacities, intentions and power. The use of a cognitive trust model allows to reason on the distrust decision to distinguish between those who are vandals and those who are low skill contributors.

The implementation of a BDI agent is proposed here with the *Jason* language. It relies on the website's changes, freely available, to perceive contributions. The agent watches patrollers' actions, namely modification or revert, and learns the trust assessment that is made towards contributors. This trust model is then used to reduce the amount of modifications to verify based on trust assessment toward their contributors.

A simulation of these assistant agents is currently being implemented in order to validate experimentally the pertinence of the decision taken by the agents: By using the contribution's history (including reverts) available on Wikipedia, we will then simulate a learning and an assistance to patrollers. The distance between assistant assessment and real decisions (from the patrollers) will then be correlated in order to evaluate a distance between both. Model parameters, like decision thresholds, can be decided experimentally by doing multiple simulations in order to reduce this distance.

A large number of wikis work the same way, thus, even if the application described here relies on Wikipedia, it is possible to transpose it on other wikis, e.g. those of the Wikimedia foundation (Wiktionary, Wikiversity, ...).

Acknowledgements

The work presented in this article is supported by the ANR in the ForTrust ANR-06-SETI-006[9] project.

References

1. Castelfranchi, C., Falcone, R.: Social trust: A cognitive approach. In: Castelfranchi, C., Tan, Y.H. (eds.) Trust and Deception in Virtual Societies, pp. 55–90. Kluwer, Dordrecht (2001)
2. Viégas, F., Wattenberg, M., McKeon, M.: The hidden order of Wikipedia. In: Schuler, D. (ed.) HCII 2007 and OCSC 2007. LNCS, vol. 4564, pp. 445–454. Springer, Heidelberg (2007)
3. Grandison, T., Sloman, M.: Trust management tools for internet applications. In: Nixon, P., Terzis, S. (eds.) iTrust 2003. LNCS, vol. 2692, pp. 91–107. Springer, Heidelberg (2003)

---

[9] http://www.irit.fr/ForTrust/

4. Zacharia, G., Moukas, A., Maes, P.: Collaborative reputation mechanisms in electronic marketplaces. In: Proceedings of the Hawaii International Conference on System Sciences (HICSS-32), Maui, Hawaii, United States of America, vol. 08, p. 8026. IEEE Computer Society, Washington (1999)
5. Sabater-Mir, J., Paolucci, M., Conte, R.: Repage: Reputation and image among limited autonomous partners. Journal of Artificial Societies and Social Simulation 9(2), 3 (2006)
6. Lorini, E., Herzig, A., Hübner, J.F., Vercouter, L.: A logic of trust and reputation. Logic Journal of the IGPL (2009)
7. Lorini, E., Demolombe, R.: Trust and norms in the context of computer security: A logical formalization. In: van der Meyden, R., van der Torre, L. (eds.) DEON 2008. LNCS (LNAI), vol. 5076, pp. 50–64. Springer, Heidelberg (2008)
8. Bordini, R.H., Hübner, J.F., Wooldrige, M.: Programming Multi-Agent Systems in AgentSpeak using *Jason*. Wiley Series in Agent Technology. John Wiley & Sons, Chichester (2007)

Evolutionary Role Model for Multi-Agent Systems

Erdem Eser Ekinci and Oğuz Dikenelli

Ege University, Department of Computer Engineering,
35100 Bornova, Izmir, Turkey
erdemeserekinci@gmail.com
oguz.dikenelli@ege.edu.tr

Abstract. In sociology, the role concept is deeply researched to predict activities of human organizations and theorized with many sub-theories. In the same direction, multi-agent system researchers use the role concept to model and program the agents behaviours, cooperations. But there is an important point missed out by the MAS researchers: evolution of the organization. In this paper, by inspiring from the efforts in sociology, we propose an evolutionary role model for coping with the evolution of the role-based multi-agent systems.

1 Introduction

The role concept are widely researched from the view points of individual behaviours and cooperation of the agents to incorporate the concept into programmable artifacts of multi-agent systems (MAS). But, when open, distributed-concurrent and unstoppable properties of the MAS[1] are considered, proposed models and released frameworks remain weak to answer question of how an agent system spreading over a wide geography can be deployed, managed and maintained. In this paper we propose an abstract role-based model to handle MAS with an evolutionary approach and paves the way of coping with these deployment, management and maintenance problems. Our model looks multi-agent organization through individual evolution and organizational evolution perspectives and determines the relations between these perspectives.

2 Evolutionary Role Model

The roots of the word of "role", although, reaches the born of the theater in antique ages. Today sociologists have converted the role concept to a deep theory to predict activities of individuals by analyzing body of knowledge about human organizations[2]. As a consequence of these researches, the role concept is defined as scripts for social conduct and depths of the concept are theorized with many sub-theories which are *Role Playing, The Self, Role Taking, Identity, Role Exit, Role Transition, Role Alternation, Role Conflict, Role Change, Role Making, Consensus and Conformity*[2,3,4,5,6,7,8].

H. Aldewereld, V. Dignum, and G. Picard (Eds.): ESAW 2009, LNAI 5881, pp. 162–164, 2009.
© Springer-Verlag Berlin Heidelberg 2009

By drawing inspiration from sociology, we propose an evolutionary role model illustrated in Figure 1. The model is divided into two different perspectives: individual evolution and organizational evolution. In the following list, states and operations of these separated perspectives are detailed.

- **Self:** The *Self* depicts all belongings of the agent and covers all properties of the agent such as beliefs, capabilities, norms, rules, goals and identities of all taken roles.
- **Role Making:** The role making is the operation of gathering the explicit knowledge of a role situated in an organization by the agent. After role making, the agent learns what the role's goals, rules, beliefs are.
- **Role Taking:** The role taking is the act of participating to a specific organization by committing the role beliefs, goals and rules.
- **Identity:** By role taking, the agent gains a new unique identity in an organization. This identity is published to whole organization and has important responsibility in communication.
- **Role Playing:** Emanating behaviours according to a role in the scope of organization with the identity of a role instance.
- **Role Alternation:** An agent can take more than one role and gain many role instances at the same time. The *alternation* is the capability of switching between these role instances.
- **Role Exit:** When an agent reaches its goals in the scope of a role, then it leaves the organization by exiting the role.
- **Role Transition:** The *role transition* is a compound operation that occurs by exiting a role and taking another one in sequential fashion. The transitions are previously defined in the organization.
- **Self-Conflict:** The *Self-Conflict* is the state of failing to play multiple roles at the same time due to conflicts. The conflict can occur between beliefs, rules, goals of different role instances, or a role instance and the self.
- **Role Change:** Role change can be defined in short as differentiation in the semantics of a role due to the changing requirements and detected conflicts.
- **Consensus:** In the consensus form, each agent, which is member of the organization, is agreed on the goals, norms, beliefs of the organization.
- **Organization-Conflict:** Conflicted organization means participant agents are dissipated and unable to cooperate with each other due to misunderstanding the semantics of role types.

As depicted in the figure of the model, whole organization is in vicious cycle between organizational conflict and consensus forms. Agents begin their lifes by taking roles whose conceptualizations are agreed on by the whole organization. But during their individual evolution they get in conflicts. Many of these conflicts can be resolved by exiting a role. But some of them requires some changes in conceptualization of conflicting role(s). After changing roles with an engineering touch, even if agent's internal coherence is obtained, the cooperation is broken down and organization is dissipated until others' recognitions are conformed to the new conceptualization of the changed role.

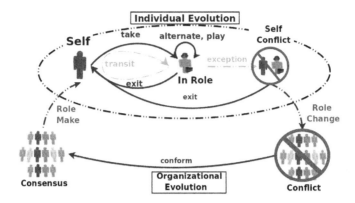

Fig. 1. Evolutionary Role Model

3   Conclusion

In this paper, we propose an evolutionary role model for multi-agent systems, which covers individual and organizational evolution, by drawing inspiration from the role theory propounded in sociology. Similar models are also articulated previously[9,10]. But, differently from these models, we define the organizational evolution and relate to the individual evolution of agents.

References

1. Jennings, N.R., Zambonelli, F., Wooldridge, M.: Developing multiagent systems: The gaia methodology. ACM Trans. Softw. Eng. Methodol. 12(3), 317–370 (2003)
2. Biddle, B.J.: Recent developments in role theory. Annual Review of Sociology 12, 67–92 (1986)
3. Coutu, W.: Role-playing vs. role-taking: An appeal for clarification. American Sociological Review 16, 180–187 (1951)
4. Stryker, S.: Identity salience and role performance: The relevance of symbolic interaction theory for family research. Journal of Marriage and the Family 30, 558–564 (1968)
5. Ebaugh, H.R.F.: Becoming an ex: the process of role exit. University of Chicago Press, Chicago (1988)
6. Turner, R.: Role change. Annual Review of Sociology 16, 87–110 (1990)
7. Aldous, J.: The making of family roles and family change. Journal of The Family Coordinator 23, 231–235 (1974)
8. Marks, S.R., MacDermid, S.M.: Multiple roles and the self: A theory of role balance. Journal of Marriage and the Family 58, 417–432 (1996)
9. Odell, J., Van Dyke Parunak, H., Brueckner, S., Sauter, J.A.: Temporal aspects of dynamic role assignment. In: Giorgini, P., Müller, J.P., Odell, J.J. (eds.) AOSE 2003. LNCS, vol. 2935, pp. 201–213. Springer, Heidelberg (2004)
10. Dastani, M., Birna Van Riemsdijk, M., Hulstijn, J.: Enacting and deacting roles in agent programming. In: Odell, J.J., Giorgini, P., Müller, J.P. (eds.) AOSE 2004. LNCS, vol. 3382, pp. 189–204. Springer, Heidelberg (2005)

Replication Based on Role Concept for Multi-Agent Systems

Sebnem Bora and Oguz Dikenelli

Computer Engineering Department
Ege University, Izmir, Turkey
{sebnem.bora,oguz.dikenelli}@ege.edu.tr

Abstract. Replication is widely used to improve fault tolerance in distributed and multi-agent systems. In this paper, we present a different point of view on replication in multi-agent systems. The approach we propose is based on role concept. We define a specific "fault tolerant role" which encapsulates all behaviors related to replication-based fault tolerance in this work. Our strategy is mainly focused on replicating instances of critical roles in the agent organization. However, while doing this, we simply transfer the critical role and the fault tolerant role to appropriate agents. Here, the fault tolerant role is responsible for coordination between replicated role instances (replicas). Moreover, our approach is flexible in terms of fault tolerance since it is possible to easily modify existing behaviors of the "fault tolerant" role, remove some of its behaviors, or include new behaviors to it due to its characteristic architecture.

1 Introduction

Multi-agent systems have recently been widely employed in solving problems faced in distributed and dynamic environments. As distributed systems, multi-agent systems (MAS) are vulnerable to failures resulting from the system crash or shortages of system resources, slow-downs or breakdowns of communication links, and errors in programming. Consequently, a fault may spread throughout a multi-agent system, and cause a degradation of the system performance and even the multi-agent system to fail. Therefore, it seems that fault tolerance is a necessary paradigm that must be inserted to the multi-agent development environment.

In most cases, replication-based techniques are employed in multi-agent systems to achieve fault tolerance such as explained in [6, 7, 8, 9, 10, 11, 12, 19, 20]. In these approaches, they replicate the agent itself by applying standard techniques used in distributed systems, although agents are more sophisticated and interactive entities.

In multi-agent organizations [18, 17], agents enact their roles and naturally, they act and communicate under their roles. Thus this affects their criticalities in the multi-agent organization. For instance, a manager role can be considered more critical role than a janitor role in a factory since the manager role has critical responsibilities in terms of the organization such as supervising and taking charge of the activities and productivity of their workers, making organizational decisions and handling a variety of problems that arise on a daily basis. There are some other responsibilities of managers such as goal setting, planning, and organizing; evaluating and analyzing; and

H. Aldewereld, V. Dignum, and G. Picard (Eds.): ESAW 2009, LNAI 5881, pp. 165–180, 2009.

providing satisfaction among the staff and the customers. If an agent enacts critical roles for the organization, it then possesses all of its roles' goals and features including its roles' criticalities. The failure of this agent affects the organization that it belongs to. To apply fault tolerance in an organization, replication is the technique we need to apply. However, we should not replicate the agent itself.

To make easy to understand why agent replication is not appropriate for fault tolerance, let us give an example. We assume that there is an agent that enacts a critical role r1 and we replicate this agent due to enacting r1. Let's say there are two replicated agents with role r1 in the organization. Then, the original agent with role r1 wants to enact role r2. We have to answer questions such as "Should the second replicated agent take up the role r2?", "How many agents do we replicate for role r2?" etc. We can increase the number of questions while expanding this scenario. Thus, we understand that agent replication is a naïve way to improve fault tolerance in MAS organization and we have to find out a new way of replication in MAS.

In this paper, we present a new approach for replication in MAS. Our method is based on role concept. Therefore, we define a specific "fault tolerant role" which encapsulates all behaviors related to replication-based fault tolerance. The fault tolerant role is assigned to the agents that enact critical roles which are identified at the design time. One of the responsibilities of the fault tolerant role is to create new instances of critical roles. Therefore, the critical and "fault tolerant" roles are transferred to appropriate agents that will enact these roles. Since the "fault tolerant" role is also responsible for ensuring coordination among replicated instances of critical roles it should be enacted by the agents that enact the critical roles.

The remainder of this paper is structured as follows: Section 2 presents the context of the work; Section 3 presents the "fault tolerant" role and how to implement role-based replication in multi-agent organizations; Section 4 describes how to determine criticalities of roles; Section 5 gives a case study; Section 6 is a review of related work on fault tolerance in multi-agent systems and finally Section 7 gives the conclusion.

2   Context of This Work

In this section, we describe the proposed architecture for role-based replication. We use the model shown in Figure 1 to describe role-based replication.

In this model, a role is one of the basic components of a multi-agent organization and it is seen as performing a goal within the organization to serve some purpose. A role has its goals, plans (a partially-ordered sequence of primitive tasks), and ontological knowledge. The concept of a goal allows specifying objectives as the desired final state to be reached. Agents are active entities that enact role(s) and achieve goals of their own roles by executing its roles' plans. A role enacting agent uses its role's knowledge via its role's plans to achieve its role's goal. For instance, as explained in [17], in order to effectively play the role of cook in a restaurant, a person has to follow work instructions, use the tools required for the role to transform the ingredients as required, and communicate with other role players. In this model, we assume that agents have their own goals, knowledge, and capabilities to enact some specific roles [26].

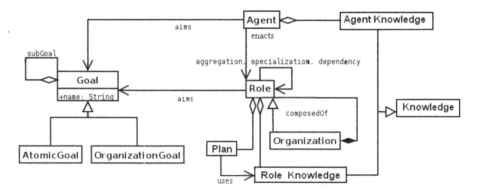

Fig. 1. The Model We Use to Describe the Proposed Architecture

If one aims to improve fault tolerance for this model, he has to identify new goals coming from fault tolerance requirements, plans to achieve these goals, and reusable services that can be used by these plans. However, we first need to present some basic concepts. A system is said to fail when it cannot meet its specification. Therefore, a deviation from the specification is considered a failure. A fault is defined as a defect that may lead to a failure. Whenever a failure occurs, a fault-tolerant system should continue to operate in a degraded fashion while repairs are being made, i.e. system should tolerate faults and continue to operate in the presence of faults. Our goal in multi-agent systems design is to construct a multi-agent organization in such a way that it can automatically recover from partial failures without seriously affecting the overall performance.

If we aim to construct a fault tolerant system, we have to answer what sort of partial failures can degrade the system's performance. Since the role concept is very important aspect of an organization in this model, the roles enacted by the agents of the organization must be avoided to be failed. We list below under what circumstances the role is failed:

1. The agent that enacts this role is crashed.
2. Some parts of communication links are crashed. Since the agent cannot communicate with agents then it will not achieve its role's goal in a timely manner.
3. Some resources can not be accessed. Since a role has rights to access resources which belong to environment.
4. There are some conflicts in the knowledge bases of the different roles of the agent. Since the agent can enact more than one role, the knowledge bases of the roles enacted by the agent can have some rules that can seriously contradict each other.
5. The agent does not have all the plans of the role it enacts.

All these situations contribute to a failure state. The failure model defines the ways in which failure may occur to provide an understanding of the effects of failures. In this work, we focus on the fail-silent model where the considered system allows only crash failures [27]. Therefore, we'll not focus on handling with items 3, 4 and 5 in this paper.

Since replication is a key technique to achieve fault tolerance in distributed and dynamic environments, we use this technique to avoid failures resulting from the failed roles. We should replicate the instances of critical roles to mask the failed roles from the organization. To achieve this, we should find agents that can take up the critical role. Then, we should transfer the critical role that encapsulates its goals, plans and knowledge to the agents.

To apply role-based replication in a multi-agent organization, there must be several services such as the replication service, the group communication service, the failure detection, and the membership service. In general, the replication service is responsible for creating new replicas and destroying some existing replicas and applying active and passive replication approaches. Active and passive approaches mainly focus on coordination between the replicas [13].

In addition to coordination requirements, the replication degree, which means the number of replicas, is a critical concept for applying fault tolerance policies based on replication. The problem is how the system will decide on the number of replicas at runtime. The replication degree can be identified adaptively or statically. In a static fault tolerance policy, this number is set to the number defined by a programmer at initialization. In an adaptive fault tolerance policy, the number of replicas of the group is determined based on resources of the system.

We have some further constraints on replication-based fault tolerance in MAS. Since the criticalities of roles may change dynamically during the system's operation and the available resources are not infinite, the number of replicas of a role instance must be dynamically updated based on the criticalities of the role as well. In order to insert fault tolerant structures to a MAS and to cope with all these constraints derived from replication, we propose a specific role called "fault tolerant role". Next, we present role-based replication.

3 Role-Based Replication

When the agent enacts a role, it behaves under this role. An agent can enact different roles from moment to moment. Each agent can enact several roles at one time beyond the basic role of AgentId. Every agent enacts AgentId role and each agent has at least that role at all times [22, 18]. For role changing, several operations such as "classify", "declassify", "reclassify", "activate", "suspend" and "shift" are introduced by Odell et al. [18]. These operations are primitive operations and come with the basic role of AgentId.

For the role-based replication, there must be several instances of a critical role (**replicas**). In the case of failure of one of replicas, there will be another replica to achieve its critical goal in the organization. In this work, we introduce the "fault tolerant" role which has some goals coming from replication-based fault tolerance requirements, plans to achieve these goals, and reusable services that can be used by these plans. This role must be enacted by all agents that enact the critical role or any role that we want it not to be crashed, since the fault tolerant role is responsible for ensuring coordination between replicas. This role provides consistency between replicas.

To simplify the understanding of the role-based replication process, we rediscuss the example given in [18] from the fault tolerance perspective. Figure 2 portrays the "Nancy" agent being classified the secretary of an executive director in the Organization B. The organization decides that her role in the company (Organization B) is very critical. Therefore, she'll enact the fault tolerant role and have some replicas. When she cannot work in her company due to some reasons, there will be nothing to worry about the organization's operation. In this case, replicas can take over her responsibilities.

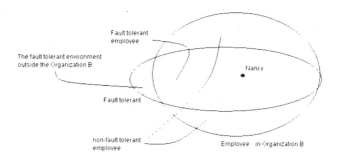

Fig. 2. Dynamic Classification in terms of Fault Tolerance (1)

Figure 3 illustrates the "Susan" agent being classified the co-secretary of an executive director in the Organization B. As defined in [18], the "Classify" operation simply adds the transferred role to other roles' group of the agent. She is the replica for Nancy's role and she also enacts the fault tolerant role. Fault tolerant role helps providing coordination between Nancy and Susan. Thus Susan has the knowledge, goal, and plan of the role of Nancy as well.

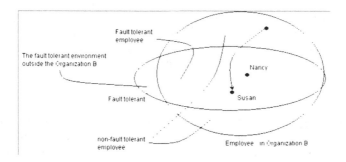

Fig. 3. Dynamic Classification in terms of Fault Tolerance (2)

In addition to operations introduced by Odell et al. [18] to deal with dynamic role assignment, we introduce some more operations: "Evaluate", "Find", "Transfer". These operations are needed due to the role-based replication process and we assume that they also come from the basic role of AgentId.

For role-based replication, the first operation is to evaluate criticalities of roles (*RoleCriticality*), if the adaptive fault tolerance policy is preferred to apply to the organization. The criticality of a role is the measure of the potential impact of the failure of that role on the failure of the organization. For this purpose, each agent that enacts the "fault tolerant" role executes a periodic plan called "calculation of criticalities of roles". In this plan, the agent periodically invokes the "Evaluate" operation and calculates the criticality of the role that it enacts. The value of *RoleCriticality* is then used to compute the number of replicas for the critical role.

For role-based replication, the next operation is to find suitable agents that can take the critical role for the replication process, if necessary. This is currently being investigated [25], and will not be considered in this paper. We suppose that there are lightly loaded agents that we can transfer the critical role to them. If there is no such an agent, we have to create new agents that can enact the critical role. After selecting or creating an agent, we have to transfer the critical role as an entity including its knowledge, its goal and plan libraries (behaviors) to the agent that will enact a given role. Therefore, "Transfer" operation is invoked. To coordinate the replicas, we also transfer the "fault tolerant" role to the agents that enact the critical role. The fault tolerant role associates with only the critical role for the coordination purpose and encapsulates fault tolerance related behaviors and provides interactions between replicas. The original agent that enacts critical role, takes up the fault tolerant role when we decide on applying role-based replication. After transferring the critical role and the "fault tolerant" role to the agents, we have to classify these roles. Thus agent enacts the critical role and the fault tolerant role (multiple classification) when it is classified.

While the agent enacts a role, this role can be either activated or suspended. To activate our new critical and fault tolerant roles, we have to perform the "Activate" operation.

Fault tolerant role is very important for improving fault tolerance in an organization since agents that enact the critical role behave under their fault tolerant roles to provide coordination between replicas. In an organization, the leader (that originally enacts the critical role) may quit the organization or it may be removed in the case of if the agent enacting this role is failed due to some reasons. Then, a replica can take over. It has all the necessary stuff such as knowledge, plans to achieve its goal. Next, we'll describe the "fault tolerant" role in detail.

3.1 The Fault Tolerant Role

Figure 4 shows a goal model for a simple fault tolerant organization in our approach. In this model, the organization includes some roles such as the fault tolerant role, a role which is critical, and some other roles. To perform role-based replication, the fault tolerant role has the goals such as "multicast to the group", "detect failures", "elect a new leader", "monitor criticalities of roles", and "adjust the number of replicas" goals. In order to achieve these identified goals, we implement their plans and the reusable services that can be used by these plans [11].

One of the reusable services is the membership service. It maintains a list of replicas of a replica group in the knowledge base of each member of the replica group. The membership service associates with a failure detection service to reach a decision

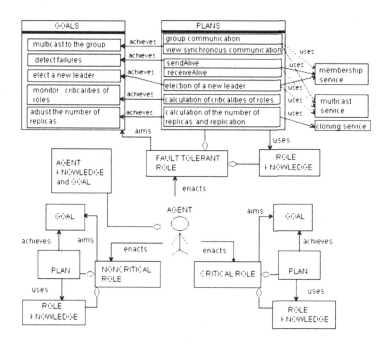

Fig. 4. A Goal Model for a Simple Fault Tolerant Organization

about the group's membership. The output of the membership service is called a
"view" [13, 14]. The reliable multicast services deliver messages to the current view
members.

Failure detection is one of the crucial aspects of any fault tolerant system to recognize a faulty component of the system. In our approach, "sendAlive" and "re-
ceiveAlive" are two plans that achieve the "detect failures" goal. In the "sendAlive"
plan, each replica in the replica group periodically exchanges heartbeats. A heartbeat
message is an "I am alive" message prepared for informing that the sending replica is
safe.

Once a heartbeat message has been received by all the replicas, then the "re-
ceiveAlive" plan is executed. In this plan, each agent waits for a new heartbeat message from the same agent that sent the previous heartbeat message. If a new heartbeat
message is not received during timeout, that replica is added to a suspect list. If all
replicas detect that replica on timeout, they place the replica in question on their suspect lists. In the case of recurrence of the same situation, the replica is deleted from
the membership lists. Timeout values are set before application starts. However,
timeout values are adapted according to observed response times. For instance, if a
replica or the connection is very slow, then the timeout value will be increased to
account for disparity; however, this may not prevent to mark a replica suspect falsely
in all cases.

Coordination between replicas is supported by a group communication service
which provides multi-point-to-multi-point communication. We assume that the MAS
development framework also supports multicasting. This feature is used to implement

the group communication service. However, this basic multicasting mechanism only delivers requests in an arbitrary order. An ordering guarantee in multicasting must be supported to develop fault tolerant systems because consistency and coordination between the replicas is constructed by performing incoming requests in order. The ordering scheme is implemented in the "group communication" plan which achieves the "multicast to the group" goal. In this plan, a group-specific ascending number is assigned to a new message whenever it is received from another agent, and then this message is multicast to the replicas in the membership lists in order to implement the semi-active replication strategy. In semi-active replication strategy, replicas are organized in a group, and all replicas execute incoming requests. One of the agent that enacts the critical role is designated as the primary (the leader) and responsible for providing responses. Therefore, consistency between replicas is ensured by processing each message.

In the passive replication strategy, replicas are also organized in a group and primary one responds to client requests. However, primary periodically updates replicas' states. If primary fails, one replica can be elected as a primary. In this work, the passive replication strategy uses the primary to order the messages as the semi-active replication strategy does, but requires a mechanism to order the views. Therefore, we have implemented the view synchronous multicast for the passive replication strategy. The inconsistency between replicas is avoided if, whenever the primary sends the update message to its replicas, either all or none of the replicas receive the message (atomicity) in the context of a dynamic membership [23]. View synchronous multicast is also implemented in the "view synchronous communication" plan. The implementation consists in delivering multiple, independent, a batch of messages between view changes. A view change occurs when a replica wants to join or leave the group, or a replica fails. In every view change, a message containing the composition of the view of the group is multicast to the group members. If the primary of the group fails, and a new view is defined, either all the replicas in new view, or none of them consider the last message of the primary. Therefore, consistency in the group will be ensured.

The replication service is the most important part of the replication-based fault tolerance approaches. To implement the replication service in our approach, the "adjust the number of replicas" goal must be achieved. The "calculation of the number of replicas and replication" plan achieves this goal by using the cloning service. In this plan, the replication degree of the group is calculated by using the value of the criticality of a critical role and the number of resources. If the replication is needed according to the result of the replication degree, then the cloning [11,15,16] service is used for replication of new replicas.

The critical roles must be identified to replicate new instances of the critical roles. To identify critical roles, the number of messages received by an agent for each role is monitored to collect some data to calculate the role criticalities. The collected data is then evaluated to take a decision on the role criticalities. The fault tolerant role is responsible for monitoring the roles and evaluating the criticalities of roles. Therefore, the fault tolerant role has the "monitor criticalities of roles" goal and the "calculation criticalities of roles" plan to achieve that goal. The criteria to be a critical role will be given in the next section.

In the proposed architecture, each role instance can be replicated many times and with different replication strategies. Each replication group has only one leader which coordinates the replica group and communicates with the other replicas. When the leader fails, a replica is selected as a new leader in the replica group. Therefore, the fault tolerant role has the "elect a new leader" goal and the "election of a new leader" plan to achieve this goal.

Next, we describe what makes an agent critical and the criticality of the role.

4 Criticality of the Role

In order to achieve effective fault handling, we have to estimate the critical roles of the organization, since the criticality of a role is the measure of the potential impact of the failure of that role on the failure of the organization. There are two cases that we must distinguish: 1) the role's criticality is static and 2) the role's criticality is dynamic. In the first case, multi-agent systems have static organization structures. Therefore, critical roles can be identified and then replication is performed by the programmer before run time.

In the second case, the role criticality cannot be determined before run time since the multi-agent systems may have dynamic organization structures. Therefore, critical roles can be dynamically evaluated at run-time. It can be done by using some prior input, or it can be done by using an observation module that collects the data [10, 11]. We can use some metrics for dynamically estimating and updating role criticalities in the organization. Within a MAS organization, the roles designate responsibilities of agents. Each role has a different impact on the operation of organization. For instance, Colman and Han distinguish types of roles in an organization: functional roles, operational-management roles and organizational management roles [17]. The concept of role captures the importance of an agent in an organization, and its dependencies to other agents.

The dependency of other roles on a specific role is another metric that can show the role's criticality. If a critical role somehow fails, the other roles, which rely on the critical role, will struggle to achieve their individual goals. The dependency on a role is derived from the number and performatives of the messages received. Guessoum et al. distinguishes six classes of performatives [12]. They also describe the influence of a message on its receiver by using symbolic values such as low, medium, high. According to this classification, we only consider messages (containing Class 1 type of performatives) [12] with a high value of influence on their receivers to determine the criticality of a role. Therefore, messages, to be considered in terms of role's criticality in our approach, contain performatives such as request, request-whenever, query-if, query-ref, subscribe.

In this work, we set a period for the organization at the system initialization. This period is called the sampling period T and actually defined over a time window $((k-1)T, kT)$, where k is the sampling instant. Considering both metrics, the criticality of a role and the number of replicas are calculated in the "calculation of criticalities of roles" and "calculation of the number of replicas, and replication" plans. The criticality of a role can be defined by the following equations:

$$RoleCriticality\ (k)=a*role(k)+b*Ratio\_req\ (k) \tag{1}$$

Ratio_req (k): The change in the number of messages sent to an agent for a specific role to the average number of messages over a number of periods;

   a, b: Coefficients for contributions of the weight of the role and the number of requests to the *RoleCriticality*.

   role(k): The value corresponding to the weight of the role at the *kth* sampling instant. The weights of the roles are explicitly defined in the role ontology before the program starts. Consider weight of each role as a numerical value within the interval (1, 10).

   After we have computed the criticality of each role, we can compute the number of replicas (*no_replicas*) of a critical role as follows:

$$no\_replicas(k+1)=\text{rounded}(rm+RM*RoleCriticality(k)) \tag{2}$$

   rm: The minimum number of replicas that is defined by programmer before an application starts.

   RM: The available resources that define the maximum number of possible simultaneous replicas. Then, the number of replicas (*no_replicas*) is used to control and update replication for each role in the next sampling period.

$$R.C=no\_replicas(k+1)-no\_replicas(k)$$

where *R.C* is the number of replicas that must be replicated if *R.C* is a positive integer or the number of replicas that must be killed if *R.C* is a negative integer. In the next we'll give the case study.

5 Case Study

Our fault tolerance approach presented in this paper has been implemented as a case study by using SEAGENT Multi-Agent framework [1, 24]. For the case study, we designed an agent system which includes some specific agents which enact the "library assistant" role (library assistant agent), or enact the "user assistant" role for querying library assistant agents. The library assistant agent manages a library and holds the library knowledge using the library ontology. Instances of this ontology hold the properties of books including name, ISBN, authors' names and keywords of the books. In our case study, each user assistant agent directly sends a book request to library assistant agents. The library assistant agent has only one plan that matches the request to the book ontology instance(s) and returns the matched books' descriptions within a FIPA-ACL message [2]. When the user assistant agent receives responses from the library assistant agents, it selects a library based on the responses and presents the result to the user. In this case study, the user assistant agents depend on the library assistant agents. Therefore, each library assistant agent is a single of point of failure. Since the library assistant agent is a critical agent for the system's operation, it must be initialized as a fault tolerant agent. In order to become a fault tolerant agent, the library assistant agent should also enact the "fault tolerant" role. The goal model of this scenario is shown in Figure 5.

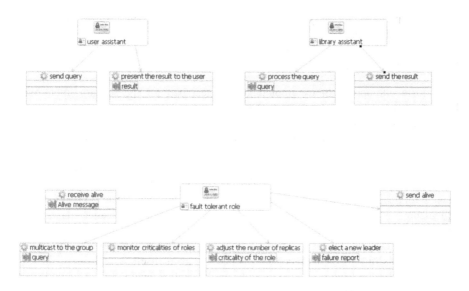

Fig. 5. A Goal Model for the Fault Tolerant Library System

In this goal model, three types of roles are given: The library assistant role, the user assistant role and the fault tolerant role. The user assistant role has the "send a query" goal to query the library assistant agent and the "present the result to the user" goal to present the results that the user waits for. The library assistant role has the "process the query" goal to process the requests and return the results. The "fault tolerant" role has the "send alive" and "receive alive" goals to implement the failure detector, the "adjust the number of replicas" goal to handle the replication process, the "elect a new leader" goal to elect a new leader when the leader fails, the "monitor criticalities of roles" goal to calculate the criticalities of roles, and the "multicast to the group" goal to implement group communication.

When we decide that the library assistant agent needs to be fault tolerant, it invokes a "classify" operation for the "fault tolerant" role, it then enacts the "fault tolerant" role. Then, it invokes a "find" operation to search for a replica candidate residing on another host. When it finds an agent to take up the "library assistant" role, it then transfers the "library assistant" and "fault tolerant" roles including their plan libraries. These all operations are performed in the "calculation of the number of replicas and replication" plan to achieve the "adjust the number of replicas" goal. When the agent on the other host classifies both roles, the agent enacts the "library assistant" role and activates it. When the agent enacts the critical role and the fault tolerant role, it and its leader periodically execute the "sendAlive" plan to implement the heartbeat mechanism of the failure detection mechanism.

Let us assume that the user assistant agent sends a query to the leader library assistant agent and apply the semi-active replication scheme. When the leader library assistant receives this query, it automatically assigns a number to this query and sends it to itself and its replica by executing the "group communication" plan to achieve group communication goal. When the library assistant agents receive this query, they process the query. The leader library assistant agent returns the result to the user assistant agent.

5.1 Evaluation of the Approach

To evaluate our approach, we implemented a test bed for the scenario mentioned above. In this test bed, we suppose that multi-agent organizations are static structures and the criticalities of roles do not change over time in such a system. Therefore, we identify that the "library assistant" role to be replicated and define the replication degree for this role before program starts. The library assistant role and some other roles having simple plans are assigned to an agent. In the first case, we employ the agent replication approach in the test bed. According to the agent replication approach, the agent is replicated due to having the critical "library assistant" role. Therefore, we implemented a test bed consisting of a library assistant agent leader, its replicas (agents) in the number range from 3 to 23, and the user assistant agent that queries the library assistant agent. In this test bed, another agent also sends requests to the library assistant agents due to their other roles. Since the agent itself is replicated, then all roles enacted by the leader are also enacted by the replica agents. In the second case, we employ the role-based replication approach in the test bed. According to our approach, the critical role and the fault tolerant role are assigned (transferred) to the agents having less workload. In this case, the test bed consists of the replica instances of the library assistant role (together with the fault tolerant role) in the number range from 3 to 23, the user assistant agent, and the leader. The user assistant agent periodically queries the agent that enacts the "library assistant" role. The number of queries sent to the agent that enacts "library assistant" role is equal to 60 for both cases. Also in the second case, the agents that enact "library assistant role" are queried by another agent for their other roles to cause workload on them. In order to see the costs of role-based replication and agent replication, the response times for queries are measured in both cases. The response time is the time it takes the user assistant agent to receive the last reply from a leader after sending its requests to the leader. In this test, we try to observe the effect of role-based replication to the overall system performance.

The agent system is implemented in the SEAGENT platform and Java Version 1.5.0. The tests are performed on two computers with Intel P4 running at 1.5 GHz and 2GB of RAM, running Windows XP. We distribute the agents to two computers and run each test ten times.

The results of the tests are illustrated in Fig. 6. The results show the average response times of the systems applying the agent replication and role-based replication approaches, as the number of replicas increases. As seen from the figure, the slopes of response times of both systems increase linearly with the number of agents in an organization. The increase in response time is expected, since it is caused by the implementation of the system on two machines. Moreover, the number of the exchanged messages increases with the number of replicas due to the multicasting of request and heartbeat messages. However, the average response times of the system applying the agent replication are much higher than the average response times of the system applying role-based replication. This result was also expected, since the agent is replicated with all its roles due to having a critical role into an agent replica group. The leader of the group multicasts requests to its group members.

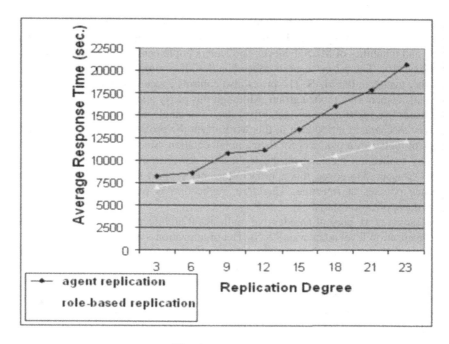

Fig. 6. The Test Results

6   Related Works

Several approaches to fault-tolerance in MAS are documented in the literature; each focuses on different aspects of fault-tolerance. Kumar et al. present a methodology than can be used to specify robust brokered architectures with capability of recovering from broker failures [3]. Their methodology is based on the theory of teamwork. In their work, brokers are organized hierarchically in teams. Brokers in teams exchange information between them and maintain communications between agents. Their approach can be only used for recovering from broker failures.

Klein proposes an approach based on a shared exception handling service that is plugged into existing agent systems [4]. This service monitors the overall progress of a multi-agent system. When a new agent is created, the "new agent registration" agent takes a description of its normative behavior and creates sentinels to look for the evidence of dysfunctional behavior. When a sentinel detects such faulty symptoms, this information is sent to a "diagnosis" agent that produces a set of candidate diagnoses. These are sent to the resolution agent that defines a resolution plan to take corrective actions.

Hagg uses sentinel agents to guard specific functions or to guard against specific states in the society of agents. The sentinel interacts with other agents using semantic addressing. Thus, it can build models of other agents by monitoring agent communication and by interaction. It can also use timers to detect crashed agents or communication link failures [5].

There are also well-known fault tolerance approaches based on replication techniques for multi agent systems. In order to increase fault tolerance and improve availability and reliability of MAS, Fedoruk and Deters implemented transparent replication via proxies [6]. The proxy as an interface handles all communication between replicas and other agents in the MAS. The proxy also controls execution in a replica group and state management of a replica group. Although this proxy approach handles fault tolerance issues in a multi-agent system, proxy itself is a single point of failure. There is no recovery mechanism introduced in this work when the proxy fails. They chose FIPA-OS agent toolkit as a platform for their implementation. Since FIPA-OS does not provide any replication mechanism, the replication server is implemented as a standard FIPA-OS agent. Moreover, this approach does not support the idea of changing fault tolerance policies at run-time. Therefore, replication is realized by a programmer before the application starts.

Guessoum et al. present an adaptive multi-agent architecture with both agent level and organization level adaptation [7, 8]. The organization's adaptation is based on the monitoring of the system's behavior. The architecture was implemented with the DIMA platform [9] and the DarX middleware [10]. In DarX, software components can be either replicated or un-replicated, and it is possible to change the replication strategy at run time. Although we also use the replication technique to implement fault tolerance policies within the organization, the main difference of our approach from this work is that our replication technique is based on role concept. In our replication technique, we do not replicate an agent due to its criticality. Because, we claim if an agent is critical in the organization, its role that it fills as a position is critical for the organization. Therefore, we transfer behavior libraries (plans) and knowledge of the critical role to an agent to become an instance of the critical role.

These approaches present useful solutions to the problem of fault tolerance in multi-agent systems. However, the entities used for handling this problem force a specific multi-agent organization and these approaches lack flexibility and reusability. On the other hand, in our case, fault tolerance requirements are identified and the behaviors that satisfy these requirements are encapsulated by the fault tolerant role. These behaviors can be used whenever we need to make an organization fault tolerant. Briefly, our approach provides flexibility and reusability to multi-agent organizations in terms of fault tolerance since it is possible to easily modify existing behaviors of the fault tolerant role, remove some of behaviors, or include new behaviors.

7 Conclusion

In this paper, we presented a new approach to replication-based fault tolerance in MAS. We define a "fault tolerant" role that encapsulates all the related behaviors to replication-based fault tolerance such as replication, failure detection mechanism, group communication service, leader election, and monitoring. Therefore, the "fault tolerant" role is responsible for replicating instances of critical roles, coordination between critical role instances and satisfying all replication-based fault tolerance requirements.

Moreover, our approach is flexible in terms of fault tolerance since it is possible to easily modify existing behaviors of the "fault tolerant" role, remove some of its behaviors, or include new behaviors to it.

References

1. Dikenelli, O., et al.: SEAGENT: A Platform for Developing Semantic Web Based Multi Agent Systems. In: The Fourth International Joint Conference on Autonomous Agents - AAMAS 2005 (2005)
2. FIPA, FIPA Specifications, http://www.fipa.org
3. Kumar, S., Cohen, P.R., Levesque, H.J.: The adaptive agent architecture: Achieving fault-tolerance using persistent broker teams. In: Proceedings of Fourth International Conference on Multi-Agent Systems (July 2000)
4. Klein, M., Dallarocas, C.: Exception handling in agent systems. In: Etzioni, O., Muller, J.P., Bradshaw, J.M. (eds.) Proceedings of the Third International Conference on Agents (Agents 1999), Seattle,WA, pp. 62–68 (1999)
5. Hägg, S.: A sentinel approach to fault handling in multi-agent systems. In: Proceedings of the second Australian Workshop on Distributed AI, in conjunction with the Fourth Pacific Rim International Conference on Artificial Intelligence (PRICAI 1996), Cairns, Australia (August 1996)
6. Fedoruk, A., Deters, R.: Improving fault-tolerance by replicating agents. In: Proceedings of 1st International Joint Conference on Autonomous Agents and Multi-Agent Systems, Bologna, Italy (2002)
7. Guessoum, Z., Ziane, M., Faci, N.: Monitoring and organizational-level adaptation of multi-agent systems. In: AAMAS 2004, pp. 514–522. ACM, New York (2004)
8. Guessoum, Z., Briot, J.-P., Charpentier, Z., Aknine, S., Marin, O., Sens, P.: Dynamic and Adaptive Replication for Large-Scale Reliable Multi-Agent Systems. In: Proc. ICSE 2002 First International Workshop on Software Engineering for Large-Scale Multi-Agent Systems (SELMAS 2002), Orlando FL, U.S.A. ACM, New York (2002)
9. Guessoum, Z., Briot, J.P.: From active objects to autonomous agents. IEEE Concurrency 7(3), 68–76 (1999)
10. Guessoum, Z., Briot, J.P., Sens, P., Marin, O.: Toward fault-tolerant multi-agent systems. In: MAAMAW 2001, Annecy, France (2001)
11. Bora, S., Dikenelli, O.: Implementing a Multi-agent Organization that Changes Its Fault Tolerance Policy at Run-Time. In: Dikenelli, O., Gleizes, M.-P., Ricci, A. (eds.) ESAW 2005. LNCS (LNAI), vol. 3963, pp. 153–167. Springer, Heidelberg (2006)
12. Guessoum, Z., Faci, N., Briot, J.P.: Adaptive Replication of Large-Scale Multi-agent Systems – Towards a Fault-Tolerant Multi-agent Platform. In: Garcia, A., Choren, R., Lucena, C., Giorgini, P., Holvoet, T., Romanovsky, A. (eds.) SELMAS 2005. LNCS, vol. 3914, pp. 238–253. Springer, Heidelberg (2006)
13. Tanenbaum, A.S., van Steen, M.: Distributed Systems: Principles and Paradigms. Prentice-Hall, Englewood Cliffs (2002)
14. Chockler, G.V., Keidar, I., Vitenberg, R.: Group Communication Specifications: A Comprehensive Study. ACM Computing Surveys 33(4), 1–43 (2001)
15. Shehory, O., Sycara, K., Chalasani, P., Jha, S.: Agent Cloning: An Approach to Agent Mobility and Resource Allocation. IEEE Communications 36(7), 58–67 (1998)

16. Decker, K., Sycara, K., Williamson, M.: Cloning for Intelligent Adaptive Information Agents. In: Rao, A., Singh, M.P., Wooldridge, M.J. (eds.) ATAL 1997. LNCS (LNAI), vol. 1365, pp. 63–75. Springer, Heidelberg (1998)
17. Colman, A.W., Han, J.: Roles, Players, and Adaptable Organizations. Applied Ontology 2 (2007)
18. Odell, J., Parunak, H.V.D., Brueckner, S., Sauter, J.A.: Changing roles: Dynamic role assignment. Journal of Object Technology 2(5), 77–86 (2003)
19. Bora, S., Dikenelli, O.: Applying Feedback Control in Adaptive Replication in Fault Tolerant Multi-agent Organizations. In: Proc. ICSE 2006 Fifth International Workshop on Software Engineering for Large-Scale Multi-Agent Systems (SELMAS 2006). ACM, Shangai (2006)
20. Bora, S., Dikenelli, O.: Experience with Feedback Control Mechanisms in Self-replicating Multi-Agent Systems. In: Burkhard, H.-D., Lindemann, G., Verbrugge, R., Varga, L.Z. (eds.) CEEMAS 2007. LNCS (LNAI), vol. 4696, pp. 133–142. Springer, Heidelberg (2007)
21. Stollberg, M., Rhomberg, F.: Survey on Goal-driven Architectures. Technical Report (2006)
22. Ferber, J.O., et al.: Agent/Group/Roles:Simulating with Organizations. In: Fourth International Workshop on Agent-Based Simulation, France (2003)
23. Guerraoui, R., Schiper, A.: Fault-Tolerance by Replication in Distributed Systems. In: Strohmeier, A. (ed.) Ada-Europe 1996. LNCS, vol. 1088. Springer, Heidelberg (1996)
24. SEAGENT, http://www.seagent.ege.edu.tr
25. Almeida, A., Aknine, S., Briot, J.P.: Dynamic resource allocation heuristics for providing fault tolerance in multi-agent systems. In: SAC 2008, pp. 66–70 (2008)
26. Dastani, M., Dignum, V., Dignum, F.: Role-Assignment in Open Agent Societies. In: AAMAS 2003, Australia. ACM, New York (2003)
27. Powell, D.: Delta-4: A generic architecture for dependable distributed computing. Springer, Heidelberg (1991)

Knowledge Management in Role Based Agents

Hüseyin Kır, Erdem Eser Ekinci, and Oguz Dikenelli

Ege University, Department of Computer Engineering,
35100 Bornova, Izmir, Turkey
{huseyinkir,erdemeserekinci}@gmail.com, oguz.dikenelli@ege.edu.tr

Abstract. In multi-agent system literature, the role concept is getting increasingly researched to provide an abstraction to scope beliefs, norms, goals of agents and to shape relationships of the agents in the organization. In this research, we propose a knowledgebase architecture to increase applicability of roles in MAS domain by drawing inspiration from the *self* concept in the role theory of sociology. The proposed knowledgebase architecture has granulated structure that is dynamically organized according to the agent's identification in a social environment. Thanks to this dynamic structure, agents are enabled to work on consistent knowledge in spite of inevitable conflicts between roles and the agent. The knowledgebase architecture is also implemented and incorporated into the SEAGENT multi-agent system development framework.

1 Introduction

In multi-agent system research domain, role concept is getting more popular from both methodology and infrastructure perspectives in last years. The main purpose behind using roles in MAS research domain is to provide an abstraction to define beliefs, norms, goals of agents and to shape relationships between the agents in the organization. But, the role concept is not new, and not firstly used by the MAS domain researchers for modeling organizations.

The role concept was introduced within the theater in antique ages to define behaviors and scripts of an actor in scenes of a part. But in the previous century, sociologists converted this simple concept to a deep theory which is comprised of systematic methods of empirical investments to predict activities of individuals, to resolve human social relationships, stratification and interactions by analyzing body of knowledge about human organizations[1]. As a consequence of these researches, the role concept is explicated as designated social part to be played, characteristic behaviors and scripts for social conduct. Albeit at a first glance it appears like that there is not so much change in the general definition of role through the ages, depths of the concept are theorized with many sub-theories (role playing, role taking, role transition, role leaving, role conflict, etc.) which do clarify the problems such as which conditions conduct a role, how an individual plays a role and what the dynamics are behind taking or leaving a role.

When the MAS researchers import the role concept to the multi-agent system theory, they pave the way of transferring all related sub-theories of sociological role theory. Already corresponds of many role sub-theories propounded

H. Aldewereld, V. Dignum, and G. Picard (Eds.): ESAW 2009, LNAI 5881, pp. 181–196, 2009.

by sociologists[2,1] can be seen in the prominent MAS researches[3,4]. But we ascertain that the fact of the self concept's importance in the role theory is disregarded in these researches. In this paper, to increase applicability of roles in MAS domain we propose a knowledgebase architecture by drawing inspiration from the *self* concept in the role theory of sociology.

The self concept, basically, denotes the word "I", which is the knowledge of physical properties, beliefs, impulses, characteristic behaviors and talents, and all other referents to the "I" [2]. But in theory, the concept is not a simple, complete structure but granulated net that is expanded and reorganized during life long evolution of the individual[5,6]. In daily life, each individual participates many organizations such as family, school, and business and gains many identities by taking different roles. In sociology, individual's participation in an organization is technically expressed as expansion of the self with the acceptance of all norms, goals and beliefs, which belong to the enacted role[6]. Additionally, when the individual moves from one participated organizations to another, the granulated form of the self is dynamically reorganized according to the identification of the individual with respect to its cognition about its roles[5,7].

The main contribution of the self concept to the role theory is depicted as clarifying the problem of resolving human behaviors in conflicting positions[7]. In detail, an individual may play more than one role in the same organization or different organizations. But, rules, norms and goals of these roles may not be completely consistent with each other, even if they are in the same organization. Furthermore, an individual can play a role, which is not congruent with her/his self, by violating self's rules and norms until reaching self goals, if there is not another way. In such conflicting positions, by the help of granulated and alterable form of the self concept, sociologists become capable of explaining the meaning of individual's behaviors[5].

Analogously to sociological role theory, in a role-based multi-agent system, agents enact various types of roles due to desire of achieving their congenital goals during their life time. Differently from the human case, in the MAS literature conflicts between agents and roles are formally expressed and highlighted as an undesired situation[3,8]. But as emphasized previously, conflicts between the roles of an organization is inevitable for the reason of looking through the different perspectives to the organization.

In the light of this idea, to make role theory completely applicable on MAS, we propose a knowledgebase architecture, which consists of dynamically arranged knowledge blocks, similar to the granulated and alterable form of self concept developed by sociologists. The proposed knowledgebase architecture has two components; active and passive knowledge. The passive knowledge is used as storage unit for all knowledge blocks of the agent. Besides, the active knowledge is a subset of passive knowledge that is arrangement of knowledge blocks which are the most relevant to the agent's active position in the organization. While consistency of the passive knowledge is not cared, active knowledge is obliged to be consistent to plan deterministically at decision making time. This architecture is implemented and incorporated into the SEAGENT multi-agent development framework[9]. SEAGENT framework is based on the OWL ontologies in a way that all artifacts of the programming paradigms are stored in the ontologies. So, the knowledgebase is implemented to manage the knowledge handled with these ontologies by the direction of the role theory and the self concept.

The remainder of this paper is structured as follows: In Section 2, we detail our knowledgebase semantics on the agent meta-model and formally declare the effects of the role operations on the knowledge. Section 3 presents the implemented architecture of the proposed knowledge approach which is incorporated into the SEAGENT multi-agent development framework. Section 4 elaborates a case study that emphasize the benefits of the proposed knowledge model. Finally in Section 5, we examine the related works before concluding with Section 6.

2   Role-Based Knowledge Semantics

In the decision making phase, the knowledgebase of the agent has the responsibility of providing information about how the agent reacts the events perceived from the environment, or how it achieves proactively its goals. But beyond providing information about plans or goals, for effective planning, the knowledgebase must also exhibit partial projection of the world encompassing the agent. Through this direction, when the world around the agent is organized with roles, the projection of the world in the knowledgebase takes form according to these roles and their relationships. Since, to handle projection of the world around the agent we define three types of knowledge blocks as granules of our knowledgebase; self knowledge, role knowledge and role-instance knowledge blocks. If it is required to introduce these blocks simply; the role knowledge block involves norms, goals, rules and beliefs specific to a role in an organization and the self knowledge block represents the agent itself in the form of congenital behaviors, norms, goals, rules and beliefs. Differently from the other ones, the role instance knowledge block handles the information of inferred rules, norms and beliefs while the agent is performing under a role. Followings of this section declares the formal semantics of these knowledge blocks.

From the point of knowledge view, the knowledge of a role $r \in R$ is a tuple $K_r = \langle G, P, \sigma_r, \pi_r, \mathbb{R} \rangle$ where, G is the set of goals, P is the set of plans that are used to achieve each role goal, σ_r specifies the facts of the role, π_r specifies the rules of the role and finally $\mathbb{R}$ represents the set of possible relations between roles. To detail semantics of $\mathbb{R}$ we use the model proposed in [10] by Kristensen and Osterbye. They ascertain three types of role relations: specialization, aggregation and dependency. Specialization is supported by extension and used to built up role hierarchies. We represent specialization as $\mathbb{R}_{spec}(r_1, r_2)$, where $r_1, r_2 \epsilon R$, and implies that r_1 extends r_2. Similarly, aggregation is used to construct role compositions and represented as $\mathbb{R}_{aggr}(r_1, \{r_x, r_y, ...\})$, where $r_1, r_x, r_y, ... \epsilon R$, and defines that r_1 is aggregated of given role set. Finally the role dependency means one role is dependent on another role for the realization of its goals[11]. In accordance with the Kristensen's work, we examine the reflections of these inter-role relations on the knowledge block relations.

Another knowledge block in our knowledge model is the self knowledge. The self defines the personal attitudes of an agent $a \in A$. Hence, we represent the self knowledge as a tuple $K_{self} = \langle G, P, \sigma_{self}, \pi_{self}, \Omega \rangle$ where, G represents the set of congenital goals of the agent, P is the set of plans that comprise the own capabilities of the agent, σ_{self} specifies the facts that the agent has about the world and himself, π_{self} specifies the rules that constraints the agent behavior and Ω represents the identity of the self.

In our model the last knowledge block is the role instance knowledge. When an agent enacts a role, it creates a unique entity, called role instance $ri \in Ri$, in the organization. We specify the role instance knowledge as $K_{ri} = \langle id, roleType,$ $enactmentType, \sigma_{ri}, \pi_{ri}, \mathbb{A} \rangle$ where id is the unique identifier of the role instance, $roleType$ represents the role to which the role instance belongs and $enactment$-$Type$ determines the degree of dedication of an agent on a role. The semantics of the enactment is detailed in [11,4] and there are four types of enactment; maximally selfish, selfish, social and maximally social, $\mathcal{T} = \{\tau_{MaxSelfish}, \tau_{Selfish},$ $\tau_{Social}, \tau_{MaxSocial}\}$. If an agent enacts a role in a selfish form this means the agent attaches higher priority to the self's rules, goals and norms. On the contrary, if the enactment is social, the agent prioritizes its role responsibilities. Finally $\mathbb{A}$ represents the set of role instances that the role instance aggregated of. In this article we use the shorter form as $k_{ri_{id}^{roleType}} \in K_{ri}$, to represent the role instance knowledge. When a role is initiated newly, it has an empty fact(σ_{ri}) and rule(π_{ri}) sets. This knowledge is composed along the life cycle of the agent via learning and inference. Also, these two concepts could be considered as an extension of the role knowledge which empower agent to objectify the role.

Consequently, we represent the agent's whole knowledge as K_a which is union of the self knowledge k_{self}, set of the role knowledge $K_r = \{k_{r_1}, k_{r_2}, ..., k_{r_n}\}$ and set of the role instance knowledge $K_{ri} = \{k_{ri_1}, k_{ri_2}, ..., k_{ri_n}\}$, $k_{self} \cup K_r \cup K_{ri} \subseteq K_a$. But, as emphasized in the introduction, consistency of entire knowledgebase K_a cannot be established due to unavoidable conflicts between self of agents and roles and between enacted roles. The granulated structure of knowledgebase enables an agent to construct the most relevant and consistent subset of the agent knowledge in accordance with its active role. Even the agent enacts various roles that are in conflict, decision making must always placed on a consistent knowledge. To provide the consistency, we separate the knowledgebase into two constituents; active knowledge(K_{active}) and passive knowledge($K_{passive}$). While passive knowledge is equivalent to the entire knowledge of the agent $K_{passive} \subseteq K_a$ and its consistency is not expected, the active knowledge is a sub-set of passive knowledge $K_{active} \subset K_{passive}$ that is arranged from the relevant knowledge blocks into a consistent form. We introduce the semantics that formally define how passive and active knowledge are managed according to the life-cycle of role-based agents in the following section.

Operational Knowledge Semantics

Through the life-cycle of a role-based agent, the agent enacts roles and performs under these roles till reaching its goals and then deacts the roles. Concurrently,

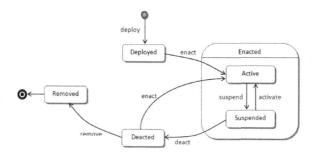

Fig. 1. Role Life Cycle

the knowledgebase also evolves together with its owner agent. In order to detail changes of the knowledgebase during the agent evolution, one must declare operations performed between an agent and a role. These operations are determined informally by Odell et al. in [12]. But Dignum et al. articulate these operations in a formal way[4]. We declare an enhanced version of the role operations in Figure-1 and within the following definitions, we formally declare the effects of these operations on the active and the passive knowledge of the agent.

Definition 1. (Deploy) An agent takes the knowledge of a role by performing deploy operation. This operation makes agent acquainted with the organizational facts, norms and goals from the perspective of a role. By this way, the agent obtains the knowledge about how the role can be performed. After the deployment, the knowledge block of the role is installed into the passive knowledge of the agent. The operation is represented as $O_{deploy}(a_1, r_1) \rightarrow K'_{passive}$ where $r_1 \in R$, $a_1 \in A$ and $K'_{passive}$ is for the evolved agent knowledge after the deployment operation. Let $\langle g_a, p_a, \Sigma_a, \Pi_a \rangle$ be the agent's passive knowledge before deploy operation and $\langle g_{r_1}, p_{r_1}, \sigma_{r_1}, \pi_{r_1}, \mathbb{R} \rangle$ is the knowledge block of the role r_1, then the deployment operation can be detailed as follows:

$$\frac{K_{passive} = \langle g_a, p_a, \Sigma_a, \Pi_a \rangle \quad k_{r_1} = \langle g_{r_1}, p_{r_1}, \sigma_{r_1}, \pi_{r_1}, \mathbb{R} \rangle \quad O_{deploy}(a_1, r_1)}{K_{passive} \cup k_{r_1} \subseteq K'_{passive} \quad K'_{passive} = \langle g_a \cup g_{r_1}, p_a \cup p_{r_1}, \Sigma_a \cup \sigma_{r_1}, \Pi_a \cup \pi_{r_1} \rangle}$$

But, in order to perform deployment operation successfully, some preconditions that comes from the relationships of the deployed role must be satisfied. If the role intended to deploy extends or aggregates from other roles, then the parent or aggregated roles should be deployed as well:

$$O_{deploy}(a_1, r_1) \Rightarrow \forall r_x \in R \left((\mathbb{R}_{aggr}(r_1, r_x) \vee \mathbb{R}_{spec}(r_1, r_x)) \wedge O_{deploy}(a_1, r_x) \right)$$

Definition 2. (Enact) By performing this operation, an agent gains a new identity and a unique instance of the role is declared to the organization. Instantiation of a role is represented as $O_{enact}(a_1, r_1, \tau) \rightarrow k'_{self}$, where $r_1 \in R$, $a_1 \in A$, τ specifies the enactment type and k'_{self} specifies the evolved knowledge block of the self after the enactment operation. This operation ingenerates a new instance of the role r_1 as $ri_x^{r1} \in Ri$ and adds this new identity to the agent's self knowledge block $k_{self} = \langle g_{self}, p_{self}, \sigma_{self}, \pi_{self}, \Omega \rangle$.

$$\frac{k_{self}=\langle g_{self},p_{self},\sigma_{self},\pi_{self},\Omega\rangle \quad O_{enact}(a_1,r_1,\tau)}{k'_{self}=\langle g_{self},p_{self},\sigma_{self},\pi_{self},\Omega'\rangle \quad \Omega \cup \{ri_x^{r1}\} \subseteq \Omega'}$$

Similar to the deployment operation, in order to perform the enactment successfully the agent follows the suit by enacting the aggregated roles:

$$O_{enact}(a_1,r_1) \Rightarrow \forall r_x \in R \ (\mathbb{R}_{aggr}(r_1,r_x) \wedge O_{enact}(a_1,r_x))$$

Besides, enactment does not cause only extending the identities in the self knowledge block. In addition, a role instance knowledge $k_{ri_x^{r1}}=\langle x,r_1,\tau,\sigma_{ri},\pi_{ri},\mathbb{A}\rangle$ is also created and inserted into the passive knowledge, $K_{a_1} \cup k_{r_1} \subseteq K'_{a_1}$. But the newly created role instance has an empty fact (σ_{ri}) and rule (π_{ri}) sets. These rules and facts are directly inserted into the role instance knowledge block or generated by inference along the activation and execution of the role instance.

Definition 3. (Activate) An important point is that, an agent may enact various roles to achieve numerous goals concurrently. Hence, a role is not played continuously. Due to the position of the agent in the organization, a role is activated at a time. The activation operation puts forward an identity of an agent to prepare it performing under a role instance. From the point of knowledge view, each activation operation causes a context switch that updates the active knowledge of the agent with respect to the activated role. The active knowledge is constructed from the most relevant knowledge blocks stored in the passive knowledge that literally reflects the activated role instance's conception of the world. Additionally, relations between roles and enactment type of the role instance significantly effects the content of the active knowledge.

Before declaring semantics of the active knowledge construction in terms of the enactment type, an important function *Construct Perspective (CP)* and logical operator $\oslash$, which are intensely used in our semantics, are required to be defined. First one is conflict resolver operator "$\oslash$", which designates the maximal subset of the former operand that does not conflict with the latter operand. For instance, let $s_1=\langle x_0,x_1,x_2,x_3,\neg x_5\rangle$ and $s_2=\langle\neg x_1,x_2,x_4,x_5\rangle$ are set of premises, then $s_1\oslash s_2=\langle x_0,x_2,x_3\rangle$ and $s_2\oslash s_1=\langle x_2,x_4\rangle$. In order to define and eliminate conflicts between entities, we utilize goal and rule conflict definitions made by Dastani et al.[4] and the semantic relations between these entities.

Construct Perspective function, on the other hand, is the root function for arranging the active knowledge from the related knowledge blocks. The function is called when the activation operation is triggered, $O_{activate}(ri_x^{r1}) \rightarrow CP(ri_x^{r1})$ where $ri_x^{r1} \in Ri$. We define $CP(ri_y^{rx})$ function for the role $r_x \in R$ and role instance $ri_y^{rx} \in Ri$, whose type is r_x, as:

$$\frac{CP(ri_y^{rx})}{K_{active}= k_{ri_y^{rx}} \cup CP^\tau(r_x) \cup \forall ri_z^{rk} \in \mathbb{A} \ (CP(ri_z^{rk}))}$$

where $k_{ri_y^{rx}}=\langle y,r_x,\tau,\sigma_{ri},\pi_{ri},\mathbb{A}\rangle$.

In order to construct the knowledge perspective of a role instance, three groups of knowledge block are added to the active knowledge. The knowledge block of the activated role instance($k_{r_i r_y^r}$) is added to the active knowledge without any hesitation of a conflict. Because, when a role is initiated for the first time, it has empty fact (σ_{ri}) and rule (π_{ri}) sets and the efforts on keeping active knowledge consistent prevents expansion of the role instance knowledge in a conflicting way. Also, the active knowledge constructor function recursively adds all aggregated role instances' knowledge, which are defined in $\mathbb{A}$, to the active knowledge. And finally, the knowledge block of the role is added to the active knowledge with the operation $CP^\tau(r_x)$. Dignum[11] defines the evaluation of the goals of an agent in accordance with the role enactment type (τ), but goals are not the only determinant on the behavior of an agent. Hence, we extend this definitions in a way that comprises every entity in the knowledge.

The function $CP^\tau(r_x)$ process in a different way for each enactment type τ and the active knowledge varies as follows:

Case 1. (*Maximally selfish enactment*) The agent only uses its own goals, and ignores any objectives of the role. But, the role enacting agent cannot try to achieve pure self goals while playing the game by the organizational rules. Hence, the agent should disregard the organizational rules. But, it still has to know at least the shared organizational vocabulary in order to communicate with the other agents. $CP^\tau(r_x)$ function for this type of enactment is:

$$CP^{MaxSelfish}(r_x) = k_{self} \cup p_{r_x} \cup (\sigma_{r_x} \oslash \sigma_{self}) \cup \forall\ r_m \in \mathbb{S}\ (CP^{MaxSelfish}(r_m))$$

where $k_{r_x} = \langle g_{r_x}, p_{r_x}, \sigma_{r_x}, \pi_{r_x}, \mathbb{R} \rangle$, $\mathbb{S}$ defines the list of specialized roles that is inferred from the role relations $\mathbb{R}$ and as mentioned before $\sigma_{r_x} \oslash \sigma_{self}$ designates the role facts that does not conflict with facts of the self knowledge block.

Case 2. (*Selfish enactment*) Different from maximal selfish enactment, the enacting agent takes as many of its role's goals and rules as possible into consideration. But self rules still have the priority, so rules of the role that conflict with the self rules are disregarded.

$$CP^{Selfish}(r_x) = k_{self} \cup p_{r_x} \cup (\sigma_{r_x} \oslash \sigma_{self}) \cup (\pi_{r_x} \oslash \pi_{self}) \cup (g_{r_x} \oslash g_{self}) \cup \\ \forall r_m \in \mathbb{S}\ (CP^{Selfish}(r_m))$$

where $k_{r_x} = \langle g_{r_x}, p_{r_x}, \sigma_{r_x}, \pi_{r_x}, \mathbb{R} \rangle$ and $\mathbb{S}$ defines the list of specialized roles that is inferred from the role relations $\mathbb{R}$.

Case 3. (*Maximally social enactment*) Agent, even though it does not firmly believe, may act for the sake of the organization's benefits. For this reason, the agent only uses objectives from the role and precisely obeys the organizational rules. Agent ignores its self goals and rules, for the duration of the role enactment.

$$CP^{MaxSocial}(r_x) = k_{r_x} \cup p_{self} \cup (\sigma_{self} \oslash \sigma_{r_x}) \cup \forall\ r_m \in \mathbb{S}\ (CP^{MaxSocial}(r_m))$$

where $k_{r_x} = \langle g_{r_x}, p_{r_x}, \sigma_{r_x}, \pi_{r_x}, \mathbb{R} \rangle$ and $\mathbb{S}$ defines the list of specialized roles that is inferred from the role relations $\mathbb{R}$.

Case 4. (Social enactment) This enactment type is similar to the selfish enactment, but herein the agent includes as many of its own goals and rules as possible but the organizational rules and goals still have the priority.

$$CP^{Social}(r_x)=k_{r_x} \cup p_{self} \cup (\sigma_{self} \oslash \sigma_{r_x}) \cup (\pi_{self} \oslash \pi_{r_x}) \cup (g_{self} \oslash g_{r_x}) \cup$$
$$\forall r_m \in \mathbb{S} \; (CP^{Social}(r_m))$$

where $k_{r_x}=\langle g_{r_x}, p_{r_x}, \sigma_{r_x}, \pi_{r_x}, \mathbb{R} \rangle$ and $\mathbb{S}$ defines the list of specialized roles that is inferred from the role relations $\mathbb{R}$.

As a special case, if there are no conflicting goals or beliefs between the self and the activated role, then the constructed active knowledge of social enactment is same with the selfish enacted role's active knowledge. In other words, if there are no conflicting rules then, $\pi_{self} \oslash \pi_{r_1} = \pi_{self}$, $\pi_{r_1} \oslash \pi_{self} = \pi_{r_1}$ and the same for the facts and goals. Hence;

$$O_{activate}(ri_x^{r1}) \rightarrow (k_{self} \cup k_{r_1} \cup k_{ri_x^{r1}}) \subseteq K_{active}$$

whether $k_{ri_X^{r1}}=\langle x, r_1, \tau_{Social}, \sigma_{ri}, \pi_{ri}, \mathbb{A} \rangle$ or $k_{ri_x^{r1}}=\langle x, r_1 \; \tau_{Selfish}, \sigma_{ri}, \pi_{ri}, \mathbb{A} \rangle$.

While active knowledge construction ensures that the agent makes deterministic decisions, occasionally agent may need to share a role specific knowledge or a know-how with another role that does not have direct relation. In such a case, agent adopts that knowledge as experience and adds the knowledge to its self knowledge. Thereby, agent can use that knowledge independent from the life-cycle and knowledge scope of the role.

Definition 4. (Suspend) Role instances goes into suspending state when none of its goals and eventually tasks are in execution and there is nothing more to do in the scope of instance. In this case, the entire active knowledge is committed back to the agent knowledge and a new active knowledge is constructed with the subsequent activation operation.

Definition 5. (Deact) Agent deacts a role instance in the case of withdrawing from a social position. Deact operation could be triggered through the achievement of all role goals or the inexpediency of the enacted role instance. This operation deallocates the role instance from the agent and represented as: $O_{deact}(a_1, ri_1^{r1}) \rightarrow k'_{self}$, where $ri_1^{r1} \epsilon Ri$ and $a_1 \epsilon A$. When the role instance's main goal is achieved, the instance is deallocated from the agent.

$$\frac{k_{self}=\langle g_{self}, p_{self}, \sigma_{self}, \pi_{self}, \Omega \rangle \quad O_{deact}(a_1, ri_1^{r1})}{k'_{self}=\langle g_{self}, p_{self}, \sigma_{self}, \pi_{self}, \Omega' \rangle \quad \Omega' = \Omega \setminus ri_x^{r1}}$$

Enacting a role and deacting the same role doesn't always end up with the same agent knowledge, because through the execution of the role instance, agent may gain experience and its self knowledge may evolve. Also, as a rule, if there is an aggregate role which is enacted by the agent, its participant roles could not be deacted.

$$O_{deact}(a_1, ri_1^{r_1}) \Rightarrow \forall r_x \in R \ (\mathbb{R}_{aggr}(r_x, r_1) \wedge O_{deact}(a_1, ri^{r_x}))$$

Definition 6. (Remove) Finally, with remove operation, the agent also loses the capability of playing the role. This operation removes the resources of a role and every instances of it from the agent. Role remove is represented as $O_{remove}(a_1, r_1) \rightarrow K'_{passive}$ where $r_1 \epsilon R$ and $a_1 \epsilon A$.

$$\frac{K_{passive} = \langle g_a, p_a, \Sigma_a, \Pi_a \rangle \quad k_{r_1} = \langle g_{r_1}, p_{r_1}, \sigma_{r_1}, \pi_{r_1}, \mathbb{R} \rangle \quad O_{remove}(a_1, r_1)}{K'_{passive} = K_{passive} \setminus (\ k_{r_1} \ \cup \ \forall ri_x^{r_1}(k_{ri_x^{r_1}}))}$$

that is $K'_{passive} = \langle g_a \setminus g_{r_1}, p_a \setminus p_{r_1}, \Sigma'_a, \Pi'_a \rangle$ where $\Sigma'_a = \Sigma_a \setminus (\sigma_{r_1} \cup \forall ri_x^{r_1}(\sigma_{ri_x^{r_1}}))$ and $\Pi'_a = \Pi_a \setminus (\pi_{r_1} \cup \forall ri_x^{r_1}(\pi_{ri_x^{r_1}}))$.

If there is an instance of the role running on the agent, the role cannot be removed, $O_{remove}(a_1, r_1) \Rightarrow \forall ri_x^{r_1} \in Ri \ (O_{deact}(a_1, ri_x^{r_1}))$. Also, in order to remove a role which is depended on by another role with the relationship types of specification and aggregation must be removed, $O_{remove}(a_1, r_1) \Rightarrow \forall r_x \in R \ ((\mathbb{R}_{spec}(r_x, r_1) \vee \mathbb{R}_{aggr}(r_x, r_1)) \wedge O_{remove}(a_1, r_x))$.

3   The Architecture

We implemented a knowledgebase architecture, which supports the semantics detailed in the previous section, and incorporated it into the SEAGENT semantic web enabled multi-agent framework[9]. The SEAGENT framework handles all its artifacts such as roles, goals and plans within OWL ontologies. Since OWL is a description logic based knowledge representation language, the SEAGENT framework provides great facilities for implementing mentioned role-based knowledge semantics. In this section, we focus on our knowledgebase implementation and position it in SEAGENT framework.

Figure-2 represents the implementation of the proposed knowledgebase architecture within the SEAGENT framework. As indicated in the figure, two vertical layers compose the overall architecture. The first layer, called Execution Layer, provides planning and execution infrastructure for the SEAGENT agents. The second one, the Semantic Web Layer encapsulates the ontologies that represents the roles, goals, rules and domain specific concepts. This layer also represents the semantic web together with the local ontologies which imports the shared concepts published in the internet. The proposed knowledgebase architecture is composed of three sub-modules: Knowledge Manager, Active Knowledge and Passive Knowledge. The Passive Knowledge module is responsible for storing all local ontologies that are used by the agent. We provide an extensible support for different physical passive knowledge persistence solutions and there are two existing implementations as TDB and RDB light weight ontology storage based on Jena API[1]. On the other hand, Active Knowledge module serves a complete and consistent knowledge subset that is arranged from the passive knowledge in accordance with the active role instance and its dependencies. In fact, this knowledge is an in-memory ontology model that imports all active role instance related

---

[1] http://jena.sourceforge.net/DB/index.html

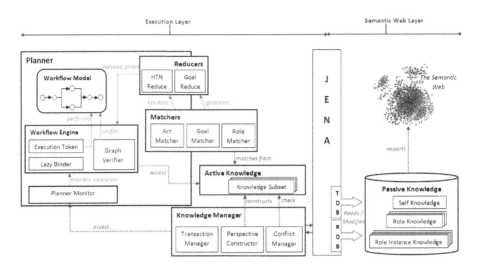

Fig. 2. SEAGENT Knowledgebase Architecture

ontologies and accessible from the tasks of the active role. Lastly, the Knowledge Manager module acts as a bridge between active and passive knowledge modules and has critical responsibilities such as, construction of active knowledge, ensuring the consistency of it and synchronization of the active and passive knowledge. To fulfill these responsibilities, the Knowledge Manager module is composed of three sub-modules that are Perspective Constructor, Transaction Manager and Conflict Manager. Following paragraphs detail the functionality of the Knowledge Manager module.

The Perspective Constructor module is in the charge of the construction of active knowledge. Figure-3 represents the algorithm that constructs the active knowledge. In accordance with the formerly proposed knowledge semantics, this algorithm takes the activated role instance as parameter and simply identifies a maximal related sub graph from a net of role and role instance relations. After the specification of role and role instances that are related with the activated role instance, their knowledge are read into active knowledge in accordance with their enactment type. This provides a consistent and well defined knowledge context, even agent enacts conflicting roles and participates in non-adaptive organizations. This knowledge serves agent a conception of world from the perspective of the active role instance.

Another important function of the Knowledge Manager is the concurrency management. Since selected storage infrastructure is a non-transactional media and we have different atomicity requirements, we implemented our own transaction management sub-system and this functionality is provided by the Transaction Manager sub-module. As emphasized previously, an agent may enact several roles concurrently (one actively at a time), and each role instance may execute several tasks in order to achieve several goals synchronously. However, the Transaction Manager module ensures that only one task can modify an ontology at a

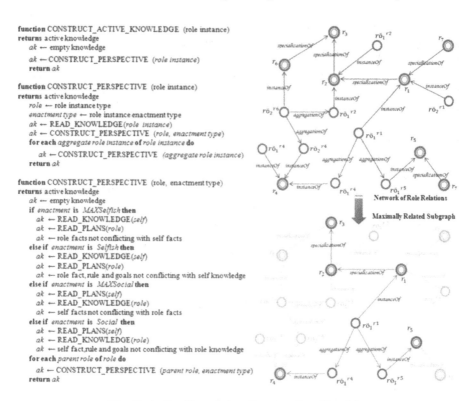

```
function CONSTRUCT_ACTIVE_KNOWLEDGE (role instance)
returns active knowledge
    ak ← empty knowledge
    ak ← CONSTRUCT_PERSPECTIVE (role instance)
    return ak

function CONSTRUCT_PERSPECTIVE (role instance)
returns active knowledge
    role ← role instance type
    enactment type ← role instance enactment type
    ak ← READ_KNOWLEDGE(role instance)
    ak ← CONSTRUCT_PERSPECTIVE (role, enactment type)
    for each aggregate role instance of role instance do
        ak ← CONSTRUCT_PERSPECTIVE (aggregate role instance)
    return ak

function CONSTRUCT_PERSPECTIVE (role, enactment type)
returns active knowledge
    ak ← empty knowledge
    if enactment is MAXSelfish then
        ak ← READ_KNOWLEDGE(self)
        ak ← READ_PLANS(role)
        ak ← role facts not conflicting with self facts
    else if enactment is Selfish then
        ak ← READ_KNOWLEDGE(self)
        ak ← READ_PLANS(role)
        ak ← role fact, rule and goals not conflicting with self knowledge
    else if enactment is MAXSocial then
        ak ← READ_PLANS(self)
        ak ← READ_KNOWLEDGE(role)
        ak ← self facts not conflicting with role facts
    else if enactment is Social then
        ak ← READ_PLANS(self)
        ak ← READ_KNOWLEDGE(role)
        ak ← self fact, rule and goals not conflicting with role knowledge
    for each parent role of role do
        ak ← CONSTRUCT_PERSPECTIVE (parent role, enactment type)
    return ak
```

Fig. 3. Active Knowledge Construction Algorithm

time via transaction. In the implementation of our concurrency control infrastructure, two-phase locking algorithm is adopted because of its simplicity and success in practice[13]. Also with the construction of our own transaction mechanism, we are enabled to redefine the atomicity of the knowledge transactions and agent goals are the best guide for this purpose. Transaction Manager commits all un-committed modifications, that are triggered by the task, in the case of achievement of the goal that the task contributes. Or, in the case of an exception that occurred during the execution of the task, all un-committed modifications are aborted. In the case of long-term goals, this approach may cause long-lived transactions that access large number of resources and this may cause deadlocks. To cope with this problem transactions can be prematurely committed within the tasks of the agent.

As a result of the agent's cognitive structure, agent learns and gains experience from its former actions. Besides, consistency of the agent knowledge shouldn't decay with this newly added or inferred knowledge. For each knowledge modification, Conflict Manager checks the consistency of the active knowledge and all suspending role instances' knowledge perspectives. Since the SEAGENT framework represents all knowledge artifacts with OWL ontologies, this consistency check is basically an ontology validation. But from the point of agent view, a concept's validity is only dependent on the agent's perception on that concept. Hence, open world assumption based inference engines are not sufficient for our requirements. We extended Eyeball[2] tool with new inspectors in order to detect and report goal and rule conflicts. When Conflict Manager distinguishes a knowledge modification that threaten the consistency of the active knowledge, it throws an exception and notifies the SEAGENT exception handler[14].

4   Case Study

This section presents a multi-organization application that is implemented with SEAGENT Multi-Agent Development Framework as a case study to emphasize and observe the benefits of the proposed knowledge architecture. In order to provide conflicting but not totally irrelevant roles to our agents, we preferred the barter domain. Figure-4 represents Corporate Barter and Barter Trade Exchange organizations' design model. The corporate barter organization, or peer to peer barter, is the most plain type of barter which is arranged between two companies who have mutually agreeable goods or services to swap evenly. Participants can openly determine the price of the goods being exchanged and offer discounts without inviting retaliation by competitors or existing customers. This type of organization is a free competition market, where every customer tries to be monopoly in its area of expertise. Hence, companies aim to dominate the market with creating competition via reducing prices and increasing product quality. Explicit representation of the corporate barter organizational rules that are applicable to the customer role are, *(ruleSet1)*:

PERMITTED(*customer* DO *overpricing(product)*)
PERMITTED(*customer* DO *underpricing(product)*)
PERMITTED(*customer* DO *offer_discount(product)*)
OBLIGED((*customer$_i$* DO *make_payment(customer$_j$, product$_i$)*)
IF(*customer$_j$* DO *make_payment(customer$_i$, product$_j$)*)
AND (*customer$_i$, customer$_j$* DO *accept_trade(product$_i$, product$_j$)*))

Similarly, barter trade exchange organization is a collection of businesses that trade their goods and services, managed by an intermediator. In this organization, businesses do not exchange goods directly as in the bilateral form of the corporate barter. Rather, barter trade exchanges is multilateral and participants only interacts with an intermediator. Another difference of barter trade exchange is the use of a form of private label currency. The customer role of this organization stimulates enactor agents to maximize their profit via increasing prices within the legal limits or reducing transportation cost by preferring nearby barter options. The rules and norms in the role description of the Customer role of barter trade exchange organization are, *(ruleSet2)*:

FORBIDDEN((*customer* DO *overpricing(product)*)
AND(*customer* DO *underpricing(product)* AND(*customer* DO *offer_discount(product)*)
IF(*customer* DO *violate_competition_legislation(product_price)*))),
OBLIGED((*customer* DO *make_payment(barter_manager, product$_i$)*)
OR (*make_payment(barter_manager, barter_dollar)*))
IF(*customer* DO *accept_trade(product$_i$, product$_j$)*)
OR *accept_trade(product$_i$, barter_dollar)*))

---

[2] http://jena.sourceforge.net/Eyeball/

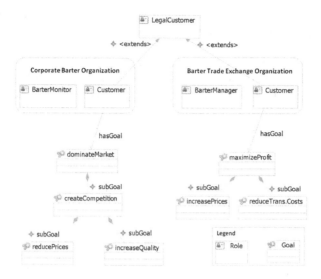

Fig. 4. Organization model

Also, both Customer roles extend from a more generic *Legal Customer* role that is supplied by a competent authority in order to ensure, without considering barter type, all customer roles respect the legislation. Such as, prohibiting barter of unmarketable goods like weapons, drugs and prostitution, or obligating companies to have appropriate license to sell goods that are permitted to be sold only by licensed sellers(such as alcohol), *(ruleSet3)*:

FORBIDDEN(*customer* DO *barter(weapon, drug, ...))*,
OBLIGED(*customer* DO *have(license)* IF(*customer* DO *barter(product)*
AND(*product* DO *require_ license(license)))*

In order to affirm the expediency of our approach, we will examine a case where a company agent participates *Corporate Barter Organization* and *Barter Trade Exchange Organization* by socially enacting both *Customer Roles* in order to achieve his self goal of consuming the company's unused stocks. Also, the self knowledge has a rule in sales as applying a fixed price to all goods and not making discounts regardless of the amount of the purchase. Similarly, he has a self rule in buying as only trading the indispensable goods, *(ruleSet4)*:

PERMITTED(*self* DO *barter(product)* IF(*self* DO *demand(product))),
FORBIDDEN(*self* DO *discount(product))*

While existing agent cognitive models refuse the simultaneous enactment of both customer roles because of their conflicting rules on pricing policies, it could be easily seen that this is not an uncommon and avoidable case. As a part of the solution that we proposed for this problem, SEAGENT agents stores both rules, as SWRL rules, and goals, as goal ontologies, into his passive knowledge. In a case where another agent, which is also participated in *Corporate Barter Organization,* makes a barter offer with a very low profit margin and even quite under the product's fair market value, our agent activates the appropriate role instance and evaluates his knowledge in order to make a decision.

With a traditional knowledgebase, both rule sets would be included in an aggregate agent knowledge and agent would query whole related and unrelated knowledge in order to make a decision. Correspondingly, while this very low profited barter is permitted by the *Corporate Barter Organization*, underpricing which violates competition legislation are banned in the *Barter Trade Exchange Organization*. Also, while *Corporate Barter Organization* permits offering discount, self of the agent adopts one-price policy:

PERMITTED(*customer* DO *underpricing*(*product*) - **from ruleSet1**
FORBIDDEN((*customer* DO *underpricing*(*product*) - **from ruleSet2**
IF(*customer* DO *violate_ competition_ legislation*(*product_price*))))
PERMITTED(*customer* DO *offer_ discount*(*product*)) - **from ruleSet1**
FORBIDDEN(*self* DO *discount*(*product*)) - **from ruleSet4**

On the other hand, in our approach with the activation of the customer role instance of the *Corporate Barter Organization,* the knowledge manager of the agent reconstitutes the active knowledge. In accordance with active knowledge construction semantics defined in previous section, this knowledge contains the active role instance's knowledge and since the enactment type is social, *Corporate Barter Organization*'s Customer role's knowledge, Legal Customer's knowledge and the subset of the self knowledge that does not conflict with the role knowledge. In the following rule-set, content of the active knowledge is shown.

PERMITTED(*customer* DO *overpricing*(*product*)),
PERMITTED(*customer* DO *underpricing*(*product*)),
PERMITTED(*customer* DO *offer_ discount*(*product*)),
OBLIGED((*customer$_i$* DO *make_ payment*(*customer$_j$*, *product$_i$*)
IF(*customer$_j$* DO *make_ payment*(*customer$_i$*, *product$_j$*)
AND (*customer$_i$*, *customer$_j$* DO *accept_ trade*(*product$_i$*, *product$_j$*))),
FORBIDDEN(*customer* DO *barter*(*weapon*, *drug*, ...)),
OBLIGED(*customer* DO *have*(*license*)
IF((*customer* DO *barter*(*product*)) AND(*product* DO *require_ license*(*license*))))),
PERMITTED(*self* DO *barter*(*product*)) IF(*self* DO *demand*(product)))

The constituted active knowledge that is clarified from conflicting and irrelevant knowledge represents the exact perception of the world of the activated role instance. Hence, this approach makes enactment of the roles which have conflicting knowledge possible and ensures the integrity of the global identity.

5   Related Work

In the agent research domain, there are some approaches which are motivated to handle inconsistent knowledge of agent by the approach of clustering[15,16]. In [16], Halpern and Fagin presents a model of local reasoning, where an agent's knowledge is handled as a "society of minds", each with its own cluster of beliefs, which may contradict with each other. In each frame of mind, the agent beliefs are consistent, but the conclusion that the agent draws in different frames of mind may be inconsistent. Differently from our role-based approach, in the model of this research, knowledge clusters are defined as non-interacting and agent can utilize only one cluster at a time. So, they develop a new modal operator to be able to define axioms that are true in all frames of the mind.

On the other hand Wassermann[15], similarly, proposes a belief base structure that simulate commonsense reasoning in an psychologically way, that amplify the RABIT system. This system consists of four modules: LTM(Long-Term Memory) that all agent beliefs are stored, STM(Short-Term Memory) which is a small subset of LTM where the reasoning (decision making) takes place, ITM(Intermediate-Term Memory) that stores the history of the reasoning process and finally RTM(Relevant-Term Memory) which is a kind of context, storing the relevant concepts. Also, an heuristic algorithm to retrieve the most relevant beliefs from a structured belief base(LTM) into the STM is introduced. But, because of the absence of a well defined context scope, we cannot affirm that the constructed STM embody the exact mental state of the agent.

Another research, that must be touched on here due to its conceptually similarity with our approach, is the VIKEF project[17]. The VIKEF project aims to create large-scale information systems that base on Semantic Web Technology. At the center of the system there is an RDF knowledge base which contains a large amount of information about documents and their contents. But, as a result of the nature of web, it is obvious that conflicting information will arise. To cope with this problem, they propose a context-based system to store semantically contradictory statements in the knowledge base. But they use relations between contexts, called compatibility relations, to gather related contexts differently from our role-based approach.

6 Conclusion

In this paper we propose a knowledgebase approach to increase applicability of role concept in the MAS research domain. While developing this role-based agent knowledgebase architecture, we dive into the depths of the role theory which is developed in consequence of sociological empirical researches. By the help of role theory, sociologists also use roles to predict human behaviors according to the body of knowledge about human organizations[1]. In the development of our knowledgebase approach, we inspire from the self concept that has an important place in the sociological role theory to resolve human behaviors in conflicting social positions.

We also implement this knowledge approach and integrate it into the SEAGENT multi-agent development framework[9]. The proposed knowledgebase architecture is separated into two parts; active and passive knowledge. Both knowledge parts consist of knowledge blocks each of which contains consistent information about agent, role or role instance. While in the passive knowledge persistence of knowledge blocks are provided, on the other hand, in the active knowledge related knowledge blocks are arranged in a consistent form to provide consistent knowledge to the agent for deterministic decision making. In Section 2, we declare the semantics of these knowledge blocks and how active and passive knowledge evolve in the life-cycle of role-based agent. To measure applicability of our approach and ensure the implemented architecture, we also develop a case study in electronic barter domain application in Section 4. Within the case study, we observe that an agent can play roles which have conflicting knowledge. In the further steps of this research, we aim to cope with management of the knowledge from the organizational perspective.

References

1. Biddle, B.J.: Recent developments in role theory. Annual Review of Sociology 12, 67–92 (1986)
2. Allen, V.L., van de Vliert, E.: A role theoretical perspective on transitional processes. Role Transitions: Explorations and Explanations, 3–18 (1984)
3. Dastani, M.M., van Riemsdijk, M.B., Hulstijn, J., Dignum, F.P.M., Meyer, J.-J.C.: Enacting and deacting roles in agent programming. In: Odell, J.J., Giorgini, P., Müller, J.P. (eds.) AOSE 2004. LNCS, vol. 3382, pp. 189–204. Springer, Heidelberg (2005)
4. Dastani, M., Dignum, V., Dignum, F.: Role-assignment in open agent societies. In: Autonomous agents and multiagent systems (AAMAS), pp. 489–496. ACM, New York (2003)
5. Marks, M.S.M., Stephen, R.: Multiple roles and the self: a theory of role balance. Journal of Marriage and the Family (1996)
6. Goffman, E.: The Presentation of Self in Everyday Life. Anchor (June 1959)
7. Stryker, S., Serpe, R.T.: Identity salience and psychological centrality: Equivalent, overlapping, or complementary concepts? Social Psychology Quarterly 57, 16–35 (1994)
8. Zhang, X., Xu, H., Shrestha, B.: An integrated role-based approach for modeling, designing and implementing multi-agent systems. Journal of the Brazilian Computer Society (JBCS) 13, 45–60 (2007)
9. Dikenelli, O.: Seagent mas platform development environment. In: Autonomous Agents and Multiagent Systems, pp. 1671–1672 (2008)
10. Kristensen, B.B., Osterbye, K.: Roles: conceptual abstraction theory and practical language issues. Theor. Pract. Object Syst. 2(3), 143–160 (1996)
11. Vázquez-Salceda, J., Dignum, V., Dignum, F.: Organizing multiagent systems. Autonomous Agents and Multi-Agent Systems 11(3), 307–360 (2005)
12. Giorgini, P., Müller, J.P., Odell, J.J. (eds.): AOSE 2003. LNCS, vol. 2935. Springer, Heidelberg (2004)
13. Bernstein, P.A., Hadzilacos, V., Goodman, N.: Concurrency control and recovery in database systems. Addison-Wesley Longman Publishing Co., Inc., Amsterdam (1987)
14. Cakirlar, I., Ekinci, E.E., Dikenelli, O.: Exception handling in goal-oriented multiagent systems. In: Proceedings of the workshop Engineering Societies in the Agents World IX. Springer, Heidelberg (2009)
15. Wassermann, R.: On structured belief bases. In: Frontiers in Belief Revision. Applied Logic Series, vol. 22, pp. 349–369. Kluwer Academic, Dordrecht (2001)
16. Fagin, R., Halpern, J.Y.: Belief, awareness, and limited reasoning. Artificial Intelligence 34(1), 39–76 (1987)
17. Stoermer, H., Palmisano, I., Redavid, D., Iannone, L., Bouquet, P., Semeraro, G.: Contextualization of a RDF knowledge base in the VIKEF project. In: Sugimoto, S., Hunter, J., Rauber, A., Morishima, A. (eds.) ICADL 2006. LNCS, vol. 4312, pp. 101–110. Springer, Heidelberg (2006)

Balancing Organizational Regulation and Agent Autonomy: An MDE-Based Approach[*]

Loris Penserini[1], Virginia Dignum[1], Athanasios Staikopoulos[2],
Huib Aldewereld[1], and Frank Dignum[1]

[1] Universiteit Utrecht - Institute of Information and Computing Sciences
P.O. Box 80089, 3508 TB Utrecht, The Netherlands
{loris,dignum,virginia,huib}@cs.uu.nl
[2] Trinity College Dublin, Computer Science, Ireland
AthanasiosStaikopoulos@cs.tcd.ie

Abstract. The deployment of agent societies —as complex systems— in dynamic and unpredictable settings brings forth critical issues concerning their design. Organizational models have been advocated to specify open systems in dynamic environments in order to accomplish the need to represent regulating structures explicitly and independently from acting components (or agents). Despite the fact that several frameworks have been proposed for the specification of organizational models, it is still a matter of design choice how to balance between regulative design and component flexibility.

We propose a design framework, discussing the advantages of having different degrees of abstraction at organizational level in the development of agent societies. That is, we illustrate how the design properties impact the flexibility of run-time systems to cope with context changes. We adopt the OperA software engineering methodology to deal with the organizational model specification, and the Model Driven Engineering (MDE) mechanisms to map concepts between different design models.

1 Introduction

To empower individuals and human organizations to achieve their goals and perform their tasks effectively, we need systems that are aware of dynamic and usually unpredictable physical and organizational/social contexts where tasks are performed. The current trend is that an increasing number of entities, from smart personal devices to legacy databases, are controlled by software agents. The deployment of agent societies in dynamic and unpredictable settings brings forth critical issues concerning the design, implementation and validation of their behavior [11,7,4]. Changes in the environment lead to alterations on the effectiveness of the organization and therefore in a need to reorganize, or at least, the need to consider the consequences of the change to the organizations effectiveness and possibly efficiency.

---

[*] This work has been performed in the framework of the FP7 project ALIVE IST-215890, which is funded by the European Community. The author(s) would like to acknowledge the contributions of his (their) colleagues from ALIVE Consortium (http://www.ist-alive.eu)

H. Aldewereld, V. Dignum, and G. Picard (Eds.): ESAW 2009, LNAI 5881, pp. 197–212, 2009.

Organizational models have been advocated to specify open systems in dynamic environments. By open we mean that components are not designed nor controlled by a common entity, and by dynamic we mean that unplanned and unspecified changes may occur at run time. That is, there is a need to represent the regulating structures explicitly and independently from the acting components (or agents). Organization models comprise structural and behavioral aspects [11,7]. Structural aspects include the formal patterns of relationships between groups and individuals, and the norms that govern their interactions, while behavioral aspects include processes, rules, activities, and operational methods. Depending on the specific situation, a change may affect the structural aspects or the behavior aspects.

Several frameworks have been proposed for the specification of organizational models. However, it is still a matter of design choice how to balance between regulative design and component flexibility. In this paper, we present some initial considerations towards the formalization of design guidelines for organizational models and apply these to the case of modeling of crisis management systems in the Netherlands [12]. The work reported in this paper is part of the general development framework within the European FP7 ALIVE project. In particular, with respect to the proposed ALIVE design framework, we discuss possible advantages of having different levels —i.e., *Organizational* and *Coordination* — in the design process of agent-based systems. That is, we illustrate how the design properties impact the flexibility of run-time systems to cope with context changes. We adopt and combine the OperA methodology [5] to deal with the organizational model specification, and the Model Driven Engineering (MDE) mechanisms [1] —i.e., MDA based transformations [8]— to map concepts between the different levels of abstraction.

The paper is organized as follows: Section 2 gives an overview of the ALIVE design framework that includes the OperA methodology and the MDE techniques. Section 3 briefly sketches a case study about The Netherlands procedures to cope with a crisis management scenario. Section 4 provides some intuitions about the effects of having a more or a less abstract organizational model specification over the (run-time) agents autonomy. In Section 5, we illustrate how MDE techniques facilitate the regulation of the level of design abstraction. In Section 6, we apply our approach to a real case study of organizational models. Section 7 provides some preliminary remarks about advantages and disadvantages of our approach. Finally, Section 8 gives some conclusions.

2   Background

2.1   The ALIVE Approach

The ALIVE project aims to apply organizational concepts to the design and implementation of service-based software systems. The main focus of the project is to create complex systems based on the composition of (existing) services, through the addition of levels of abstraction. The project extends the current trend in service-oriented engineering by combining the latest in coordination and organization mechanisms and model driven design to create a framework for software and service engineering for "live" open systems of active services. An overview of the project's architecture is given in figure 1.

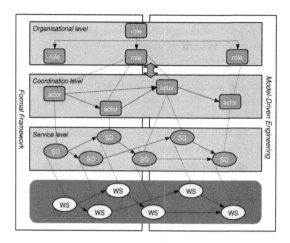

Fig. 1. The ALIVE framework for software and service engineering

- The *Service Level* (SL) augments and extends existing service models with semantic descriptions to make components aware of their social context and of the rules of engagement with other services.
- The *Coordination Level* (CL) provides the means to specify, at a high level, the patterns (workflows) of interaction between services, using a variety of powerful coordination techniques from recent European research in the area.
- The *Organization Level* (OL) provides context for the other levels – specifying the organizational rules that govern interaction and using recent developments in organizational dynamics to allow the structural adaptation of distributed systems over time.

The advantage of added levels of abstraction to the design process of systems based on the composition of services is two-fold: 1) it is more intuitive to think in organizational structures and interactions while designing complex interactions for services, and the addition of these layers of abstraction allows for a gradual (fluent) transition from the system as foreseen to the actual implementation; 2) when changes happen in the environment (e.g., specific services become unavailable) the added levels of abstraction are an explicit representation of the conceptual steps made at design, thus giving additional information on why certain interactions (between the services) are as they are, which enables the system to dynamically cope with the changes.

OL and CL have different philosophies: CL takes a bottom-up approach to modeling, by describing the behavior of the system as a plan workflow by describing the individual behavior of agents and specifying their activities. OL takes a top-down view, by describing the objectives of an organization. OL defines the desired result of the collective behavior, whereas CL describes the practice (i.e., the individual activities and interactions) that leads to that result. The difference in the viewpoints becomes clear when we compare the models used at OL and CL, as detailed below.

In the rest of this paper, we focus our attention on OL and CL. Specifically, we illustrate how different degrees of design abstractions at OL and CL may be affected by context changes that force the system to adapt.

The Organization Level of ALIVE. The *Organizational Level (OL)* defines the organizational structure of the society, describing roles and interactions, as intended by the organizational stakeholders. The OL specification is based on the OperA framework [5]. OperA enables the specification of abstractions, suitable both to model and study existing societies, as well as to develop new systems that participate in an organizational context. The main focus of OperA enable a suitable balance between global aims and requirements agent autonomy, their coordination needs, and environmental stakeholders' needs.

At the OL, social structures (describing roles and their relationships) as interaction structures (describing abstract patterns of interaction) and norms (describing organizational rules and requirements) are specified. These form the basis for the design of the coordination layer, by providing the organization information that agents will require to enact roles in the organization.

The Social Structure specifies objectives of the society, its roles and what kind of model governs coordination. The Social Structure is typically depicted in a role-dependency graph (e.g., Figure 2). Normative structures describe how to shape the freedom of role-enacting agents within the organization. While the Social Structure diagram deals with organizational objectives and social responsibilities between organizational roles, and the Normative Structure describes the regulations that hold in an organizations, the Interaction Structure specifies how to fulfill responsibilities and to achieve objectives, while still remaining compliant with a normative dimension (cf, Figure 6). Interaction Structure diagrams specify a partial ordering of the activities within the organization defined in terms of scenes and scene transitions. It abstracts over how the activities are done, but defines in which order what is supposed to happen such that organizational objectives are met without violating any organizational rules.

Interaction Scenes describe a scenario of activity, that is, how roles can interact and evolve. A scene is described by its players, results and the norms regulating the interaction (cf, Figure 6.(B)). Within a scene, *landmarks* define important states in the scene execution, that is, states that must be reached in any interaction between players to achieve a scene result. Landmark patterns provide a partial ordering of scene states (cf, Figure 6.(C)).

The Coordination Level of ALIVE. The OL provides the overall organization design that fulfills the stakeholders requirements. However, it does not specify how to structure groups of agents and constrain their behavior by social rules such that their combined activity will lead to the desired results. Coordination can be defined as the process of managing dependencies between activities [9]. That is, one way to coordinate is to manage functional dependencies. In this sense, coordination refers to task sharing and management, such that individual and shared goals are achieved. Another view is that of the system as an organization where dependencies are captured through supervision (e.g. influence, authority, etc.) and collaboration (e.g. teams) relationships between agents. In this sense, coordination refers to the specification of power and authority relations between agents.

2.2 Model Driven Engineering

Model Driven Engineering (MDE) [1] refers to the systematic use of models as primary artifacts throughout the Software Engineering (SE) development process. A model-driven approach to development is generally based on the Model Driven Architecture (MDA) [8] that is an initiative from OMG[1] specifying a framework of open standards and related technologies. The framework is built upon the metamodel foundation in order to enable a standard specification and inter-operability mechanism for tools. So systems and applications are formalized with metamodel descriptions and are visualized by models as metamodel instantiations. Actual code implementations are created automatically by applying predefined transformations from source models to target models and implementation languages.

In the context of this paper, MDE specifies the organization and coordination layers, upon which special purpose tools (editors) are created, allowing the modeling and instantiation of corresponding models. Moreover, constraint rules in the form of OCL expressions are attached to the metamodels to validate models during instantiation as well as transformations are applied to integrate ALIVE across its layers.

3   Motivating Scenario

Incident Management refers to the activities of an organization to identify, analyze and correct hazards. The Netherlands has an extensive crisis management structure to respond to incidents that affect public order. A layered model, the Coordinated Regional Incident-Management Procedure (GRIP), is a nationwide emergency management procedure based on the severity of the disaster, and allows local, regional and national authorities to take action where necessary. The aim of the procedure is to enable the adequate response to the situation, with a minimum level of disruption of the public life. The procedure is currently used by emergency services, different layers of government and government agencies. Table 1 gives an overview of reach and procedures of the different levels.

These GRIP procedures are a motivating use-case for ALIVE as a scenario in which changes in the environment affect organizations [12]. Following the ALIVE method, a distinction is made between organizational structures, specified in the OL (i.e. the structural aspects of the system), and coordination activities, specified in the CL as multi-agent systems (i.e. the behavioral aspects of the system). One aim of ALIVE is to support smooth transition between different disaster levels and maintain consistency of operation, by providing a flexible formal model for the GRIP procedures.

The organizational model describes the abstract purposes of the system. That is, the organizational model describes the objectives and requirements for the organization; it describes the reason for which the organization is created and/or laws or regulations imposed on the organization by external institutions. In the GRIP procedures these can be, for instance, the overall objective to "solve crises" (holds over all possible environments) or abstract maintenance goals like "minimize casualties", "minimize structural

---

[1] Object Management Group, see http://www.omg.org/

Table 1. GRIP levels of incident management

Phase	Affected area	Coordination
GRIP 0	Day-to-day routine operations	-
GRIP 1	Incident of limited proportions	Duty officers
GRIP 2	Incident with a definite effect on the surrounding area	Local commander
GRIP 3	Threatened well-being of (large groups of) the population within a single municipality	Mayor
GRIP 4	Province or country level	Queen's Commissioner

damage", and "minimize cost". There are obviously, many different ways in which to specify these issues.

Design decisions taken at OL have consequences for the possibilities at CL. For example, assume that at OL it is explicitly defined that *evacuation of casualties* is a task of the *medics* role and to be done using an *ambulance* by a team of exactly 3 players (the *driver*, the *nurse* and the *first-aid specialist*). This choice gives a very precise description to the CL on how to deploy agents for this task and how to define a concrete evacuation plan. On the other hand, it can be decided at the OL that *evacuation of casualties* is the objective of the crises-solvers. This leaves open the possibility, in case of need, to request a bystander to use her car to take some casualties to the hospital, which may be more efficient if no medics are around. However, such a design decision requires a more complex solution at CL, given that less handles are provide about which are the capabilities and requirements of specific agents, who must be endowed with the capabilities to reason about their position in the organization.

Abstract organization models are flexible and robust as they can accommodate many changes in the environment; however, these models may not give enough information to generate an efficient coordination model. This would be the case of the GRIP 'free' model depicted in Figure 2. Similarly, concrete organization models are more efficient as they describe capabilities and requirements in great detail but will need to be reorganized in face of environmental changes. This implies the specification of a detailed

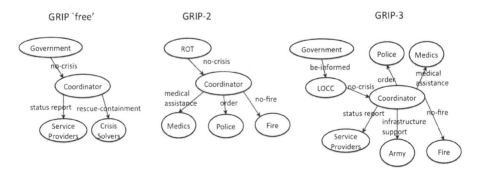

Fig. 2. Possible organizational models at different levels of abstraction, by OperA's Social Structure diagrams

organizational model for each GRIP level, as the models for GRIP-2 and GRIP-3 in Figure 2 plus the reorganization rules to change between these models. The issue is thus to decide when to choose a flexible and robust organizational model, and when to choose a highly descriptive and efficient model.

4   Balance Regulation and Flexibility

As discussed in the previous section, at the highest level of abstraction, organization models represent all institutional norms with the minimum constraints for agents. At the lowest level of abstraction, organizations describe one, proven, process that guarantees full compliance to organizational norms and objectives. In [7] and [11] a formal description in terms of graph theory is proposed for quantifying to what extent organizational structures enjoy specific characteristics such as robustness, flexibility and efficiency. These formal properties can be used to determine the level of specificity of the organizational model. That is, given different organizational models, it can be determined which one provides the highest flexibility, and which one the highest efficiency.

Basically, the spectrum of choices concerning the level of abstraction of the organization model ranges between the following two extremes:

Most Abstract. The organization model consists of only one role, which has one objective corresponding to the global objective of the organization, and as norms all the organizational norms. This requires the Coordination Level (CL) to have the capabilities to interpret such description in the context, and decide on the best transformation into concrete plans and activities.

Most Concrete. The organization model includes many roles with detailed objectives and sub-objectives. Interaction scenes and the partial ordering of scenes provide all the details needed to generate a complete plan that fixes activity such that there is no room for interpretation. Structures at CL can be obtained by a translation mechanism and therefore there is no need for decision making capabilities at CL.

As detailed by examples in the next sections, different degrees of abstraction reflect also on the single agent autonomy required to accomplish organizational objectives. Intuitively, if more detailed specification is given at OL, less alternative ways (autonomy) for agents at CL to achieve the organizational objectives are left. So, despite the fact that we often desire agents to be highly autonomous (e.g., see [4]), we also expect agents to adhere to institutional norms that regiment their activities and, hence, reduce their autonomy. The OperA modeling language adopted at OL does not have the goal of guaranteeing agent autonomy but rather of coping with the given autonomy. Nevertheless, by the separation of concerns along three levels (*organizational*, *coordination* and *service*), the ALIVE design framework helps designers to better regulate agent autonomy simply intervening in the specification of each level. Of course, the autonomy property is also often used as an indicator to establish the system flexibility to adapt to context changes, as discussed next.

5   MDE to Guarantee Flexibility-Regulation Balance

This section describes a concrete MDA approach to support the design of organizational models with different degrees of abstraction as well as the modification of their underlying coordination model as a result of an organizational adaptation. As it is explained, the design property impacts the flexibility of run-time systems to cope with context changes. That is, the adaptation process of the run-time system may require changes either within models at CL —e.g., agents' workflows— or within both CL and OL —e.g., agents' workflows and the organization's Social Structure. Figure 3 outlines in terms of MDA concepts, the two principal modeling scenarios discussed along the paper.

As it is illustrated in the first case (Figure 3.(A)), the abstract GRIP 'free' organizational model is capable to effectively capture both scenarios of GRIP-2 and GRIP-3 (at OL) with no modifications. As a result this design solution provides ultimate flexibility and dynamicity for the OL. While, the coordination models need to be modified to reflect changes on agents and workflows involved. In this case both GRIP-2 and GRIP-3 coordination models are associated with the same abstract organizational model making the generation process rather generic, so agents playing the same role are treated similarly ignoring their specific/individual capabilities and requirements.

In the second case, the escalation of scenario from GRIP-2 to GRIP-3 requires both the modification (with new organizational roles and regulations) of the organizational models and their corresponding coordination models. This more concrete design approach may compromise adaptation flexibility, however it provides more elaborate mappings among the organizational and coordination models, thus providing more elaborate workflows due to enhanced regulations.

In MDA, the OL and CL dependencies are formulated with model driven mappings (relations). The mappings are specified with a transformation language, among the corresponding elements of the OL and CL metamodels shown in Figure 4 and Figure 5 respectively. As illustrative examples, the mappings among `sceneToAgents`, `playerToAgent`, `landmarkToCompositeTask` and `sceneResults` have been specified. So, the transformation process can be initiated from the `sceneToAgents` mapping that creates a number of agents from the players of a scene. The rule in turn applies a mapping among a player and an agent, which based on the interaction patterns identified in the scene for that player creates a number of ordered task lists. A particular ordered task list is derived from the *from* and *to*

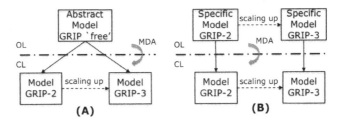

Fig. 3. Modeling alternatives at OL: (A) an abstract model and (B) a detailed model for every crisis situation

landmarks that are mapped to composite tasks, and a flow that connects tasks as a result of the partial order is created. Similarly the results (e.g., sub-objectives) of a scene are mapped to workflow tasks.

```
mapping sceneToAgents(in s: OL::Scene, inout wf:Workflow) {
  var agents:= s.players->collect(pl| map
  playerToAgent(agentNames, pl, s));
}
mapping playerToAgent(in agentName:String, in pl:OL::Player, in
  s:OL::Scene, inout wf:Workflow):Agent{
  name := agentName; play := pl.playerID;
  participate += object CL::Partition{
    agent := result;
    task += s.interactionPattern->collect(x|
    map createOrderedTaskLists(x, wf)); };
}
mapping createOrderedTaskLists(in lp: OL::LandmarkPattern,
  inout wf:Workflow):Sequence(CompositeTask){
  var partialOrders := lp.landmarkOrder;
  result := partialOrders->collect(x:OL::PartialOrder|
  map createOrderedTaskList(x, wf));
}
mapping createOrderedTaskList(in po:OL::PartialOrder,
  inout wf:Workflow):Sequence(CompositeTask){
  var ct1 := map landmarkToCompositeTask(po.from);
  var ct2 := map landmarkToCompositeTask(po.to);
  var flow := object Flow{};
  ct1.outgoing->append(flow); ct2.incoming->append(flow);
  wf.edge +=flow; result +=ct1; result +=ct2;
}
mapping landmarkToCompositeTask(in l:OL::Landmark):CompositeTask{
  result := object CL::CompositeTask{
  name := l.name;};
  ...}
mapping sceneResults(in s:OL::Scene, inout wf:Workflow):
  Sequence(SimpleTask){
  result+= s.results->collect(x| x.stateDescription->
  map toSimpleTask());
  ...}
mapping OL::PartialStateDescription:: toSimpleTask():SimpleTask{
  name:= self.stateDescription;
  ...}
```

When an abstract organizational model is used as a source of the mapping definitions only a few elements are resolved, associated with general capabilities. In the second case where the source model is more elaborate the mapping can produce more detailed Agent specifications with specific capabilities.

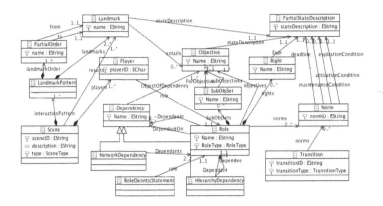

Fig. 4. OperA Meta-Model fragment

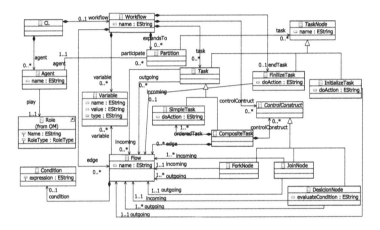

Fig. 5. Coordination Meta-Model fragment

6   Organizational Structure Design

This section provides some details about how to use the modeling language of our ALIVE design famework. According to Figure 3, the focus is on how context changes may affect the whole system, considering both a more and a less abstract organizational model at OL. The features of the ALIVE design framework are illustrated by the crisis scenario through some examples of MDA transformation rules.

6.1   Abstract OL

This is the case where at OL the designer provides an organizational model that abstracts from the GRIP crisis situations, i.e., as shown by *GRIP 'free'* model of Figure 2. The abstraction level adopted for dealing with the social structure of the organization

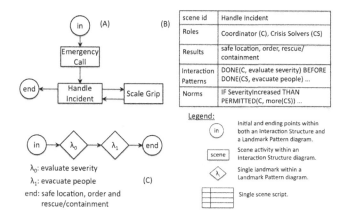

Fig. 6. Modeling fragments at OL: (A) Interaction Structure, (B) scene script for `Handle Incident` and its (C) landmark pattern, referred to the *GRIP 'free'* model of Figure 2

also reflects onto its interaction structure, as pointed out by Figure 6. Figure 6.(A) defines a partial ordering of activities (scenes) within the organization to fulfill the main objective `no-crisis`. Moreover, within each scene, the designer may describe how roles interact and evolve, expected results and norms regulating the interactions, as shown in Figure 6.(B) and (C).

In the abstract OL, the landmark pattern provided for the scene `Handle Incident` only specifies two important objectives (landmark states) to be achieved by role enacting agents within the scene execution. In particular, each agent that enacts the role of `Coordinator` has at least to reach the state `evaluate severity` and each agent that enacts the role of `Crisis Solvers` has at least to reach the state `evacuate people` in order to correctly fulfill the scene results. This level of details are quite far from what actual agents require at CL to effectively deal with a `Handle Incident` activity (a complex task) within a crisis scenario. For example, Figure 7 gives an idea of how complex the workflow of agent tasks can be[2] at CL to deal with the expected results from scene `Handle Incident`, i.e., safe location, street order, rescue and containment.

Thus if we apply the transformation description (`sceneToAgents`) upon the organizational model, an incomplete coordination model is derived. Therefore, even if some OL concepts can be mapped into the CL, a lot of information is missing and has to be captured within the CL, e.g., by providing agents that embed more complex activities than required. That is, the more abstract the OL specification, the more freedom for the agents at CL to choose the way to fulfill organizational objectives. For coping with the crisis situation of GRIP-2, a possible workflow required at CL —mainly to achieve the results required by scene `Handle Incident`— is described by Figure 7. It is worth noticing that the single landmark `evacuate people` —λ_0: specified at OL— is mapped into three main CL workflow tasks —

---

[2] This design concept 'task' is used to model both an agent's complex plan and an agent's simple atomic action, as for the scope of this paper the distinction is not relevant.

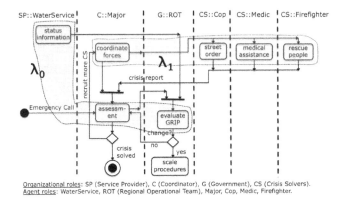

Fig. 7. Possible workflow model at CL to deal with the scene Handle Incident of Figure 6 when severity is at GRIP-2

status information, assessment and evaluate GRIP—belonging to the roles Service Providers, Coordinator and Government respectively, reflecting the more complex level of details as well as the extended freedom given to the agents in order to achieve an objective.

In the case of a transformation, the landmark evacuate people produces a composite task with corresponding agents, which are derived from the corresponding players of the scene. However, the composite task cannot be decomposed further into two simple tasks as such details are not provided yet. Moreover, in GRIP-2, the expertise of several agents is needed to cope with the crisis, e.g., agents Cop, Medic and Firefighter comply with and enact the role Crisis Solvers and how they should coordinate with each other is not detailed within the landmark patterns of scenes. So, workflow constructs such as ForkNode and JoinNode cannot be created to impose the ordering of single tasks that are created from the result mapping (sceneResults). According to our crisis management scenario, we describe here a possible context change that forces the whole ALIVE organizational setting to adapt. In particular, we discuss how these changes impact design models provided at CL and OL as illustrated in Figure 3.(A).

Scenario 1. *While the crisis organization is involved in a GRIP-2 level of a floodwater incident, the river that crosses a big city has breached its banks. This causes the roads into (or out of) the incident location to get blocked and cannot be used for wounded and people evacuation any longer. This context change also forces the Government to scale up to the GRIP-3 level.*

The regulation imposed by the organizational model *GRIP 'free'* —i.e., see Figure 2 and Figure 6— remains still valid to cope with Scenario 1. Nevertheless, as partially described by Figure 7, this workflow is not suitable anymore for the new crisis situation and a new workflow model is needed at CL. For example, new agents playing roles along with new rights come to play at GRIP-3 of incident handling, e.g., as the mayors of the affected towns are coordinated and supervised by a regional coordinating team (LOCC) that keeps the Minister of Internal Affairs (Government) informed about the actual crisis situation, i.e., see the social structure diagram of Figure 2.(GRIP-3). In this case, the transformation process (`playerToAgent`) is parameterized from domain knowledge as follows: `playerToAgent('Major', C)` and `playerToAgent('LOCC', C)`.

Finally, with MDA many of the normative rules defined in OL models can be translated into OCL rules in CL models, so the generated coordination models can be validated after a transformation or an adaptation process.

6.2 Specific OL

In this section, we discuss the case where at OL the designer provides an organizational model specifically tailored to a crisis situation, e.g., let us consider the case of GRIP-2. A possible resulting model is defined by the social structure of Figure 2.(GRIP-2) and by the interaction structure of Figure 8 but except for the scene `Mobilise` along with any reference to the role `Army`, as it comes to play within the crisis only at GRIP-3 and GRIP-4.

The more accurate level of details also is reflected by landmark patterns of scenes, as partially shown in Figure 8.(C). That is, an MDA transformation can produce the workflow of Figure 7 as almost a straight interpretation of the OL model. For example, the previous freedom at CL of choosing the three agents —Cop, `Medic` and `Firefighter`— to deal with `Handle Incident` activities at GRIP-2 is lost. In fact, now by the landmark pattern of Figure 8.(C) the need of the three agents along with their required abilities is precisely defined by:

$DONE(P, street\_order) BEFORE$

$(DONE(M, medical\_assistance)\ AND\ DONE(F, no\_fire))$

So, the transformation of scene results (`sceneResults`) will produce a detailed workflow fragment of tasks with the imposed ordering and concurrency derived from the landmark pattern. Moreover, instead of the previous generic role of

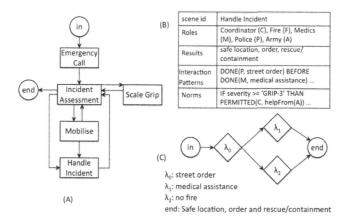

Fig. 8. Modeling fragments at OL: (A) Interaction Structure, (B) scene script for `Handle Incident` and its (C) landmark pattern, referred to the *GRIP-3* model of Figure 2

`Crisis Solvers` (CS) played by three different agents —`CS::Cop`, `CS::Medic` and `CS::Firefighter`— now the workflow is more elaborated with `P::Cop`, `M::Medic` and `F::Firefighter` where `P`, `M` and `F` corresponding to well defined organizational roles `Police`, `Medics` and `Firefighter` respectively, along with their required abilities and rights.

Considering the previous Scenario 1, the context change forces the organization to adapt but this time the organizational model proposed in Figure 2.(GRIP-2) is not valid anymore to deal with GRIP-3. The change from GRIP-2 to GRIP-3 introduces some new organizational roles and changes in the hierarchical structure of the role interactions. For example, the National Operational Coordination Center (`LOCC`) of the Dutch Ministry of Interior and Kingdom Relations comes into play with the responsibility to monitor and support the activities of the pool of majors involved into the crisis. That is, the proposed model for GRIP-3 (see Figure 2) considers a local dimension for the `Coordinator` that is enacted by any involved major along with the required local handling forces. Moreover, within the organizational model of GRIP-2 there is no role (e.g., `Crisis Solvers`) that may abstract on possible `Army` enacting agents needed at GRIP-3.

7   Consequences for Agent Design

Role description as provided by the OL modeling is a "position" to be filled by a player [10]. At CL, roles will be (temporarily) assigned to players. For example, in GRIP 1, the role of crisis coordinator is assigned to the first official to arrive on the scene. A role may be temporarily unassigned, without necessarily leading to a failure in the operation of the system. From the perspective of the organization it does not matter whether policewoman Alice or policeman Bob take the coordinator role, as long as they both have sufficient capability. The ability to dynamically bind different players to roles gives the organization a degree of adaptability in meeting changing goals and environments.

A role player who is bound to a role in an organizational structure needs an ability to perform the assigned role. This capabilities include [2]:

– Execution of function defined by the role or imposed by role relationships, including the ability to use resources available to the role.
– Ability to communicate, as a proxy for its role, with players of other roles.
– Ability to reason about what plans and activities can be used to achieve role objectives (landmark states).

In particular this last capability requires different skills, depending on the level of abstraction of the OL specification. From the perspective of a role player, the role description provides a, more or less abstract, definition of the organizational knowledge and skills required to adequately perform the role. That is, different levels of abstraction of OL models have consequences for the capabilities required from CL agents, i.e., in its operational knowledge or know-how. Role players need to evaluate the context and determine fulfillment of the role. This demands observation and reasoning skills for the agents in order to adapt to different contexts and determine plans and operational activities to enact the role. Communication between agents is necessary, and robustness of the system is rather dependent on the monitoring process. Nevertheless, when agents are designed for a specific role, they cannot accommodate large changes in the context.

Taking the crisis management scenario as an example, we can identify the following characteristics of the different abstraction choices:

Case 1. Abstract emergency management description at OL.

In this situation, the crisis management model at OL is abstract enough to incorporate all GRIP situations. Specific models for each GRIP level need to be defined at CL, but they still have to adhere to those regulations inherited from OL by MDA transformations.

 – Advantages: Only requires organizational verification for one model, MDA model transformations guarantee link between OL and CL. Furthermore, dynamic changes are dealt with at CL affecting only the current GRIP model, enabling a stable OL model. Less regulations inherited from OL allows agents more freedom to search for optimized ways of achieving organizational objectives.
 – Disadvantages: There is a need for CL-designers to be able to acquire the lacking OL specification, e.g., manually and/or by other design tools. Hence, the CL-designer has also to be a domain expert in order to correlate agent capabilities with organizational objectives and norms.

Case 2. Specific GRIP descriptions at OL.

 – Advantages: The verification of each GRIP is done at OL level (e.g., making use of OperettA verification capabilities [6]). The CL model is explicitly generated for each GRIP, limiting the need of acquiring context information at CL.
 – Disadvantages: Change dynamics are required at OL which implies a more complex change strategy, as changes at OL have consequences for all models at CL. Interpretation of GRIP at CL is fixed by the OL-CL transformation, which means that it is not possible to incorporate specific agent capabilities.

Another important issue is the evolution of situation knowledge. If we keep the knowledge coupled to a role, then it can be transferred to any agent enacting that role (e.g. when the role of coordinator moves from police officer to mayor). If we keep knowledge at agent level, then explicit 'debriefing' is needed when roles change. Comprehensive solutions for this issue require complex agents that are able to reason about their own objectives and desires and thus decide and negotiate their participation in an organization [3].

8 Conclusions

The proposed work shows features and discusses the applicability of a design framework for software and service engineering of systems deployed in highly dynamic contexts. We illustrated that the modularity (levels: OL, CL and SL) of our design framework helps designers in separation of concerns, making it easier and more precise to regulate agent autonomy by simply intervening in the specification of each level. Moreover, we focused on how context changes may affect the system flexibility to adapt, considering both a more and a less abstract organizational model at OL. We adopt and apply the

OperA methodology to deal with the organizational model specification, and the MDA transformation techniques to map concepts between the different levels of abstraction at OL and CL. We motivate and actually apply our ideas within the case of modeling of crisis management systems in the Netherlands.

References

1. Brown, A.W., Conallen, J., Tropeano, D.: Introduction: Models, Modelling and Model Driven Architecture (MDA). Springer, Heidelberg (2005)
2. Colman, A., Han, J.: Roles, players and adaptive organisations. Applied Ontology: An Inter. Journal of Ontological Analysis and Conceptual Modeling (2), 105–126 (2007)
3. Dastani, M., Dignum, V., Dignum, F.: Role assignment in open agent societies. In: AAMAS 2003. ACM Press, New York (2003)
4. Dignum, M., Weigand, H.: I am autonomous, you are autonomous. In: Nickles, M., Rovatsos, M., Weiss, G. (eds.) AUTONOMY 2003. LNCS (LNAI), vol. 2969, pp. 227–236. Springer, Heidelberg (2004)
5. Dignum, V.: A Model for Organizational Interaction: based on Agents, founded in Logic. PhD thesis, Universiteit Utrecht (2004)
6. Dignum, V., Okouya, D.: Operetta: A prototype tool for the design, analysis and development of multi-agent organizations. In: Proc. AAMAS 2008, Demo Track (2008)
7. Grossi, D., Dignum, F., Dignum, V., Dastani, M., Royakkers, L.: Structural aspects of the evaluation of agent organizations. In: Noriega, P., Vázquez-Salceda, J., Boella, G., Boissier, O., Dignum, V., Fornara, N., Matson, E. (eds.) COIN 2006. LNCS (LNAI), vol. 4386, pp. 3–18. Springer, Heidelberg (2007)
8. Kleppe, A., Warmer, J., Bast, W.: MDA Explained: The Model Driven Architecture— Practice and Promise. Addison-Wesley, Reading (2003)
9. Malone, T., Crowston, K.: The interdisciplinary study of coordination. ACM Computing Surveys 26(1) (March 1994)
10. Odell, J., Nodine, M., Levy, R.: A metamodel for agents, roles, and groups. In: Odell, J., Giorgini, P., Müller, J. (eds.) AOSE 2004. LNCS, vol. 3382, pp. 78–92. Springer, Heidelberg (2005)
11. Penserini, L., Grossi, D., Dignum, F., Dignum, V., Aldewereld, H.: Evaluating organizational configurations. In: IEEE/WIC/ACM International Conference on Intelligent Agent Technology, IAT 2009 (2009)
12. Quillinan, T.B., Brazier, F., Aldewereld, H., Dignum, F., Dignum, V., Penserini, L., Wijngaards, N.: Developing Agent-based Organizational Models for Crisis Management. In: Proc. of the 8th Int. Joint Conf. on Autonomous Agents and Multi-Agent Systems (AAMAS 2009), pp. 45–51. ACM Press, New York (2009)

Cooperative Sign Language Tutoring: A Multiagent Approach

İlker Yıldırım, Oya Aran, Pınar Yolum, and Lale Akarun

Department of Computer Engineering
Boğaziçi University
Bebek, 34342, Istanbul, Turkey
{ilker.yildirim,aranoya,pinar.yolum,akarun}@boun.edu.tr

Abstract. Sign languages can be learned effectively only with frequent feedback from an expert in the field. The expert needs to watch a performed sign, and decide whether the sign has been performed well based on his/her previous knowledge about the sign. The expert's role can be imitated by an automatic system, which uses a training set as its knowledge base to train a classifier that can decide whether the performed sign is correct. However, when the system does not have enough previous knowledge about a given sign, the decision will not be accurate. Accordingly, we propose a multiagent architecture in which agents cooperate with each other to decide on the correct classification of performed signs. We apply different cooperation strategies and test their performances in varying environments. Further, through analysis of the multiagent system, we can discover inherent properties of sign languages, such as the existence of dialects.

1 Introduction

Sign language is the natural means of communication for the hearing-impaired. These visual languages are based on *signs*, which are a combination of hand gestures, facial expressions, and head movements. A sign that is composed of hand gestures is called a *manual sign*, whereas the head movements or facial expressions are called *non-manual signal*. Teaching these signs to others is an important, but a difficult task. A person can improve her performance of signs only with frequent attempts and feedback. To automate the teaching of sign languages, an automated sign language tutoring tool called *SignTutor* has been developed [1]. The aim of this system is to help users learn isolated signs by watching recorded videos and to enable them to try those signs on their own. The system records a user's video while she is performing a sign. After analysis of the user's sign performance, the system gives the user feedback on her performance. The system can recognize manual signs as well as non-manual, complex signs, which include hand movements and shapes, together with head movements, and facial expressions. The system uses a classifier for recognition, by which it can compute a similarity score with a level of certainty for the user's sign performance. This classifier is the key component in deciding whether the

H. Aldewereld, V. Dignum, and G. Picard (Eds.): ESAW 2009, LNAI 5881, pp. 213–228, 2009.

user has performed the sign correctly. SignTutor is specialized for Turkish sign language.

The current system is a stand-alone application. That is, each system has its own data and own set of classifiers and there is no communication between different instances of the system. Hence, two students that are practicing the same set of signs on different stations cannot use each other's data or feedback. This is an obvious disadvantage. Intuitively, different systems will have varying data and varying performances of classifiers. That is, a system may classify sign A correctly, but may be incompetent in classifying sign B, whereas a second system may have complementary expertise. It is most appropriate for these systems to cooperate with each other when making decisions.

This challenge can be addressed by a traditional approach in which there is a centralized database and a classifier, where every tutoring system acts as a client. Clients then need to to be connected in order to facilitate tutoring. This architecture is not plausible in our situation, because first, we know that the clients may not be online all the time, and second, videos may belong to certain individuals who do not want to share them on a central database.

Accordingly, we propose to encapsulate each instance of the SignTutor in an agent. Agents are distributed geographically, but will be able to communicate with each other over the Internet, forming a cooperative multiagent system [2]. Each agent is associated with a local database of signs and a classifier. An agent can improve its classification performance due to its own experience. An agent may decide to include a practice sign in its training data or a sign language teacher may add new training data. Moreover, agents can help each other classify signs by exchanging classification requests. Thus, even when an agent's own classifier is not trained to classify a sign accurately, it can collect answers from others and decide autonomously. Since agents have their own local databases they can make a decision even when they cannot or do not want to communicate with other agents. However, realizing this multiagent system comes with challenges. The most important one is that when agents have varying expertise in different classes, it is not immediately clear whom to ask for help. Accordingly, we study different cooperation strategies deeply to understand their strengths and weaknesses in different environments.

The rest of this paper is organized as follows: Section 2 formalizes the problem of identifying agents to cooperate with. Section 3 explains different cooperation strategies that have been developed to help agents decide on sign classification. Section 4 evaluates these cooperation strategies on real sign language data. Section 5 explains how important sign language properties can be inferred from a multiagent system. Finally, Section 6 discusses our work with comparisons to the literature.

2   Problem Definition

In this study, rather than focusing on how agents can improve the capability of their own classifiers, we are interested in the problem of cooperation for making

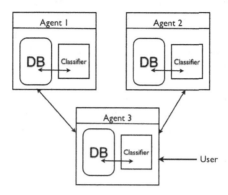

Fig. 1. A setting for multiagent architecture for Turkish sign tutoring tools

better decisions for incoming classification requests. We illustrate the problems of cooperation associated with our architecture on a simple setting. Figure 1 depicts a possible setting for cooperative multiagent architecture, which consists of three agents that can communicate with each other. Each agent has a classifier and this classifier is trained with data in the database associated with it.

As described above, the tutoring tool aims to make people learn sign language on their own. The tutoring tool shows videos of signs as queried by the human learner. A sign language learner requests the agent to recognize her performance, V_{human}, and decide whether it is an instance of sign class C_{claim}. The agent then queries a subset of other agents, A_Q, in the system by communicating to them V_{human}, for their top m class predictions, $P_i^{(1)}, ..., P_i^{(m)}$, with associated scores, $S_i^{(1)}, ..., S_i^{(m)}$ and certainty values, $C_i^{(1)}, ..., C_i^{(m)}$ for all $i \in A_Q$. Now, the agent has to decide if V_{human} belongs to C_{claim} by combining predictions, scores and certainty values of all queried agents. Therefore, the problem is to design cooperation strategies in our architecture, which enable agents to effectively combine results of other agents and to achieve better classification performance than it would do on its own.

3   Cooperation Strategies

In our context, cooperation strategies are expected to enable each agent achieve better tutoring, which corresponds to increased predictive accuracy in recognizing performances of human learners. As discussed above in Section 2, predictions, scores and certainties of other agents are available to each agent by communication. Therefore, we develop cooperation strategies that exploit data gathered through communication.

A valid interpretation of the cooperation strategy problem is classifier combination. In this view, the agent that is to make the decision is responsible for gathering predictions of other agents and applying any classifier combination

method, such as voting and score fusion. In Sections 3.1 and 3.2, we further
elaborate state-of-the-art classifier combination methods [3].

Another suitable interpretation for the cooperation strategy problem is teammate modeling in cooperative multiagent learning, where agents model each
other in order to make good guesses about their future behavior [4]. In our case,
each agent in our system, by communicating predictions for human performances
maintain probabilistic models of each other. Each agent, then, uses these models
of other agents in the system to decide which agents to query for a given human
performance, and how to combine responses of these agents to make a better
prediction next time. We propose two probabilistic methods, one incorporates
prior knowledge to build a model, and the other uses observations coming from
interactions. The details of these methods are explained in section 3.3.

3.1   Voting

Voting is a common method for combining classifiers, and has proven useful
many times in the literature [5,6]. While applying voting schemes as cooperation
strategies, we consider responses coming from other agents as votes, and the
decision making agent which is responsible to respond to the user (the agent
that is queried by the human learner) is responsible for counting the votes in
terms of a specific scheme, and making the decision accordingly. We call this
agent the decision maker. For instance, in our sample setting seen in Figure 1,
the user performs a sign, which is captured by agent 3 as V_{human}, and the user
also claims that she performed an instance of the sign class C_{claim}. Following
this, agent 3 queries both agents 1 and 2 to collect their votes for the class of
sign to which V_{human} belongs. Among several voting schemes we study majority
voting, weighted voting and Borda count schemes. If at the end of counting of
votes, agent 3 decides that the performance V_{human} belongs to the class C_{claim},
then it responds verbally as OK, and otherwise as $WRONG$ to the user.

Majority voting. Majority voting is the application of majority rule, which
selects the one of two choices with more than half of the votes to make a decision [7]. To apply the majority rule, the decision making agent, agent 3 in our
sample setting, needs to retrieve the top predictions, $P_i^{(1)}$, for all $i \in A_Q$, the
agents that are queried (in this case agents 1 and 2). There are two outcomes of
majority voting, OK or $WRONG$. A vote $P_i^{(1)}$ is counted for OK if it is equal
to C_{claim}, and counted for $WRONG$ otherwise. The one which has more than
half of the votes is the final decision. In case of a tie, the decision maker selects
one of the possibilities randomly.

Weighted voting. The weighted voting scheme is based on the idea that not
all voters are equal, but instead, each voter has an associated weight and her
vote is counted according to this weight. This time, the decision maker collects
certainty values (which corresponds to weights) and predictions for their top
choices, $C_i^{(1)}$ and $P_i^{(1)}$ respectively for $i \in A_Q$. The decision maker needs to
count the weighted votes as follows.

$$R = \sum_{i \in A_Q} K * C_i^{(1)}$$

where

$$K = \begin{cases} 1 & \text{if } P_i^{(1)} = C_{claim} \\ -1 & \text{if } P_i^{(1)} \neq C_{claim} \end{cases}$$

and

$$\text{Final Decision} = \begin{cases} OK & \text{if } R \geq 0 \\ WRONG & \text{if } R < 0 \end{cases}$$

One problem associated with weighted voting is the assessment of weights. Without elaborating on this problem, we simply make agents assess a certainty value for their votes as $C_i^{(1)} = S_i^{(1)}/S_i^{(2)}$, where, $S_i^{(1)}$ is the score calculated for top prediction, $P_i^{(1)}$, by agent i and $S_i^{(2)}$ is the score of the second prediction, $P_i^{(2)}$.

Borda count. Borda count is a voting scheme, in which voters rank candidates (or a subset of candidates) in the order of preference. Each candidate's score is the summation of points—the higher the position of the candidate in the rank of a voter, the higher the score—over all voters. The winner in Borda count is the candidate with the maximum score.

In Borda count, the decision maker collects the top k predictions, $P_i^{(1)}, ..., P_i^{(k)}$ from each agent $i \in A_Q$, the subset of agents that are queried. Each position in a rank of k predictions has a specific score. For instance if $k = 3$, a possible scoring could be 15 points for the first position, 10 and 5 points for the second and third positions, respectively. After counting the total score for each class, the one with the maximum score is selected. If the selected class is C_{claim}, then feedback is generated as OK, otherwise it is generated as $WRONG$. In our experiments we set $k = 3$, and scores as 3 points for the first position, 2 points for the second position, and 1 point for the last position in the rankings.

3.2   Score Level Fusion

In score level fusion, instead of the predictions themselves, the scores (confidences, likelihoods, and so on) of the prediction, coming from different experts, are fused to give the final decision [8,9]. Several combination rules, such as sum rule or product rule, can be applied to combine data coming from different sources in order to achieve better inference. Here, we apply sum rule for score level fusion.

The decision making agent gathers predictions, $P_i^{(1)}, ..., P_i^{(k)}$, and their associated scores, $S_i^{(1)}, ..., S_i^{(k)}$ for the top k choices for all agents $i \in A_Q$. For instance, in our sample setting in Figure 1, once the decision maker, agent 3, receives the data coming from agents 1 and 2, it can proceed to apply score level fusion methods to generate the user feedback. In our experiments we set $k = 3$.

Given that the decision maker has $P_i^{(1)}, ..., P_i^{(k)}$ and $S_i^{(1)}, ..., S_i^{(k)}$ for all $i \in A_Q$, score fusion by sum rule calculates new integrated score for each sign class as follows:

$$sumScores(P_i^{(j)}) = sumScores(P_i^{(j)}) + S_i^{(j)} \quad \forall\ i: i \in A_Q \text{ and } 1 \leq j \leq k,$$

where $sumScores$ is a vector of size of the number of different sign classes, and it is initially all 0s. The position of the maximum value in $sumScores$ is the decision of the decision making agent. If the decision is the same as C_{claim} then the feedback is generated as OK, and otherwise as $WRONG$.

3.3   Modeling Agents

As we have discussed earlier, the aim of cooperation strategies is to enable agents to achieve better tutoring, i.e. increased predictive accuracy in recognizing human performances. Agents in our architecture are heterogeneous in the sense that their classifiers are trained using different databases, and they aim to improve via experience. The heterogeneity of agents in the system could be of advantage if a proper cooperation strategy is designed.

Strategies we have proposed up to now do not actually take advantage of agents' being heterogeneous. For instance, in majority voting and Borda count schemes, the decision-making agent totally ignores differences among agents, and acts as if everyone is equally knowledgeable for all queries. Although in weighted voting each agent's vote is counted according to their certainty values, one's evaluating its own weight may not always be a good choice. For instance, among other reasons, weights gathered this way have no meaning in terms of relative certainty of two agents, because they are all generated independent from others by all means. Similarly score fusion techniques also suffer from the same case of being relatively unnormalized.

One can exploit the heterogeneity of the system by designing a strategy in which each agent models others explicitly in terms of what they know and how well they know what they know, or in other words a strategy by which each agent models expertise of other agents. Once an agent has modeled expertise of other agents, it can query them accordingly, and still end up as a better tutor than it would otherwise be. We now propose two different approaches for modeling other agents in the system, the Observation-based model, a simple model of counting success and failure times in previous predictions by each agent for each sign class, and the Bayesian model, on top of the Observation-based model, incorporating some prior knowledge related with success of others for each different sign class[1].

Observation-based model. In multiagent games, a simple model for modeling other agents in the system to predict their future behavior and achieve coordination is called fictitious play, in which agents maintain empirical distribution

---

[1] In terms of our modeling approaches, we do not need to consider the exploration versus exploitation tradeoff, because agents can only explore when extra data for modeling others are available. When such data is available, agents use this data to update all models they maintain.

of previously observed behavior for each agent, and use these distributions to predict behavior of others. As shown previously and repeated many times, in many settings, fictitious playing agents can achieve coordination [10].

In our work, we use the same idea to model predictive accuracy of other agents in the system for each class of sign. But in our case, agents need to communicate with each others training data sets to build up models of predictive accuracy. More specifically, agent i has a data set D, which consists of performance instances (videos) for different sign classes. Agent i queries a set of other agents, A_T with D and collects their top predictions $P_i^{(1)}$ for each item in D. Using these predictions, agent i calculates an empirical distribution for each agent j in A_T in terms of how accurate agent j is in predicting an instance of sign class c, which is the reliability R_i^c. For each sign class c and for each agent i the reliability is calculated as follows:

$$R_i^c = \frac{TP}{TP + FA} \tag{1}$$

where TP is the number of times agent i predicted an instance of the sign class c correctly (number of true positives), and FA is the number of times the agent predicted c when it was not c (false accepts).

Agents can use their Observation-based models in combining responses to make a better decision. For instance, an agent can decide to stick to prediction of a particular agent in a particular sign class based on its reliability. Formally, an agent decides based on its Observation-based model as follows. The agent collects the top prediction, $P_i^{(1)}$, for all agents $i \in A_Q$, a subset of all agents that are queried. A value for each sign class is calculated using reliability of all agents in their predicted class:

$$Value(P_i^{(1)}) := Value(P_i^{(1)}) + R_i^{P_i^{(1)}} \tag{2}$$

where $R_i^{P_i^{(1)}}$ is the reliability of agent i in sign class $P_i^{(1)}$, and $Value$ is a vector of size of number of sign classes. The decision making agent then, averages each item in $Value$ depending on the number of agents that predicted that particular sign class. The agent makes its decision as the position of the maximum in $Value$.

To illustrate Observation-based modeling strategy we study an example on our sample setting as seen in Figure 1, where agent 3 models agents 1 and 2 for three different sign classes, namely "Study", "Study regularly", and "Study continuously". For each of these three classes, agent 3 queries both agents for 5 instances (Hence 15 instances are used for modeling at total). Table 1 shows reliability values calculated by agent 3 according to Equation 2. For example, agent 1 responded correctly four out of five times for the "Study" class, whereas agent 2 only answered two out of five correctly for the same class.

The values in Table 2 are obtained after normalization of reliability values among agents. Now, having calculated normalized reliability values of others, agent 3 will decide for a test item by querying other agents. Suppose that, agent 1 decides that this test item belongs to the third class, "Study continuously",

Table 1. Reliability values of both agents for three classes before normalization

Reliability	Agent 1	Agent 2
Study	0.8	0.4
Study regularly	0.6	1
Study continuously	0.8	0.6

Table 2. Reliability values of both agents for three classes after normalization

Reliability	Agent 1	Agent 2
Study	0.67	0.33
Study regularly	0.38	0.62
Study continuously	0.57	0.43

whereas, agent 2's decision is the second class, "Study regularly". After collecting responses of both agents, according to its models, agent 3 favors agent 2's decision (agent 2's value of 0.62 is greater than agent 1's value of 0.57).

Bayesian model. A rather important point in modeling is that the more accurate the models of others, the better decisions made out of others' responses. Especially if observations are scarce, (i.e. due to cost or availability), agents can achieve better modeling if they rely on their prior information regarding other agents in the system. In our system, the observations between agents that are useful for modeling are really rare. Therefore, incorporating prior information turns out to be critical and could be of help.

In the Observation-based model, agents only use their interaction history for other agents, and build their models only according to their observations. One can extend this approach by incorporating the available a priori information in a Bayesian fashion. For instance, a relevant prior information about different sign classes is their similarity with each other. On top of the observations collected, augmenting the prior information, which says that a particular pair of similar signs are more likely to be confused with each other, can increase accuracy of models.

In our model, several subsets of sign classes are very similar in each other.[2] This similarity a priori says that an agent is more likely to confuse the class of a sign with another class which is similar to the real class. More formally, let S be the class of all signs, and $Conf_1, ..., Conf_\kappa, ..., Conf_n$ be disjoint confusion sets, such that $S = Conf_1 \cup ... \cup Conf_\kappa \cup ... \cup Conf_n$. Then, we say that any instance of sign s in $Conf_\kappa$ is more likely to be confused with another instance of a sign in $Conf_\kappa$, than it is to be confused with an instance of a sign in the set $S - Conf_\kappa$.

---

[2] In our Bayesian model, a priori, each agent takes it for granted that every other agent is likely to confuse a pair of similar signs. But instead, there could be other types of priors and each agent could have a specific distribution over these possible priors.

We quantify how much two classes of signs are confused with each other as follows: Let $Conf_\kappa = s_1, ..., s_j, ..., s_c$, and let $R_i^{(s_j)}$ be the reliability of agent i in class s_j as described in Section 3.3. We calculate the posterior reliability of agent i in sign class s_j as follows:

$$PR_i^{s_j} = R_i^{s_j} - \frac{\sum_{s_h \in Conf_\kappa}(1 - R_i^{s_h})}{|Conf_\kappa|} \tag{3}$$

where $|Conf_\kappa|$ is the cardinality of the set $Conf_\kappa$. This formula says that to calculate the posterior reliability, we decrease the reliability of agent i in sign s_j by the average unreliability of agent i in signs in $Conf_\kappa$. The underlying intuition is that if agent i is wrong in its prediction of s_j, then the reason is its unreliability in predicting the true class s_{true} where both s_j and s_{true} are certainly in $Conf_\kappa$.

Once posterior reliability values are calculated, the decision making agent can proceed as in the Observation-based model. But this time, the decision maker adopts the prediction of the agent with the highest posterior reliability without averaging them. Therefore, the decision maker does maximum a posteriori (MAP) estimation over the posterior reliability distribution of other agents. In other words, the decision making agent is more likely to stick to the prediction of the agent which is not only reliable in terms of the sign class of its prediction, but also reliable in the sign classes that are likely to be confused with that of prediction.

Having formally described Bayesian model, we know illustrate how it works by following our example above at the end of Observation-based model, Section 3.3. Firstly, notice that the three classes we selected, "Study", "Study regularly", and "Study continuously" all belong to the same confusion set. Table 3 shows posterior reliability values calculated by agent 3 according to Equation 3 and Table 1.

Values in Table 4 are obtained after normalization of posterior reliability values in Table 3 again for each sign and over all agents. Again, agent 3 is to test the same data item as in Observation-based model. Before studying what Bayesian model predicts, here we reveal that the test item belongs "Study regularly" class. Therefore, Observation-based model actually fails to predict the test item correctly (its prediction is "Study continuously").

Same as the Observation-based model example, agent 1 decides that the test item belongs to the third class, "Study continuously", whereas agent 2 decides it belongs to the second class "Study regularly". Our Bayesian model believes that

Table 3. Posterior reliability values of both agents for three classes before normalization

Posterior Reliability	Agent 1	Agent 2
Study	0.5	0.2
Study regularly	0.4	0.5
Study continuously	0.5	0.3

Table 4. Posterior reliability values of both agents for three classes after normalization

Posterior Reliability	Agent 1	Agent 2
Study	0.71	0.29
Study regularly	0.44	0.56
Study continuously	0.63	0.37

a posteriori agent 1 is more reliable than agent 2 in terms of their decisions, hence it predicts that the test item belongs to the third class, "Study continuously", which is the correct prediction (agent 1's value of 0.63 is greater than agent 2's value of 0.56).

4   Evaluation of Cooperation Strategies

We evaluate the performance of our cooperation strategies on a dataset of 19 signs (We use exactly the same dataset used in [1]). For each sign, the dataset consists of five repetitions from eight different subjects. We measure the performance of each cooperation strategy by the predictive accuracy of the decision making agent. We also compare the performance of decision making agent with the performance of each single agent queried. We perform our analysis in several experiments. All results reported are average of five runs for each experiment (See Table 5 for a summary of each experimental setting).

Table 5. Summary of experimental settings, see text for details

	# of				
Setting	Trained agents	Random agents	Semi-oracles	Quarter-oracles	Total
One	2	-	-	-	2
Two	2	2	2	-	6
Three	2	4	-	4	10

In the first set of experiments, we examined how cooperation strategies perform given there is a very limited number of agents to query. In this setting, there are two agents which are trained with performance instances of several subjects. And there is one decision making agent, which is responsible to query others and combine their responses (See Figure 1 for an instance of the first setting). In this setting, we make up test sets using performance instances of one subject. We train the first of two agents using instances of four other subjects, and the second agent is trained by performances of three subjects. There is one overlapping subject that we use to train both agents, therefore at total, data from six subjects are used to train classifiers of the two agents. Performance instances of one of the remaining two subjects are used by the decision making agent to model other agents. The instances of the remaining last subject is left for the test. We apply eight-fold cross-validation to generate test and training sets. For example, in a fold, we use instances from subject one (95 instances) for

Table 6. Test results for the first setting

Subjects	Agent 1	Agent 2	Majority Voting	Weighted Voting	Borda Count	Sum Rule	Obs.-based based M	Bayesian Model
1	0.68	0.68	0.64	0.66	0.67	0.67	0.69	0.71
2	0.77	0.78	0.65	0.81	0.76	0.79	0.78	0.80
3	0.76	0.60	0.54	0.62	0.67	0.63	0.73	0.75
4	0.76	0.73	0.59	0.77	0.78	0.78	0.72	0.79
5	0.59	0.47	0.34	0.57	0.58	0.60	0.40	0.47
6	0.81	0.72	0.65	0.79	0.80	0.80	0.71	0.76
7	0.62	0.68	0.49	0.68	0.71	0.64	0.66	0.62
8	0.77	0.64	0.52	0.80	0.72	0.77	0.68	0.74
Avr	0.72	0.66	0.55	0.71	0.71	0.71	0.67	0.70

test, and use instances from subjects two, three, four and five (380 instances) for training first agent, and use instances from subjects five, six and seven (285 instances) for training the second agent, and use instances from subject eight (95 instances) to train the decision making agent for the models of the first and second agents.

Table 6 tabulates the performances of cooperation strategies as they are employed by the decision making agent by querying two agents. First, we see that although the decision making agent has no valid classifier to recognize any instance of 19 signs, it achieves equally successfully as the other two trained agents. Second, our results suggest that all cooperation strategies perform comparably, except the majority voting scheme. But in terms of teammate modeling strategies, we can still see the availability of prior information results in a slightly higher performance (Bayesian modeling is slightly better than Observation-based model). Actually, modeling approaches come with a cost, which is the cost of extra training data and the necessary interactions to build models of others. Given this cost, we can infer that voting and fusion methods are more preferable when compared to modeling in this particular setting.

In real settings, it is more likely that there will be more than two agents to query, and their predictive accuracy (reliability) in any given sign class is expectedly variant. In a second set of experiments we run our cooperation strategies on a more realistic setting to see the performance of our cooperation strategies and whether modeling pays off. For this purpose, this time in addition to a single decision making agent, and two trained agents (among which the dataset distributed as described for the first experiments), two random agents and two semi-oracle agents are also involved. A random agent responds to a given query by one of 19 classes randomly. It also generates second or more predictions, as well as corresponding scores and certainty values again randomly. In contrast, a semi-oracle agent can recognize a set of sign classes perfectly, whereas it performs just like any random agent for the rest of the signs. In our setting, the first semi-oracle is perfect in the first ten signs, whereas the second semi-oracle is perfect in the remaining nine signs.

Table 7. Test results for the second setting

Subjects	Majority V	Weighted V	Borda C	Sum Rule	Obs-based M	Bayesian M
1	0.17	0.17	0.80	0.74	0.94	1.0
2	0.15	0.14	0.85	0.80	0.95	1.0
3	0.14	0.15	0.88	0.79	0.89	0.98
4	0.17	0.15	0.87	0.78	0.94	0.99
5	0.07	0.12	0.80	0.71	0.79	1.0
6	0.17	0.17	0.87	0.79	0.94	1.0
7	0.08	0.14	0.88	0.73	0.77	0.96
8	0.15	0.13	0.86	0.77	0.94	1.0
Avr	0.14	0.14	0.85	0.76	0.89	0.99

Note that our second setting is different from the first setting in that there are significant number of agents in the system who are not reliable at all for a given sign. In Table 7, since in majority voting scheme we blindly count the votes, majority voting ends up with a poor performance due to votes coming from unreliable agents. The situation is the same for weighted voting as well.

Interestingly, Borda count and score fusion by sum rule achieve relatively better performance. In Borda count, since each agent responds with its top three choices, and since the higher a sign class in a rank the higher its counted score, the effect of random agents is less, whereas the correct predictions (both from semi-oracles and trained agents) are reinforced due to scoring. In the light of our results, we can say that Borda count scheme is more robust to unreliable sources of information when compared to other common voting schemes. See [11] for a detailed discussion on robustness of the Borda count and its variants.

A similar effect is also observed for score fusion by sum rule. In this case, again each agent reports its top three choices alongside with its corresponding scores. The difference from Borda count is that the scoring is calculated by each agent on its own. Since the higher a sign class is in a rank, the higher its score, this method can also eliminate unreliable information and continue with more reliable ones.

The best performing strategies are teammate modeling methods, namely Observation-based and Bayesian modeling, in which the decision making agent explicitly models other agents in terms of their predictive accuracy for all sign classes. The explicit modeling enables the decision maker to avoid unreliable responses, and only consider information coming from reliable sources. For instance, in the Observation-based model, the decision maker is more likely to decide an instance in one of top ten signs following the first semi-oracle agent, and more likely to decide as the second semi-oracle for an instance from the last nine signs. Bayesian model brings it further by including the prior, and achieves to reveal the oracle for most of the time. We conclude that it definitely pays off to explicitly model others in the system, if not every agent in the system are comparably reliable, and there exists unreliable ones.

To examine further effects of the size of the system, and information distribution among agents, we test our methods in a third set of experiments. In this

Table 8. Test results for the third setting

Subjects	Borda C	Sum Rule	Observation-based M	Bayesian M
1	0.77	0.61	0.93	0.85
2	0.72	0.58	0.98	0.96
3	0.73	0.60	0.97	0.95
4	0.77	0.58	0.96	0.95
5	0.69	0.53	0.81	0.82
6	0.79	0.59	0.95	0.89
7	0.69	0.57	0.81	0.82
8	0.71	0.52	0.93	1.0
Avr	0.73	0.57	0.92	0.91

case, in addition to one decision making agent, and two trained agents, there are four random agents and four quarter-oracles. A quarter-oracle perfectly recognizes one fourth of 19 signs, in particular the first quarter-oracle is perfect in sign classes between 1 and 5, the second is perfect in 6 to 10, the third is perfect in 11 to 15, and the fourth quarter-oracle is perfect in 16 to 19. Quarter-oracles respond randomly for the signs in which they are not perfect.

This time, we only compare Borda count and score fusion by sum rule with Observation-based modeling and Bayesian modeling. The results in Table 8 show that it becomes more and more preferable to pay the cost of modeling as the size of the system increases and variations in the reliability of agents increase.

5   Discovering Sign Language Properties

Languages have inherent properties that are useful to discover. One such property is the existence of dialects. The term dialect corresponds to a specific form of a language that belongs to a particular geographic region or social group [12]. Sign language contains many dialects. Although dialects are mostly due to geographical separation, dialects—in terms of particular signs—can as well be observed among different signers in the same region. Before continuing, to avoid ambiguity, we consider dialects at the level of a sign, and if there are dialects for a particular sign, then it means this particular sign is signed in at least two different ways.

Since dialects are very common in sign language, it is an important question for linguists to understand the nature of dialects. Actually the first step in the study of dialects is to discover them. Here we propose and evaluate an automated method to discover dialects using the models generated by agents in Observation-based and Bayesian modeling strategies.

First we assume that for a particular sign, an agent only knows one way of signing it, even if the sign has dialects. Now consider a sign with two different dialects. Since an agent, which can recognize one dialect, cannot recognize the other dialect, we can separate the set of agents in the system in two in terms of which dialect they recognize. More formally, the set $Dial_1$ has the agents that can recognize the first dialect, and the set $Dial_2$ contains the agents that can only recognize the second dialect. Due to our assumption that $Dial_1$ and $Dial_2$ are separate, if one can find such disjoint sets of agents in terms of recognizing one particular sign class, it can be inferred that this sign has at least two different dialects known in the system.

A way to extract such patterns of sets is to use models generated by agents for Observation-based and Bayesian modeling. We can generate set of reliable agents for each sign using a threshold reliability value out of model of a decision making agent. Formally, T_i^c is the set of reliable agents for the sign class c for the decision making agent $i \in A_D$, the set of decision making agents. If the sign c has only one dialect known in the system, and each decision making agent $i \in A_D$ models the same set of other agents A_Q, then we expect $\cap_{i \in A_D} T_i^c \neq \phi$. But on the other hand, if there are at least two dialects of the sign c known in the system, then it follows that $\cap_{i \in A_D} T_i^c = \phi$.

To experimentally test our method for discovering dialects in the system, we run an additional fourth set of experiments. In this case, there are two decision making agents, two trained agents, two random agents and two semi-oracle agents. In addition to the 19 signs, we include a 20th sign, which has two different dialects in the system. One trained agent is trained for the first dialect and one semi-oracle is perfect in the first dialect. On the other hand, the other trained agent is trained for the second dialect and the other semi-oracle is perfect in the second dialect.

For each decision making agent, any agent i is in the set of reliable agents for a particular sign if the reliability of that agent i for that particular sign is greater than a threshold value, which we set as 0.6. For all 20 signs, we find the cardinality of the intersection of set of reliable agents for the decision making agents 1 and 2, $T_1^c \cap T_2^c$, where $1 \leq c \leq 20$. We observe that this cardinality is 0 only for the sign 20. Therefore we infer that the sign 20 has at least two dialects known in the system.

6   Discussion

We introduced a cooperative multiagent system for sign language tutoring. Each agent in our architecture represents a SignTutor [1] that can improve itself due to experience and by exchanging decisions with each other. On this architecture, we proposed several cooperation strategies that differ on whom to request experiences from and how to combine incoming answers.

As a cooperation strategy, firstly, we adopted several voting methods (majority voting, weighted voting, and Borda count), which are widely and successfully used in combining classifiers. Secondly, we applied score fusion by sum rule, which has proven useful in many pattern recognition problems. And lastly, we proposed two teammate modeling methods. Observation-based modeling strategy explicitly accounts for the reliability of other agents in the system using previous on purpose communication (On purpose in the sense that they interact to model each other using a portion of training data). The other teammate modeling method, the Bayesian modeling strategy, incorporates the available a priori information in order to model others better.

At first, we observed that the decision making agent performs comparably for all cooperation strategies in a toy setting, where there are two agents that are more or less equally reliable. But in more realistic settings, where there are more agents and they are not equally reliable, modeling strategies—although they are costly when compared to other strategies—perform the best. Therefore, for the decision making agent, it pays off to model others when there are agents with unknown reliabilities. We also showed that by analysis of the set of reliables of different agents, we can discover dialects of a sign known in the system.

Yolum and Singh [13] show that agents by modeling and updating models of others can achieve trustworthy service selection. In their model, agents model others in the system and direct their queries accordingly. Similar to our model, a model of an agent has several components, and they are updated depending on the interaction with that particular agent. But, rather than a statistical model, they assign a value between 0 and 1 for each component for each agent, and updating these values corresponds to an increment or a decrement over them.

To make agents cooperate more effectively, Chalkiadakis and Boutilier [14] employ Bayesian learning in order to better model others in the system and predict their future behavior more accurately. They show that Bayesian agents achieve better coordination in stochastic environments when compared to fictitious play, which is similar to our Observation-based model, and several previously proposed heuristic strategies.

Parker [15] also uses confusion matrix of a classifier as prior information to combine rankings coming from several non-homogeneous learners. He assumes that the confusion matrix of a classifier is a predictor for this classifier's future behavior, and he uses these behavior predictions in combining and achieves better error rates. In this study, predictions about future behavior of classifiers are done only upon the prior, but, in contrary to our modeling approaches, there neither exists an explicit statistical model nor the prior is updated due to observations.

Currently, we are collecting a larger database of human performances for a larger collection of signs in Turkish sign language. Therefore, we will have the chance to test our cooperation strategies also on this upcoming database. We are also working on other possible priors in addition to the confusion matrix. Lastly, we are searching for other properties of sign languages and methods to discover these properties on our architecture.

Acknowledgement

This work has been partially supported by The Scientific and Technological Research Council of Turkey (TUBITAK) under grants 107E021 and 105E073.

References

1. Aran, O., Ari, I., Akarun, L., Sankur, B., Benoit, A., Caplier, A., Campr, P., Carrillo, A., Fanard, F.: Signtutor: An interactive system for sign language tutoring. IEEE MultiMedia 16(1), 81–93 (2009)

2. Wooldridge, M., Jennings, N.R.: Intelligent agents: Theory and practice. Knowledge Engineering Review 10(2), 115–152 (1995)
3. Kuncheva, L.: Combining pattern classifiers: methods and algorithms. Wiley-Interscience, Hoboken (2004)
4. Panait, L., Luke, S.: Cooperative multi-agent learning: The state of the art. Autonomous Agents and Multi-Agent Systems 11(3), 387–434 (2005)
5. Kittler, J.: Combining classifiers: A theoretical framework. Pattern Analysis & Applications 1(1), 18–27 (1998)
6. Melvin, I., Weston, J., Leslie, C.S., Noble, W.S.: Combining classifiers for improved classification of proteins from sequence or structure. BMC Bioinformatics 9(1), 389 (2008)
7. Weiss, G.: Multiagent systems: a modern approach to distributed artificial intelligence. MIT Press, Cambridge (1999)
8. Aran, O., Burger, T., Caplier, A., Akarun, L.: A belief-based sequential fusion approach for fusing manual signs and non-manual signals. Pattern Recognition (2008)
9. Gokberk, B., Akarun, L.: Comparative analysis of decision-level fusion algorithms for 3D face recognition. In: Proceedings of the 18th International Conference on Pattern Recognition (ICPR), vol. 3, pp. 1018–1021 (2006)
10. Robinson, J.: An iterative method of solving a game. Annals of Mathematics, 296–301 (1951)
11. Van, M., Erp, S.L.: Variants of the borda count method for combining ranked classifier hypotheses. In: The Seventh International Workshop on Frontiers in Handwriting Recognition, pp. 443–452 (2000)
12. Jewell, E.J., Abate, F.: The New Oxford American Dictionary. Oxford University Press, Oxford (2001)
13. Yolum, P., Singh, M.P.: Engineering self-organizing referral networks for trustworthy service selection. IEEE Transactions on Systems, Man and Cybernetics, Part A 35(3), 396–407 (2005)
14. Chalkiadakis, G., Boutilier, C.: Coordination in multiagent reinforcement learning: A bayesian approach. In: Proceedings of the 2nd AAMAS, pp. 709–716 (2003)
15. Parker, J.R.: Rank and response combination from confusion matrix data. Information Fusion 2(2), 113–120 (2001)

Assistance Layer in a P2P Scenario

Jordi Campos[1], Maite López-Sánchez[1], and Marc Esteva[2]

[1] MAiA Dept., Universitat de Barcelona
{jcampos,maite}@maia.ub.es
[2] Artificial Intelligence Research Institute (IIIA) CSIC
marc@iiia.csic.es

Abstract. Usually, MAS design and implementation involves a coordination model that structures agent interactions and an infrastructure in charge of enacting it. We propose the term Coordination Support to denote the services offered by this infrastructure. Such services can be grouped in different layers. We propose an additional Assistance layer devoted to assist coordination rather than just to enable it. This layer is illustrated by means of a Peer-to-Peer sharing network (P2P) scenario, so that the benefits of our proposal can be empirically evaluated.

1 Introduction

As a general illustration of the proposed *Coordination Support* concept[1], with an accent on the *Assistance Layer*, we present a P2P sharing network scenario. In this scenario, a set of computers connected to the Internet (peers) share some data. The performance is evaluated in terms of time and network consumptions during the sharing process. We model this scenario as a MAS where peers are agents with a certain organisation. Its role capabilities and their net of relationships constitute its *social structure*. Also, we assume they are organised to pursue the following goal: all *peers* get the data by consuming minimum time and network. Moreover, they follow some social conventions. Specifically, peers use a simplified version of the BitTorrent protocol[2] to interact and a norm to limit their network usage. This norm can be expressed as: $norBW_{DL} =$"a peer cannot use more than $\mathtt{max_{BW}}$ bandwidth to share data".

2 Assistance Layer

To provide assistance functionalities, we have implemented our proposed 2-LAMA architecture [3], which places a *meta-level* (ML) on top of a previously existing *domain-level* (DL). Accordingly, the P2P MAS constitutes the *domain-level* whilst the *meta-level* consists of a set of agents we call *assistants* organised to aid peers. Each *assistant* provides a subset of peers (cluster) with the following functionalities:

Information. It consists on providing agents with necessary and useful information to participate: the description of current norms and the identifiers of

H. Aldewereld, V. Dignum, and G. Picard (Eds.): ESAW 2009, LNAI 5881, pp. 229–232, 2009.
© Springer-Verlag Berlin Heidelberg 2009

those other peers interested in the same data. An *assistant* supplies this information to new peers joining its cluster and to all peers in its *cluster* whenever this information is updated. Norm descriptions are sent by means of "`norm <norm_id> <definition>`" messages, whereas information about peers are sent with "`interested <peer> [,<peer>]*`" messages.

Justification. It justifies the effects of agent actions due to social conventions: involves providing explanations about why some messages have been filtered out due to the application of a norm. We assume Internet Service Providers (ISP) are equipped with an infrastructure mechanism that filters out messages that violate norms. This approach is not unrealistic since, nowadays, there exist ISP initiatives to improve P2P distribution systems. Specifically, *assistants* supply justifications to their peers by sending a "`justification '<orig_message>' action 'filtered out' reason 'norm <norm_id>'`" message.

Advices. It consists in suggesting plans to contact other *peers*. Based on network communication times, *assistants* recommend the subset of agents to be contacted by a newcomer *peer*. Each *assistant* generates these plans based on partial information it receives from its *clusters*. This information consists of communication times and data possession. At *meta-level*, *assistants* communicate among them to share a summary of this information. Consequently, each *assistant* has detailed information about its *cluster* and an overview about the rest of the *domain-level*. *Assistants* use this information to estimate which are the shortest paths among data sources and destinations. Accordingly, they recommend *peers* to contact those other *peers* that are in these shortest paths [3]. by sending "`contact <peer> [,<peer>]*`" messages.

Adaptation. In updates system's organisation to improve its design purpose achievement. Our *meta-level* adapts the *domain-level* organisation by changing its bandwidth norm $(norBW_{DL})$. It changes the bandwidth limit $(\mathtt{max_{BW}})$ at certain time intervals. As this limit increases, the time to share data decreases since more network is used to transmit it. However, a large increase of network usage can saturate it and, as a result, increase time instead of reducing it. *Assistant* agents observe its *cluster* network usage and suggest to vary this limit in order to increase the usage without achieving network saturation (see [3] for further details). Then, *assistants* need to agree on the next value of $\mathtt{max_{BW}}$. In current implementation, each *assistant* computes the average of all suggested $\mathtt{max_{BW}}$ and communicates it to its *peers*.

3   Implementation and Results

We have implemented a prototype [3] of our P2P proposal in Repast Symphony [4]. Our actual P2P scenario is composed of 12 *peers* grouped in 3 different *clusters*, each one having its own assistant. Figure 1 depicts the underlying network topology composed by peers (p), assistants (a), routers (r) and links among elements (lines with an associated bandwidth).

We tested three MAS approaches: `Brute-force-no-ML`, a MAS without ML in which all *peers* contact all the others to request the datum; `2-LAMA-AgAss`, our proposed architecture providing *agent assistance* through information, justifica-

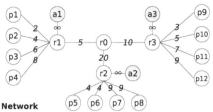

Fig. 1. P2P network topology

Table 1. Results using different approaches

MAS approaches	c_t	c_n
Brute-force-no-ML	1325.97	69884.3
2-LAMA-AgAss	1146.38	25089.2
2-LAMA-AgAss-OrgAss	876.43	18854.5

tion, and advice services but without norms; and 2-LAMA-AgAss-OrgAss, previous approach plus an *organisational assistance* to adapt the $norBW_{DL}$ norm. We use a simplified version of BitTorrent protocol in each one of them. Table 1 shows the time (c_t) and network (c_n) consumed by these approaches. c_t is the number of time units required to distribute the datum among all *peers*, whereas c_n is the number of network units consumed during this same period (the network units consumed by a single message depends on its length and its transportation latency). Obtained results show that adding a *meta-level* (2-LAMA-AgAss) saves network consumption, since it advises *peers* to contact only a subset of them. This reduction also means there is less network saturation, so messages travel faster and c_t is slightly decreased. Moreover, if we add the bandwidth limit norm and let the ML adapt it depending on network status (2-LAMA-AgAss-OrgAss) then, the savings become significantly greater for both measures. Over all, simulations show positive results of social structure advices and norm adaptation.

4   Conclusions

This paper suggests to include an additional Assistance layer when developing MAS. We illustrate this new layer in a P2P sharing network scenario. The results show the *Assistance Layer* improves system's performance, especially when adapting MAS' organisation. In fact, we regard run-time assistance as a new research line in MAS. Assisting agents about current coordination model can simplify its development and let them be more effective and efficient. On the other hand, adapting a MAS organisation to varying circumstances can help to keep its original purpose.

Acknowledgements. Work funded by IEA (TIN2006-15662-C02-01), AT (CONSOLIDER CSD2007-0022), and Marc Esteva's Ramon y Cajal contract.

References

1. Campos, J., López-Sánchez, M., Esteva, M.: Assistance layer, a step forward in Multi-Agent Systems Coordination Support. In: AAMAS 2009, pp. 1301–1302 (2009)

2. Cohen, B.: The BitTorrent Protocol Specification, `http://www.bittorrent.org`
3. Campos, J., López-Sánchez, M., Esteva, M.: Multi-Agent System adaptation in a Peer-to-Peer scenario. In: ACM SAC 2009 - Agreement Technologies, pp. 735–739 (2009)
4. North, M., Howe, T., Collier, N., Vos, J.: Repast Simphony Runtime System. In: Agent Conference on Generative Social Processes, Models, and Mechanisms (2005)

Navigational Web-Interfaces from Formal Tropos Specification

Komminist Weldemariam

Center for Information Technology, FBK-Irst,
via Sommarive 18, Trento 38100, Italy
sisai@fbk.eu

Abstract. This paper presents a method of building executable and interactive application interface prototypes from requirements. The specification of the requirements uses i* and Formal Tropos languages.

1 Introduction

A methodology for automatically generating prototypes from requirements that are specified using Formal Tropos (FT) [1] language is presented. FT follows the agent-oriented requirements modeling concepts. It allows to specify the structural and behavioral aspects of a system in the form of actors, goals, tasks, resources, softgoals and dependencies. The specification is then iteratively verified and refined using NuSMV [2] tool, for the consistency and completeness checking. The verified requirements are then passed to our tool for generating the actual prototypes, which can easily be embedded in web application.

2 Prototype Generation

We summarize our prototype generation framework in three steps (detail can be found in [3]). First we model and validate the business logic. During which we identify, model, and specify requirements. More specifically, we represent the actors of the system, their goals, and dependencies using i* [4] or Tropos [5]. We derive FT specification for the corresponding visual models. The FT specification is then mapped into an intermediate language using T-Tool [6] for formal analysis. T-Tool calls the NuSMV [2] engine for formal validation. Secondly, we derive relational database structures from FT specification. During which we capture structural and behavioral properties of the system from validated FT specification and map them into relational database structures with stored procedures and functions. Finally we integrate the relational structures and application service interfaces. During which we generate skeletons of application service interfaces from verified requirements so that the stakeholders can directly interact with the prototype.

Our prototype generator schema produces an architecture that comprises of application navigational interfaces, stored programs and functions, and application database models. The model part of the architecture resembles the model

H. Aldewereld, V. Dignum, and G. Picard (Eds.): ESAW 2009, LNAI 5881, pp. 233–235, 2009.

view control (MVC) architecture. It contains the structural aspect of the prototype in the form of relational structure. The stored procedures and functions contain the behavioral aspects of the prototype in the form of behavioral constraints managed through Java Server Pages (JSP) and relational procedures. The application interface is organized as a set of web-based interfaces with navigational features that capture user and system interactions. The user interacts with the application interfaces. The interactions are captured and stored into the database model. The stored procedure observes the runtime state of the database model and controls the view accordingly.

3   Capturing Application Data Models

Information related to the structural and behavioral aspects of the system are derived from the verified FT specification. We organized such information in the form of relational models.

Related to the structural aspect we extracted *actor list*, *goal list*, *goal hierarchy*, and *dependancy list*. The *actor list* is a one to one mapping of actors to their respective root goals. An actor is associated with exactly one root goal, which is formalized in outer layer of the FT specification through a goal or task specification. The *goal list* is a representation of a goal decomposition for every actor. The decomposition is done from the point of view of the actor who committed for its fulfillment. The *goal hierarchy* represents the hierarchy of a goal in the form of a collection of $< supergoal, subgoal >$ tuples. Finally we capture the dependencies between two actors in the *dependancy list*, where the depender's goal depends on dependee actor's local activities.

Behavioral aspects of the objects in the model and dependencies among them are essential for rapid application service prototyping. They are annotated in the inner layer of FT specification to capture the circumstances on the goal creation and fulfillment as constraints. Further, they allow to capture pre- and post- conditions on tasks and sub-tasks creation and fulfillment. We captured two relational tables that model both constraints, namely the *goal creation* and *goal fulfillment* relational structures. The *goal creation* captures the creation constraints for each goal. It is generated from the inner layer of FT specification through an analysis of goal creation properties. Whereas, the *goal fulfillment* captures the fulfillment constraints for each goal. Like the goal creation relation, the goal fulfillment is generated with the same analysis strategy. However, unlike that it uses fulfillment constraints.

4   Integrating Relational Models and Interfaces

The structures mentioned in the previous section are then further analyzed in the second pass to generate service interfaces for application prototyping. The goals which are to be achieved are made unavailable from the service interface once they are fulfilled. Application service interfaces may be easily generated from relational model through the following strategy.

- *Top Level Interface.* An interface is displayed for every root goal for every actor. They are organized by actors role. If the top level interface is navigated, the root goal corresponding to the interface is said to be created in the system. The pre-condition for navigation must attain true value for created flag of the goal which is being navigated.
- *Creation of subgoal interfaces.* A subgoal interface is displayed as soon as creational constraints of the subgoal are satisfied and the super goal is being analyzed. Subgoal instance is created once the super goal interface is navigated.
- *Goal status the display.* Upon navigating through a specific goal subgoal are created, and based on it's fulfillment conditions, its completion status is also displayed.

5   Conclusion

A strategy for modeling and generation of application service interfaces from agent based specifications is discussed. We address interactions between product users and service interfaces, and interdependencies among services. Application interfaces are generated by applying *actor as roles* interpretation. Actor's role equips the actor to interact with the system through an interface corresponding to the responsibilities of the role. In order to find responsibilities, a view of *goals as responsibilities* is taken. A service interface per actor role is generated. A service interface is a collection of goals, or responsibilities of the given actor role. Goal dependencies result in service dependencies. The runtime interface interactions with the relational database model is supported by the MySQL stored procedures and functions.

References

1. Pistore, M., Fuxman, A., Kazhamiakin, R., Roveri, M.: Formal Tropos: Language and Semantics. Technical Report 4, University of Trento (November 2003)
2. Cimatti, A., Clarke, E., Giunchiglia, E., Giunchiglia, F., Pistore, M., Roveri, M., Sebastiani, R., Tacchella, A.: NuSMV Version 2: An OpenSource Tool for Symbolic Model Checking. In: Brinksma, E., Larsen, K.G. (eds.) CAV 2002. LNCS, vol. 2404, p. 359. Springer, Heidelberg (2002)
3. Weldemariam, K.: An Agent Oriented Approach for Rapid Application Prototyping. Master's thesis, Indian Institute of Technology, Bombay, Powai, Mumbai-400076, India (August 2006)
4. Yu, E.S.-K.: Modelling Strategic Relationships for Process Reengineering. PhD Thesis, Dept. of Computer Science, University of Toronto, Toronto, Canada (1995)
5. Giunchiglia, F., Mylopoulos, J., Perini, A.: The Tropos Software Development Methodology: processes, models and diagrams. In: AAMAS 2002: Proceedings of the first international joint conference on Autonomous agents and multiagent systems, pp. 35–36. ACM, New York (2002)
6. Pistore, M., Kazhamiakin, R., Roveri, M.: T-Tool Tutorial. Technical report, University of Trento (2003)

ALIVE: A Framework for Flexible and Adaptive Service Coordination[*]

J.S.C. Lam[1], W.W. Vasconcelos[1], F. Guerin[1], D. Corsar[1], A. Chorley[1], T.J. Norman[1],
J. Vázquez-Salceda[2], S. Panagiotidi[2], R. Confalonieri[2], I. Gomez[2], S. Hidalgo[2],
S.A. Napagao[2], J.C. Nieves[2], M. Palau Roig[3], L. Ceccaroni[3], H. Aldewereld[4],
V. Dignum[4], F. Dignum[4], L. Penserini[4], J. Padget[5], M. De Vos[5], D. Andreou[5],
O. Cliffe[5], A. Staikopoulos[6], R. Popescu[6], S. Clarke[6], P. Sergeant[7], C. Reed[7],
T. Quillinan[8], and K. Nieuwenhuis[8]

[1] University of Aberdeen
[2] Universitat Politécnica de Catalunya
[3] Tech Media Telecom Factory SL
[4] Universiteit Utrecht
[5] University of Bath
[6] Trinity College Dublin
[7] Calico Jack Ltd
[8] Thales Nederland B.V.

Abstract. There is a large body of research on software services, but the issues of communication and dynamic reconfiguration have received little attention, as have adaptation to environment and dynamic combination of service building blocks into new applications. Here, we present the approach of the FP7 ALIVE project to the use of formal models of *coordination* and *organisation* mechanisms to deliver a flexible, high-level means to describe the structure of interactions between *services* in the environment. Our aim is to create a framework for services engineering for "live" open systems of active services. We propose to build on the current activities in service-oriented engineering by defining three levels: (i) An organisational level models the organisational structure of executing and interlinked services and the context around them. (ii) A coordination level provides flexible ways to model interaction between the services. (iii) These two levels connect with existing (semantic) Web services, which contain semantic descriptions to make components aware of their social context and of the rules of engagement with other services.

1 Introduction

New generations of networked applications based on the notion of software services which can be dynamically deployed, adjusted and composed will make it possible to create radically new types of software systems. These systems shall be able to communicate and reconfigure flexibly at runtime, adapt to their environment and dynamically combine sets of building block services into new applications. In order to achieve

---

[*] This work has been performed in the framework of the FP7 project ALIVE IST-215890, which is funded by the European Community (http://www.ist-alive.eu)

H. Aldewereld, V. Dignum, and G. Picard (Eds.): ESAW 2009, LNAI 5881, pp. 236–239, 2009.

this objective, the ALIVE project aims at providing a semantic-based and context-aware framework by bringing together the leading edge methods from two highly promising areas – Coordination Technology and Organisational Theory. The project will adopt the latest Semantic Web technologies to connect to existing service-oriented systems. The ALIVE framework combines model driven development with coordination and organisational mechanisms, providing support for live (that is, highly dynamic) and open systems of services. We will demonstrate the implemented framework which validates and tests the ALIVE approach in three use cases from three industrial partners respectively: dynamic crisis management, communication in entertainment domains and dynamic orchestration of distributed services on interactive community displays.

2 ALIVE Framework

The ALIVE framework aims to support the design, deployment and maintenance of distributed systems by (1) allowing the coordination, reorganisation and adaptation of Web services, (2) following operational constraints defined in the organisation level; and (3) adapting to the dynamic nature of Web Services at runtime.

2.1 Organisation Level

The organisational model views an organisation as a social system, and describes what the aims and the concerns of the organisation are with respect to the social system. The OperettA tool[1], an Eclipse plugin, is an organisational modelling tool. Its function is to create and manage the organisational model of a given distributed system. The designer is able to design the whole organisational level of a given distributed system through abstract concepts such as objectives, roles, obligations, violations, sanctions and high-level interaction diagrams that only identify critical states (called landmarks) and landmark patterns. The organisational model is specified in terms of four structures: (1) The *social structure* specifies objectives of the society, its roles, role dependencies and what kind of model governs coordination (see Fig. 1 (B)). (2) The *interaction structure* describes interaction moments, as scene scripts, representing a society task that requires the coordinated action of several roles, and gives a partial ordering of scene scripts, which specify the intended interactions between roles (see Fig. 1 (A)). (3) The *normative structure* expresses organisational norms and regulations related to roles. (4) The *communicative structure* specifies the ontologies for description of domain concepts and communication illocutions.

2.2 Coordination Level

The *coordination level* provides a means to specify the patterns of interaction between services, and to transform the organisational representation coming from the organisational level into service-oriented workflows. The Coordination Design Tool are created (as Eclipse plugins) for administrators to design the whole coordination level of a distributed system by means of actors, tasks, workflows and workflow coordination

---

[1] http://www.cs.uu.nl/research/projects/opera/

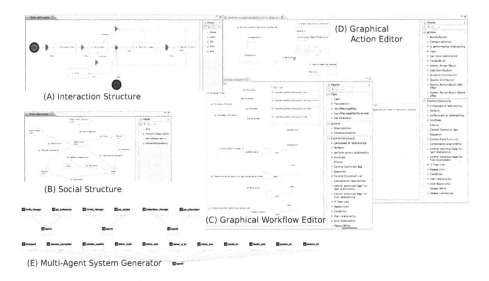

(A) Interaction Structure

(B) Social Structure

(C) Graphical Workflow Editor

(D) Graphical Action Editor

(E) Multi-Agent System Generator

Fig. 1. Screen shots from Eclipse: (A) & (B) Interaction and Social Structure Editor in OperettA; (C) Graphical Workflow Editor; (D) Graphical Action Editor; (E) Multi-agent System

mechanisms. The tools also support the generation of the agents that will perform the actual coordination tasks and the inspection of predefined and generated workflows. The Graphical Action editor (see Fig. 1 (D)) produces machine processable action descriptions, which can be used by other components, such as the workflow synthesis and agent tab. A workflow is composed of a sequence of steps, where each step is associated with an action and input bindings for the inputs of that action, along with a link to the next step in the workflow. Generated workflows are initially used by the workflow editor (see Fig. 1 (C)), which supports visualisation of a workflow, editing of a workflow, and uploading/downloading of a workflow to/from the workflow repository. Workflows are subsequently used by the agents for enactment. The multi-agent generator (see Fig. 1 (E)) takes the OperettA model and the actions defined for the organisation and creates an initial multi-agent system where every role in the organisation is assigned to an agent and the actions are distributed to the agents according to the role. The Planning agent chooses a plan and sends it to all the coordination level agents; each agent enacts the actions it is responsible for. The agents run in the AgentScape[2] platform.

2.3 Service Level

The *service level* supports the semantic description of services and the selection of the most appropriate service for a given task. It also effectively supports higher level and dynamic service composition. The service design tool is used to generate or inspect service descriptions, edit service templates and register them in the service directory. It also connects with the service matchmaking tool (a human interface to the match-

---

[2] http://www.agentscape.org/

maker component), allowing administrators to search for services matching a given task description or implementing a given service template and registering it in the service directory. The service setup tool is used to check and modify the setup of the running environment, including the URIs of different resources, facilitating components, pre-defined services and service containers. Sometimes the administrator may want to manually change an automatically selected service for another that is considered more suitable (for reasons not modelled within the ALIVE framework); in this case the service matchmaking tool is used to search for services that match a given task description (by using the matchmaker component).

The Monitor Tool covers the three levels. It allows administrators to inspect the status of a system's execution, and to keep track of the events generated at execution time and inspect how the system handles them. The tool aggregates and analyses event logs related to the execution of services, the fulfilment of coordination plans and the achievements of role and/or organisational objectives; and hence feedback is provided to the organisational model and workflow generation.

An Organisational Adaptation Simulator for P2P Networks

Jordi Campos[1], Marc Esteva[2], Maite López-Sánchez[1], and Javier Morales[2]

[1] MAiA Deptartment, Universitat de Barcelona
{jcampos,maite}@maia.ub.es
[2] Artificial Intelligence Research Institute (IIIA), CSIC
{marc,jmorales}@iiia.csic.es

Abstract. Organisational centred multi-agent systems (MAS) have proved to be effective to regulate agents' activities. Nevertheless, population and/or environmental changes may lead to a pour fulfilment of the system's purposes, and therefore, adapting the whole organisation becomes key. This paper presents a MAS simulator devoted to test organisations with self-adaptation capabilities in P2P scenarios. More specifically, our simulator implements different sharing P2P methods –some of them with self-adaptation– and so, it can be used as a testbed for comparing them.

1 Introduction

This paper presents a simulator for testing organisation adaptation mechanisms in P2P scenarios. In order to endow an organisation-based MAS with self-adaptation capabilities, we propose to incorporate a meta-level in charge of adapting system's organisation. Hence, we call our approach Two Level Assisted MAS Architecture (2-LAMA) [1]. In this context a P2P system is modelled as an organisation, with a social structure among peers, and a set of protocols and norms that regulate the sharing process. On top of the P2P system, that we call domain-level, we add a distributed meta-level which perceives information about its status and uses this information to adapt peers' social structure and norm values. Meta-level adaptation is based on system performance, which is measured by the time peers spent to share data and the network consumption in such a process.

The simulator, that we have implemented using Repast Symphony, can model the whole process, implements different sharing methods, and help in the analysis of system's behaviour. In the rest of the paper we present the system architecture in section 2, the implemented sharing methods in section 3 and the graphic user interface in section 4.

2 Simulator Architecture

The simulator architecture allows to model both agents (*agent-level*) and the transport of messages among them (*network-level*). On the one hand, the p2p

H. Aldewereld, V. Dignum, and G. Picard (Eds.): ESAW 2009, LNAI 5881, pp. 240–242, 2009.

module represents the conceptual model defined by the 2-LAMA targeted to drive the simulation at *agent-level*. Among others, it provides facilities to create state-based agents, and to define a problem (number of peers, who has initially the datum, etc). This module is divided into two layers, the *domain-level* composed by peers, and the *meta-level* containing the assistants that implement adaptation services.

On the other hand, the `netsim` module drives the simulation at *network-level*. It provides facilities to transport messages among agents, to define different network topologies, and to collect statistical information about network status. The network level simulates message transport as a packet switching network. We assume that peers are connected to different ISPs. Hence, we define an individual link that connects each peer to its ISP, and some aggregated links among ISPs. The latency of a message between agents depends on the number of links, their *bandwidth* and the current traffic through them.

During simulations the tool generates log files containing all occurred events. The simulator includes a module for facilitating the analysis of simulation results. For this purpose, this module processes the generated logs extracting relevant information, which is later on displayed in different types of graphics. Hence, this can be used to compare the time spent to share the data in different configurations, or using different sharing methods.

3 Sharing Methods

The simulator offers alternate sharing methods. This way, they can be executed over the same initial configurations and their results can be compared. Currently the tool includes two sharing methods without meta-level, and two different methods with meta-level. The two methods without meta-level are a brute-force algorithm, where peers contact all other peers, and a single-piece version of the BitTorrent protocol (BT). Regarding methods using a meta-level, the tool includes the 2-LAMA approach with just *social structure* adaptation, and the 2-LAMA approach with *social structure* and *norm* adaptation Hence, it allows to compare the performance of our adaptation approach with respect to methods without meta-level.

We used the BitTorrent protocol as a base to design the protocol in our 2-LAMA P2P approach, so both protocols are similar. The main difference is that BT does not have a distributed *meta-level* but a single agent (*Tracker*) that informs just about connected *peers*. Consequently, *peers* do not receive any further assistance to share the datum, and are restricted to use the algorithm in [2]. In contrast, the 2-LAMA approach without *norm* adaptation includes a *meta-level* with *assistant* agents. In this method, assistants just adapt the social structure among peers —i.e. their overlay network. Hence, norm values remain unchanged during the whole simulation. Finally, in the 2-LAMA approach with *social structure* and *norm* adaptation, assistants update both the social structure and norm values during the simulation.

4   GUI

In order to display up-to-date visual runtime information of the evolution of our P2P simulation, an advanced GUI has been created as an extension of the Repast GUI. Figure 1 depicts a GUI screenshot that illustrates its general appearance. The **Control toolbar** (1) pertains to the original Repast GUI and allows to play the simulation, pause it or execute it step by step. On the left area, the **Legend panel** shows information about what represents each object of the layout (2), the colours of the different messages exchanged among agents (3), whether they are visible or not, and if execution will pause upon sending this kind of messages (4). All these options can be modified by users. Thus, the legend allows an easy identification of each object and message to interpret what is happening in the simulation at every moment The **Runtime P2P Network layout** (5) shows the elements of the simulation and the communications among them. Peers and assistants are drawn according to the network topology, while messages are displayed as arrows among them with the corresponding colour defined in the legend panel. Finally, the **Resume layout** (6) displays how the data has been distributed among the different peers. It highlights completed peers and displays arrows connecting source and receiver agents. These arrows are labelled with the time step at which the datum was received.

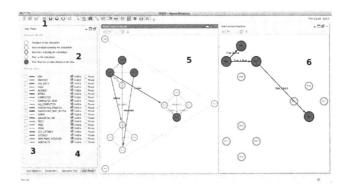

Fig. 1. 2-LAMA P2P Simulator Graphic User Interface

Acknowledgements. Work funded by IEA (TIN2006-15662-C02-01), AT (CONSOLIDER CSD2007-0022), and Marc Esteva's Ramon y Cajal contract.

References

1. Campos, J., López-Sánchez, M., Esteva, M.: Multi-Agent System adaptation in a Peer-to-Peer scenario. In: ACM SAC 2009 - Agreement Technologies, pp. 735–739 (2009)
2. Cohen, B.: The BitTorrent Protocol Specification, http://www.bittorrent.org/beps/bep_0003.html

PreSage-MS: Metric Spaces in PreSage

Hugo Carr[1], Alexander Artikis[1,2], and Jeremy Pitt[1]

[1] Electrical & Electronic Eng. Dept., Imperial College London, SW72BT
[2] National Centre for Scientific Research "Demokritos", Athens 15310

Abstract. We consider adaptation in open systems, i.e. systems without global objects or common objectives. There are three related issues: how to make the degrees of freedom (DoFs) transparent to all agents, how to define a 'fair' process for performing adaptation, and how to retain some control over the adaptation to avoid, for example, undesirable configurations. We represent the specification DoFs in terms of a metric space, and define, in a uniform and consistent way, a mechanism for 'moving' between points in the metric space which is both 'fair' to the agents and avoids unacceptable moves or points in the space. This approach is demonstrated by the platform PreSage-MS, which allows a designer to specify and animate an adaptive open multi-agent system in terms of a metric space and norm-governed rules for 'moving' in that space.

1 Introduction

Open systems [1,2] performing organisational adaptation must define in advance which DoFs may be adapted at runtime. Taken in isolation a DoF of a protocol specification does not have any meaning; systems need to specify both the adaptable and non-adaptable aspects of the system. As well as the parameters for adaptation it is also necessary to specify the mechanism for adapting these parameters, ideally in the same formalism. In open systems, it has been shown that an action language such as the Event Calculus is an effective means of establishing such a description [1], and for specifying protocols for adaptation which are representative and 'fair' [3].

However, a system which has full access to its own specification may adapt in damaging ways and in practical terms must be constrained. Artikis et al have demonstrated [4] how the rules of an adaptive system can be represented as a specification point (SP) in a metric space. SPs which represent dangerous or unstable positions can be excluded from the space. This can be encoded using normative positions (power, permission and obligation) and thus represented in the Event Calculus. As such, we have a single unifying formalism describing the specification space, the adaptation mechanism and its constraints.

In this paper, we present the multi-agent system (MAS) animator PreSage-MS which serves as a tool to investigate how the specification of DoFs affects long term system utility. Depending on which DoFs are available during a simulation,

H. Aldewereld, V. Dignum, and G. Picard (Eds.): ESAW 2009, LNAI 5881, pp. 243–246, 2009.
© Springer-Verlag Berlin Heidelberg 2009

adaptation may become stagnant, chaotic, stable, or periodically stable. By experimenting with different sets of DoFs, designers can balance control versus flexibility.

2   PreSage-MS

PreSage-MS is a framework written to facilitate the design and implementation of a multi agent organisation that can adapt its own specification at run-time. The platform takes an open approach to MAS design and implements a formal description of the protocols and rules of behaviour in the event calculus. PreSage-MS represents an integration of the MAS-simulation platform PreSage [5] and the preliminary work done by Apostolou and Artikis on metric spaces in Java [6]. As an example, we implement a general voting protocol in the Event Calculus as an adaptation mechanism and consider a system's resource distribution method as a DoF. Below we define the name of the DoF (line 1), the possible values it can take (line 2), and its initial value (line 3).

```
1  dof( resource_distribution ).
2  dofValues( resource_distribution, [ priority, vote, random] ).
3  intially ( active(resource_distribution) = priority).
```

This DoF is subsequently adapted through the voting protocol, specifically when 'A' declares the result of the vote. A new active predicate is initiated containing the value of the DoF voted for by the agents (line 4). The calculation of the winner has been abstracted into the vote_result predicate (line 7) and is based on which votes have been cast (line 6). This operation can only occur if 'A' has the institutional power to perform such a declare (line 5).

```
4  initiates( declare(A, Result), active(resource_distribution) = Result, T) :-
5      holdsAt( pow( A, declare(A, Result) ), T),
6      holdsAt(votes_cast = Votes, T),
7      vote_result(Votes, Result).
```

When these rules are unified with an action history, the system can derive the normative positions of the agents, and the respective legal actions. We have included an Event Calculus plugin to provide a window listing the active predicates and the action history. This has been complemented with a manual animator in which the user can examine all legal actions in the current timecycle. Each legal move has been implemented as a button which may be used to force an institutional action at the current timecycle. This can be seen in Figure 1.

The transition from a Current Specification Point (CSP) to a desired specification point (DSP) will generally be guided using the predefined distance metric coupled with a machine learning technique. To aid the design of a system based on such a distance we have included a plugin (Figure 2) which measures how far away a DSP lies with a range of metrics including weighted and unweighted Euclidean, and weighted and unweighted Manhattan. In addition to this the visualiser plugin maps a graph of all of these legal jumps based on the maximum threshold distance the system may deviate from any SP. Using these graphs a path can be planned towards what the agents collectively consider to be the optimal SP.

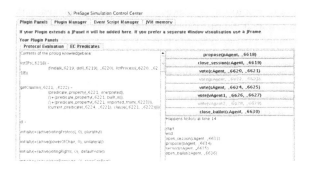

Fig. 1. Plugin listing the Prolog predicates along with a set of legal actions for the current time point and the action history

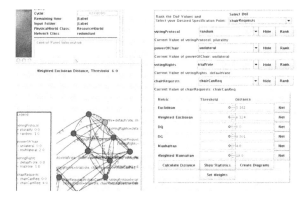

Fig. 2. Plugin measuring the distance between specification points and a graph of legal moves. The discoloured node corresponds to the CSP.

3   Conclusion

Necessary aspects of adaptation in open systems can be uniformly described in the Event Calculus. We have developed PreSage-MS, which combines agent simulation with metric spaces to facilitate the animation of run-time behaviour of such systems. Furthermore, as PreSage-MS is specified in a uniform object language, designers may even experiment with runtime adaptation of the metric space itself, resulting in a hitherto unexplored form of meta-adaptation.

References

1. Artikis, A., Pitt, J., Sergot, M.: Animated specifications of computational societies. In: AAMAS 2002, July 2002, pp. 1053–1062 (2002)
2. Hewitt, C.: Open information systems semantics for distributed artificial intelligence. Artificial Intelligence 47, 79–106 (1992)

3. Pitt, J., Kamara, L., Sergot, M., Artikis, A.: Voting in online deliberative assemblies. In: ICAIL 2005, June 2005, pp. 195–204 (2005)
4. Artikis, A.: Dynamic protocols for open agent systems. In: AAMAS 2009, pp. 97–104 (2009)
5. Neville, B., Pitt, J.: Presage: A programming environment for the simulation of agent societies. In: Hindriks, K.V., Pokahr, A., Sardina, S. (eds.) ProMAS 2008. LNCS, vol. 5442, pp. 88–103. Springer, Heidelberg (2009)
6. Apostolou, M., Artikis, A.: Evaluating dynamic protocols for open agent systems. In: AAMAS 2009, May 2009, pp. 1419–1420 (2009)

Normative Multi-Agent Organizations
A Programming Language and Its Interpreter

Mehdi Dastani

Utrecht University
The Netherlands

Abstract. Multi-agent systems are viewed as consisting of individual agents whose behaviors are regulated by organization artifacts. This abstract presents a programming language, which is designed to implement norm-based organization artifacts, by means of an example and explains the execution behavior of the language interpreter.

In order to achieve the overall objectives of multi-agent systems, the behavior of individual agents and their interactions should be regulated/coordinated. Existing approaches advocate the use of organizational models, normative systems, and electronic institutions to regulate the agents' behaviors and interactions [3,4,6]. Norm-based artifacts regulate the behavior of individual agents in terms of norms being enforced by monitoring, regimenting and sanctioning mechanisms. Generally speaking, the social and normative perspective is conceived as a way to make the development and maintenance of multi-agent systems easier to manage, e.g., OperA [2], AMELI [3], and $\mathcal{M}$oise$^+$ [5].

A declarative programming language to implement norm-based organization artifacts is presented in [1]. It provides programming constructs to specify 1) the initial state of an artifact, 2) the effects of the agents' actions that can be monitored by the artifact, and 3) the applicable norms and sanctions[1]. The interpreter of the programming language is based on a cyclic process. At each cycle, the observable actions of the individual agents are monitored, the effects of the actions are determined, and norms and sanction are imposed if necessary. Below we give a brief presentation of the programming language by means of a simple example, discuss the data types for specifying norms and sanctions, and finally describe the execution behavior of the built interpreter.

The (initial) state of a normative organization artifact is constituted by two disjoint sets of facts: *brute* and *institutional* facts. Brute facts specify the brute state of the artifact (e.g., "John has submitted a paper with 18 pages."), which may for example be the state of the environment shared by the agents. Institutional facts specify the normative state of the artifact (e.g., "John's submission

---

[1] The individual agents are assumed to be implemented in a programming language, not necessarily known to the artifact programmer. However, it is required that the observable actions of the agents can be monitored by the artifact.

H. Aldewereld, V. Dignum, and G. Picard (Eds.): ESAW 2009, LNAI 5881, pp. 247–249, 2009.

violates the 15 page limit."). The brute facts are initially set by the programmer by means of a Prolog program. As a consequence of an agent's action, the atomic brute facts can change during the artifact's execution. The institutional facts are only created and modified during the artifact execution since no initial institutional facts can be specified. They are created and modified based on the (brute and normative) state of the artifact and the applicable norms. The effect of an agent's observable action is specified by means of a pre- and a post-condition, each considered as a set of brute literals (positive or negative brute facts). A precondition is evaluated with respect to the brute state of the artifact and the postcondition is used to update the brute state of the artifact. Norms are represented by counts-as rules [4], which ascribe "institutional facts" to "brute facts". For example, in a paper submission system, a counts-as rule may express the norm "a submission with more than 15 pages counts-as a violation". Institutional facts are used with the explicit aim of triggering system's reactions (e.g., sanctions). Sanctions are implemented as rules too, but follow the opposite direction of counts-as rules. A sanction rule determines which brute facts will be brought about by the system as a consequence of the institutional facts. Typically, changing the brute state of an artifact (e.g., an agent's environment) by adding brute facts to it corresponds to imposing sanctions (e.g., issuing fines).

The example in Figure 1 illustrates the implementation of a small part of a paper submission system. The initial brute facts represent the facts that `virginia` is one of the workshop chairs and that there are four registered authors. The rest of the facts declare the lists of submitted papers and the reviewers that are assigned to papers (both lists are initially empty). We also have some background knowledge, represented by Prolog rules, used to determine if the assignment of papers to reviewers are conflicting (e.g., if an author should review its own paper). The declaration of the initial brute facts is followed by the specification of two actions to monitor: `uploadPaper` and `assignReviewers`. The execution of the first action adds a paper to the list of submitted papers, and the execution of the second assigns one reviewer to each paper. The first action is assumed to be performed by an author and the second by the chair. Action specifications are followed by counts-as and sanction rules. The first counts-as rule states that a submitted paper with more than 15 pages is a violation and the second rule indicates that conflicting assignments should be regimented. The special atom `viol` indicates a regimented state that cannot be reached. A counts-as rule with `viol` in its consequent means therefore that a state satisfying its antecedent should be avoided. This is done by not realizing the effect of the observed action and thereby preventing the application of the counts-as rule. Finally, the sanction rule indicates that a page limit violation should be sanctioned by issuing a fine of 25 euro.

The execution of this artifact program monitors possible actions performed by either a registered author or the workshop chair. In particular, performing the action `uploadPaper(john, p1, 18)` by the author `john` adds paper `p1` to the list of the received submissions (initially empty) resulting in the brute fact `submittedPapers([ [john,p1,18] ])`. The result is evaluated with respect

```
Facts:
    workshopChair(virginia).
    registeredAuthors([john, mary, eva, peter]).
    submittedPapers([]).
    reviewersPapers([]).
    conflict([],Rs,[]).
    conflict([(A, Id, Pages)|T], Rs, [A|R]):- member((A, Id), Rs), conflict(T,Rs,R).
    conflict([(A, Id, Pages)|T], Rs, B):- conflict(T, Rs, B).
    empty([]).

Effects:
    { submittedPapers(Rs), registeredAuthors(As), member(A,As) }
        uploadPaper(A, Id, Pages)
    { not submittedPapers(Rs), submittedPapers([(A,Id,Pages)|Rs]) }

    { workshopChair(A), reviewersPapers(OldPRs) }
        assignReviewers(A,PRs)
    { not reviewersPapers(OldPRs), reviewersPapers(PRs) }

Counts-as rules:
    submittedPapers(As) and member((A,Id,Pages), As) and Pages > 15   => viol_pageLimit(A).
    submittedPapers(Rs) and reviewersPapers(Res) and conflict(Rs, Res, X) and not empty(X) => viol.

Sanction rules:
    viol_pageLimit(A)    => fined(A,25).
```

Fig. 1. An example of norm-based organization artifact program

to the counts-as rules causing the generation of the page limit violation and adding `viol_pageLimit(john)` to the normative state of the artifact. Finally, the interpreter evaluates the normative state of the artifact with respect to the sanction rule adding the brute fact `fined(john,25)` to the brute state of the artifact. This brute fact indicates that a fine of 25 euro is issued for john. Suppose `mary` and `peter` upload their papers as well resulting in the brute fact `submittedPapers([[peter,p3,12], [mary,p2,14], [john,p1,18]] )`. Also assume that the workshop chairs decide to assign papers to reviewers by performing the action `assignReviewers( virginia,[ [peter,p1], [john,p3], [mary,p2]] )`, indicating that papers p1, p2, and p3 should be reviewed by `peter`, `mary` and `john`, respectively. The performance of this action, however, will be prevented since otherwise the second counts-as rule can be applied causing the generation of the special regimentation atom `viol`.

References

1. Dastani, M., Tinnemeier, N.A.M., Meyer, J.-J.C.: A programming language for normative multi-agent systems. In: Dignum, V. (ed.) Multi-Agent Systems: Semantics and Dynamics of Organizational Models, ch. 16. IGI Global (2008)
2. Dignum, V.: A Model for Organizational Interaction. PhD thesis, Utrecht University, SIKS (2003)
3. Esteva, M., Rodríguez-Aguilar, J.A., Rosell, B., Arcos, J.L.: Ameli: An agent-based middleware for electronic institutions. In: Proc. of AAMAS 2004 (2004)
4. Grossi, D.: Designing Invisible Handcuffs. PhD thesis, Utrecht University (2007)
5. Hübner, J.F., Sichman, J.S., Boissier, O.: Moise+: Towards a structural functional and deontic model for mas organization. In: Proc. of AAMAS 2002 (2002)
6. Jones, A.J.I., Sergot, M.: On the characterization of law and computer systems. In: Deontic Logic in Computer Science (1993)

Hybrid Teams in Virtual Environments: Samurai Joins the Training Team

Jurriaan van Diggelen, Tijmen Muller*, and Karel van den Bosch

TNO Defense, Safety and Security
Soesterberg, The Netherlands
jurriaan.vandiggelen@tno.nl, tijmen.muller@tno.nl,
karel.vandenbosch@tno.nl

Abstract. This paper demonstrates a virtual environment where mixed human-agent teams are used for team-skills training.

Keywords: Human-Agent Teams, Team Training, Cognitive Modeling.

1 Introduction

Training team skills forms an essential part of the education of many professions which demand a tight collaboration, such as medical, military, or fire fighting. Usually, this is done by team training drills with a (potentially large) number of participants, each playing a dedicated role in a given scenario.

The demonstrator described in this paper intends to provide a different approach. We have developed a game-based platform in which some team-members are played by humans, and some team-members are played by software agents. In this way, team training can be made less costly, as not all roles have to be fulfilled by humans anymore. Furthermore, it can be better tailored to the specific learning objectives of a specific individual, as we can more precisely control the team behavior of artificial team members than that of human team members (which may be trainees themselves).

We use the game SABRE [3], which is a Virtual Environment (VE) based on the commercial game Never Winter Nights, which has been developed by NATO for training military team skills. Normally, SABRE is played by a group of humans which collaboratively explore a village to find weapons hidden by terrorists. In this project, we implemented a software agent, called *Samurai*, and allowed it to participate in a team of human SABRE-players as an equal team-member.

Samurai is based on the agent programming language 3APL [3], where agents are defined in terms of cognitive concepts such as goals, plans and beliefs. To endow an agent with the desired team characteristics, we also added organizational notions to the framework, such as roles, workflows, and team goals.

---

* The first two authors are listed alphabetically and should be regarded as having made an equal contribution.

H. Aldewereld, V. Dignum, and G. Picard (Eds.): ESAW 2009, LNAI 5881, pp. 250–253, 2009.

The next section describes Samurai's different types of team behavior. Section 3 describes the implemented prototype. Section 4 concludes the paper.

2 Teaming Up with Samurai

Most simply, a team is a group of people working together to achieve a common goal. This requires team members to maintain *common ground*, to be *mutually predictable*, and to be *mutually directable* [2]. Related literature reports different ways in which these properties can be implemented in artificial team members, with different levels of sophistication. In an elementary way, we have implemented them in Samurai as follows. Samurai maintains common ground with the other team members by actively sharing relevant pieces of information with them. Mutual predictability is achieved by applying an organizational structure to the team, which is commonly known by all participants, and provides a shared basic understanding of how the different participants are performing their share of teamwork. Mutual directability is implemented by a *request* protocol, which allows one agent to ask another agent to perform an action.

Whereas we believe these properties to be essential for team membership, *how* these properties reveal themselves in behavior may vary. By explicitly modeling such differences in artificial team members we can expose trainees to different types of team behavior. For all three aspects discussed above, we can configure Samurai in either *provocative* mode or *unprovocative* mode. When Samurai maintains common ground in a provocative way, it sometimes refrains from sharing relevant information. This invites the trainee to learn to actively collect relevant information. When mutual predictability is implemented in a provocative way, Samurai is not (fully) organization aware. This invites the trainee to improve the collaboration with Samurai by communicating his or her own roles. Provocative mutual directability means that Samurai will not blindly follow up a request from the trainee. Instead, the trainee should convince Samurai that that the requested action is in its own interest too, or in the team's interest.

3 Team Training Environment

We assume that an agent's behavior can be modeled by specifying *beliefs*, *goals* and *plans*. Following the agent programming language 3APL [1], we assume that the relation between these three notions is specified by practical reasoning rules (or *PR-Rules*). When an agent enacts a role in the organization, it adopts the corresponding PR-rules, which is then known by all other agents in the organization. These other agents can decide which information qualifies as relevant to an agent, by inspecting its organizational PR-Rules. Because also human behavior is specified in this way, Samurai can decide which information is relevant to a human trainee, and subsequently share it with the trainee.

The coupling between the agent (Samurai) and the virtual environment (SABRE) is depicted in Figure 1. A screenshot of the application is depicted in Figure 2.

The Samurai and SABRE processes run in parallel. At the Samurai side, the process starts when new information is obtained from SABRE. This may be about actions being finished or new observations. This information may be exchanged with others, and may lead to new actions. Actions are executed at the SABRE side by calling game scripts. In this way, the higher level planning of actions is implemented in the agent, while the lower level implementation of these actions is implemented in the VE.

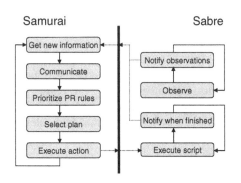

Fig. 1. Agent-VE coupling

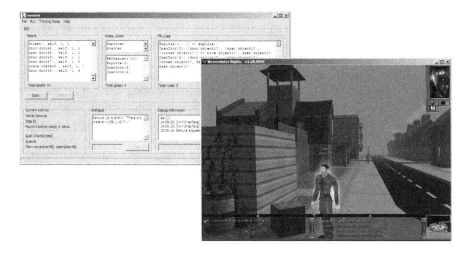

Fig. 2. Samurai's internal workings (left); Samurai in the VE (Right)

4   Conclusion

This demonstration paper describes our approach to applying virtual team members in training scenarios. Samurai can be configured to exhibit different types of team behavior which may be more or less challenging to the trainee. In the future, we plan to perform experiments to test the effectiveness of our hybrid training environment on human learning.

References

[1] Hindriks, K.V., de Boer, F.S., van der Hoek, W., Meyer, J.-J.C.: Agent programming in 3APL. Autonomous. Agents and Multi-Agent Systems 2(4) (1999)

[2] Klein, G., Woods, D., Bradshaw, J.M., Hoffman, R.R., Feltovich, P.J.: Ten Challenges for Making Automation a Team Player. In Joint Human-Agent Activity. IEEE Intelligent Systems 19(6) (2004)

[3] Leung, A., Diller, D., Ferguson, W.: SABRE: A game-based testbed for studying team behavior. In: Proceedings of the Fall Simulation Interoperability Workshop (SISO). Orlando, FL, September 18-23 (2005)

Joint Activity Testbed: Blocks World for Teams (BW4T)

Matthew Johnson[1], Catholijn Jonker[2], Birna van Riemsdijk[2], Paul J. Feltovich[1],
and Jeffrey M. Bradshaw[1]

[1] Florida Institute for Human and Machine Cognition,
40 South Alcaniz, Pensacola, Florida, USA
[2] EEMCS, Delft University of Technology, Delft, The Netherlands
{mjohnson,pfeltovich,jbradshaw}@ihmc.us,
{c.m.jonker,m.b.vanriemsdijk}@tudelft.nl

Abstract. This demonstration will be the presentation of a new testbed for joint activity. The domain for this demonstration will be similar to the classic AI planning problem of Blocks World (BW) extended into what we are calling Blocks World for Teams (BW4T). By teams, we mean at least two, but usually more members. Additionally, we do not restrict the membership to artificial agents, but include and in fact expect human team members. Study of joint activity of heterogeneous teams is the main function of the BW4T testbed.

Keywords: Joint Activity, Coordination, Teamwork.

1 Introduction

This demonstration will be the presentation of a new testbed for joint activity. The domain for this demonstration will be similar to the classic AI planning problem of Blocks World (BW) shown in Figure 1. BW has been a popular test domain with the Planning community because of its simplicity and was borrowed by the Distributed AI (DAI) and Multi-Agent Systems (MAS) community to study distributed planning and coordination. We extend BW into what we are calling Blocks World for Teams (BW4T). Teams consist of at least two, but usually more members. Additionally, we do not restrict the membership to artificial agents, but include and in fact expect human members. Study of *joint activity of heterogeneous teams* is the main function of the BW4T testbed.

Fig. 1. Basic Blocks World

H. Aldewereld, V. Dignum, and G. Picard (Eds.): ESAW 2009, LNAI 5881, pp. 254–256, 2009.
© Springer-Verlag Berlin Heidelberg 2009

2 Blocks World for Teams (BW4T)

In order to study joint activity of heterogeneous teams in a controlled manner, we extend the basic BW problem in a few ways. First, instead of having only one player, as usual in BW, for BW4T we allow multiple players as in the DAI and MAS work. Our approach is different in that players can be combinations of both human and artificial agents. Second, instead of having all the blocks visible on a table, we hide them in a series of rooms. Agents can only see blocks that are in the same room as they are. This feature is added to force the coordination to be explicit, i.e., to force coordination through communication. Coordination can frequently occur through observation of the environment and non-verbal cues. While implicit coordination is another valuable area of study, these cues can be very difficult to detect and measure. Restricting the visibility will force explicit communication. A restricted chat window is provided for communication. By controlling the goal and the communication options, we can influence the need for coordination and type of coordination available during the joint activity.

2.1 The Environment

Figure 2 shows the basic setup: a number of colored boxes are hidden in a number of rooms that have one or more doors. In Figure 2, we show twelve rooms arranged in three rows of four, containing a number of red, white and blue boxes.

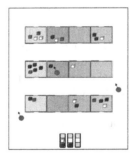

Fig. 2. BW4T basic setup with everything visible

2.2 The Players

Each player in BW4T controls an avatar in the environment. The players must navigate their avatar around the world and perform simple pick-up and drop-off actions. Human team members use a simple keyboard and mouse interface. Players communicate through a restricted chat like interface. The messages are restricted to a domain relevant set to bound the interpretation problem for artificial agents and still allow for a very diverse set of coordination techniques by the players. Players have their own interface and are restricted as to what they can see. As an example, consider a two player BW4T example shown in Figure 3. Players, depicted by their red circle avatars, can only see the contents of the room they are currently in and do not see the other players or their status except through communication.

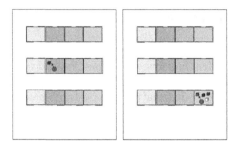

Fig. 3. BW4T - 2 player example

2.3 The Game

At the bottom of the interface, as shown in Figure 2, there is a set of bins. The bins depict the color pattern required. The team goal is to fill each bin to match the specified pattern as fast as possible. Players may "carry" only one block at a time. To retrieve a block, each player must maneuver its avatar into the various rooms, to find the block of interest. Then the player must navigate to the block of interest to "pick it up" and maneuver the robot into the goal area to "drop it off" in the appropriate bin.

3 Related Work

While there have been plenty of MAS testbeds, it is rare to find a testbed specifically designed for arbitrary sized heterogeneous (human and agent) teams. This testbed is similar to MICE (Michigan's Intelligent Coordination Experiment) [1] in that it addresses a simple domain. BW4T is similar to Gamebots3D [2] in that we focus on human participation. While its initial domain is a simple one, we expect to add more domains with increased complexity in the future.

Acknowledgments. The work is partially supported by the ADA CTA.

References

1. Durfee, E.H., Montgomery, T.A.: MICE: A Flexible Testbed for Intelligent Coordination Experiments. In: Proceedings of the 1989 Distributed AI Workshop (1989)
2. Adobbati, R., Marshall, A.N., Scholer, A., Tejada, S.: Gamebots: A 3D Virtual World Test-Bed For Multi-Agent Research. In: Proceedings of the Second International Workshop on Infrastructure for Agents, MAS, and Scalable MAS (2001)

Author Index

Akarun, Lale   213
Aldewereld, Huib   116, 197, 236
Alvarez-Napagao, Sergio   116, 236
Andreou, D.   236
Andrighetto, Giulia   1
Aran, Oya   213
Artikis, Alexander   243

Blancke, David   113
Bora, Sebnem   165
Bradshaw, Jeffrey M.   254
Burgemeestre, Brigitte   68

Campennì, Marco   1
Campos, Jordi   229, 240
Carr, Hugo   113, 243
Ceccaroni, L.   236
Chorley, A.   236
Clarke, S.   236
Cliffe, O.   236
Confalonieri, R.   236
Conte, Rosaria   1
Corsar, D.   236

Dastani, Mehdi   247
De Vos, M.   236
Dignum, Frank   116, 197, 236
Dignum, Virginia   84, 197, 236
Dikenelli, Oğuz   162, 165, 181

Ekinci, Erdem Eser   162, 181
Esteva, Marc   229, 240

Feltovich, Paul J.   254
Ferber, Jacques   15

Gil, Yolanda   132
Gleizes, Marie-Pierre   33
Gomez, I.   236
Groth, Paul   132
Guerin, F.   236

Herzig, Andreas   148
Hidalgo, S.   236
Hindriks, Koen   98

Hübner, Jomi Fred   148
Hulstijn, Joris   68

Johnson, Matthew   254
Jonker, Catholijn   98, 254

Kamphorst, Bart   84
Kleerekoper, Anthony   113
Kır, Hüseyin   181
Krupa, Yann   148
Kühn, Eva   17, 65

Lam, J.S.C.   236
López-Sánchez, Maite   229, 240
Luck, Michael   132

Maurel, Christine   33
Migeon, Frédéric   33
Miles, Simon   132
Modgil, Sanjay   132
Morales, Javier   240
Morandini, Mirko   33
Muller, Tijmen   250

Nieuwenhuis, K.   236
Nieves, J.C.   236
Norman, T.J.   236

Oren, Nir   132

Padget, Julian   49, 236
Palau Roig, M.   236
Panagiotidi, S.   236
Penserini, L.   236
Penserini, Loris   33, 197
Perini, Anna   33
Pitt, Jeremy   113, 243
Popescu, R.   236

Quillinan, T.   236

Reed, C.   236

Sergeant, P.   236
Sesum-Cavic, Vesna   17, 65
Staikopoulos, Athanasios   197, 236

Tan, Yao-Hua   68
Traskas, Dimitris   49

van den Bosch, Karel   250
van Diggelen, Jurriaan   250
van Riemsdijk, M. Birna   98, 254
van Wissen, Arlette   84
Vasconcelos, W.W.   236

Vázquez-Salceda, Javier   116, 236
Vercouter, Laurent   148

Weldemariam, Komminist   233

Yolum, Pınar   213
Yıldırım, İlker   213